KAREN HORNEY

Gentle Rebel of Psychoanalysis

KAREN HORNEY

Gentle Rebel of Psychoanalysis

JACK L. RUBINS

Weidenfeld and Nicolson
London

To Renate, Marianne and Brigitte
  without whose help this book could not
  have been as it is.

To my wife
  for her forbearance and support during
  the years of searching and writing.

CONTENTS

INTRODUCTION

It is a strange experience to try to recreate the life story of a person now dead. During the seven years that I have worked on this book, I have often had the curious feeling of vicariously reliving Karen Horney's life and times. I have in truth walked the streets of Blankenese and Hamburg, of Freiburg and Berlin, of Chicago and New York, looking for traces of her passage. But the magic of my imagination transmuted the places and time. It was not the 1970's. Instead I felt I was living in the turbulent, exciting Berlin of the Weimar decade, experiencing the persecution of the Jewish psychoanalysts during the early Nazi period, sitting in the analytic classes in Chicago in 1930, participating in the past squabbles—today so unimportant but then so emotionally charged—of the New York Psychoanalytic Institute and the Association for the Advancement of Psychoanalysis. In my mind I have discussed philosophy, religion, literature or politics in innumerable evening gatherings. At times I have become so involved that I have felt like a real member of her family, perhaps even to the point of assuming an unwarranted familiarity with her daughters. If I have done so, I apologize to them for it.

The attempt to "re-create" another person's life is part of the daily activity of a psychoanalyst. This involves, in the basic sense of that term, exploring, understanding, experiencing and rendering again, hopefully in an original, more truthful way. It excludes good-bad value judgments and distortions, whether conscious or unconscious, of the past or present. It means laying bare and confronting facts and feelings, activities and attitudes that may be pleasant or unpleasant, valued positively or negatively, admired and wanted or despised and rejected. It means revealing the person as a total human being, in true-to-life flesh and blood, with assets and strengths as well as foibles and frailties. Every analyst is aware of how difficult this task can be, even when the person is describing his own self and past history. Everyone resists, wishes to hide those aspects of himself which do not conform to the idealized self-image he needs to hold and to present to others. His memories too must accord with the traits and attitudes making up this favorable picture of his personality and life-style. Therefore only some past events will be recalled; others will be conveniently forgotten. The emotional significance and impact of some memories will be exaggerated in a positive sense, that of others, in a negative sense. Some will be remembered in much detail, others minimized, passed over lightly or factually distorted. This often depends on the feeling associated with either the present trait being described or the past event being recalled: guilt, embarrassment, humiliation, shame, fear, hate, disapproval, joy, pleasure, pride, love and so on.

If all these reactions are present in the living person, more or less motivated to confide and reveal himself, how much more difficult the task is with a person dead twenty-five years, who lived during the seventy years before that. Now one must depend on witnesses prone to the same unwitting distortive tendencies, each with his own version of the truth. Other factors intervene as well. These were evident in the interviews I conducted with some hundred people in several countries and different parts of this country.

Some at first quoted the proverb *"De Mortuis nil nisi bonum"*—speak only good of the dead—to rationalize their unwillingness to confide. Usually they later agreed to cooperate. Others could remember little. Unfortunately time does blur the memory, adding to the subjective distortion. The public image that had to be maintained while Horney was alive and the legend that has arisen since her death were also influences. Some who wished to maintain the myth requested that only positive aspects be revealed. Others urged that the undertaking be dropped; it would only disturb the status quo. Better that her memory and work fade away and be forgotten. Still others urged the same thing for a different reason: It would be impossible to write a completely truthful biography of Horney, to get to her "roots." They supported Mark Twain's remark that "biographies are but the clothes and buttons of the man— the biography of the man itself cannot be written."

From the outset, I envisioned this book as a jig-saw puzzle. Every interview, every document, every bit of information was an added piece. Every confirmation of a previous bit locked the piece into place. So did each contradictory version of the same event, when the two could be presented side by side. The more pieces one had, the truer the picture;

it was no different from a psychoanalysis except that the tools differed: documents and witnesses instead of direct observations. While it may not be possible to get the total or innermost essence of the person, the more one has, the closer one comes to it. In any event, as a psychoanalyst, I have long been committed to the proposition that truth is preferable to any legend or false image. A true story could be written, provided the same clinical objectivity could be retained.

And yet, in spite of all these obvious difficulties and caveats, the writing of psychohistory has nearly become a parlor pastime. Some recent books have been well-documented, detailed, honest and valuable contributions to our knowledge. Most have been superficial or biased or incomplete. I am not speaking here of the inherent bias of the descriptions given by witnesses, but rather of the slant given by some authors. The author may emphasize or play down certain aspects of the subject's life story or personality because of his own needs or blind spots. Or he may make inferences, interpret motives, in keeping with a particular theoretical stance that is not generally acceptable or valid, and thus fall prey to the ever-present danger of fitting the person into some particular theory—be it psychoanalytic or any other.

Why then still another such biography? My original motives for writing this were fortuitous. In 1970 I was asked by a publisher, through the Association for the Advancement of Psychoanalysis, to bring out a book of significant papers written by Horney and her followers during the twenty years since 1950. I accepted what I saw then as simply an interesting assignment. When I realized that the publication date would correspond to the twentieth anniversary of her death, I felt that such a commemorative volume would best be completed with a short biographical study. So it was done.[1] It was only in gathering material for this original short study that I became aware of certain factors that demanded a more comprehensive biography. One was the lack of personal information about Horney and her early life. Only two brief biographical sketches existed at the time, Joseph Natterson's in *Psychoanalytic Pioneers*[2] and Harold Kelman's in *Helping People: Karen Horney's Psychoanalytic Approach*.[3] The former is quite incomplete, with few details of her personal life and attitudes. The latter suffers from the usual limitations of a biography written by someone who has been closely involved with the subject. While such an author may have greater knowledge of the person's experiences, he may be biased or, as in the case of the second sketch, he may gloss over his own role and influence on the subject. This will depend on the extent to which he can be self-perceptive and self-revealing, as opposed to presenting himself in a favorable light.

Karen Horney's reserve about herself contributed to the paucity of material about her life. She was a very private person, not easy to know intimately or deeply. She seldom spoke of her past or of her profound feelings, even to her closest friends or family. When she did so, it was in fragmentary remarks.

A second reason for this book lay in the disappearance of Horney's name from psychoanalytic literature dealing either with the history of psychoanalysis or with feminine psychology, the subject she was so prominent in during her earlier years. It was as if her name had been expunged and history rewritten in the best party-line tradition. Some of the older orthodox analysts who were known to have had contact with her even refused to speak to me or answer my letters when I mentioned my interest. I could only surmise why. Perhaps some intense hostility or similar emotion, originally felt for her or her ideas, was being perpetuated. Or perhaps they were afraid of being connected with her, of being contaminated, so to speak. Perhaps her theories were even then thought to be a threat to the classical Freudian views and therefore to be avoided. This, despite the fact that her books are now in their eighteenth printing and still selling in large quantities, are being used as texts in many university courses in psychology, sociology and psychoanalysis, are regarded as classics, and are responsible for bringing many people into personal analysis.

A third reason was the growing interest in Horney in a different quarter, namely in the woman's liberation movement. I am certain that she herself would have denied being a feminist, at least in the current sense of the term. Yet she certainly fought for the upgrading of women's status, for genuine pride in being a woman, for the equality of men and women. But it was primarily as a sociopsychobiological human being rather than for any special women's rights or for political, vocational or economic position. Her rebellion was against the Victorian ethos, the tradition of the patriarchal family, which she felt to be perpetuated wrongfully in the Freudian concepts of family sexuality. Now her name was beginning to appear occasionally in articles about psychoanalysis, not for her contribution to analytic theory—others were often given credit for her ideas—but as one of the early women in the analytic movement.

I therefore felt the need to fill the gap about her personal life, past and present, to correct the historical record of her role in the development of psychoanalysis, and to clarify her position on women. Furthermore, knowing her theories well, having used them for thirty years and written extensively on their application and relevance to the present social situation, I wondered whether they might be related on the one hand to her own development and personality, and on the other to the cultural conditions she lived in. To demonstrate such a relationship, and clarify it if it existed, was another reason for the book.

That the subjects she chose to write on and her conceptual interpretations of them did reflect the changes in her personal attitudes and feelings has not detracted from their proven clinical validity. It is a truism that every writer portrays something of himself in his writings. Yet this need not diminish the truth or the originality of his findings. One of Horney's abilities was precisely that: to transcend her own inner conflicts and apply her insights to others in a generalized fashion.

During the many interviews I conducted, several overall impressions struck me forcefully. One was the range and intensity of feelings Horney elicited in others. They ranged between extremes, from pan to panegyric, from condemnation and disdain to admiration, even adulation. She was called everything from an excellent, most perceptive clinical psychoanalyst to not an analyst at all—a polite professional synonym for "charlatan." And yet, even though all the people I spoke to knew her in some way, few based their opinions on more than a superficial knowledge of her work. In some instances they were based on hearsay or rumor.

Second, I was impressed by the variety of ways she was experienced by different persons. This was astonishing, even allowing for the subjective needs and biases of the witnesses. Thus, she was described variously—and contradictorily—as both frail and strong, open and reticent, aloof and "with you," distant and close, caring, motherly and uncaring, unsympathetic, loving and unloving, dominating and self-effacing, manipulative and compliant, a leader and a follower, fair and mean. From such characterizations, the impression emerged that she was not only changeable and constantly changing, but indeed a complex personality. She needed to encompass and unify many diverse and conflicting traits, apparently with constant struggle. But no one who knew her was unaffected by her; all spoke of her with passion. All agreed that she exerted a strong influence upon them. Her charisma—that most misused and difficult to define of words—was evident. It was not an outspoken domination through authority nor was it hauteur. It was simply an aura generated by her very presence, in spite of the external plainness of her person. Yet she was apparently unaware of the effect she had on others, and when it was called to her attention, she would deny it, was perhaps threatened by it.

A third impression was that although many persons thought they knew her well, each was aware of only a small aspect of her being. She kept much of herself submerged. Although many called themselves friends, the depth and intimacy of these relationships was questionable. She had few lifelong friends. She made friends easily but could discontinue the friendship as easily.

Which was the true Karen Horney? All were true and even more.

As to her work itself, this book is not intended to be a scholarly analysis or discussion of her theories. I have tried to present all her papers and books in summary form, but the emphasis has been on her person; her work comes through as a product of her personality and of her external milieu—to the extent that she herself was a product of her family and cultural environment. Her work must therefore be seen—both in its development and in its final form—within the context of her times, albeit filtered, as it were, through her personality. Her life encompassed part of the Victorian epoch, the golden decade of Weimar Germany, the Nazi tyranny, two world wars, and modern America. It confronted European traditionalism and conservatism with American avant-gardism and freshness. Just as Freudian psychoanalysis was iconoclastic with respect to classical psychiatry and to social mores in general in 1920, so Horney's psychoanalysis was iconoclastic with respect to Freud's "classical" theories in 1940. She was a bridge builder between the psychobiological man of Freud's psychology and the sociocultural man of today. Although she did not foresee it, she foreshadowed the present emphasis on ego psychology and social psychiatry. As the social psychiatrist Robert Coles has pointedly remarked, today her "revisionism" strikes us as pure common sense. Her ideas have not obtained any momentous, out-right acceptance but they have largely become part of our present psychological knowledge. Many have been taken up by psychoanalysts today, discovered, so to speak, without credit being given her. The concept of self-realization (which has become the basis for several schools of psychology), the importance of pride and pathological self-idealization in neurosis, the concept of neurotic narcissism, the significance of a realistic and broad patient-doctor relationship in therapy and the role of specific noninstinctual interpersonal attitudes are a few instances. In any event, one cannot do justice to her work or to its impact on psychoanalytic thought by evaluating them summarily.

At this point I would like to acknowledge my debt and express my gratitude to all those colleagues and friends who generously confided to me their memories, conversations, experiences and personal documents relating to their contacts with Karen Horney. The story here told is based on these many interviews and extensive correspondence. It is factual, allowing of course for the vagaries of memories. Where inferences or speculations are made, it has been so stated.

Those who contributed are:

DR. GUNTER AMMON (*Berlin, Germany*)
DR. FRANCES ARKIN (*Miami, Fla.*)
DR. NICHOLAS BARBARA (*Hewlitt, N.Y.*)
DR. VALER BARBU (*New York*)
MR. LEONARD BARSCHALL (*New York*)
DR. BENJAMIN BECKER (*Forest Hills, N.Y.*)
DR. MILTON BERGER (*New York*)
DR. IRVING BIEBER (*New York*)
MRS. DOROTHY BLITZSTEN (*New York*)
DR. WALTER BONIME (*New York*)
DR. MEDARD BOSS (*Zurich, Switzerland*)
PROF. YVON BRÈS (*Sceaux, France*)
DR. ALBERT BRYT (*New York*)
DR. ELIZABETH (BURCHARDT) CLEMMENS (*New York*)
DR. ROBERT COLES (*Cambridge, Mass.*)

MRS. CORNELIUS CRANE (*New York*)

DR. RALPH CROWLEY (*New York*)

DR. GEORGE DANIELS (*New York*)

DR. RICHARD DEMARTINO (*Philadelphia*)

DR. LOUIS DEROSIS (*New York*)

DR. HELENE DEUTSCH (*Cambridge, Mass.*)

DRS. ELSE AND FELIX DURHAM (*New York*)

MRS. VLADIMIR ELIASBERG (*Belmont, Cal.*)

DR. HARMON EPHRON (*Princeton, N.J.*)

MRS. HANNA FENICHEL (*Los Angeles, Cal.*)

DR. ANNA FREUD (*London, England*)

PROF. ERICH FROMM (*Locarno, Switzerland*)

DR. HARRY GERSHMAN (*New York*)

DR. GUSTAVE GRABER (*Berne, Switzerland*)

DR. ALEXANDER GRALNICK (*New York*)

DR. BERNDT GRAMBERG-DANIELSEN (*Altona, Hamburg, Germany*)

DR. MARTIN GROTJAHN (*Beverly Hills, Cal.*)

DR. ERNEST HARMS (*New York*)

DR. B. JOAN HARTE (*New York*)

MME. MARGARETHA HONEGGER (*Zurich, Switzerland*)

DR. LOUIS HOTT (*New York*)

DR. CHARLES HULBECK (*Locarno, Switzerland*)

MRS. ESTA (BRODY) HUTTNER (*New York*)

DR. MORRIS ISENBERG (*Forest Hills, N.Y.*)

DR. EDWIN KASIN (*New York*)

DR. NORMAN KELMAN (*New York*)

DR. WERNER KEMPER (*Berlin, Germany*)

DR. AKAHISO KONDO (*Tokyo, Japan*)

DR. KARL KORNREICH (*Harrison, N.Y.*)

DR. LAWRENCE KUBIE (*Towson, Md.*)

MRS. ELIZABETH LANCASTER (*New York*)

PROF. HAROLD LASSWELL (*New Haven, Conn.*)

MRS. GERTRUDE LEDERER-ECKARDT (*New York*)

DR. DAVID LEVY (*New York*)

MRS. MARIE LEVY (*New York*)

DR. GEORGE LEWIN (*New York*)

DR. DANIEL LIPSCHITZ (*New York*)

DR. SANDOR LORAND (*New York*)

MR. STEFAN LORANT (*Lenox, Mass.*)

DRS. YELA AND HENRY LOWENFELD (*New York*)

DR. PAUL LUSSHEIMER (*New York*)

PROF. GERHARD MAETZE (*Berlin, Germany*)

MRS. ELLI MARCUS (*New York*)

DR. JUDD MARMOR (*Los Angeles, Cal.*)

DR. ALEXANDER MARTIN (*Old Lyme, Conn.*)

DR. EUGENE MARX (*New York*)

DR. CLARA MAYER (*New York*)

DR. MARGARET MEAD (*New York*)

DR. JOHN MILLET (*New York*)

DR. RUTH MOULTON (*New York*)

DR. HANS MULLER-BRAUNSCHWEIG (*Geissen, Germany*)

MR. AND MRS. OTTO NEUMANN (*Queens Village, N.Y.*)

DR. ELKE (MULLER-BRAUNSCHWEIG) NEUSPIEL (*Ottawa, Canada*)

MRS. JANET (FREY) NIMMO (*Miami, Fla.*)

DR. MARVIN OPLER (*Buffalo, N.Y.*)

DR. ABE PINSKY (*Brooklyn, N.Y.*)

DR. FRANCES (STRELTZOFF) PIZITZ (*New York*)

DR. ISIDORE PORTNOY (*New York*)

DR. SANDOR RADO (*New York*)

PROF. DAVID REISMAN (*Cambridge, Mass.*)

MRS. PAULETTE (GODDARD) REMARQUE (*Ronco, Switzerland*)

DR. SIDNEY ROSE (*New York*)

DR. HILDA (FRANKEL) ROSENBERGER (*Jerusalem, Israel*)

DR. ERNST SCHACHTEL (*New York*)

DR. DAVID SCHECHTER (*New York*)

DR. HERTA SEIDEMANN (*New York*)

DR. LESTER SHAPIRO (*Rockville Centre, N.Y.*)

DR. J. WILLIAM SILVERBERG, JR. (*White Plains, N.Y.*)

MRS. ESTHER SPRITZER (*New York*)

DR. ERWIN STRAUSS (*Lexington, Ky.*)

MRS. KATHERINE (KELMAN) SUGARMAN (*New York*)

MR. JAMES SULLIVAN (*Washington, D.C.*)

MRS. ROSE (LANDERS) TANNENBAUM (*New York*)

MRS. HANNAH TILLICH (*East Hampton, N.Y.*)

DR. BELLA VAN BARK (*New York*)
PROF. URSULA VON ECKARDT (*San Juan, Puerto Rico*)
MR. WOLF VON ECKARDT (*Washington, D.C.*)
DR. EDITH (VOWINKEL) WEIGERT (*Silver Spring, Md.*)
DR. FREDERICK WEISS (*New York*)
MRS. GERTRUDE (TERMER) WEISS (*Newton, Mass.*)
DR. RITA (HONROTH) WELTE (*Cleveland, Ohio*)
DRS. ANTONIA AND SIMON WENKART (*New York*)
MRS. BARBARA WESTCOTT (*Rosemont, N.J.*)
DR. WANDA WILLIG (*New York*)
DR. ERICH WITTKOWER (*Toronto, Canada*)
DR. ALEXANDER WOLF (*New York*)
DR. ELEANOR YACHNES (*Brooklyn, N.Y.*)
DR. GARY ZUCKER (*New York*)
MR. CARL ZUCKMEYER (*Saas Fe, Switzerland*)
DR. BERNARD ZUGER (*New York*)

My special thanks are due to various secretaries, librarians and libraries, for their help in researching source material. These include:

MRS. MARY ROLFE and MRS. JANET NIMMO of the Association for the Advancement of Psychoanalysis
MS. RUBINTON, MS. REYNOLDS, MS. TAYLOR and MS. WOLPE and the library of the New York Psychoanalytic Institute
MR. JAMES MONTGOMERY, librarian, and the New York Psychiatric Institute
MR. ALBERT TANNLER and the University of Chicago Library, Special Collections Division
MR. KENNETH A. LOHF and the Butler Library, Columbia University, Manuscript Division
MS. DOROTHY PROVINE and the National Archives and Records Service
MR. ROY BASLER and the Library of Congress, Manuscript Division, Freud Collection
Springer Verlag, Hamburg, Germany
The American Institute for Psychoanalysis and the Association for the Advancement of Psychoanalysis, for permission to consult their files for historical material

KAREN HORNEY
Gentle Rebel of Psychoanalysis

I
PROLOGUE

As I turned into the entrance of the New School that wintry night in December 1946, I was struck by the long line of cars double-parked. This was highly unusual; double parking was generally not permitted except to take on or let off students. Even more unusual were the uniformed chauffeurs waiting in several of them. I did not connect them then with the lecture to which I was going. I thought some important personage, perhaps a visiting politician, was speaking at the school. Then as I entered the immense main auditorium I was again surprised, at the size of the audience. Though the room was crowded, I managed to find a seat fairly close to the podium.

The audience varied in age from teen-age college students to a sprinkling of elderly persons, with most in their thirties or forties. Their dress ranged from the carefully cultivated sloppy and casual of the college types to the sophisticated elegance of the obviously well-to-do. With the loud hum of conversation, the atmosphere seemed charged with a current of expectation and eagerness. It was a contrast to the usual staid psychoanalytic lectures I had been attending and which I had been expecting tonight.

I had come to hear Karen Horney as part of my search for direction in the future. My group of residents in the Bellevue Psychiatric Hospital that year was three times as large and somewhat older than the usual yearly crop. Most of us had recently returned from military service overseas, after having had firsthand contact with suffering and disability—medical or psychiatric. Although already much disillusioned by our experiences, we were all still moved by our private illusions that we could change the society which had given rise to the recent holocaust. We little realized that for most of us, these feelings were based on the imagined omniscience and omnipotence of youth, needed to cover our real naiveté, inexperience and indirection. We were all dedicated to psychiatry, which we idealistically believed would be the panacea to bring about this change.

And yet most of us felt that the psychiatry we knew was inadequate and imperfect, was a base metal that still needed the gold of analytic psychotherapy. We were all trying to decide which psychoanalytic school to join, which analytic theory to learn. The discussions we were accustomed to hold nightly only prolonged our indecision. I had attended many lectures to hear proponents of each view pontificate on their ideas. Among the many books I had read, Horney's first two works had stood out as intelligent, clear and free from the usual professional jargon—yet they were not totally convincing.

Therefore as I sat waiting I felt skeptical and wary. Would her lecture, like all the others I had heard, consist of the same time-worn clichés, abstruse generalities, God-given psychoanalytic theories or case histories tailored to fit the theoretical concepts?

The hubbub died down suddenly as Horney rose and stepped to the podium. She walked slowly, rather heavily and tiredly. And yet there was a kind of jaunty bounce to her gait that belied her seeming heaviness. She wore a plain brown dress, unadorned except for a small white collar to set it off from her browned neck. Her body was short and stocky, without obvious feminine contours. But in spite of the squarish solidity, she somehow gave me the impression of being small and frail. At first view, her face appeared plain, somewhat nondescript, all flat planes. Deeply tanned, her complexion melded with the color of her dress. Topping an oval face, her short-cut curly hair was of a mottled gray, though the light gave it a bright silvery shine. Her smallish straight nose ended in a slightly uptilted button. Her mouth seemed a little too long to be harmonious with the rest and the folds from its corners up to her nose cast deep shadows, accentuated by the play of light from above. It was difficult to estimate her age: Her skin was unlined except for the small crow's-feet at her eyes. An aura of youthfulness—or perhaps more accurately, of agelessness—hung over her. I judged her to be about fifty, though I later learned she had passed sixty.

As she stood there for a long moment, holding the edges of the podium, her dark eyes looking down on her notes, I had the impression of someone slightly afraid, stiffening her back in defiance of the audience or the world. Then as she raised her eyes she seemed to have a faraway look, like someone drawing into herself to gather strength.

She began to speak without any preliminary rising inflection in her voice, as if she were simply continuing some previous unsaid but understood message. Her voice was deep, almost husky, slow and low and rather uncertain at first, yet clearly audible in the absolute silence. She had a noticeable accent, difficult to identify exactly but certainly more Germanic than anything else, and at times she had some difficulty in finding the right word. But as she continued, an amazing change—at least to me—appeared to be taking place.

Her voice became stronger and took on assurance as she talked. Yet it was not loud, not strident; it remained quiet and gentle, albeit warm and vibrant. She left her notes and began to move out to the side so that eventually she was standing free to face the audience. She was serious and obviously concerned deeply with her subject. Her face lit up, especially those eyes, so that she seemed to be radiating enthusiasm and hope. Her voice took on a note of impassioned appeal without changing its tone of serenity. She stood erect now, appeared taller. I would have sworn that she had grown by at least a foot.

I do not remember the subject of her talk in detail, but it was not the usual psychoanalytic lecture, not the usual case history described or explained in scholarly language. She spoke of elemental passions, of love and hate, of ambition and self-contempt, of honesty and self-deception, of good and evil, of stagnation and growth—in short, of very human qualities in very human beings. What had so often been so complex and difficult to understand now seemed understandable in apparently simple terms. At times I felt she was looking directly at me, into me, appealing to me. She was describing *my* feelings and conflicts. I wondered how she could know me so perceptively. Automatically I remembered incidents when I had experienced the reactions she was mentioning. I felt a sudden clarity, a sudden awareness and a reassurance from within.

Almost astonished, even a bit ashamed of my reaction, I looked around. Everyone I could see bore the same rapt expression. They were caught in the same thrall as I. Then when she suddenly ended, the mood persisted for a prolonged moment of silence, a time the audience needed to recover, before it was broken by the long and loud applause. This loud reaction pleased and annoyed me at the same time. I left quickly before the questions began.

I went home profoundly moved and confused. I had been touched on a level more emotional than intellectual. I could not understand clearly what had happened. I felt admiration and awe for Horney. But my basic skepticism kept reasserting itself, preventing me from accepting these feelings. It made me angry at myself for being so easily swayed. How had this occurred? Was there something about Horney which had affected me so? Or was it the subject matter that provided me a key of entry to myself? Had her impact upon me—and upon the audience—been a kind of hypnosis, to which I had been particularly receptive in my state of indecision? I did not think so. Hers was no great oratory, no demagoguery, even though her low-keyed, down-to-earth style was convincing. I had heard other spellbinding speakers; she was not like them. Perhaps she represented some primeval Ur-mother, offering strength, tender loving care or surcease. Perhaps she had communicated an implicit message of optimism and hope—the hope of resolving our deepest human conflicts. Or was it simply some kind of personal charisma, a presence, that mysterious quality often referred to but never quite defined?

All these questions assaulted me at that time. And they continued to haunt me long afterward. I did not know the answers then. Yet at some deep level of my being, I knew one thing. From that experience I had made a decision without realizing it. I had decided to seek the answers by taking the step that was to shape and give direction to my entire future: to learn more about that woman and her ideas.

II
THE TIME AND PLACE

"Feelings and attitudes—normal and neurotic—are to an amazingly high degree molded by the conditions under which we live, both cultural and individual inseparably interwoven."

—*The Neurotic Personality of Our Time*

This is where she was born: the small village of Blankenese, about twelve miles west of Hamburg on the north bank of the Elbe. The time: September 16, 1885, toward the end of the Victorian era. At this point, the river widens into a small bay, about three miles across. Standing on the pebbly shore, one can see the massed cranes of the huge Hamburg shipyards pinpointing the sky off to the left. In the channel the great ocean-going steamers—stately white passenger ships or careworn freighters—pass regularly in review, plowing the waters on their way from the city to the sea. The small excursion boats, scurrying like waterbugs, make their eternal triangular rounds from the city to Cranz across the river and thence to the village here. Each arrival disgorges or picks up its boatload of milling tourists, who then scatter into the restaurants, the small hotels or the uphill streets. The little fishing dories are gone today; only a few wait forlornly in their anchorage or lie overturned on the strand.

The bank rises steeply, sloping up to the tops of the two low hills, one on each side of the town, and to the lower ridge between them. The pastel stuccoed houses hug the hillside, curving in double lines to follow the winding cobblestoned streets that lead down to the waterfront from the crest. The houses are square and squat, as solid and unchanging as the citizens; yet in their brown, yellow, pink or gray pastel shades, every window adorned with its bright flower-bedecked windowbox, each has a beautifully fresh, fragile, quaint look. Their appearance belies their age. Many still have the thatched roofs of yesteryear or the traditional Blankenese half-doors.

Coming from the city, the main road, the Elbechaussee, follows the shoreline closely, zigzagging gently. Reaching the town, it curves inland

[5]

behind the Muhlenburg Hill, to circle around the main square in front of the station. This is the center of the village. From here, the main street—the Bahnhofstrasse—descends toward the river. The Elbe road, now become the Blankeneserstrasse, follows the crest through the village until it finally turns northwestward across the fertile Holstein plain. In the village north of this road, the villas are newer and larger, each with its own plot of lawn and yard. To the south, on the steep slope side, the houses are aligned in banked contiguity, separated only by small flower-covered cement terraces. Between the adjoining rows run narrow flights of steps branching out laterally here and there—a veritable honeycomb to delight the children playing their games of hide-and-seek or cowboys-and-Indians, much as they did in the past.

Time flows gently in the village. To be sure, some things have changed. The town is now officially a suburb of Hamburg, included within its geographical limits. An electrified train and bus lines connect it with the metropolis. It has grown threefold, and crowds of commuters travel to and from the city daily. A line of automobiles can be found parked in front of the small shops along the main street on weekends or during the evening home-from-work hour. And yet the atmosphere is of a world removed from the hustle and bustle of the nearby city and seems as it was a hundred years ago. The pace of living is slow: People move slowly, think slowly and speak slowly. That one waits for service in the shops or restaurants is taken for granted. People seem to be slow to react emotionally. They tend to be taciturn and reserved and reflect before talking. Their German is slow-paced, low-toned, a poorly enunciated dialect similar in intonation and phrasing to the neighboring Danish. Indeed, the people here are said to be kith and kin—ethnically, culturally, emotionally and temperamentally—to the northern peoples, the British and the Scandinavians. Tradition is important here. Pride in custom and the heritage of the past is evident everywhere, from the homes to the picturesque old-fashioned clothes often seen on the streets, especially on Sunday. Even in the crowded weekly street market, shouting is seldom heard; voices tend to be restrained and low.

The seagoing tradition remains strong in the village. The ship-building yards for which the town was famous until 1900 are gone now. But every village elder, every homespun historial will tell you of the famous schooners and sloops built here that sailed under many flags to every port. The museum contains models of many of these; and their captains are memorialized in the statues in the parks. The fishing fleets formerly based here are gone also, except for a few hardy individuals who still go out daily. Yet in other ways the tradition is maintained. An important seamen's school trains many of the region's young men in the skills of the seagoing life. Many, if not most, children have small boats and sailing is taught regularly. Ship captains, active and retired, often come to live here, where they can be close to their ships. Just as Captain Berndt Wackels Danielsen had come before them.

The Danielsen name was well known in Bergen, Norway, in the mid-nineteenth century. A statue of Dr. Cornelius Danielsen stands in front of the town hall. Although a physician, he is remembered for his interest in many fields. He helped found the city museum and theater. His medical research into the effects of fish on human diet led to sweeping changes and modernization of the important fishing industry. Most significant, however, was his work on leprosy. He is credited by some with having discovered the *bacillus leprae* even before his compatriot, Hansen. In fact, he founded the well-known research institute where the latter worked.

His brother, Lars, though less glamorous, was no less known and respected in the community for his work as a master watchmaker. But Lars's son, Berenth Henrick Vackels Danielsen, born in 1836, did not wish to enter his father's bourgeois and sedentary trade. Stimulated by his uncle's work with the fishing industry and by his city's great seafaring tradition—it had been a major center in the ancient Hanseatic League—he was restless. Being boxed into a shop or tied down to a workbench was not for him, even though it would mean earning a decent and respectable living. He felt the call of the sea; he had to be a seaman. He had been influenced by the strict religious outlook of his family—and was not the sea one of God's greatest creations? The really big opportunities for seamen lay with the great German shipping lines, centered in Hamburg, so, after marrying a local girl, Berenth migrated there.

From what one can see in a photograph of him, perhaps in his forties, standing on a deck, dressed in oilskins, blown by the wind, he must have been a tall, dashing, handsome man. He has a look of self-confidence, of command, the look of someone who has mastered not only the elements but his peers as well. His blue eyes could be frightening, as Karen Horney was to recall. He rose through the ranks from able seaman in the Kosmos Line to commodore with the Hamburg-American Line (HAPAG) when the two lines were merged. After some years he became a German citizen and Germanicized his name. Berenth Vackels became Berndt Wackels, generally known as Captain Wackels, the simple surname he preferred. Four children issued from his marriage: Agnes, Astrid, Gideon and Enoch. His wife died when he was in his early forties. His children were in their teens at the time. Although he may have been seeking someone to mother them when he met and married young Clotilde Van Ronzelen some three years later, the children seem to have been out on their own already. But, as is often the case, they never really accepted their father's new wife, and resented Berndt and little Karen, when they were born, as well. This attitude probably contributed to the later marital difficulties of their parents.

To complement her father's Nordic strain, Karen's maternal lineage was Dutch-German. Clotilde was also descended from a well-known family. Her father, Jacobus Johannus von Ronzelen, an Amsterdam hydraulic engineer and architect, came to Bremen as a young married man, apparently at the invitation of the city council. He was named Director of the City Planning Commission. He was responsible for the building of the great port facilities at Bremerhaven, which stand even today as his monument. After his wife died, leaving him with four young children, he married young Marie von Camerer from Stuttgart. Unfortunately, she too died giving birth to their second child, a daughter Clotilde. He remarried a third time and had several more children. It was this last wife who raised the entire brood of children, supplying inexhaustible tender loving care. Karen was to recall this step-grandmother as a symbol of the giving maternal figure, a most positive influence on her life.

Clotilde, Karen's mother, was about twenty-seven when she married Captain Wackels, eighteen years her senior. One may ask why this young woman, described as proud, beautiful and intellectual, would have accepted such a situation. According to the social standards of the time, the marriage was eminently suitable. Both families were of good lineage. The Captain was a pious, God-fearing man, who could quote passage and verse from his well-used family Bible, if need be. True, he was somewhat gruff and masterful, but was this not fitting for a sea captain, accustomed to command from the bridge? And if he was not an intellectual and lacked certain genteel finesses, still he was mature and had attained a respectable status in his career. Besides, his work had a certain glamour and worldliness, even a hint of the adventurous. He had traveled far, to exotic places, and could tell stories well. He offered financial security and social stability. Though he might often be away on his trips, he could still provide for a substantial household, with even a maid to help care for the children.

In addition, Clotilde was at an age when marriage was a necessity if she was not to remain a spinster. As to the age difference, the patriarchal marriage was entirely in keeping with the Victorian ethic, which became enshrined in Germany as the *Kinder, Küche und Kirche* tradition. The husband was intended to be the absolute master of the home. The proper place of the wife was in the home; household affairs were her domain, independent work was taboo. Respectability, propriety and appearance were all important.

Berndt and Clotilde's first child, a son Berndt, was born in 1881, followed by Karen, four years later. But alas, the couple's eighteen-year difference in age was to be more than matched by their differences in personality.

III
CHILDHOOD AND ADOLESCENCE

"Basic anxiety can be roughly described as a feeling of being small, insignificant, helpless, deserted or endangered in a world that is out to abuse, cheat, humiliate, betray, envy . . . and special in this is the child's feeling that the parents' love, their Christian charity, honesty, generosity . . . may be only a pretense. If the child is fortunate enough to have a loving grandmother, an understanding teacher, some good friends, his experience with them may prevent him from expecting nothing but bad from everybody."

—The Neurotic Personality of Our Time

From as far back as she could remember, Karen felt that her brother Berndt had been treated differently than she. It was difficult to understand when she was little. Of course he was a boy, which could account for it but still did not explain it. Was it because as a boy he was built differently; or because people simply felt differently about boys than girls; or because he had qualities she didn't have, like charm, daring and good looks?

When Berndt was born, the parents' marriage was still new and fresh, filled with hope. The relationship between Wackels and Sonni—as Clotilde was affectionately called—was still that of newlyweds, carrying over the romantic ideals of the courtship days. Their firstborn, a son, fulfilled the tradition of carrying on the family name. He was wanted and welcomed and his parents' darling; he represented their hope for the future. He was indeed a delightful child: attractive, fair, charming, friendly.

When Karen arrived four years later, the situation was quite different. The relationship between her mother and father had changed. The differences in personality had been exacerbated by their daily life together. The qualities that could have first been seen as positive or as mere idiosyncrasies through the veil of their romantic idealization, may well have become irritants in later reality. Karen questioned whether she had really been wanted.

Wackels was a stern, righteous, religious man. The Evangelical creed, perhaps even more so than it is today, was a fundamentalist one, clearly distinguishing right and wrong, black and white, as defined by the Biblical truths. And these had to be imposed with zeal. Believe in them and you could be saved. Wackels was an avid Bible reader when he was at home. All that was wrong, forbidden, was to be repressed or chastized. He was a dominating, imperious man, accustomed to being obeyed and resentful of contradiction or what he felt to be disrespect. He was given to long silences, sometimes devoted to his Bible-reading, sometimes simply expressions of his anger; or to outbursts, when he might even throw his Bible at Sonni as if better to impress her with its words. In fact, perhaps after witnessing such outbursts, the children later used to call him *der Bibelschmeisser* (Bible-thrower) behind his back.

His feelings toward the children could also have been influenced by his attitudes toward the two sexes—defined in part by religious beliefs. Did not the Bible declare the woman to be secondarily created from the man; was she not subject to temptation in the Garden and thereby the source of evil? What was permitted the male could not be tolerated in the female. His son Berndt would be allowed freedom, privilege, education; these were not necessary for his wife or youngest daughter.

Sonni did not agree with these beliefs and attitudes. The extreme differences in their personalities gradually became contradictions, then conflicts and antagonisms. Inheriting the Dutch tolerance, she was a freethinker who could at first take a half-deprecating, half-accepting attitude toward his silences and religiousness. Beautiful, more sophisticated, more intellectual and better educated than he, she had different social and intellectual needs from his. It may have been difficult for her to remain the subservient female, the housewife. Wackels was willing enough to provide a maid to do the housework; yet when Karen was somewhat older and the maid was out, Wackels would answer Sonni's complaints with the remark that Karen could stay in to do the household chores. With such conflict and argument, his frequent absences must often have been a relief, even though his emotional presence filled the home and influenced everyone—especially Karen.

[11]

Karen's relationship with her father and her attitudes toward him seem to have been quite ambivalent. On the one hand, she needed and sought affection and attention from him. She admired and respected him, often visiting his ship. He took her on several longer trips with him—at least three and possibly more. One was when she was between the ages of two and three, another at about the time she reached puberty. During the latter trip they went as far as the Falkland Islands, around Cape Horn, and up the west coast of South America to San Diego. These voyages engendered in her a love for travel and a zestful curiosity about exotic places. Much later, perhaps from a vantage point of greater maturity, she was to speak of him in rather sympathetic terms. She appreciated his gusto and his enjoyment of life at a deep-down earthy level. He also brought her gifts from faraway places, which she was to recall with much pleasure. In later years she was apt to refer to "the captain and his ship" as expressing a positive, self-fulfilling attitude. In one lecture in 1942, when she was describing her own deep love for psychoanalysis, she compared it with the way a "captain feels about his ship. He knows its deficiencies and its assets and loves it regardless of any faults it may have." She even took to wearing a captain's-style cap for a while in the twenties, indicating a positive affinity—conscious or unconscious—for him. Physically she resembled him more than her mother, and friends would remark—especially when she wore the cap—how much she looked like him. His wish to have her on his trips surely bespoke, at the least, a fatherly interest and care, if not outright affection and love.

On the other hand, Karen also felt her father to be awesome and intimidating. She often was to recall "his frightening blue eyes." He was definitely stern, repressive and demanding. Karen felt that she was rejected by him, or at least less loved than her brother, throughout her childhood and adolescence. And yet, even when this feeling was greatest, for instance when he objected to her schooling—for her the sharpest hurt of all—she did not feel unadulterated anger or vindictiveness. Her attitude remained an admixture; as she used it in her diary when she was fourteen, the expletive "my precious father" carried a bitter-sweet tone, an irony, the mixture of anger and affection.

By contrast, Karen's relationship with her mother was a close, loving one. In spite of Berndt's favored position as the first-born child and the male, she felt a special warmth and devotion toward and from Sonni.

Perhaps this was because she was a girl and her mother could identify with her less favored position. Sonni seems to have supported and protected Karen against her father, particularly in her desire for education and in obtaining the means of procuring it. Perhaps, too, Sonni saw in her daughter's talents and wishes a means to fulfill vicariously her own thwarted ambitions. As they grew a little older the children formed a kind of protective alliance with their mother against their father. Later, in retrospect, she was to feel that her mother had demanded admiration, which she, as a compliant child, had felt compelled to give.

There are few factual details about Karen's earliest childhood. In pictures taken when she was about three, she appears to be a sturdy, beautiful child, with short blonde hair in a Buster Brown cut. Most striking in her photographs at this time as well as throughout her adolescence is the serious expression on her face; rarely is she smiling. Her head is usually tilted back slightly, chin raised in a proud position. The eyes look out with the reflective cast of the thinker. In several early pictures she is with her dolls. Her favored one at age three was a little sailor doll, in a photograph taken when she was twelve the dolls are dressed in costumes from various countries, probably gifts from her father. She had a strong need to give care, at first to her dolls and later to her patients.

In two of her books she transparently described a few significant events in her early childhood. Until the age of about eight she was a clinging, compliant little girl, "like a little lamb." Even so, she was unable to get the affection she desperately yearned for, that she needed for reassurance, from her parents. At eight she even placed some of her toys on the street for some poorer child to find, telling no one about it. Being self-sacrificing was her way of being good. But she changed at nine after Berndt drew away from her. She became not only ambitious but secretly rebellious. She would get revenge. Thereafter she decided to participate in the other girls' little intrigues involving some unsuspecting teacher, even leading some of them.

She had entered the local elementary school (*Volkshule*) at kindergarten. Still remembered fondly by oldsters of the town, it was then only recently built and the pride of the community. Its teachers were carefully selected for their background and social qualifications. They used the latest educational methods and all the current educational material, and instructed the students in the proper social attitudes as well. For little

Karen, school soon became a refuge, an outlet and a passion. This may have been partly an escape from the oppressiveness of her home environment. But in addition, she was possessed by an unusually intense native curiosity and zest for learning. Then there was another factor: her basic sense of inadequacy, related primarily to her feeling that she was physically unattractive. As she said years later to her daughter, "If I couldn't be beautiful, I decided I would be smart." This in spite of her being, in reality, a strikingly beautiful young girl.

Whereas her need to be smart had previously been a reaction to the lack of affection from her parents, it became a fierce ambition after her brother rejected her as well. Until then she had been strongly attached to him, with much sexually tinged tenderness. As he entered puberty, he became self-conscious about this affection. For Karen it was not only a loss, it was a blow to her pride as well; she felt ashamed and humiliated.

On the advice of the family doctor, her parents interpreted her dejection as due to her inability to keep up with her school work. They decided she was probably in too advanced a class. So after a summer vacation to get her away from the supposed strain of school, they had her put in a class one year lower. From then on she showed a driven ambition, vowing that she would always be first in her class. This interest in school and her obviously high intelligence impressed Sonni, who tried to encourage it. It was less appreciated by her father.

Karen had become an avid and omnivorous reader almost as soon as she had learned to read and she remained one throughout her life. Her favorite reading during these early years were the popular novels of Karl May, the German Zane Grey. He described the adventures of a young German lad wandering in the American Southwest among the Indians, prospectors, cowboys and cavalrymen during the mid-eighteen hundreds. Of the Indian chiefs the hero met, Winnetou, Chief of the Apaches, was the greatest. The two became tribal brothers by exchanging blood, according to tribal custom. These books achieved a tremendous popularity and thrilled millions of German children for over five generations, even though the author never left Germany. They pictured the downtrodden Indians sympathetically, with dignity. Karen used to play out the various roles with her closest girlfriend, Tutti, usually taking the part of Winnetou for herself. She would invent props for their adventures, such as the little flag sewed for the leader that was found in her box of childhood treasures after her death. Indeed, she later recalled with much pleasure how she and Tutti had gone through a highly dramatized ritual ceremony of blood sisterhood, each pricking her finger and mixing the drops—as Winnetou had done.

Tutti was the nickname of Gertrude Ahlborn, one of her earliest and dearest friends. They remained close throughout their lives, passing through the typical adolescent quarrels, angry separations and tearful reconciliations. Tutti went into teaching and social work and may have influenced Karen in her short-lived decision to become a teacher when she was fourteen. Tutti moved to Göttingen to continue her studies, apparently when Karen was in medical school there. Afterward they continued to correspond and visit, and Karen regularly sent Tutti each of her books.

After finishing elementary school, Karen entered a *Klosterschule*—a private parochial school, essentially a convent school—in Hamburg. At about this time, the family moved into the Eilbek section of the city, probably to be nearer the school. This section was a substantial, middle-class residential section, dominated by the immense Eilbek city hospital. As convenience dictated, many of the hospital staff and attending doctors lived there and medical offices abounded. It was also but a short walking distance to the Alster, the beautiful estuary of the Elbe where each Sunday it was customary for neighborhood families to go sailing in their small sailboats and little excursion boats, or to go strolling or riding in their carriages around the elegant lake drive.

Before 1900, such a parochial school usually included the equivalent of our junior high and high school (*Mittelschule* and *Hauptschule*), and went through age eighteen. On entering, children were usually questioned about their previous religious education and background; if this was considered inadequate, tutoring might be required. For Karen, such a requirement would not have presented a problem; on the contrary, it would have pleased her parents, especially Wackels. Heavy emphasis was placed on religious studies—history of religion, Bible study, theology—along with philosophy, literature, history, mathematics, German, French and English. No subjects were taught that were not tolerated by the church. Thus, some elementary natural science was permitted in some schools, but certainly not human biology. Strict discipline, obedience to teachers' authority and maintenance of propriety were enforced. In those schools that were co-educational, boys and girls were separated.

After entering the school, Karen seems to have gone through a phase of enthusiasm for religion. In part this was a form of self-surrender to the highest authority, in part it was due to her zest for learning. But it was also due to another trait which was to express itself many times in her later life. This was her tendency to become totally involved in whatever subject she was concerned with at the moment.

In addition, other factors were now motivating her as well. She was entering adolescence, maturing rapidly. Her interest in her various subjects was influenced by the attitudes of her teachers and by her reactions to them. As is so often the case with the idealistic, daydreaming adolescent, she went through romantic crushes on some of her teachers. One of these was her Bible teacher, Herr Schultze. In her diary she refers to him as her "beloved," her "adored," totally idealizing and idolizing him. During these infatuations, she loved profoundly, felt emotions profoundly and was devastated profoundly by rejection—whether real or conjured from within the depths of her exquisitely sensitive spirit. And yet, however much we might be inclined to dismiss these sentiments as only teen-age puppy love, in retrospect they were most significant. The attitudes involved—intense adulatory affection, idealization, fear of invoking rejective anger—seemed to presage similar attitudes later on toward other men. They also bespoke an intensity of inner emotion that would rarely be exposed thereafter. Finally, they again indicated a fertility of imagination.

When she was twelve, Karen made a momentous decision. She decided she would study medicine. What motivated her is largely a matter of speculation. Thirty years later, during a newspaper interview, she recalled that it was because she had been impressed by "a nice country doctor." This was the same expression she used to describe the father of the semifictitious patient, Clare, in her later book *Self-Analysis,* which suggests that she may have been partly referring to herself therein. Were she or her parents treated by such a doctor during some minor illness? Was it another instance of a similar idealizing relationship during this impressionable age? Was the choice an unconscious reaction to deep feelings of something needful within herself, so that she identified and empathized with the helpless ill—as do many youngsters who go into the caring professions?

Whatever the answer, this decision presented problems. It would require changing her course of study. The *Klosterschule* curriculum of religious studies was not acceptable as preparation for medical school.

What school to choose? The regular *Gymnasium* emphasized the humanities, Latin and Greek, but did not give enough science courses, an absolute requisite for medicine. The *Realschule*, in contrast, stressed the sciences but lacked the courses in the humanities and literature that Karen loved, as well as Latin, which she also needed. This was more for the specialized scientific professions like engineering. There remained the *Realgymnasium* for girls. This provided a broader course of study—the sciences and humanities, philosophy and logic, Latin and a modern language and some mathematics, but did not require Greek. That would be the best. She would still have to take an entrance exam, the *Aufnahmprüfung*—not too much trouble for a bright student. But she might get only partial credit for her *Klosterschule* studies and lose some time. In fact, since one usually graduated from the *Realgymnasium* (which included two years of the equivalent of our college) at eighteen, and Karen finished at twenty (in 1906), she actually did require an additional period of make-up time.

Another obstacle was the tuition, even though her books would be free. Not only would her father's financial help be needed, but she would also have to have his permission to go. This would be difficult to obtain in view of his objections to higher education for girls. He could always argue that obligatory schooling for most Hamburg children did not go beyond age fourteen (the *Bürgerschule*) and only rarely up to eighteen (*Hauptschule*).

As she had feared, her father did refuse her the *Realgymnasium*—at first.

By the time Karen reached thirteen, many changes had occurred in her feelings, attitudes and personality. While some of these were typical of every pubescent girl, some were atypical, even remarkable. For one thing, she began to keep her secret diary.* This in itself is not unusual for the shy, sensitive girl who does not have the opportunity or inclination to confide in others. What is unusual is the length of time she kept it—until she was twenty-four. Her diary was her confidante, with whom she carried on a personal dialogue, even though, as with an old friend whom we see only occasionally but with whom we feel in close contact, she wrote in

---

* Recently discovered among her papers. The quotations here are taken from excerpts written or publicly spoken by her daughters, at the Association for the Advancement of Psychoanalysis and the American Academy of Psychoanalysis.

it only intermittently, sometimes weekly, sometimes at yearly intervals. There is an almost four-year gap from 1906 through 1909, between the ages of twenty and twenty-four, during her medical-school years and courtship. The gap is partly filled in by letters she wrote to her then husband-to-be, which he kept and passed on. In fact, at one point in them she refers to them as her "living diary." Her own words provide an insight into her personality and emotional development. The style of writing is innocent, intimate, revealing. Thus she writes, "Dear Diary, I have been unfaithful to you. A whole year has gone by since I last confided in you. . . . there is an endless amount to tell [you]." The last entry is the inclusion of a letter to her psychoanalyst terminating her analysis. To her dear pages she confided her hopes, her ideals, her plans and especially her problems and doubts.

From her diary entries it is evident that one trait emerging in her at this time of pubertal change was a growing skepticism. She was beginning to doubt and question the concepts she had previously accepted as given. This derived as much from her intense innate curiosity and need to explain things for herself as it did from a basic earthy pragmatism. She seemed to have difficulty in understanding and accepting abstract or metaphysical notions. And since she was so immersed in religious studies at the time, it was inevitable that her doubts should focus on religion. For instance, she writes, "Was Jesus truly God's son or was he a human being who simply represented a divine principle?" She could not understand such a mixture of God and man. She turned to her brother Berndt for a clarification. When he explained that since Jesus was the strongest embodiment of a divine element present in everyone, he was therefore [the] man closest to God, she felt uplifted: "Something like a stone fell from my heart . . . He became dearer to me."

At another point she questioned the miraculous reappearance of Jesus to his disciples, given in the Bible as proof of His resurrection. She asked whether this luminous vision might not have been a subjective hallucination of Paul, due to his overwrought emotional state. Perhaps this was an early forerunner of her interest in emotional explanations of behavior.

Her rebellious doubting continued during her entire early adolescence. At the time of her confirmation, she not only resented having to go to church but was filled with doubts about all her religious beliefs. "My religion is in a desperately sad state. Questions and doubts bother me, which no one can solve for me. What is God? Is God personal? Is he a God of love?" The discrepancy between the Christian ideals she was being taught and the attitudes she found in her home was too painfully striking to her.

Of course, she associated the religious authorities, God and her minister, with the authority of her father. At fifteen her despair and anger at him reached its greatest depth. She wrote, "It must be grand to have a father one can love and esteem. The Fourth Commandment stands before me like a specter, with its 'Thou shalt.' I cannot respect a person who makes us all unhappy with his hypocrisy, egocentricity, crudeness and ill-breeding." Pouring out her anguish after her confirmation, she noted "indescribable days for Mother and us under the fearful domination of the master of the house and our pastor. Pen and paper would rebel against writing down anything so coarse and mean. Confirmation was no blessing for me. On the contrary, it was a great piece of hypocrisy, for I professed belief in the teachings of Christ, the doctrine of love, while carrying hatred in my heart (and for my nearest at that). I feel too weak to follow Christ. Yet I long for the faith, firm as a rock, that makes oneself and others happy. He who was love, the pure one, hovers before me as a glorious ideal."

Yet even though she could confide such angry and hostile feelings to the intimacy of her diary, it was still too difficult to come out with them openly. Nevertheless, such questioning and skepticism, even rebellion, were positive signs of her maturating, her independence. Today we would consider such changes in attitude an aspect of normal adolescent growth, part of the search for identity. But in the context of her times, of the strict moralistic religious environment she had been raised in, it was indeed a daring stance for a girl of fourteen. In effect it constituted a profound questioning of her deepest roots and background, of basic concepts she had been trained to value highly, of her very identity. This could not have been an easy step to take. It also meant contradicting—rebelling against— her father and his edicts, "standing up to the frightening gaze of my father's blue eyes," as she later confided to her friend Franz Alexander.

At the same time she needed to ask her father's permission and support for further schooling, which he was strongly resisting.

But even more painful, as she notes in the diary, because it had to be repeated daily before her classmates, was facing the disapproval or anger of her beloved teacher toward her doubting. Dealing with such disapproval or anger was apparently an emotional problem for her then, and it remained one. Perhaps her need and quest for her father's love, displaced onto other father-figure authorities, constituted one dynamic source of this problem.

Another trait she developed at this time was the ability to set clearly defined goals for herself, along with a directness in going after them. This required a determination and persistence most remarkable for a young girl. One example was her desire to study medicine. When Wackels first refused permission for her to go to the *Realgymnasium,* she set up an alternate plan. She would go into teaching for three years until she could manage to go into medicine on her own. In the meantime she would bring to bear upon her father and mother all the influence she could muster. This same persistence and directness was to be evidenced many times in her later life.

That she did develop this kind of skeptical rationality and realism at fourteen was surprising, considering the equally intense romanticism and fantasy-making tendency she also possessed. Only a scant while before, she had still been inventing situations for her dolls; then living out in her imagination the exploits of her Indian friends; and finally experiencing the emotions of her crushes. The coexistence of these two tendencies in her personality speaks for a puzzling dichotomy, which she had to encompass. As she grew older, a change occurred in her romanticizing—possibly due to her reality-oriented intellectuality. Thus, at about fifteen, she wrote, "I tell myself stories all the time, now more than ever. This story telling is really amusing. I picture to myself the story of my choice. As characters I choose my crushes, and myself as chief character. The main story is apt to be the same, but each time I weave in whatever I have experienced or read."

While her imagination was still playing a significant role in her activities, there was now a difference. She had an awareness of the process of creating her imaginary world. She was no longer actually living in her imagination but had moved away from it as on-going experience, to become more of an intellectual observer. Later on, in her theory, she was to recognize the considerable significance of these attitudes—living in imagination and intellectualization—by defining them as defensive methods for providing inner harmony. But at that time, however much her down-to-earth realism and rationality may have been needed to cushion her frustration or disappointment, they also lessened the beautiful spontaneity and youthful exuberance that had shone through in her diary.

Nevertheless, in spite of his reluctance to help her at first, her father was eventually brought around. First, several of her mother's friends convinced Sonni, who then tried to persuade him. Then brother Berndt, now committed to go to law school, intervened. He had heard a lecture on the "woman question" praising advanced schooling for girls. He communicated these views to Wackels. Karen's Aunt Klara likewise added her weighty influence. Finally, Karen gave her father a written statement—in verse, no less—promising him that if he would only help her through the *Realgymnasium* she would ask nothing more of him. This won the day. And in her diary she poured out her happiness.

She entered the *Realgymnasium für Jungen Mädchen* in September 1901, her young dream come true. The new school was different from anything she had known before. At first she found it confusing, overpowering. Then as she got used to it her basic objectivity and sense of humor reasserted themselves. She could even begin to comment on the foibles of her teachers. She saw them as individuals, some interesting, some boring, some clear, some almost incomprehensible. She soon had to find out what learning really was. It was hard work, but she enjoyed it nonetheless.

In a photograph taken at this time, her face still carries the imprint of a striking young adolescent beauty—fine-featured, with a thin, straight patrician nose, high rounded cheekbones and a chin just beginning to take on the softly rounded contours of womanhood. And yet, as she was later to recall, she did not appreciate this subtle beauty. She did not feel beautiful. She often felt unlovable and unloved.

At about this time, the family moved from the city proper to the village of Reinbeck, about fifteen miles east of Hamburg. In 1900—much as it is today—this was a suburban town of modest one- and two-family houses. Its situation in farming country combined rural tranquillity with the advantages of city life nearby. As it was about a half hour's train ride for Karen to commute to school her parents must have judged her mature enough and worldly enough to be away from home.

Until now her developing sexual urges had apparently not been a problem. Her idealized crushes on men had been so purely intellectual that they had not involved her on a more physical or interpersonal level. She had accepted the standard sexual repressions and prudery so characteristic of that time: One must be unconcerned about such things. At seventeen, however, such feelings and interests could no longer be denied. She began to wonder not only about relations between men and women, but also, as she noted in her diary, about male and female homosexuality. She was enlightened by her schoolfriend Alice, and found the implications of it all quite troubling. Then, with her typical pragmatism, curiosity and directness, she paid a visit to the Hamburg red light district—along the famous Reeperbahn—to observe what she could of people's behavior there. In her diary she asked herself whether a girl should have sexual relations before marriage or wait until she truly loved a man. She was now further questioning the strict code of morality she had been raised on. She wrote how Shakespeare's dictum helped her resolve the turmoil she was feeling. " 'There is nothing either good or bad but that thinking makes it so.' All our morals are either nonsense or immoral. Will this ever change? The dawn of a new time is breaking."

However, breaking out of the confining restrictions of her moral code was not easy. She expressed her struggle and all-powerful longing in a beautiful and moving poem in her diary. In it she pictures herself buried, as if in a dungeon beneath the stone debris of an old castle. She is able to burst out to see, to know, to enjoy everything, singing a jubilant song to freedom and light. But she is then haunted by uncertainty about the goal she is seeking. Finally she realizes and accepts that life is only "watchful searching without complaining, and restless seeking. Rest is synonymous with imprisonment—but life does not know it. No weary resignation; that is life. Dare to accept it." She voices the same message later in her book *Self-Analysis:* ". . . the idea of a finished human product not only appears presumptuous, but even, in my opinion, lacks any strong appeal. Life is struggle, striving, development and growth . . . certainly its positive accomplishments are important, but also the striving itself is of intrinsic value. As Goethe has said in *Faust,* 'whoever aspires unweariedly is not beyond redeeming.' "

In spite of these inner struggles and her feelings of self-doubt and transitory depressions, she continued to devote herself wholeheartedly to her studies. Literature and drama were her special passions. Shakespeare, Goethe, Ibsen, Stendhal, Hugo, Zola, Balzac, Neitzsche, all those who dealt with the human comedy, delighted and stimulated her. In her later writing, she was apt to quote them, and to discuss their work in her seminars and courses on literature and psychoanalysis. When she was about sixteen, she was so taken by drama that she considered becoming an actress. She even took special tutorial courses in acting and declamation, presumably to help her overcome inhibitions in speaking before an audience. Years later, when her daughters were grown, she was to recall that at this time she had had three ambitions: to be a doctor, an actress and a mother. She achieved two, and in her daughter's career she found fulfillment of the third. Her basic English courses gave her a blessed foundation for her later adopted language. She was aware of how bright she was and proud of it.

By the time she reached seventeen, her period of religious doubt was coming to an end. Of course, she had not only doubted her religious background and principles, she had also questioned her general self-worth. She felt different from other girls, inferior. Now she began to take a stand against this self-derogatory attitude, scolding herself in her diary for feeling the way she did. "My ordinariness is evident in my wanting very much—how pedantic—to know what I am in the religious, moral sense. Christian, deist, pantheist, monist, atheist? Berndt says that developing larvae like me describe themselves best as 'skeptics.' " She was to remain agnostic throughout most of her life, at least until her sixties.

Yet in spite of this moderation of her self-criticism and greater self-acceptance, her tendency toward self-analytic questioning was to become and remain one of her most notable personality traits. In her own words she describes this subtle transformation a short time later. "I really shouldn't read anything, no books but only myself. For one half of my being lives, the other observes, criticizes, is given to irony. Things look so devastated in me that I myself cannot burrow my way through the labyrinth. And yet: I am beginning to burrow. I often think I see the light toward which I am struggling. Then again I get deeper into chaos. Before my confirmation, I made my last attempt to pray. The same words came: Lord, give me truth. I now know no one can give me this, but only through my own work will I get a clear view."

Her personality was changing in other ways too, at this time. Her expansiveness—previously expressed mainly in her ambitiousness and competitiveness with Berndt—was now coming out in another way. Her social life increased, she became more gregarious. She was dating now and several young men were attracted to her. Some of her friends of this period are known by name. Tutti, Alice and Ida Behrmann were girlfriends; Rolfe and "Losche" (Louis) Grote were boyfriends. Perhaps this change was the result of the internal struggle she had recently been experiencing; or perhaps her personality had first changed as part of her developmental growth and this change had then precipitated the struggle.

In a photo of her at eighteen she is no longer an adolescent. She has the contours of a mature woman. Her expression is determined and resolute, her eyes have a defiant, proud look, her compressed lips and head tilted back seem to be challenging the world, to be saying that she will succeed in spite of everything. And so she did.

She had no difficulty with the *Abitur*—the standardized *Gymnasium* final examination, commonly known to students as the *Matura*. But then the problem of entering medical school had to be faced. Admission to medical school in Germany in 1906 was not as difficult as it is today; almost all applicants were accepted as long as they were German citizens. For a woman, though, it was much harder, even though Karen had the required marks. Another problem was where to go. There are many reasons why Karen might have chosen Freiburg-im-Breisgau. Hamburg did not yet have its own university medical school. Furthermore, it was an old tradition for German medical students to attend several different universities for their basic sciences, their preclinical and their clinical studies. Karen had traveled during the previous three years and had had the opportunity to see different cities and compare them. Freiburg was a well-known and respected Catholic medical school; many students from northern Germany went there. It was noted for its large anatomical museum and laboratories and for the respected pathologist Professor Ashoff. Berlin was still the greatest center of medicine in Germany, but that was because of its great hospitals, and therefore for clinical studies. As all the state schools had the same curriculum, one could easily change after a few semesters without losing credit. As a clincher, her friend Louis was also going there. It was probable that this influenced her decision.

Leaving the family home presented a mixed blessing. Her father was now in his late sixties and his tyrannical behavior, his irascibility, his tirades had become accentuated with age. Karen's mother could apparently take it no longer; in August 1904 she had left him, taking the children with her back to Hamburg. The move required them to be self-supporting. Karen had already promised she would no longer seek or accept financial help from her father. It was a difficult time for them. For a year and a half they lived in sublet furnished apartments. Wackels withheld financial help apparently to put pressure on Sonni to return. Both Karen and Berndt helped out by tutoring. Then, when it was time for Karen to enter the school in Freiburg, her mother went with her while Berndt went on to Berlin.

IV
THE MEDICAL STUDENT

"That many-faceted thing called love succeeds in building bridges from the loneliness on this shore to the loneliness on the other one. These bridges can be of great beauty, but they are rarely built for eternity and frequently they cannot tolerate too heavy a burden without collapsing. Here is the other answer to the question posed of why we see love between the sexes more distinctly than we see hate—because the union of the sexes offers us the greatest possibilities for happiness. We therefore are naturally inclined to overlook how powerful are the destructive forces that continually work to destroy our chances for happiness."
—"The Distrust Between the Sexes"

"Education for women" was the rallying cry throughout Germany at the turn of the century. The subject generated even more passion and polemics than the issue of suffrage. Women were speaking in public forums in every city, led by such feminists as Helen Lange, Minna Caur and Gertrude Baumer. One such lecture in Hamburg had, in fact, impressed Berndt and favorably influenced Karen's father, so breaking down any remaining resistance he might have had to Karen's own further education. Newspapers and magazines carried many messages for and against the education of women. Even so liberated a playwright as W. S. Gilbert, however much he poked fun at Victorian restrictions, still hesitated about education for women when he wrote in *Princess Ida:* "A Woman's college! Maddest folly going! What can girls learn within its walls worth knowing?" A hostile article by Nietzsche, "Why I Hate Women," and a favorable one by Joachim Weichert in the Viennese newspaper *Die Zeit,* "Should Women Be Educated?" attracted much literary attention. (The latter was reprinted in the leading Moscow literary journal in 1905, the week of the abortive uprising. It was cited in turn by a Viennese socialist newspaper as an indication of how far Russia was out of step with the social realities of other countries.)

Prior to 1890 women had not been permitted to study at the German universities. In 1892, when Herman Grimm demanded that they be allowed to attend lectures in Berlin, his motion had been refused. Although women had been permitted to take the *Abitur* from the state *Realgymnasiums* after 1893, they still could not enter the universities. The universities of the state of Baden—including Heidelberg and Freiburg—were the first to accept women in their science and medical schools. In fact, in 1904, only two years before Karen entered medical school, the professor of anatomy in Berlin had politely but firmly escorted one young woman from the anatomy class before a demonstration apparently considered too risqué for feminine viewing. Officially women were permitted to pursue such studies in Prussian universities (including Berlin) from about 1906 on. Yet even though Freiburg was one of the first medical schools to admit women, Karen was the only woman in her group of seven in the photograph taken to celebrate their passing the preclinical examination.

She arrived in Freiburg with Sonni in May 1906.

Freiburg was then a city of perhaps 60,000 persons, much smaller than Hamburg, yet most beautiful and picturesque, situated about twelve miles from the Rhine. The waters of the Dreisam River flowed through the streets of the town in little canals. The ramparts of the old city were laced with footpaths that gave opportunity for delightful walks above the vineyards planted below; the Black Forest was only a few minutes away. In the center of the city, its medieval heritage was evidenced by the ducal and archepiscopal palaces, the ornate town hall, and the Kaufhaus, or merchants' hall. The stately Gothic cathedral, with its serene Holbeins and Baldungs and stained glass windows, was a place where students would sometimes go just to meditate.

The small but famous Ludovico-Albertina (Ludwig-Albert) University dated back to the sixteenth century under the Jesuits. Its old buildings were well preserved and hallowed by tradition. The medical faculty was rather small, and there were about a hundred students at that time. Most of them lived in the student quarters near the school, in furnished rooms or boarding houses. Karen's mother rented an apartment and took in a few students as boarders. Although tuition was low for the courses, it was still difficult to make ends meet. Karen earned some money by tutoring other students.

Ida Behrmann, Karen's friend from Hamburg, alone in the city and lonely, was one of the boarders who came to live with them. She was the daughter of a well-to-do Jewish family, who had been and remained fast friends with Karen. Louis Grote was also a boarder. Ida later married Louis, who, like Karen, went on to Berlin to finish his studies. Ida and Louis were Karen's witnesses at her own marriage. After graduation Louis eventually went on to become the physician-in-charge of a private hospital in Frankfurt and, still later, professor-in-charge of an important Dresden hospital. He made a reputation as a medical historian, writing a series of books on the lives of well-known physicians of the time.

Student life in Freiburg was all that Karen had imagined. In the university district, the students were well known and given special privileges—lower prices in the shops and street cars, and amused tolerance for their exuberance. Dr. Jacob Nahum, a physician still practicing today, recalls the student atmosphere of that time. "It was the summa university for many young students, very well known. But you didn't go for studying. The lectures were there, but it was not only for learning or exams. It was to become acquainted with medicine. The students had a good time. There was a feeling of freedom. You could fly there, not like in a big town. Like a bird in a cage who gets free. There was little competition. The students wanted nature, freedom, studying and at the same time a good time."

Here at last was the freedom Karen had yearned for, that she had celebrated in her diary. Classes still had to be attended, course material had to be studied, yet in reality the demands were not that heavy. Not for a woman with her intellectual capacity. Besides, no examination was required until the end of the first five semesters, with plenty of time to prepare. However, other factors could have contributed to the pressures she experienced, not so much because of the course of study but as a result of her reaction to the new situation. Being the only woman in that male-dominated atmosphere must have been difficult, especially for a woman with her ambitions. Other women in similar situations have described such experiences. It would have been necessary to compete, to prove that she could do as well as, if not better than, her male counterparts. We know that Karen was competitive, for instance with Berndt. She had turned to studying, to using her intellectual gifts as a means of surpassing him.

If being in the minority was a disadvantage in her academic work, it could only have been an advantage in her social life. Here she not only had her friends from Hamburg, but she soon met Oskar Horney, who was visiting his boyhood friends Karl Muller-Braunschweig and Walter Honroth, who were studying there. All three had come from the same region in the state of Braunschweig (Brunswick), between the towns of Hessen and Hildesheim. Although Oskar remained only a short while in Freiburg, he often came to visit during that first year.

The Horney name is a historic one and can be traced back to the thirteenth century. In a medieval chronicle, the Horneis are described as a family of well-to-do farmers in the Brunswick region. The Barons Hohenrode (Honroth), knights and robber-barons who owned a castle in the foothills of the Harz Mountains, ambushed a wagon train loaded with produce and goods belonging to the Horneis and "slew their servants and men." Hardly a propitious beginning for what later became a long and enduring family friendship.

Oskar Horney was a strikingly handsome young man: tall, slender, with light-brown hair and small, almost classic features. He usually sported a full mustache, with a trimmed but wispy goatee; this, along with his thin, gold-rimmed pince-nez glasses, gave him a slightly severe, meticulous, bookkeeperish, yet still elegant appearance. The expression in his eyes could add a stern quality to this impression; and yet at times they showed a tender and appealing look. He tended to hold himself so straight that one of his friends described him as resembling a "Prussian lieutenant." He had a rather high-pitched voice which could strike one as incongruous on hearing it for the first time. Then majoring in economics at the University of Brunswick, he was reputed to be a brilliant thinker and a gifted planner and organizer. Chess was a favorite pastime, although—at least in those student days—he was not one-sidedly intellectual. He enjoyed physical sports as well, especially Ping-Pong and tennis, a somewhat exclusive sport for those times. He was intensely competitive at sports and seemed to have a need to win. In spite of a superficial emotional restraint and a basic conservatism, he had a playful sense of humor. At parties or with children, he could always be relied on for the fun, entertainment and games.

It is easy to see how Karen would have been attracted to him. His emotional strength, intellectual ability and dominating personality were very much a reflection of similar traits in herself. He could provide the strength which she could lean on and depend upon, satisfying her own underlying dependency needs. Indeed, Oskar was attractive to and attracted by women in general—which could have added to his desirability in those days of student socializing.

Karen, too, seems to have been popular with the young men of the group. Karl Muller-Braunschweig was one of these. Much later, when reminiscing about this period with a colleague, he recalled having remarked that if Oskar was not going to marry Karen, then he, Karl, would have done so himself. Although tall, blond and handsome, he differed in many ways from Oskar. He spoke slowly and reflectively, in a low, deep voice. In contrast to Oskar's penchant for mathematical and logical reasoning, he preferred the speculative and the philosophical. He had begun his college studies in Munich in philosophy, with special emphasis on Kant and Kierkegaard. But he had a broad range of other interests, including art and theology. Many of his college friends were artists. Later, after he had switched to psychiatry, he continued to be fascinated by religion. Even after going into psychoanalysis, he worked with ministers and organized a group of pastoral "healers." Oskar considered Karl's interest in art frivolous, although he could appreciate his philosophy as long as it remained logical and rationalistic. For Karen, Karl's interest in religion must have furnished a common bond, particularly since this interest seems to have derived in both cases from their attempts to resolve the doubt and conflicts created by the intensely religious atmosphere of childhood. Their discussions were lively and sometimes heated. They made a strong impression on Karen and she was to recall them with much pleasure. In fact, in her later writings she often quoted Kierkegaard and, in 1930, gave a course on his work.

From September 1906 until the end of 1907, while Oskar was still finishing his studies in Brunswick, Karen kept up a constant correspondence with him. She poured herself into her letters, much as she had done with her diaries. These letters were kept as mementoes and today they shed much light on her feelings and attitudes at that time. They were not merely emotional outpourings, love letters, expressing her longing to be with him. They were also intellectual continuations of the discussions the two had shared in Freiburg. In fact, the intellectual bond seemed to overshadow the emotional closeness. This is not to say that she did not reveal her feelings in her letters, in particular her changing attitudes toward her mother. She was taking Sonni down from her idealized place on the pedestal. She now saw her as a basically good person, but somewhat cold-hearted, with a lack of self-control and exaggerated feelings of independence. These were qualities Karen did not find to her liking. Obviously her attachment to her mother—her own dependency needs—were chafing. She was experiencing the normal conflict of late adolescence between dependency and independence.

During this same time, another of her most cherished attitudes was being challenged, her feelings about her adored bother Berndt. He had become a handsome, charming young man, suave and gallant, with a way with the girls, though still a serious student. While he was at law school in Berlin, he wrote long letters to Sonni, in an affectionate, half-teasing tone, as if addressing a girlfriend, admonishing her not to go out too much and to be good. Though he constantly promised to come see her and to help her financially, he always found some excuse not to. Karen began to feel some doubt about him, to wonder how responsible he really was. Some disillusionment was beginning to set in.

The two years passed swiftly. Wackels died quietly during this time, of typhoid fever. Karen's half-brother Enoch came with the news and she later recalled how sympathetic and helpful he had tried to be. Until then she had intensely resented her four half-brothers and -sisters. She had felt that they had turned her father against her mother and herself. Besides, had he not encouraged, even financed their education while refusing any assistance to Sonni, Karen and Berndt? This was particularly true of Enoch: He had become an archaeologist and for a time worked in a museum. On another occasion, Enoch arranged to show her around a local museum—always one of her favorite pastimes—a friendly gesture that she remembered affectionately. Perhaps too, now that she was achieving her own educational goals, her envy and consequent resentment of Wackels's favored treatment of Enoch had begun to soften. In any case, this was one time she was to remember him as more human.

In September 1908 she took her *Physikum*, the examination on preclinical subjects, which she passed without difficulty. In the commemorative class photograph, dressed in the formal conservative white bouffant blouse and long black skirt, Karen has an uncertain half-smile, is biting her lip. She gives the impression of being ill at ease and timid. Most significantly, while the six boys are carrying student swagger sticks—emblems of the

German male student arrogance—Karen is holding a skull crooked in her arm, symbol of the head and intellect.

By this time, Oskar had transferred to the University of Göttingen to continue his studies in economics and political science. During the Michaelmas vacation (September 29), after Karen's examinations but before the beginning of the next semester, she and Sonni moved to Göttingen as well. Some of Karen's friends from the boarding house, including Ida and Louis, accompanied them. Here her medical school work became more demanding. In addition to the more advanced lecture courses in pathology, pharmacology and bacteriology, she also had to attend the "polyclinics" in medicine, surgery, gynecology and obstetrics, in combination with the textbook study of these subjects. These were general out-patient clinics for the indigent, where the medical students had their first contact with real live patients.

For Karen this surely represented a most significant, even a climactic step in her development. We know that she had an intense emotional need to care for others, even as she had cared for her dolls. Until now her notions about medicine had been idealized, abstract and theoretical, from the books; now it was becoming reality, human. The impression this confrontation with the suffering clinic patients made on her was later expressed in a statement on the importance of clinical medicine: The clinic, she said, could best impart the special skills needed for observation of the living, suffering human being, the experience of his sickness and compassion for it, the sense of responsibility for his helplessness, and above all, the will to heal. She seemed to have a special feeling—or need—for clinic work, manifested by her desire to be affiliated with a clinic. Thus, she was first attached to the Lankwitz Clinic, next stayed at the Berlin polyclinic for psychoanalysis for ten years, then unsuccessfully tried to start a similar clinic in her own institute, and was overjoyed when a public clinic bearing her name was finally about to be established.

The time in Göttingen flew by. Few specific details are known of this period. Karen's childhood friend Tutti came to Göttingen during this time to study social work. She eventually married a university professor there and settled down. Karen corresponded regularly with Tutti, sent her her books, and visited her.

In a later curriculum vitae Karen wrote simply that she had decided to go to the University of Berlin for the winter semester of 1909–1910. The spring semester ended in July. Oskar apparently finished his studies and took his final exam (*Staatsexamen*), but it is not known whether he did so in Göttingen or Berlin. Karen writes further, "on the 31st October, 1909, I was married to Oskar Horney, *Dr. rer., pol.*" The Grotes were their witnesses. Karen was now twenty-four, mature and confident in some ways, naive and uncertain in others. During the preceding three and a half years she had neglected to write in her diary. If the diary was her confessional, the outlet for her problems and difficulties, for her disappointments and doubts, then these years were the happiest of her young life.

V

BERLIN 1910: MARRIAGE AND MEDICINE

"It would not be going too far to assert that . . . conflict confronts every woman who ventures upon a career of her own and who is . . . unwilling to pay for her daring with the renunciation of her femininity."
—"The Overvaluation of Love"

Berlin, 1909: the young couple full of love, hope, enthusiasm and determination.

Berlin in 1909 was the hub of Germany, important and imposing. The city was bustling and booming and growing, the *Berliner Tempo* accelerating. Its population was increasing rapidly as students and workers, intellectuals and artisans, talented innovators and followers flocked into the city from all over Germany and from abroad. Berlin was like a magnet for the young, the energetic and the ambitious, for anyone seeking opportunity. Careers could be had for the taking in business and finance, in the theater, film and dance, in art and literature, science and medicine. The immigrants included many soon-to-be-illustrious names in all of these fields, and all of them quickly became Berliners. There were Czechoslovak, Russian, French and English colonies mixing in the polyglot cafés, and a new American community numbering several thousand. Electric trolley lines to the suburbs replaced the old horse-drawn trams and an extensive new subway system, begun in 1906 as a short hop from the Potsdamerplatz to the zoo, reached to the outskirts of the city in a few years. Private automobiles had been multiplying like mushrooms since 1902; by 1910, there were almost four thousand taxis, *Kraftdroschken* (and a new dial telephone exchange as well). The elegant center of the city was crowded with the obviously, or at least apparently, affluent, but the industrial slums were also spreading in the outlying districts. The *Mietkasernen* were typical, hollow tenement blocks built around a central courtyard, often filled with small factory buildings and more overcrowded

[34]

apartments, the whole gloomy honeycomb of courts and archways filled with workers, children, noise and confusion. The more prosperous factory workers or bourgeois white-collar workers lived in better apartment houses as much as an hour's ride from the center of the city.

People were glad to be Berliners—cosmopolitan and sophisticated. Their habits were still old-fashioned and conservative, their entertainment and diversions relatively simple, family oriented. They strolled on the avenues or sat in the cafés. Many families had their own little gardens, *Schrebergarten,* clustered in little colonies, *Laubenkolonien,* in the middle of the city, to which they went to work or simply to sit in the sun. Or they walked in the then rural Tegel or the Grunewald, or along the banks of the Havel, where trout fishing was popular. There was swimming in the Wannsee, where Europe's largest open-air swimming pool was constructed in 1908. Most men had favorite corner cafés, *Eckkneipen,* with a preferred table, or *Stammtisch,* where they chatted and toasted everything with neighbors. The great Berlin Sportspalast was opened to provide mass entertainment with its bicycle races.

The atmosphere of Kaiser "Willem's" (as he was popularly known to Berliners) reign had been one of unchanging traditionalism, combined with Bismarckian-Prussian authoritarianism, even though this had been disguised under the euphemism "state democracy." True social-democratic and liberal movements existed, but they were not recognized officially as political groups. The former called themselves "journeymen without a fatherland" and the latter "secret Germany"; they were most active in Berlin, with its large working-class population. Social and moral standards still emphasized the Victorian virtues—or covert vices. Nevertheless modernist movements were developing in many fields.

In art, the traditional neoromantic trend as well as the turn-of-the-century Art Nouveau were being challenged by Impressionism and then Expressionism. Mies van der Rohe, Walter Gropius and Le Corbusier were already developing their experiments in functional architecture in their workshop-school, foreshadowing the later Bauhaus. In the theater, Max Reinhardt staged the longest Shakespearean festival ever produced. The fledgling movie industry was expanding rapidly; early short and primitive moralistic (or pornographic) films were getting longer, and offstage voices were being replaced by printed titles. Many small theaters were being transformed into local cinemas. Rainer Maria Rilke published his poems and Thomas Mann his *Buddenbrooks,* both enjoying enormous circulation.

Berlin was the center of German—indeed of all European—medicine. Students came not only from throughout the country but from many other countries including the United States to spend some time at the university. In American medical circles, a year of post-graduate work in Berlin was considered the ultimate, most prestigious training possible. The great hospitals of the city—the Charité, Virchow, Friedenhain, Moabit, Urban, Lankwitz, Wittenau, Children's—provided an inexhaustible source of patients and types of illness for students and attending staff. The medical school was housed in and around the Königliche Charité, the general hospital. It was an agglomeration of amorphous buildings, some old and ivy-covered, some more modern and recently constructed. It made up a small, irregular community that spread over into the side streets and had satellite clinics in more distant hospitals in the city.

The faculty list contained some of the most notable names in the history of medicine. Rudolf Virchow, usually considered the father of cellular pathology, had signed a state petition to outlaw anti-Semitism. Friedrich Kopsche, in anatomy, had written one of the best textbooks in Europe. Gustav von Bergmann had an international reputation in medicine. Ferdinand Sauerbruch, in surgery, innovated many surgical techniques and later became notorious as Surgeon-in-Chief of the German army. Krückmann, the opthalmology professor, was to become known for his refusal to give the Hitler salute when he declared "no politics" in his classes. Karl Bonhoeffer's psychiatric service in the Charité—and Theodor Ziehen's before him—was one of the foremost in the world, where many future psychiatrists trained. The neurology text of Herman Oppenheim was a classic of its kind for fifty years.

Karen began her final year here in the Charité in October 1909 with a crowded schedule. Lectures in special pathology, bacteriology and pharmacology were combined with clinical work in pediatrics, otorhinolaryngology, medicine, surgery, obstetrics and gynecology. The material was interesting enough and the clinical contacts satisfying, but they required much studying and time. There were still very few women in the course, perhaps five per cent. Even though there were no longer any official restrictions against women students, some of the professors still held the traditional prejudiced view of career women, especially in medicine.

After finishing his law studies at the university, Oskar found employment with the Stinnes Corporation, an up-and-coming investment firm. The meteoric rise and fall of the still young Hugo Stinnes was to become a saga in the history of German high finance and industry. Although born of a well-to-do family, he worked in the coal mines as a youth before studying to be a mining engineer and then going into his grandfather's coal business as a clerk. First dealing in coal, he bought his first coal mine in 1895 and he continued to buy and buy—usually on borrowed money. By 1910 he owned numerous mines in the Ruhr and consolidated his other holdings into an industrial empire: coal-barges, coal-carrying steamships, a bank, iron and steel mills. One colleague recalled that he might come to the office dressed in workman's clothes and boots, which—with his swarthy skin and black beard—gave him the look of a worker or provincial businessman. And yet, even though he was a wizard in his complex business dealings, he ran his businesses from little slips of paper stashed in his pockets. They contained his accounts, details of his companies' transactions, the names and numbers of his customers. Although constantly active, running, telephoning, doing everything for himself, he still needed an organization and someone to run it for him. Oskar Horney hitched his wagon to Stinnes's star. With his intelligence, economic and legal background, industriousness and organizational ability, he advanced rapidly. By 1915, Karen wrote that he had become the *General-Sekretar* of the organization, an administrative-executive position equivalent to manager or director of operations. One may assume that his career was as demanding and time-consuming as Karen's.

The combination of her medical studies with her housekeeping chores was probably as burdensome to Karen as it has proven to be for so many other physician-housewives since then. At least today there are special concessions in course schedules made in some medical schools for women students. The presence of Sonni in the home certainly would have been a help, even though a parent in a newlywed couple's home can at times be intrusive.

Karen completed her clinical semesters by the summer of 1910, but then had to prepare for her final examination. That fall she discovered she was pregnant. Berndt came to visit often and she seemed to depend on him again as she had as a teenager.

She was feeling depressed, chronically tired and lethargic. Perhaps this was partly due to the sheer strain of overwork; perhaps it was some emotional conflict related to her career choice, feeling indecision between the socially acceptable female role of homemaker and the then deviant professional role; perhaps she was also feeling some disillusionment about her marriage, sensing some discrepancy between what it was and what she had imagined it would be. In a paper in 1934, she was to write revealingly, "Conflict confronts every woman who ventures upon a career of her own and who is . . . unwilling to pay for her daring with the renunciation of her femininity."

During her final semester, both she and her friend Karl Muller-Braunschweig, who had just finished his medical studies, had attended the neuropsychiatric clinic of Professor Herman Oppenheim. Karl decided to seek psychoanalytic help from a young analyst who often came to the clinic, a Dr. Karl Abraham. Most probably he discussed this with Karen and influenced her to go into analysis herself at this time.

Then, as an additional emotional trauma, Sonni, then sixty-one, became critically ill in February 1911. She had a stroke shortly after a birthday party Karen had given for Berndt, perhaps brought on by excitement. She died a week later. Shortly afterward, in March 1911, Karen gave birth to her first child, Brigitte. One can only imagine the welter of emotions she must have felt. Death and birth, loss and separation, sadness and joy, creation and love.

Her analysis during this tumultuous period may have sustained her to some extent. Nevertheless, however supportive it might be, every analysis inevitably produces stress and conflict, since it deals with deep-seated emotional problems, often going back to childhood. Karen's ambivalent feelings toward her father, her dependency upon her mother and her struggle to free herself from this dependency, her long-standing resentment at playing a secondary role to her brother, the conflict within herself between the roles of assertive professional woman and the compliant childbearing homemaker—all these had to be confronted.

Karen later calculated that she had spent some five hundred hours in analysis. At the now prescribed frequency of five sessions per week, her analysis with Abraham would have lasted about a year and a half. However, psychoanalytic techniques and treatment at that time were not as structured as they later became. As many analysts today still remember, it was often a hit-or-miss process, with the need for a further session depending on how the patient worked that day and what material was brought up. The sometimes striking "therapeutic" changes that occurred were often purely intellectual and transitory and were not in fact truly integrated into the patient's experience and personality.

There is no doubt, however, that Karen did change. Whether that change was totally positive is a moot question. In her diary, to which she had returned while pregnant, she expressed her depressed feelings and her doubts. During her analysis, the tone of her writing changed: She seemed to have lost her youthful exuberance and spontaneity. Her comments became more stereotyped and couched in analytic terms. In short, she was becoming acculturated to the psychoanalytic world—one might even say indoctrinated—much like the child who loses some of his playfulness and exuberance when he has to learn to conform to cultural mores during growth. Perhaps in losing the depressive emotion, she had to lose some of her healthy emotionality.

The conclusion of her analysis was apparently not satisfying to her. She was still troubled by depression and inertia. The last entry in her diary was the termination letter to Abraham. She raised the question of whether analysis should not do more than simply elucidate old, childhood issues. She asked, "Does not the real work begin after the analysis? The analysis shows one her enemies but one must battle them afterwards, day by day. I was inclined to be satisfied with the theoretical understanding. But perhaps it is only meant to put the weapons into one's hands. Then the doctor would have to make his influence count in this direction, do more positive educational work. But I cannot force myself to work when I am tired. The power of my moral will is insufficient for that."

She was thus raising a question that was later to prompt the search for a new form of analysis. Neither thorough recall of infantile experiences nor the explanation of one's attitudes in terms of Freud's psychoanalytic theories was sufficient to eliminate one's distress. Something more was needed to deal with the here-and-now symptoms or feelings. Of course, the concept of "working through," of relating awareness to current life experiences and thereby changing them, was not well understood at that time. Karen's feelings of depression continued to recur from time to time and her ambivalent feelings toward older men, including Karl Abraham himself, remained.

In the winter of 1911, Karen presented herself for her state medical examination. Her friend Lisa Honroth was later fond of relating to her own daughter how Karen had succeeded in taking the exam. In spite of the prejudice of some of her professors against women in medicine, she had been given a special lenient examination schedule—usually several grueling, uninterrupted weeks of oral and practical tests—to allow her enough time between tests to go home to nurse Brigitte. Lisa admired Karen's ambition and determination to succeed. She considered her the model of the successful emancipated woman and would often pay her the ultimate compliment: "Karen thinks and works like a man."

After her examination, she spent the first four months of 1912 doing her medical internship under Professor August Frankel at the Urban Hospital (Berlin Städtische Krankenhaus am Urban), one of the large general hospitals in Berlin. This was followed by eight months in the Lankwitz Sanatorium.

In the western suburb of Lankwitz, just a short ride from the city, stood the Lankwitz Kuranstalt, a large and venerable municipal neuropsychiatric hospital. The main building on the Victoriastrasse and its smaller ancillary buildings housed 375 patients, and were surrounded by lovely grounds where they could wander. Although officially under the auspices of the city of Berlin and the province of Saxony, it was funded by the *Krankenkasse*—the equivalent of health insurance—set up by the Social Democrats. Dr. Henry Lowenfeld, now a practicing psychoanalyst in New York, who worked there at this time and who was later to meet Karen again under vastly different circumstances, still recalls the atmosphere: "The patients were generally poor. Neuroses and psychoses—one saw a lot, and learned a great deal. We were supposed to work very hard from early morning until six. We only got room and board, but we earned some extra money by writing reports for the insurance." The Lankwitz neuropsychiatric clinic gained a considerable reputation under its chief, Dr. Kurt Loewenstein.

Across the street, however, was a section given over to about 175 private patients, where Karen worked. This had begun as a small private sanatorium for the treatment of women's mental illness (Privat-Heil-und-Pflegeanstalt "Berolinum" für Weibliche Geisteskranke). Under the guidance of its director, Dr. James Fraenkel—or simply "Papa" Fraenkel, as he was popularly known—it had grown into a sizable complex of pavilions and houses. When it was combined with the Municipal Hospital in 1906, it became the largest private mental hospital in Germany. Karen was recommended to Dr. Fraenkel by either Oppenheim or Abraham (the two were cousins) or both; the Jewish neuropsychiatrists of the city all knew each other and formed a sort of unofficial community. Indeed, there was probably some family relationship between Fraenkel and the two cousins.

The atmosphere here was different from that of the main building. For one thing, while the main building housed indigent patients, only private patients came here. Then too, here the residents were paid a stipend, small but significant nonetheless. The sanatorium atmosphere was more homey and familial, and the physicians lived on the premises. Papa Fraenkel was a genial, kindly man of fifty-five, a benevolent fatherly type even if a conservative traditionalist. He was liked by everyone. He had a placid, imperturbable personality and seldom complained when his meals were interrupted—as they so frequently were—by calls for advice. His family often mingled with the doctors and patients. His daughter, Hilda, then a young teenager and now a practicing psychiatrist in Jerusalem, wandered about among the young residents and attended their meetings. She can still remember Karen's diffidence and enthusiasm, and more impressive, how serious a worker she was.

Freud himself hospitalized or consulted on the cases of several patients in the Kuranstalt. He would come and go by bus and the staff would try to gather around to hear his remarks. The proponents of psychoanalysis were still struggling for its acceptance by the traditional psychiatric community. Dr. Otto Juliusberger, the medical director, was in favor of the new psychoanalytic approach and encouraged its practice in the hospital. He had, in fact, written a paper in 1908 called "Contribution to the Theory of Psychoanalysis," which Abraham had sent on to Freud. He was one of the first to join the new Psychoanalytic Society. But, as Abraham mentioned to Freud, Juliusberger's chief, "Papa" Fraenkel, was opposed to psychoanalysis, at least at that time. (His daughter recalls that a while later he finally accepted the new doctrine even though he never practiced it or considered himself an analyst.)

Karen remained here until the end of 1912. Apparently she was so impressed with Lankwitz that she was to return two years later. Even though she had received her Medical Qualifying Certificate (*Approbation als Ärztin*), she still needed her medical doctorate degree. In Europe one did not receive the M.D. degree on graduating medical school or passing the state medical examination; a physician still had to write a doctoral thesis, which usually took several years. It meant finding a faculty professor as a sponsor, and accumulating suitable case material and/or clinical training to prepare the thesis. Psychiatry and neurology were closely related then; psychiatry was mainly organically oriented. Practitioners of both specialties often called themselves "nerve specialists" (*Nervenärtze*). A stint in a good neurological-psychiatric service was almost obligatory. The question for Karen was, Where to go? It was a choice between the two most highly regarded neuropsychiatric services in the Charité—the outpatient clinic of Professor Oppenheim and the in-patient service of Professor Bonhoeffer. She decided she would go to both. She first became an assistant in Oppenheim's clinic.

Herman Oppenheim was one of the few Jews ever to have held a full professorship. But it was a titular appointment only; as a Jew, he was not eligible for an official professorship in a university clinic. Therefore his clinic was considered "private," even though it was within the Charité. His textbook on neurology had been a Bible for a generation of physicians, assuring him an impressive reputation. It was most important for the psychoanalysts to secure his support. They tried constantly, even though he remained opposed to psychoanalysis for many years. For example, at one meeting of the Berlin Society for Psychiatry and Neurology in 1908, Abraham related how he tried to win him over. He recalled that mentioning Freud's name would have been "like a red rag to a bull." Instead he concentrated on several issues raised in his paper, "The Effects of Intermarriage Between Relatives on Neurosis," which Oppenheim could accept, and he played down such controversial topics as infantile sexuality. He tried to convince Oppenheim on a few points at every meeting. Another tactic was to draw sympathy by allowing opponents to make themselves ridiculous with their rude denunciations of psychoanalysis. Abraham did not have much of a psychoanalytic practice yet and his several days weekly at the clinic were spent locating suitable patients. He was grateful for the private patients Oppenheim referred to him for analytic treatment, with increasing frequency as time passed. In his letters to Freud, he described some of the symptoms exhibited by the patients in the clinic— tics, migraine, backaches, sexual "neurasthenia," coughing, hysterical attacks—and complained of how little understanding the orthodox psychiatrists had of such cases.[1] But the attitude in the clinic gradually became more tolerant, allowing for some speculation along psychoanalytic lines, although the concepts of infantile sexuality had still not found favor. By the end of 1909, Abraham's practice was almost full, and the next year he was referring patients to Max Eitingon, another young disciple of Freud who had recently arrived there. It was there in the clinic that Karen had first met Abraham and become interested in analysis, both for patients and for herself.

Seeking a sponsoring professor to direct her thesis, Karen turned to Karl Bonhoeffer. She began to work under him at the end of 1913, after a year in Oppenheim's clinic.

It was practically an unwritten law that every budding neuropsychiatrist in Berlin must work in Professor Bonhoeffer's service before completing his training. It was the choicest and most sought-after appointment, not only for the academic lectures but for the clinical material as well. Foreign students, including many Americans, also vied to get in. Several of the assistants who worked there during this period—Fred Weiss, Charles Huelsenbeck, Edith Vowinkel, Morris Isenberg, Frances Streltzoff, Herta Seidemann, and Paul Lussheimer—were to meet Karen later, either in the analytic school or in America. The staff numbered about forty at the time, including attending physicians, assistants and auditors, though not students.

Bonhoeffer himself was a pleasant man, easy to get along with, although rather reserved and quiet, a trait that was often reinforced by the awe in which he was held by most of the staff. However, he did not hold himself aloof at all and would often invite his young assistants to his home out in Grunewald for informal evenings. Professionally he had a special feeling for, and humane way with, the schizophrenic patients on his ward rounds, which the students admired. He could easily interview even the most disturbed patient. Once one of the younger students accidentally locked herself in an isolation room with a violent, agitated patient and could not get out without her forgotten passkey. After she was let out thirty minutes later, Bonhoeffer asked whether she had been afraid of the patient. She responded that she had not, whereupon he gave a lecture on the relationship between doctor and patient, stressing the psychotic's intuitive—or unconscious—awareness of interpersonal attitudes. This antedated Sullivan's similar concepts by some forty years.

Though of a rather religious background, Bonhoeffer was a liberal in his personal and political outlook, although more traditional in his scientific views. He disliked upsetting the status quo by accepting extreme ideas. This accounted for his lack of enthusiasm for psychoanalytic theory, though, as Abraham wrote, he was "not in principle opposed to the idea . . . he is no friend of psychoanalysis, but he is not an enemy on principle and certainly not an unfair one. He openly admits that his arguments against it are emotional and completely unscientific but that he accepts much of it."[2] Numerous Jewish assistants were accepted on his staff, an exception to the explicit or implicit anti-Semitism of most of the faculty. His son Dietrich, who became a minister, was to suffer the consequences of opposing the Nazi regime not many years later.

Abraham himself applied to the medical school for an official faculty appointment, at first for a lectureship, then for a professorship in psychoanalysis. Freud sent letters of recommendation to several influential faculty members. In his correspondence with Freud, Abraham often mentioned that Bonhoeffer was favorably inclined, but the appointment did not go through, probably due to the resistance of other faculty members. Only Siegfried Bernfeld, among the analytic group, ever received such an appointment.

Karen applied for Bonhoeffer's sponsorship at a time when he, like many others, was interested in the post-traumatic syndromes. He suggested these as a topic for her thesis. The mere fact that he agreed to sponsor her work indicates that he had a sympathetic interest in her. Perhaps he was influenced by her early religious background which she had described in her application and interviews.

The large number of assistants in Bonhoeffer's neuropsychiatric service permitted an atmosphere of freedom and lack of pressure in which to work. There was time to be absent if need be. And Karen did need time and freedom just then—she became pregnant again in 1913 and gave birth to her second daughter, Marianne, that year.

The Horneys lived in a garden apartment complex on the Waldmannstrasse in Lankwitz, in which several of their friends also lived. Karl Muller-Braunschweig, and his new wife, Karen's young friend Josine Ebsen, also originally from Hamburg, were among them. Another couple were Walter Honroth, now an architectural engineer, and his wife, Lisa, both old friends of Oskar's from Braunschweig. The two Horney daughters and the Honroths' daughter, Rita, all played together on the grounds surrounding the apartment house. In fact, Oskar was Rita's godfather, and he never forgot her birthday. Lisa, a Jewish student from Breslau, was studying writing and became a prominent journalist and novelist during the postwar years. She considered herself rather "liberated" for that time, but in her eyes, Karen, the practicing physician and psychoanalyst, had reached the ultimate heights. Walter's slightly younger bachelor brother, Otto, was another member of their coterie, and three other brothers often visited. Still another couple were Karl (Kalli) and Elizabeth (Lissie) Marx. He was a chemist who became one of the directors of I. G. Farben. His lively, vivacious blonde wife, was a *Kunstgewerbleren*, an artist who specialized in textile design and interior decorating. Their daughter, Gerda, the same age as the other girls, added to the children's group; they were to remain friends for many years.

Social life was active and pleasant for the group, with evening gatherings and weekend tennis. In spite of her heavy workload both in the hospital and at home, and her fatigue and depression, Karen participated enthusiastically. Rita Honroth, now a practicing child psychiatrist, recalls those get-togethers before and during the war years and even into the twenties. All intellectuals, they ranged in their passionate discussions over politics, religion, art, philosophy and psychoanalysis. It was, in effect, a continuation of similar debates from their university days. Lissie Marx was attending art school and entertained some of the struggling artists later associated with the Bauhaus—Gropius, Klee, Kandinsky; Karl Muller-Braunschweig also introduced some of his theological friends. These activities and acquaintances brightened and stimulated Karen, reinforcing interests that were to emerge periodically throughout her life.

Social relationships in the group, among both the married and single members, were light-hearted, flirtatious and sexually liberated. In today's terminology, they would probably have been called swingers. Girlfriend- or wife-swapping was much in vogue in Germany at that time, antedating a similar social phenomenon in this country by some sixty years. Short-lived liaisons were frequent, as often with the knowledge of the spouse as without. According to one of the group, "It was almost taken for granted that the men had their affairs—perhaps as proof of their virility. The mistresses were often relatives or friends of the wives, and there was a certain amount of openness, tolerance and laissez-faire; friendships continued, appearances were observed and social intercourse did not seem to be interfered with. The wives, by and large, were not as active sexually but they too had their flings and no one got too upset about that either." Perhaps this behavior was a rebellion against the Victorian prudery of the 1890's. Yet it was still largely covert, not yet reaching the degree of openness of Weimar sexual mores.

As Ernst Johann and Jorg Junker have noted in their book on German cultural history, this type of social behavior was widespread from 1900 to 1914, especially in the large cities like Berlin. Daughters of upper-middle-class families who wished to escape domestic confinement and parental restrictions turned to a kind of bohemian existence by becoming habitués of literary cafés or artist's ateliers. Some women bohemians were of noble background, like Franzeska, Countess of Reventlow, and the poet Else Lasker-Schuler. Their public lives contradicted the customs and standards of the times. Still others were intellectuals, taking advantage of the emancipation achieved by the feminist movement. Lou-Andreas Salomé, who became involved in the psychoanalytic movement in 1912, was a notable example.

Not that Karen could have been considered a bohemian. On the contrary, at this time she appeared to be strongly family- and home-oriented. In a photograph taken about 1913 with Oskar and Brigitte, Karen is holding her second daughter; her face bears a soft expression of loving tenderness; she is the epitome of the caring maternal figure.

In 1914, after completing her stint at the Charité, Karen returned to work at the Lankwitz Kuranstalt. The Kuranstalt was closer to home; the work atmosphere was relaxed and undemanding, and here Karen would have the opportunity to examine many interesting cases and to apply some of her psychoanalytic ideas as well. She was grateful for the ease while it lasted; in 1916 she was pregnant again. She gave birth to their third daughter, Renate, in November 1916. However, before this occurred, she was able to find a suitable subject for her thesis. With the help of her chief, Juliusberger, she prepared and submitted it at the end of 1914. It was accepted and published in January 1915, with due thanks expressed to Juliusberger and reference to the previous work of Bonhoeffer.

The thesis itself was a straightforward, unremarkable case study, demonstrating that an interesting but atypical psychosis can occur following head injury. The case presentation and Karen's explanation of it were organically oriented, in keeping with the traditional psychiatric approach espoused by Bonhoeffer. A psychoanalytic explanation would probably have been too iconoclastic, even for Karen. One has the impression that she had no intention of producing a creative original work; the thesis was simply a formal prerequisite for the degree, to be accomplished as quickly as possible.

Nevertheless, it was inevitable that some of Karen's creative questioning should have crept in. In her closing comments, she considers the problem of causality of mental illness. She asks whether the underlying pathology—in this case, cerebral arteriosclerosis—or the precipitating trauma—a severe blow on the head—was primary and responsible for the symptoms. Obliquely she was raising an issue that was to provide a focus for her doubts about Freudian theories thirty years later. It was the classic question of the primacy of nature versus nurture, of seed versus soil, of the instinctual basis versus the environmental superstructure.

Yet in spite of the ordinariness of her thesis, it was to have the unforeseen result of bringing Karen to the attention of some of the senior psychiatrists and psychoanalysts. The subject of post-traumatic psychoses foreshadowed impending events, namely the effects of the war and the interest generated in the post-traumatic war neuroses. The controversy over whether these syndromes were organic or psychological in origin was soon to become heated.

VI
INTERLUDE:
THE WAR YEARS

"Effective prosecution of war requires a huge army on both home and fighting fronts. A child understands war in terms of life in his own home. . . . The alterations of the stability of family life and everyday routine are upheavals which are a disturbing force to children of all ages. Physical desertion of the child as a result of the necessities of war has its emotional counterpart of deprivation and neglect. The full force of these events will be felt—not now—but in years to come."

—*"Children in Wartime"*

In August 1914 Germany entered the war and general mobilization was ordered. The next four years were to bring profound changes in Karen, in her life and in her circle of friends.

Karen's relaxed schedule at the Lankwitz Kuranstalt, which allowed her time to be home with the children, did not last long. As the psychiatric war casualties began to come in, Papa Fraenkel first offered one pavilion of 60 beds as a war hospital (*Vereinslazarett*) in 1915. By 1918, 250 beds were occupied by war casualties. The entire staff had to work doubly hard as part of the war effort. The attending psychiatrists—at least the males—were officially assigned to the war hospital although whether Karen was is not known. The military functions of the unit were placed under a navy medical officer, Dr. König.

As German war production was activated, the Stinnes conglomerate expanded rapidly. With the country needing matériel and transportation facilities, his coal mines, iron and steel mills, shipping lines and banks became invaluable. At one point he even offered to take over the entire war matériel supply. Though the offer was refused, he still commanded a large share of German industrial production. As Stinnes expanded, Oskar's fortunes prospered accordingly. With Karen's workload even heavier

[48]

and Oskar's income considerably increased, it is probable that it was at this time that she began to employ the first of the governesses that her daughters were later to complain about.

Toward the end of 1915, the family was able to purchase their own house, first in Dahlem—where Renate was born—and a short while later, with Oskar becoming still more prosperous, at No. 15 Sophie Charlotte-strasse in Zehlendorf, a fashionable suburb in the southwestern section of the city, near the Grunewald and Havel Lake. They were to remain there until 1926. The property included about three acres of garden and grounds. Across the way was a small meadow with a pond, a little hill, down which the children could slide or ski, and a small woods beyond. Her daughters recall that Karen always preferred nature and the outdoors; cold or hot, they had to be outside. The back-to-nature movement was popular at the time in Germany and the outdoor life was acclaimed as the best thing for growing children. The girls would wander through the woods on weekends and later on, after school, with or without Mochen— as they soon nicknamed Karen. Karen enjoyed growing flowers there and for a while participated in a flower-arrangement group with some of her friends. Most of all, she loved the garden and was soon an ardent gardener, planting, weeding, composting, growing vegetables, fruits and berries along with her flowers. She grew much of their own food and put up in preserves during August whatever they couldn't eat. The fall cleanup time was a big occasion, when the children would all dance around the bonfire of old stalks and leaves. One memorable year, the police came on a neighbor's complaint to make them put it out.

Even though the earlier Lankwitz group was now dispersed—the Honroths had moved to Berlin-Grunewald, the Muller-Braunschweigs into the city proper, the Marxes first into the city and then out to Dessau—they still maintained close social contact and visited fairly often.

Karen now had to rely regularly on a housekeeper or governess to help care for the children so that she could get to the hospital for her work or to write. In 1917, Brigitte, at six, was entering public school; Marianne, four, entered kindergarten. They were already missing Karen's time and attention; they protested her physical and emotional absence and resented the series of governesses. Both she and Oskar firmly advocated independence and self-sufficiency for children. No taking them by the hand; no coddling. By the age of four they were taking a twenty-minute walk, unaccompanied, to the kindergarten. By the age of five this included not only a thirty-minute walk but a train ride as well.

Karen was to write later that her children had received a "good psychoanalytic upbringing." Presumably this meant helping them to pass through the prescribed psychosexual stages with good eating habits, proper toilet training, avoidance of excessive oedipal attachments, emotional independence and adequate sexual enlightenment so as to avoid undue fixations. As with most intelligent young mothers, she would have found in her own children a most significant learning experience, her living laboratory. As early as February 1912, Abraham wrote to Freud that Karen had presented to their little informal group a report, her first, on handling the young child. "For once, the paper showed a real understanding of the material, unfortunately something rather infrequent in the papers of our circle."[1]

As far as her daughters can now recall their earliest childhood experiences, they agree that each of them had a quite different personality. Brigitte, or Biggi, was the most dominating, somewhat willful, the leader. Marianne, or Janne, describes herself as having been rather shy and timid, usually the "goody-goody," more introverted and intellectual. A degree of rivalry between the two was to be expected, except when they allied themselves against their little sister, Renate. Like the others, she too had an affectionate nickname, Nacki or Naci. As the youngest, she was out of things during this early period, too small to be of importance. As she grew up, however, her sisters would tend to tease her. She remembers herself as a tomboy, the most active, running, climbing trees, getting into childish scrapes. All three daughters recall that Karen usually had a laissez-faire or detached attitude toward their concerns, although at times she seemed to have an uncanny ability to tell when they were lying to get out of some difficulty. They simply could not lie to her, for she would always see through their ruses. However, she was not the family disciplinarian; Oskar had that function. At times he was not above spanking them, using a leather strap, a crop, or even a stick.

Methods for raising children had not essentially changed since the nineteenth century. One very popular source book, used by and on several generations of German children, was *Der Struwwelpeter*. This was a German translation of a moralistic English classic, *Slovenly Peter*, an illustrated book of verse originally written by an English physician for his own children. It described the mishaps and misbehavior of the child and the severe punishments meted out, in frightening detail. Parents were advised to be strict, authoritarian and punitive toward their children. This book is remembered by Karen's children because an incident occurring in the Horney home at this time reenacted one of Struwwelpeter's mishaps. While sitting at the Christmas dinner table Marianne tipped back her chair a bit too far and fell over backwards. Clutching the tablecloth, she pulled a brand-new dinner service and the entire Christmas dinner onto the floor. Marianne screamed loudly as Oskar spanked her in an adjoining room with a dog whip, while Brigitte too wailed in sympathy. Their little friend Rita was terrified. Karen reacted calmly—in fact, did not react—accepting the whole scenario.

Karen terminated her analysis in 1912 and although she was disappointed with its results, she remained fascinated by psychoanalytic principles. And in spite of her ambivalent feelings toward Abraham, from 1911 on she attended his weekly "Freudian evenings." Beginning in 1908, these had at first been small, intimate, unofficial gatherings at his home. After 1911 they had become regular meetings of the Berlin Psychoanalytic Society. As new members joined the group, Karen's circle of personal friends grew and shifted more toward those interested in analysis. Abraham's private practice developed rapidly; by 1909, as he wrote to Freud, his time was largely taken up by psychoanalytic patients referred by other doctors or friends, or by medical candidates. After 1912, his practice became "overwhelming, ten hours a day, exhausting," but he was finding it "scientifically arid" at times. He missed having a fellow-worker with whom he could discuss things on a personal level. Karen had been one of his most gifted analysands. She was willing to work and had a flair for writing, was enthusiastic for their cause. She admired Abraham in many ways in spite of the resentment she carried over from her analysis, having transferred to him some of the feelings she had had toward her father. It was therefore quite understandable that in 1915 she became secretary to the fledgling group. But an even more pressing, practical reason was that by then most active members of the Berlin psychoanalytic group were being mobilized into military hospitals. Abraham was sent to Allenstein, Ernst Simmel to Poznan, Max Eitingon to Hungary. Someone was needed who could remain in Berlin and competently handle immediate correspondence.

As the war dragged on, living conditions in Berlin deteriorated. By the winter of 1917, coal was in such short supply that everyone—including the city authorities—had to cut down. Most staples were severely rationed, and milk, eggs and fats were almost completely gone. Those who could afford the more expensive and nonrationed foods, like fancy poultry and some fruits and vegetables, fared somewhat better for a while, but even these became unavailable by the end of 1917. Karen was better off than many, with her own garden vegetables and those sent by Oskar's mother from the family farm. The privations were weakening, exhausting to everyone, especially the children of Berlin. For children above six, milk could be bought—when it could be found—only with a doctor's certificate of absolute need. When she was almost seven, Brigitte developed a small pulmonary tubercular lesion. The standard treatment then was a rest cure at high altitude. After several months in bed, she was sent to a sanatorium at Bellaria, near Davos, high in the Swiss Alps. About six months later, Marianne was also placed there, in a local boarding school. She recalls the unsettling effect this separation from home and parents had upon them. Many of the other children there spoke Romansch, the difficult language of the Grisons valleys. When the children returned to Berlin at the end of 1918, Brigitte was cured and Marianne was speaking Romansch instead of German.

In the meantime, among the new friends Karen found in the Berlin Psychoanalytic Society were Heinrich Koerber, a co-worker at Lankwitz, Iwan Bloch, and later Hans Liebermann and Max Eitingon.

Bloch was President of the Medical Society for Sexuality (Ärtzliche Gesellschaft für Sexualwissenschaft) and a co-editor of its journal, *Zeitschrift für Sexualwissenschaft*. As a subject for serious medical study, sexuality was just beginning to free itself from the taboos and prejudices of the Victorian era. A few physicians had been studying sexual functions, sexual relationships and sexual problems; these included psychiatrists like Auguste Forel, Havelock Ellis and Richard Krafft-Ebing, and a few so-called sexologists like Albert Moll, Magnus Hirschfeld and Bloch. The latter were looked on with suspicion by other medical practitioners, considered to be on the fringe of the profession. Attracted by psychoanalysis's misinterpreted emphasis on sexuality, they had been among the first to join in the new Freudian evenings in 1908. However, as Freud wisely pointed out in a letter to Abraham, they were more interested in physical sexuality than in the psychosexual concepts of psychoanalysis. Their own society was organized in 1913; Freud became a member on Abraham's advice, but soon lost interest. The sexologists did not remain long with the analytic group either.

In February 1917, Bloch invited Karen to speak before his society. Her friend Heinrich Koerber would discuss the theoretical concepts of psychoanalysis at the preceding meeting. Karen would limit herself to psychoanalytic technique.

This meeting was her first important formal paper.[2] The audience was a mixed one: nonanalyst physicians, psychologists and interested nonprofessionals. Some were there sincerely to learn about the new field, others to be titillated by the promise of sexual revelations. Some of the medical professionals were skeptical if not outright hostile, as was usually the case with psychoanalytical presentations in those days. As Karen noted in her introduction, Koerber's previous paper had raised many objections to which she would respond.

The style and language of her paper are clear and succinct, even then showing the ability to express complex concepts in simple terms that was to characterize all her later writings.

She began by discussing the uses of free association, symbolic dream interpretation and slips in speech or behavior to understand unconscious activity and motivation. But to discover unconscious motives is not the main task or the main difficulty of analysis. The role of infantile feelings toward the parent which are irrationally transferred onto the analyst is most significant. Such transference can at first be favorable to the progress of the analysis but can later become an instrument of resistance. Removal of resistance is even more important than correctly interpreting unconscious needs and motives. After describing the various clinical manifestations of resistance, she notes that unrecognized resistance can lead to failure of the analysis, whereas incorrect interpretations are less serious; they will often be corrected by the patient. This principle was to become a basic tenet of her approach years later, that is, to attack blockages first.

Even with the transferential relationship, analytic dependency should not be unduly encouraged, and in any event, must be resolved before termination. Analyzing unconscious motives for conflict is more important than giving advice or making decisions for the patient, which may encourage his dependency. He must be enabled to become the active agent in his own decisions. As to the timing of interpretations, they should not be offered until a transference relationship is established. Even then, they will only be effective when the patient has already come close to understanding the unconscious motives through his own efforts.

Karen was particularly concerned about the analysis of physicians, a concern which was later to preoccupy her for some time. The indications for analysis were still limited, she admitted. One such prerequisite was the ability to form a "workable positive transference."

One comment may have been relevant to her own situation at that time: "Many a marriage that might have floundered because of the neurosis of one of the partners has become more healthy through analysis because the patient became able to direct his forces toward his marital partner, forces previously fixated upon infantile models." One can only speculate whether and to what extent she might have been referring to herself.

She then concludes: "Obviously not even analysis can change constitution. It can liberate a person whose hands and feet are tied so that he may freely use his strength again, but it cannot give him new arms and legs. But it has shown that many factors that he had believed to be constitutional are no more than consequences of blockages of growth which can be resolved."

In this statement she was calling attention to both the limitations and potentials of psychoanalysis. She knew of its limitations from her experience with her own analysis and her subsequent disappointment. She was cautioning against expecting too much from it, against neurotic excessive and magical expectations that could only lead to disillusionment. On the other hand, she was also confirming its potentialities. She was accepting the notion that individuals were constitutionally different from one another and would bear this unique individual endowment throughout their lives, whether analyzed or not. At the same time, Freud's psychoanalytic concept of "constitution" referred to a basic instinctual makeup of the individual, the "bedrock" of personality beyond which analysis could presumably not go. But she was rejecting the idea of an immutable and invariable "constitutional," e.g., psychosexual, development, which would lead to therapeutic pessimism. In its place she was introducing the concept of human growth, an innate constructive force, which was later to become a keystone of her own theories.

And this was the optimistic, life-affirming credo of a young woman of thirty-one, still only a novice in psychoanalysis. It was a small first step on her tortuous road.

VII
THE BERLIN PSYCHOANALYTIC INSTITUTE AND SOCIETY: EARLY PERIOD

"If you had enjoyed the questionable good fortune of living within an analytic circle, then you might understand this awareness better. Because here we are no less hypocritical than elsewhere, only a little different. Above all it appears repeatedly as a silent presupposition that the 'neurotic' has all these embarrassing complexes. It is like the religious Christians and their 'We are all sinners,' which can become very uncomfortable if you point out to them some concrete examples of their sins."

—*Letter to Georg Groddeck*

From a scientific viewpoint, the second International Psychoanalytical Congress at Nuremberg in 1910 had been a success. Freud spoke glowingly on the "Future Prospects of Psychoanalysis." But from an interpersonal and organizational viewpoint, problems and differences had surfaced. Freud, suffering from the previous prolonged resistance to psychoanalysis and his own ostracism, realized the need for psychoanalysts to come together in a more organized way. This was necessary not only for mutual support but also to maintain high standards of practice. Unfortunately when Sandor Ferenczi—speaking for Freud—offered this proposal, he also made possibly derogatory remarks about the quality of the analysis being practiced in Vienna. Furthermore, he suggested that all future papers would have to be approved by the president of the new organization. The objections from the members were so strong that Freud had to mollify them. He agreed to retire from leadership of the Vienna group, turning the presidency over to Alfred Adler. Adler, one of the senior and most respected members of the Viennese analytic group, had long been one of Freud's closest followers. For the preceding two years, since publication of his book on organ inferiority, his unspoken differences with Freud had been growing more evident. At the 1910 meeting, Freud's preference for Carl Jung had exacerbated this situation. According to Ernest Jones, Freud's biographer, Adler was now the leader of the rebellion of the Viennese group against Freud.[1] Freud also agreed to a new psychoanalytic journal, the *Korrespondenzblatt*. Carl Jung became the new president of the International Psychoanalytic Association. But none of these changes lasted very long.

The Berlin group was the first to become an official branch organization, with Karl Abraham as its president. The unofficial Freudian evenings, carried on since 1908 with four regular members, now became meetings of the Berlin Psychoanalytic Society. Nine official members were listed in 1910. It grew ever so slowly; some left and until 1912 there were only five members: Abraham, Bloch, Hirschfeld, Koerber and Juliusberger. Karen joined at about this time, toward the end of her analysis with Abraham.

As Ernest Jones has detailed in his biography of Freud, the five prewar years were characterized by intense opposition from the nonanalytic world and by dissension within the analytic movement itself, including the defections of Alfred Adler, Wilhelm Stekel and Carl Jung. To be an analyst was considered the equivalent of being a sexual pervert, it was misinterpreted as advocating complete sexual license. In Berlin, the leading opponents were Professor Herman Oppenheim; Theodor Ziehen, the professor of psychiatry; Ostewald Bumke, the neurologist; and Professor Franz Van Lushen, a psychiatrist. When Bonhoeffer replaced Ziehen in 1912, the situation eased somewhat, but not completely. In 1914, Freud was asked to submit a paper by the Berlin medical faculty on the psychoanalytic view of neurosis for a new encyclopedia. At the same time Alfred Kutzinsky, Bonhoeffer's assistant, was also asked to write one on the same subject following the traditional viewpoint. Kutzinsky's article was accepted.

By a curious turn of events, the war helped to win over this opposition. The military authorities were greatly concerned by the large numbers of casualties caused by post-traumatic, or war, neuroses (then called shell shock). Typically, these men developed various bizarre disabling symptoms after being exposed to exploding shells. In 1916 Dr. Oppenheim published a book explaining that these reactions were due to an organic injury to the brain, a form of concussion at a distance.[2] But these views were premature. Karen had unwittingly become involved in this issue when, in her thesis, she had asked the most pregnant question: Could there be something in the patient's previous condition, whether organic, temperamental or psychological, which predisposed the patient or predetermined such symptoms?

Ernst Simmel tried to apply psychoanalytic principles to understand these cases and used hypnosis to treat them. He and Ferenczi presented their results at a psychoanalytic meeting in Budapest and published the results in 1918.[3] Ernest Jones, in England, was working on the same problem and arriving at the same conclusions. Even Bonhoeffer was beginning to appreciate the psychoanalytic viewpoint. He held that the traumatic symptoms were "psychoneurotic fixations, dissociation phenomena, which have been rendered possible through the resultant splitting off of the violent emotion." But he could not accept the psychological cause completely; he had to hedge by noting that "the possibility of a psychopathological condition being evoked by psychogenic factors is the criterion of a degenerative condition."

However, when Jones wrote Freud about these ideas, it still required the master's logical mind to provide a theoretical analytic explanation. "It is a question of conflict between two ego ideals, the customary one and the one the war has compelled the person to build. The latter is concerned with relations to neurotic objects (superior officers and comrades) . . . equivalent to a cathexis of a new object. It might be called choice of an object not consonant with the ego. The theory would be that a new ego has developed . . . and the former ego tries to displace it. There is a struggle within the ego instead of between ego and libido, but that comes to the same thing."[4] Their definitive conclusions were published in a collection of papers by Ferenczi, Abraham, Simmel and Jones in 1919, with a foreword by Freud.[5] Stimulated by this work, they decided to open a clinic in Berlin to continue its application.

As its members returned after the war, the Berlin Psychoanalytic Society was reanimated. Psychoanalysis had proven itself practical for the masses, even if under special conditions. The previously beleaguered psychoanalysts came home full of new ideas and enthusiasm. The roster of the society now included such additions as Hans Liebermann, Ernst Simmel, Felix Boehm and Emil Simonson. In April 1919, Karen presented a clinical paper entitled "Fantastic Infantilism in a Borderline Case,"[6] apparently a study of one of her first private patients.

Karen began her private practice of psychoanalysis in the spring of 1919. She changed her official title from Neuropsychiatrist (*Nervenärtzin*) to Specialist in Psychoanalysis (*Fachärtzin für Psychoanalyse*). The office she opened at 202 Kaiserallee was ideally located in a four-story gray stone building, studded with balconies and double windows; the neighborhood was fashionable enough for a young doctor's office without being exclusive. The wide boulevard was lined with trees on both sides, yet streetcar lines and a double-decker bus provided easy transportation for patients. It was only a short distance from the Psychoanalytic Polyclinic-Institute and close to the crowded center of the city in the direction of the zoo. At the same time, just two blocks away was the Wilmersdorf Stadtpark with its tennis courts, lake and walks—so peaceful for a stroll during lunch hour.

Karen also began to see a few patients in her home in Zehlendorf. The children remember how heavy velvet drapes were hung behind the vestibule to separate the small waiting room from their living quarters. And how they had to be quiet, tiptoeing around when a patient was there. Karen saw patients at home perhaps two or three hours every other day. The general economic situation was so bad then that few people could afford to pay for analysis. The patients that came to her house were mostly referred from Lankwitz, usually seen without charge.

Sometimes a patient would work as gardener or handyman in exchange for services. Neighbors were at first startled by the "*Irren*" ("nuts"), as they were called, around the house, until they grew accustomed to them. One, in particular, was a male transvestite who dressed as a woman to work as a maid. He caused gossip for a while and much amusement—or understandable confusion—among the children. It turned out subsequently that he was not really a "patient" but a man trying to avoid military service. Karen had been fooled!

In the city the senior analysts in the group, like Abraham, Eitingon and Juliusberger, and later Georg Groddeck, began to refer patients. In spite of her analytic specialization, Karen remained interested in some physical problems of her patients, especially the women, who appear to have made up the majority of her practice. For instance, in her letters to Groddeck, she discussed the use of various hormonal treatments for female symptoms such as premenstrual tension and menopausal distress.

She was, nevertheless, becoming more outspoken in the Berlin Society on purely psychoanalytic matters. In June 1919, in a short paper entitled "The Psychoanalysis of Psychoanalysts" (*Zur Psychoanalyse der Psychoanalytiker*), she raised the question of training analysis. How was it different from therapeutic analysis? Who would do the training of candidates aspiring to become analysts? What special qualifications would be required for such training analysts? These questions were already becoming significant to the group, as they were engaged in preliminary discussions about the new clinic.

At the 1918 International Psychoanalytic Congress, Freud had voiced his hopes for some means of making psychoanalysis available to the indigent. "Sometimes, with the conscience of society awakened, we are reminded that the poor have equal rights to psychological help in the way help is already given to surgical cases; that neuroses endanger the health of the population just as tuberculosis does; and that dealing with them cannot be left only to the individual but requires the help of the entire population. Then institutions will open, clinics will be created where people trained in psychoanalytic thought will care for those given to drink; and women who break down under their burdens, and children who have no choice between confusion and despair, can all be helped to better functioning. The therapy will be without cost. It may take a long time until government acknowledges its responsibility. Present conditions may lead to procrastination and private humanitarian institutions may have to take care of such patients, but sooner or later it has to come to this point." The new Berlin clinic was the response to these hopes.

Simmel had many ideas about a clinic and Abraham contributed others. Someone was needed who could implement them in a practical way. Eitingon was the man; he was the only one of the group who did not need to depend on his practice for his livelihood and who had the financial means necessary for such an undertaking.

Max Eitingon was only four years older than Karen, though with his balding forehead and steel-rimmed glasses he looked older than that. He was born in Russia, the son of a fur dealer. His family had become fairly well off after several of his relatives had emigrated to the United States. After completing his studies in Zurich and serving a psychiatric residency under Eugen Bleuler at the famous Burghölzli Psychiatric Hospital, he had become interested in psychoanalysis. In 1906 and again in 1909 he had spent two or three weeks in Vienna being analyzed by Freud, sometimes while they walked together around the city. He finally settled in Berlin in 1909 at the urging of Abraham, intending to remain only one year. This eventually stretched into twenty-four years. Until the war he had not been notably active in the group, as Abraham had often commented to Freud in his letters. He was slow in building his practice and even by 1912 would only occasionally accept an analytic referral; but by 1914 he was working largely with analytic patients. Extremely loyal and devoted to Freud, he was eager to carry out his wishes. Abraham respected his intellectual ability, noting that he had "an almost unfailing knowledge of the literature." However, Jones wrote that Freud did not have an equally high regard for his intellect. Mild-mannered, shy and reserved, Eitingon tended to stutter at times under pressure. He became fast friends with Karen and a frequent visitor at their house. The children recall his formal friendliness, courtly behavior and impeccable dress. He would so often bring a bouquet of roses to the house that they nicknamed him "Der Rosenmax."

He shouldered the burden of setting up the clinic with much effort and energy. There was a shortage of centrally located space, but with the help of the Minister of Culture he was able to obtain a large, somewhat musty six-room apartment. Changes were necessary. Special permission had to be obtained to use the apartment as a clinic. The two front rooms were fairly large, typical *Berliner Zimmer*. Behind them were the kitchen and finally a long corridor onto which the bedrooms opened. The building was in the shape of an unequal-armed U with a court in the center, from which the tunes of an organ-grinder might sometimes float up during an analytic session. Freud's son, Ernst, came from Vienna to take charge of the interior decorating and furnishing.

Starting during the summer of 1919, the group held many meetings to discuss and plan the organization and operation of the clinic. Finally, on February 14, 1920, the new Poliklinik was officially opened. As Freud visualized—and later stated in the tenth anniversary report of the clinic—

the functions of the Poliklinik were threefold: "to make available our theory to that great group of people who suffer from their neuroses no less than the rich but who are not in a position to pay the cost of the therapy; to present a situation in which analysis can be theoretically taught and the experiences of the older analysts conveyed to the students eager for knowledge; to bring to perfection our knowledge of neurotic illness and therapeutic techniques in application and testing under new conditions."

That these goals were altruistic is certain, but they were not only that. They were also intended to advance Freud's own theories and the psychoanalytic movement. (It is interesting that exactly the same goals were proclaimed for the Karen Horney Clinic, almost verbatim, thirty years later.)

In his opening statement, Eitingon proudly described the Poliklinik's installation and staff. There were five treatment rooms, of which the largest would serve both as conference room and meeting place for the Berlin Psychoanalytic Society. One room was the waiting room and one was set aside for the house physician, a young assistant, Fräulein Smeliansky. She, Eitingon—the nominal director—and Simmel were full-time workers, putting in as much as fourteen hours daily. Karen, Liebermann, Felix Boehm, Karl and Josine Muller-Braunschweig and Hanns Sachs made up the rest of the staff. Each agreed to take on one case for analysis and to otherwise be "available for service as needed."

The opening course was a three-week series of lectures by Abraham entitled "Selected Chapters of Psychoanalysis," which began on March 5, during the Kapp putsch. About forty people braved the general strike to attend the first lecture, including, in addition to the staff, interested professionals and representatives from the city authorities, courts and youth organizations.

The atmosphere was not without strain, however. Eitingon, in his first report, noted that the project originally encountered some skepticism among Berlin colleagues, but rapidly began to win sympathy as it got results. Franz Alexander also commented that the young analysts felt isolated from other doctors: "The medical profession, including psychiatry, had no use for psychoanalysis. Its rejection was complete." When he entered the Poliklinik he had to give up his university clinic work and go into "professional exile as a student."

This nucleus of treatment analysts expanded during the next two years. From Budapest came Melanie Klein and Jeno Harnik; Franz Alexander, Ada Schott and Hans Lampl joined after finishing their training at the institute. By the end of 1922 there was a total of eight permanent analysts working almost full-time.

The original teaching faculty numbered six, each of whom taught in their special areas of interest: Abraham in introductory psychoanalytic theory, Simmel in war neuroses, Eitingon in the use of psychoanalysis in a clinic setting, Liebermann in obsessive-compulsive neuroses, Sachs in dream theory and in psychoanalysis and the arts. Karen was assigned the topic of psychoanalytic treatment in medical practice. This was considered to have particular importance, as the group wished to entice interested new physicians into the field. Within three years this curriculum had broadened out as new instructors were appointed. Felix Boehm lectured on perversions, Karl Muller-Braunschweig on readings in Freud. Several analysts came from other cities for short periods as guest lecturers: Helene Deutsch came from Vienna to speak on special forms of neurosis, such as hysteria, and Geza Roheim came from Budapest to speak on psychoanalysis and ethnology.

In addition to her teaching and clinic work, Karen was deeply involved in the organization of a training program and course curriculum for the different categories of students, i.e., medical students, practicing psychiatrists, nonpsychiatric physicians. She worked first with her old friend Karl Muller-Braunschweig, then with Hans Liebermann, and later with Sandor Rado and Siegfried Bernfeld, who was primarily concerned with training teachers and other nonmedical professionals. By 1922 a training course which could be completed in a year and a half had been set up.

In the spring of 1921, Franz Alexander became the first candidate to complete his analysis. He was then working in Bonhoeffer's clinic and was analyzed by Sachs. Franz was to become a most significant person in Karen's life. During these first two years, twenty-five such training analyses were completed, including nineteen physicians, five teachers and one ethnologist. One of these, a young medical student named Frederick Weiss who was analyzed by Alexander, was to become a close friend of Karen's and an important influence in her life.

The concept of a training, or didactic, analysis was still not clearly defined and had been actively debated in the group ever since Karen had brought it up in her 1919 paper. Should the analysis be different for those who were ostensibly "healthy" and only wished to use it to treat others, or for those who presumably had only an intellectual interest in it? What constituted health? Was it the absence of specific symptoms such as anxiety or fears or sexual difficulties or somatic discomforts? Character neuroses and characterological symptoms were only beginning to attract attention. It was not until 1924 that courses began to be given on character development by Abraham or on disorders of character by Liebermann. Alexander, in particular, was interested in the "psychoanalysis of the total personality" as a new approach. These views exerted a great influence on Karen's thinking and were later to help form her own concepts of the neurotic personality.

During the first two years, however, such considerations were not of major importance in accepting candidates. Everything was informal and on a personal basis. If a physician was interested in being analyzed, he was usually welcomed. He needed only the verbal recommendation of one of the senior analysts of the group. Courses were given at night; anyone could attend. Prerequisites were vague or nonexistent. A personal analysis might or might not be required. What was there to analyze if the person declared himself without problems or symptoms? Even if required, the analysis could be carried out intermittently or irregularly, on evening walks for a few weeks, as in Eitingon's case; or perhaps to deal only with residual symptoms, like Karen's recurring depressions. This all had to be standardized or at least based on more definite criteria.

Another issue was how to teach the young candidates the actual clinical application of psychoanalytic principles. Didactic courses on therapeutic technique were obviously inadequate. The need for some sort of supervisory or control analysis was evident. But how could one observe and supervise the therapy without intruding on the analytic situation itself, without violating the delicate doctor-patient relationship? These questions were to preoccupy the group for at least five years; in fact they continue to concern psychoanalytic training institutions today.

In September 1920, most of the group journeyed to the Hague for the sixth International Psychoanalytic Congress. The four-day meeting was well attended—about one hundred and twenty members and guests—in spite of the economically troubled times and the financial hardships most of the delegates were experiencing. Freud was there and Karen met him.

Joan Riviere describes his "pale face . . . stooping shoulders . . . and lean but broad sturdy figure . . . and in his stern expression and firm jaw a reserve of dignity and inner strength, a tenacity; but apparently bored by the meetings."[7]

For Karen two presentations stood out as highlights of the meeting. One was Karl Abraham's paper, "Manifestations of the Female Castration Complex," in which he cited the problems of a number of women patients he had analyzed and explained them psychoanalytically. One of these patients appeared to resemble Karen herself. He pointed out that there were several possible ways a woman might react to the fear of castration by her father. In the normal reaction, she could replace the wish for a penis like her father's with a wish for a child. In the neurotic reaction, she could repress the wish to take a man's role and become homosexual. Or she could unconsciously wish to avenge herself on castrating men by developing such character traits as frigidity, sadism or simply contempt for men. These remarks both stimulated Karen's thinking and troubled her. After her return to Berlin she began to compose a reply to Abraham, which she presented in a paper a few months later.[8]

The second highlight of the meeting for Karen involved Georg Groddeck, who was to become her mentor, her informal therapist, her ideal and her good friend. Often called the father of psychosomatic medicine, Groddeck had written an article three years previously relating forces within the unconscious—which he called the It (Das Es)—to somatic disease.[9] Although he had not had any official analytic training other than self-analysis beginning at age forty-three (he was now sixty-four) or been involved in any official organization (except for a brief membership in the Berlin Society), he still considered himself a psychoanalyst. In his private sanatorium in Baden-Baden, he had developed a strange, unorthodox "psychic treatment" of his patients, often with surprisingly successful results. At the Congress, Freud had asked him to speak spontaneously about his ideas. "I am a wild analyst," he declared before going on in a rambling, disconnected way about how visual difficulties were always the expression of emotional conflicts. This speech shocked or dismayed almost all the analysts there and alienated many of them. They had just been decrying the dangers of untrained persons practicing psychoanalysis, of precisely those wild analysts he had declared himself to be. All were shocked except Rank, Ferenczi, Simmel and especially Karen. She applauded and was delighted at his candor and simplicity, which was often her reaction to self-revelation of this kind.

Perhaps she also admired and felt drawn to him because she recognized in him a kindred spirit, with some of the creative, innovative and rebellious qualities she herself possessed. Iago Galdston was later to call this quality "the giftedness of the maverick," one apart from the herd. Groddeck was indeed aloof and individualistic, yet he admired Freud in a personal way and expected personal recognition—much as a son might feel toward a busy father.

Some of his ideas also appealed to Karen and were to influence, or become part of, her later theories. He emphasized the unity of the mind and body, and preferred the concept of self to the Freudian ego. "The sum total of an individual human being, physical, mental and spiritual, with all its forces, the microcosmos, the universe which is man, I conceive of as a self. I call this the It. We know that no man's ego has had anything to do with the fact that he possesses a human form, is a human being. Yet we immediately assume that this being is an ego and can be made responsible for what he is and does. Still we know that the humanity of his being was never willed by his ego. He is human through an act of will . . . of the It."

Groddeck saw the unconscious as a more pervasive and more powerful force than Freud did. "The It is a power by which we are lived while we think we live. . . . The It shapes the nose as well as the hand just as it shapes thoughts and emotions." The basic unconscious striving toward health is present in everyone, even the sickest person. "Health and sickness are its forms of expression. No one is altogether ill, there is always some part which remains sound, even in the worst illness; and no one is altogether well, there is always something wrong, even in the perfectly healthy. The It never uses either of them alone, always both at once."[10]

Furthermore, as Lawrence Durrell was to comment in 1948, whereas Freud spoke of curing neurosis, Groddeck spoke of liberation through self-knowledge. Disease as an entity did not exist except as the expression of man's total personality. Disease was a form of self-expression.[11] Such holistic, humanistic and optimistic concepts were most congenial to Karen, and in modified form were to be integrated into her theory.

Even though Freud admitted the validity of Groddeck's unconscious somatic forces, he had difficulty accepting this "positive" healing tendency. In 1920, he wrote critically that Groddeck "took our mutual, undefined and easy-running unconscious and gave it all sorts of positive qualities which grew out of a secret source of self-realization." He disagreed with Groddeck's "Panpsychism, which amounts almost to mysticism" and claimed that Groddeck "despised reason and science, even though it neither disturbed me in the enjoyment of your writing nor confused me in the estimation of your original finds."[12]

Karen was to recall later that a statement Groddeck made during a conversation at this meeting had set her off on her train of thought about male psychology. He had commented that "men are really afraid of women." This had arisen in connection-with a previous, equally significant observation that little girls are female from the beginning and that penis envy, while present, is not a powerful force of the It. "If the It wanted women to have penises, they would have them."[13]

On their return to Berlin, even while the group concentrated on the Poliklinik, the activities and meetings of the Berlin Society continued. Karen took part, although she had other concerns as well. In October 1920 she presented a short paper, "Marriage Problems and Psychoanalysis." Although the paper was couched in objective terms, Karen's choice of subject apparently indicated strains in her own marriage. She still wished to resolve her problems and make the marriage work if possible. She decided to reenter psychoanalysis with Hanns Sachs, who had only recently begun to take private analytic patients.

Why she chose Sachs remains open to speculation. His article "The Wish To Be a Man" appeared in the *Zeitschrift* in November 1920. It referred to a sexually inhibited young woman whose wish to be a man could be related to unconscious castration/mutilation fears that were traceable back to conflicts about her father. It was sympathetically written; perhaps it struck a sensitive chord in her.

She had been working closely with him on the Poliklinik's training program. Of the seven members of the "Committee" (the semisecret inner circle of psychoanalysts, to whom Freud had presented symbolic signet rings), only Sachs and Otto Rank were not physicians. Sachs seemed set apart in other ways as well: He had studied law and was primarily interested in art and literature, philosophy and the social sciences (as was Karen). Ernest Jones described him as a highly cultured man, typically

"Viennese" in his outlook and particularly aware of his Jewish origins, a gifted raconteur with a special fondness for Jewish jokes. Although devotedly loyal to Freud, he was uninterested in, even bored by, organizational matters and the political aspects of the movement. According to Helene Deutsch, he was hypersensitive about being told what to do by others. Perhaps because of this, he was apathetic at times and thus of the seven had the least contact and least intimate relationship with Freud. At the 1918 Congress in Budapest, he had become quite ill with a lung disorder. Freud had thought him doomed. But he had recovered, after a cure at Davos, and had settled briefly in Switzerland. He had come to Berlin in 1919 and begun to practice psychoanalysis the following year.

In his analytic work, he usually followed the classical technique strictly: The analyst serves an objective mirror-function and rarely speaks. At that time, he seldom prolonged an analysis more than six months. He devoted himself primarily to training analyses, having been the first member of the group assigned this task. This was one of the reasons why he could not present clinical papers as often as the others. He was scrupulous about the confidential nature of his sessions with the candidates, which limited the case material available to him. He practiced in his small apartment, where his dining room also served as his waiting room. Some of his colleagues felt that although he had a good grasp of analytic theory, he was lacking in clinical experience.

Karen remained in analysis with him for the first six months of 1921. This work seems to have crystallized some of her feelings about herself, as a person and as a woman. She began to develop her ideas about feminine psychology. These had been stimulated by Abraham's paper at the recent Congress, by Groddeck's remarks and possibly by Sachs's little article. By November 1921 she had thought them through well enough to present a short talk to the Berlin Society, which then had twenty-two members attending. She entitled it "Contribution to the Female Castration Complex." It was, in effect, a reply to Abraham. Whether or not the other members agreed with her, they were sufficiently impressed to recommend that she present an extended version to the forthcoming International Congress.

At the Hague it had been decided to hold the next meeting in Berlin in the fall of 1922. This was intended to be both a recognition of the work the group there was accomplishing, and a stimulus to encourage them to continue it. The atmosphere at the institute in early 1922 was expectant and busy. Not only did the Berlin group have to make all the necessary arrangements for the Congress, but several wished to present papers, including Karen. Everyone was excited.

Everyone except Hans Liebermann. At the end of the war he had succeeded Karen as secretary. She liked him personally and respected his intelligence. In fact, he became one of her closest friends. Usually a shy, self-effacing man, he was becoming even more withdrawn. Although he attended all the meetings and taught a course, he wrote and spoke little. He suffered from intermittent dizziness and fainting spells, probably due to a chronic infection of the inner ear resulting from his war experiences. In January 1922, because of this illness, he was unable to continue as secretary and Eitingon took over. Liebermann's disability seemed to endear him to Karen; when they were together at meetings or on trips or when he visited her home, she gave him special attention and care. This concern for suffering was an attitude we have already seen in her treatment of clinic patients. But there was another quality about him that appealed to her. She wrote to Frau Groddeck a few years later that the analysts she most respected and admired—Simmel, Ferenczi and Liebermann—all in some way formed an attachment to Groddeck, in contrast to the others, who resented him. Perhaps they saw him as the outsider, the underdog, rejected by those in the establishment. Certainly Liebermann, even though he participated in the teaching program, was not on the executive council and is not generally considered one of Freud's principal disciples, any more than Karen is. Perhaps it was Groddeck's air of being different, nonconformist, even rebellious that he empathized with.

The meeting in Berlin was a momentous occasion for Karen. It was her debut, her first formal presentation before the official psychoanalytic community, her peers as well as her elders. In her paper she was expressing not only her own personal, original ideas—that would take courage enough—but even daring to challenge some of the ideas of both Freud and her first analyst, Abraham. Besides, Freud himself was to chair her session. This surely would have added to her tension, and by the same token, would have demanded even more fortitude. She was unaware of Freud's mood; he felt a growing concern over the friction among some of the members of his committee, "disunion," as Jones described it.

The meeting, with Ernest Jones presiding, was a great success. It drew the largest audience yet: 256 persons, of whom 112 were psychoanalysts. Of the latter, the largest contingent came, of course, from Berlin. Karen presented her paper, "The Genesis of the Castration Complex in Women," on the first afternoon. It stimulated much discussion of a generally friendly nature. Abraham's paper on melancholia was outstanding.

Freud himself presented some new ideas in a paper entitled "Some Remarks on the Unconscious." He described unconscious aspects of the nonrepressed ego, a revision of his previous theory which had visualized the unconscious in terms of repressed libidinal forces. It was the beginning of ego psychology, soon to be developed in his book *The Ego and the Id*. A short time before, in a letter to Ferenczi, he had hinted that the new concepts would have something to do with Groddeck.

Groddeck's presentation on the second day of the meeting was of greater interest to Karen than any of the others. His paper was entitled "The Flight into Philosophy," but it touched on one of the basic tenets of Freud's psychology—the nature of the unconscious. Here Groddeck amplified on his belief that the previously held concept of the unconscious did not adequately explain all its phenomena. He proposed to designate all the unconscious forces by the term *Es* (It). He believed "all the manifestations of life in man—his outward form, his structure, the alterations and functions of his organs, his actions and thoughts, his psychic and physical diseases . . . to be merely different phenomena in which the *Es* is manifested." This paper was well prepared, better organized than the previous rambling speech at the Hague and generally well received, indeed so well that Freud took over the term *Es* to denote his concept of the id.

Meeting Groddeck at a dinner afterward, Karen was seen to "regard him with affection, warmth and respect." After the meeting, she began a correspondence and friendship with him that was to last until his death.

She was soon to need him in a more personal way. A few months after the meeting, during the winter of 1922–23, her brother Berndt came down with a pulmonary infection, probably pneumonia, and died. He was only forty-one at the time. Karen was plunged into a deep depression. Groddeck's *Das Buch vom Es* was published at this time and he sent her a copy with an explanatory letter, perhaps because he had felt a special rapport with her at the Congress. Karen had appreciated Groddeck's sympathetic interest at the Congress and turned to him for comfort now.* In

* Although it has been suggested that she spent a short time resting in his sanatorium on an "analyst's vacation," according to his secretary there is no evidence in the records that she actually did so.

fact, reading Groddeck's book seemed to help pull her out of her depression.

During this trying period, she nevertheless continued with her work, both in her office and in the Poliklinik. The clinic was feeling the effects of the financial pinch at this time. Until now, all the working analysts had been asked to donate treatment time for one patient in analysis; this was obligatory if they wished to remain affiliated with the clinic. Few patients were able to pay for treatment. Some of the analysts still recall today how they would give the patients money for carfare or even lunch. They smile when they think of what a heresy this would have been considered in terms of the strict rules governing the classical analytic relationship. Any direct financial contribution toward clinic expenses, however, was on a purely voluntary basis. In February 1923, the members of the society decided that a standing fund was needed to continue the clinic's development. It was voted to tax members four percent of their monthly earnings—or the equivalent of one day's income—from their private analytic practices to sustain the clinic.

In March, the Poliklinik was renamed the Psychoanalytic Institute of the Berlin Society to emphasize its training function. A faculty council or training committee of six—Abraham, Eitingon, Muller-Braunschweig, Sachs, Simmel and Horney—was set up to work on these issues. In 1924 Rado was added, and in 1927 Alexander, after Abraham's death. One of its functions was the screening of all new applicants for their suitability to become analysts; Karen was appointed a screening analyst, a task she accepted in spite of her depression. Perhaps this even contributed to bringing her out of it.

In addition, in April she presented a short paper, "The Discovery of Childhood Traumas by Psychoanalysis"; Liebermann also spoke on the same topic. Her concern with this subject suggests that she was still working out for herself some of the problems with her early relationship with Berndt which were involved in her depression.

Then in July, while on vacation, she was finally able to answer Groddeck:

> *Thank you somewhat belatedly for your letter. Since I had to spread my libido on three girls, a husband and a considerable household in addition to my analytic work, my personal wishes had to be postponed until I was able to enjoy*

this idyllic tranquillity here. Out of grateful narcissism I wanted to compliment you on your new writing, but I needed peace and quiet to read your book, Vom Es. I am pleased to have the opportunity to enjoy the effect of the sand dunes, sea breeze and blue sky.

Your train of thought was brought close to me through two occurrences: the death of my brother, which in the beginning I considered as something totally senseless—he belonged to those people who seem to burst with the joy of living. In the face of this, after many weeks I arrived at the conclusion: something in him had wanted to die. That insight I tend to accept in general and I have only one suspicion about it, and that is that it is too much of what we want to believe.

It seems to me on the whole that you smuggle omnipotence back into the Es. But the good thing is exactly this, that you had the courage to make something out of your fantasies of omnipotence. And with this I arrive at the point which has pleased me most in your book, and that is the grandiose candor (Dr. Abraham would say that this is really only exhibitionism) with which you include yourself within this whole confusion. That is splendid.

She then went on to reveal that she was becoming aware of, and having some misgivings about, some of the attitudes of her colleagues.

If you had enjoyed the questionable good fortune of living within an analytic circle, then you might understand this awareness better. Because here we are no less hypocritical than elsewhere, only a little different. Above all, it appears repeatedly as a silent presupposition that the "neurotic" has all these embarrassing complexes. It is like the pious Christians and their "We are all sinners," which can become very uncomfortable if you point out to them some concrete examples of their sins.

She then brought up the issue she had discussed with him both at the Hague and again in Berlin, which he had mentioned in his last letter: the relationship between the little girl and her parents, and its outcome in the woman's attitudes toward men. Both Abraham and Sachs had attributed women's sexual problems to conflictive early feelings of the daughter toward the father.

> *I gave a lot of thought to the concept mentioned in your letter, namely the attitude toward the mother—and that actually both sexes have this primary female object. I consider it rather one-sided that the emphasis is always on the attitude toward the father, with a footnote always explaining that for simplicity's sake only the attitude toward the father is mentioned but that it would also apply to the attitude toward the mother. But it does not also apply to the attitude toward the mother. In fact some fundamental differences between men and women must be attributed to this fact. I find it difficult to determine whether homosexuality is really more prevalent among women. I think it is less repressed among women as an aim-inhibited goal. Perhaps the more pronounced male narcissism stems from that. I have the impression men are more easily hurt and more vulnerable in their feelings of superiority. One can say that the woman does not even demand this superiority in her own inner self. But why does the man emphasize his superiority so much? I find it so typical that, for instance, the penis-envy phenomena are so well recognized, but their origin in the Oedipus complex is generally overlooked.*
>
> *I am also working now specifically on the problem of the rejection of the child—in connection with a miscarriage that I saw in my practice. This was the second point in your book that aroused my interest.*
>
> *With best regards,*
> *Your Karen Horney*

This was the beginning of her interest in the problem of penis envy, which was to eventuate in her distinction between primary and secondary penis envy. But even more important, it presaged a new direction in her intellectual development that would emerge years later, namely a focus on the importance of interpersonal attitudes.

During the rest of 1923 and into 1924, the Berlin Society was again preoccupied with problems of standardizing analytic training. Karen participated in several special meetings on the subject. It was determined that the minimum requirements for membership in the society would be, in addition to a recognized personal analysis, regular attendance at meetings and the presentation of an analytic paper. It was felt that the matter was important enough to be brought up at the next meeting of the Congress at Salzburg in April 1924. Karen was delegated to represent the group, along with Eitingon and Sachs. About twenty members of the Berlin group went along. Two Hungarian artists, Robert Bereny and Olga Szekely-Kovacs, were commissioned to draw caricatures of the most prominent analysts present. Karen was depicted as rather heavy-set, barely smiling, with a listless expression, her hair drawn tightly back from a center part into a bun over each ear.

She did not speak at the meeting. Her good friend Hans Liebermann did; it was the only time he ever addressed a Congress. His topic was the monosymptomatic organ neuroses. In distinguishing between the usual psychoanalysis (libido analysis)—which would worsen the physical symptoms—and ego analysis, he was in effect, expressing a new concept. Karen was delighted with him; this was the innovative, maverick quality she admired.

But even more important than the scientific papers at the meeting were the events occurring backstage, the shadow behind the friendly greetings. Freud did not attend because of an attack of influenza; it was the first such meeting he had ever missed. Abraham was at last elected president of the International Psychoanalytic Association, a long overdue honor. Now the rift between Rank and Ferenczi and the rest of Freud's intimate group had become so acute that the Committee was dissolved. An undercurrent of gloom permeated the meeting. The conflict was temporarily shelved when Rank left for America for a teaching-speaking engagement. But it was not resolved; he began to write back about his new personal technique, which could produce miraculous results in a few months. The others grew even more doubtful. Ferenczi returned to the fold but this too was to be only temporary.

Back in Berlin, a number of analysts in other parts of the country wrote in to express interest in the new clinic and the organization. It was decided to hold the first Assembly of German Psychoanalysts in October

1924 in Würzburg. Most of the Berlin group went and a total of forty-eight persons attended. Simmel reported on the progress of the Berlin Institute. Sachs spoke on "Instructional Analysis," as didactic analysis was then called. Karen did not speak at this meeting either. Whether this was because she was not asked or because she did not wish to is not known. She certainly was active in other ways.

She had been named to a newly formed public relations committee, set up in response to requests from outside organizations for speakers. In October she addressed the National Society of Women Social Workers on "What Can Psychoanalysis Contribute to Women Engaged in Social Work?" In November she spoke before the Professional Organization of Kindergarten Teachers on possible applications of psychoanalysis to teaching. Following both lectures there was a spirited discussion, with considerable opposition from the leading older members of the audience but with marked positive interest and enthusiasm from the younger women.

Both within the Berlin Society and outside, she was becoming associated with women's problems and issues. For instance, she taught courses on "Frigidity and Other Women's Sexual Disorders" (1925–26) and on "Psychoanalysis and Gynecology." Although her style of speaking was calm, slow and restrained, always focused on the psychological and psychoanalytic, she somehow generally aroused lively responses in her audiences—almost entirely women. This was to provoke a negative reaction among her colleagues and to give her a reputation for being too outspoken that she was at a loss to understand.

In spite of all these outside activities, life in the Berlin Institute was a cloistered, incestuous one. Even within the broader International Association, with all its ramifications, interest was focused mainly on the group itself. The outside world was significant only insofar as it affected the fortunes of the movement.

But Karen was becoming even more involved with outside events. The year 1925 was supposed to be a good year, a hopeful year. It was the year the disastrous inflation was halted and the mark stabilized; the year Hindenburg was elected president on a promise to provide a conservative government and a return to traditional social values; and the year Adolf Hitler was released from prison and began his climb to power.

VIII
BERLIN, 1920:
THE WEIMAR FERMENT
–EARLY YEARS

"We think of a man having a 'happy marriage' who ruins or hurts his wife by failure in his work, or who increases his work or the time spent in it far beyond the real necessity, thereby withdrawing himself from his wife and any marriage conflicts. The questionable result is that conflicts will not be solved, only concealed. A favorable consequence may be that life-destroying effects may be thereby mitigated."

—"Roots of Some Typical Conflicts in Marriage"

Berlin 1920: At the end of the war, most people in Berlin were demoralized and depressed. They had had enough, they were fed up. Those who had remained at home were fed up with the privations and suffering; those who had been fighting at the front and now came streaming home were fed up with dirt and death. Many could not believe they had been defeated, and those who could not deny it, could not yet fully accept it. And then there was the widespread guilt felt by so many, which added to the bitterness. The peace treaty not only put an enormous material burden on the country, but even worse from the psychological view, ascribed all war guilt to the Germans.

The Germans themselves needed someone to blame—and they first blamed the government. Actually the wartime government had been toppled by the "revolution" of the leftist Spartacists under Karl Liebknecht. Paradoxically, the socialist elected government, led by Friedrich Ebert, allied itself with the right-wing monarchists and militarists. Months of street fighting between the "Reds" and "freecorps" of socialist "Whites" finally culminated with the murder of Liebknecht and his associate, "Red

Rosa" Luxemburg, as the leftists were defeated. The political vacuum was at last filled by the still-shaky Weimar Republic.

The 1920's began with another threat, this time from the right: the government takeover by Wolfgang Kapp—the famous Kapp putsch. As government officials fled Berlin they issued a call for a general strike. It was almost complete. Kapp ruled for only one week over a silent, darkened, motionless city. People stayed home from work, off the streets; all vehicles stopped; water, light and power and other public services were shut off. In the end Kapp was left without popular support. Most Berliners were bored or frightened or, especially in the case of the workers, hostile. Officials refused to obey his orders. His effort fizzled out quickly, almost comically. It was during this time that the Berlin Poliklinik opened. The municipal authorities attended. When government representatives attended such functions at that time, it was a Berlin witticism to ask, "of what government?"

No wonder so many flocked to the clinic. Of the thousands of former soldiers, many still retained residues of their war neurosis; many were still depressed, angry, bitter at having been deceived—as they perceived it—by promises that the new government was unable to keep. Out of that same need to blame some other convenient scapegoat, there arose among many a sort of national myth: Germany and the German people were not responsible for the debacle. They had been "stabbed in the back" by others. The newspapers spoke of a Catholic "Black International" or a Communist "Red International" or behind even these, a Jewish "Yellow International." Such feelings were not limited only to soldiers or to men.

During the war when their men were away, women had taken over many male jobs. They had driven taxis, trucks and municipal vehicles, and invaded the offices as secretaries, had operated trolleys and buses, had wielded picks and shovels on construction sites, had cleaned the streets and collected garbage, had worked in the subways, had become nurses and social workers. After the war they went to college in unprecedented numbers; many new evening courses were offered. The returning men soon reclaimed their jobs and their places in the universities. Unemployment was still high, though it was gradually declining. But the old order had changed and the change was to become accelerated in a short time. Many of the younger women were joining the old prewar youth movements like the *Jugendbewegung*, but were now becoming feminist

[77]

activists. New women's rights movements such as the *Frauenrichtlerinnen* and the *Frauenbewegung* were springing up. These were not primarily role-oriented women's rights movements like those of today. They often had political overtones, generally leftist, appealing to women workers to liberate themselves from rightist, conservative political attitudes or capitalist restrictions. They followed the tradition of Rosa Luxemburg, Bertha von Suttner, and later, Käthe Kollwitz and Lou Andreas-Salomé. In 1922 official equality for women in academic life was finally achieved with the appointment of the first woman college professor in Germany, in chemistry.

The German economy declined steadily between 1920 and 1923, primarily because of the ruinous war reparations demanded in both currency and raw materials, which led to the French occupation of the Ruhr coal mines and industrial plants. The mark fell in value, slowly at first, then with increasing momentum. Inflation set in, slow and bearable at the beginning, since wages rose with prices; but by 1923 it became an unimaginable runaway flight. Money became worthless, especially as one of the presumed remedies, the unlimited printing of more money, simply aggravated the situation. Innumerable stories have come down of people who were paid wages in suitcases or who withdrew their savings in wheelbarrows, only to find it worth next to nothing the following day. Karen's daughter Renate remembers how she used to play with billion-mark notes with her dolls.

Unemployment rose precipitously; some felt there was just no reason to work if earnings had no use. The traditional work ethic vanished. Hunger was commonplace and the lowly turnip, the stinging nettle, acorn and chicory weed became staples—just like during the war. The incidence of depression, suicide, malnutrition and related diseases, like avitaminosis and tuberculosis, rose rapidly. Some say that the situation was even worse than during the last year of the war and the terrible winter of 1918–19. Particularly hard hit were all those on fixed incomes: retirees on fixed pensions, handicapped veterans, widows living on savings, teachers, civil servants and professionals, especially doctors. The security of the entire middle class and much of the working class was wiped out. Even in the more genteel neighborhoods, "respectable" people could be seen silently begging.

Anyone with access to real property, gold or foreign currency lived high. A flourishing black market and a barter market arose. While many went hungry, others, known as "Schieper," made money; they hoarded stocks of foodstuffs which they then sold to buy gold, jewels, paintings, foreign currency or other valuables. Some people traded their few possessions of any value, even their clothes, for daily needs. Such barter markets existed in every neighborhood, and when the police would move them on, they quickly reopened, flourishing like ubiquitous weeds. Even some psychoanalysts accepted objects of value in exchange for their services. At the height of the inflation, psychoanalytic practice fell off, as was to be expected, while clinic attendance rose. Some analysts had to do other kinds of work; for instance, Henry Lowenfeld, Karen's Lankwitz colleague, gave anatomy lessons to Chinese students.

The two Congresses were held during this period. Most of the German analysts could not have afforded the trip to the Hague Congress. It was only because of a liberal financial subsidy from their Dutch colleagues that they were able to go. The economic situation also contributed to the choice of Berlin in 1922. The non-German members benefited from the currency exchange. The difficult conditions of practice and living were one of the chief topics of personal conversation among the members at that time. While the Poliklinik was surfeited with poor applicants for analytic therapy, private practice declined and lower fees had to be asked. Every analyst—even Freud—sought foreign patients for the higher fees and hard currency.

The poor grew poorer and the rich richer. Hugo Stinnes was one of the latter. During the war his investments and enterprises prospered; his coal, steel and shipping had been needed. After the war they became a crucial factor in the reparations payments. In fact, he accompanied the German delegation to the first reparations conference as the representative of the mine owners. There he made a belligerent speech starting with the words "I rise to look my enemies in the eye . . ." He was not affected by the national economic disaster because of his widespread foreign investments, such as his bank in Holland and his international shipping interests. He borrowed foreign money to buy innumerable failing German firms at ridiculously low prices. At one point in 1924, it was estimated that he owned over two thousand companies. His conglomerate became a financial empire. But it was a shaky edifice, built and held together precariously by credit. It needed only one crack to fall.

As Stinnes's general manager, Oskar benefited accordingly and his fortunes rose during these years. His personal investments also flourished. For a short while, in 1920 or '21, the family was able to purchase a huge convertible; they even briefly had a chauffeur. Renate recalls one occasion on which Oskar drove the family to the beach. Traveling over unpaved, rocky and dusty country roads, they finally arrived at the seashore, after several flat tires. There were so many jellyfish in the water that they couldn't even wash off the dust and had to return home immediately. After several more flat tires, they arrived home so disgusted and tired that Karen decided that would be the last automobile ride for her. Although she accepted rides in a car after that, she never purchased one until many years later in America.

During this time Karen continued to work at Lankwitz as a part-time attending psychiatrist until her practice in the city began to fill up, along with her part-time work in the clinic. The few Lankwitz patients she saw in her home, and some in the city as well, were usually not charged a fee. Other analysts did the same during this period.

Anger against the war and the demoralization resulting from it were also manifest in the arts and humanities. In both literature and art, Dada came to Berlin in late 1917 and lasted until 1922. However, as Willy Verkauf, one of its early participants, has pointed out, it never actually existed as a movement, as an organization or as a tendency in art. It had no prescribed principles; it was more a state of mind. It had started in Zurich in 1916, in the back-alley Cabaret Voltaire. Life during the war years had become intolerable for many young artists and creative thinkers. "Reason appeared to have been abandoned by humanity. . . . Dadaism had to fulfil a mission for crazed humanity. . . . It proclaimed nonsense as the weapon against any sense imputed to the war. Dada negated all the values until then considered sacred and inviolable, ridiculed fatherland, religion, morality and honor, and unmasked the values that had been made idols of. The great anguish caused in sensitive artistic natures by the senseless massacres exploded in the dadaist outcry, in the abrupt and uncompromising defiance of bourgeois logic which was blamed for the war and later for the resulting chaos."[1]

Dada was brought to Berlin by a young artist, George Grosz, and his close friend, the young artist-poet-writer Richard Huelsenbeck. In his savagely satirical drawings, Grosz attacked and held up to ridicule the middle classes, the businessmen, the militarists, "bourgeois morality," capitalism, militarism.[2]

Huelsenbeck (later Hulbeck) had studied philosophy, sociology and psychology in Munich and Paris prior to 1916, and then had worked with Bleuler, Jung and Geza Roheim in Zurich through 1917. Extremely bright, widely traveled and well read, and without any political belief other than what might be called a nonviolent anarchism, it was he who said, "Dada is German Bolshevism." Marcel Janco, another of the early adherents of Dada, described him then as "a poet. Like every poet he affected a slight limp. He had a shock of light hair and would get up with a slender cane in his hand, brandishing it like a rowdy. He was an expressive, activist poet and flooded the hall with his abandon, flinging out his verses like so much invective. He was aggressive and aware of his power. He looked like a fighting cock and became the antagonist of Tzara. Wherever he was, poetry would flow profusely, the fight was in full progress. He left us one day, much too early, to satisfy his taste for travel, for women and for a thousand other interests."[3]

After the war, Dada lost its bite and its relevance, but by sweeping away traditional forms it opened the way for a wave of new creative expression in all the arts—painting, architecture, films—and the physical sciences.

On completing his medical studies in Berlin in 1922, Huelsenbeck worked in Bonhoeffer's service for three years. He first met Karen at a psychoanalytic meeting and shortly afterward, when he was interviewed at the Berlin Institute, where he attended her classes five years later. Impressed by her intelligence, he was first drawn to her by an intuitive sense that she was an individualist, a rebel, just as he was a revolutionary. He recalled that they did not discuss psychoanalysis at that time. Instead he spoke of his travels around the world, his interest in cultural psychology, and of his realization that his interest in Dada represented a personal search for some impossible ideal. She seemed intrigued and friendly and shared all his experiences with pleasure. Neither could foresee that they would meet again in New York twenty years later, that she would "save his life," professionally speaking, or that they would become good friends.

What he did foresee was that Dada—if not in its form, at least in its spirit—would continue to exert a strong influence on literature, philosophy and the other humanities.

An important event in this postwar artistic renaissance was the appearance of the first consciously expressionist motion picture, *The Cabinet of Dr. Caligari,* in 1919. It ushered in a productive period of creative filmmaking that dealt with the same grist that psychoanalysis was concerned with: the criminal mind, guilt, punishment and absolution, unconscious motives, emotionality, symbolism, the ways of love. Karen was tremendously impressed with some of these films, not only because of their artistic qualities and the psychological issues they raised, but also because of the times and places they recalled for her. Thirty years later, in America, whenever she felt lonely, she would track down a revival house showing one of these old German films, perhaps less for the films themselves than for the haunting memories they evoked.

In the theater, too, a group of young dramatists and writers—Georg Kaiser, Erwin Piscator, Max Reinhardt, Bertolt Brecht—began to produce plays with expressionist or social significance, and often a leftist orientation. Like Dada, this trend rebelled against tradition, rationalism and objective reality. It appealed to fantasy, the bizarre, the unconscious.

As one significant result of all these developments, acting began to become a most desirable profession and there emerged a whole series of young, attractive and talented actors and actresses. These were the ideals for young Brigitte, then seeking a career.

A new school of philosophical psychology, existentialism, also appeared in 1919 with the publication of Karl Jaspers's Worldview Psychology (Die Psychologie der Weltanschauungen). Although this was not really a new philosophy, since it extended the ideas of Immanuel Kant, Sören Kierkegaard and Edmund Husserl, it arose anew out of the postwar despair and suffering. Karen had read these works, had debated them with her friend Karl Muller-Braunschweig in medical school and again with Sachs and Liebermann during their soirees at home. These ideas were also to have a significant influence upon her later thinking.

If Karen and Oskar were drifting apart during these difficult early postwar years, apparently the marital strains were not outwardly evidenced in the home. There was no quarreling. Karen seemed to pride herself on not showing her feelings, a trait that was to become more marked as time went on. She would not allow any friction or conflict between herself and her husband to affect the children.

She would not interfere with their growing up, with their comings and goings. But the children felt that this noninterference might have bordered at times on neglect: Their clothes were often too long or too short, their stockings did not fit. A governess was no longer needed now that they were all in school, and the maids did not look after them personally.

The children did not stay long in the local elementary school. After their return from Switzerland, both Brigitte and Marianne had trouble readjusting. Janne had become so shy, so fearful of teachers and so easily intimidated that she needed special help. For the next three semesters she had to have special tutoring. Karen heard of a new private experimental school in the neighboring suburb of Dahlem and the children were soon transferred there. Here they were permitted to work on their own chosen subjects, at their own pace. The girls rode there daily on their bicycles. Janne remembers the school excursions into the woods; it was the first time she had good friends and really enjoyed life. But for her it did not last. For some mysterious reason, at least as she perceived it, she was taken out before she was twelve and sent to a Quaker Fellowship School in Gland, Switzerland, overlooking Lake Geneva. Perhaps Karen selected this new school because it was dedicated to the ideal of promoting freedom, peace and friendship among students of different national backgrounds, pacifism and avoidance of conflict. It was a private school, preparatory for high school, where the students were taught in small groups.

Biggi decided to drop out of the Dahlem school and take up dancing as a career. Karen agreed, provided she would take some academic courses too; she hoped Brigitte would go into gymnastics, perhaps become a teacher. So between the ages of twelve and fifteen Biggi attended a well-known dancing school and took private lessons. But she was not a scholar; she did not wish to spend three years studying. She wanted to become a dancer quickly or, if possible, to work in pantomime. It was a short step from pantomime to a new ambition of going into the theater; she was convinced that she would not have to study to become an actress.

Renate, the youngest, had trouble staying in school from the beginning. Playing, having a good time, came first, studying afterward. The modern experimental school was of no help. Neither were private tutors. She was even sent to her paternal grandfather, a retired schoolmaster, in the hope that she would accept some lessons, some discipline from him. As a last resort, she was finally sent for psychoanalysis with Melanie Klein. She spent as much time crawling under the couch as lying on it, or holding her hands over her ears to spare herself the sexual interpretations. But one thing it did do for her; it aroused her interest in sexual words, which she otherwise knew nothing about. She got the idea of writing them everywhere, and sending obscene letters to neighbors. This finally convinced Karen that this torturous psychoanalysis would have to stop.

Home life, however, was not all work or school. True, Karen was most often out working, or writing when at home. Then, for instance, if Renate played with her dolls or made noise around her desk, she would send her out to climb trees. But she still saved some time for the children. On Thursdays, when the maid was off, the girls remember her teaching them how to cook delicious chocolate or white sauces, or scalloped potatoes. She was not musically inclined and seemed to dislike classical music. On one occasion, later, when some friends were visiting and someone put on a classical long-playing record, she remarked with a typical pun: "Will someone take off that long-suffering record?" The family did have a piano. Though she never studied music, Karen learned to read notes well enough to play simple folksong melodies. It was a joy for the children to spend an all too rare evening around the piano singing folksongs and carols. Christmas, in particular, was a joyous time. Renate, more than her sisters, remembers the preparations, the cooking and baking, the candles, trimming the tree; and then the excited moment of the presents, the Christmas dinner and the carols.

Oskar loved games with the children—Ping-Pong, chess, cards, bocce, mah-jongg or just romping. The girls recall the birthday parties or weekends when he was home from work. Oskar even got himself a magic kit and liked to give home performances. And yet, while they enjoyed romping with him, their pleasure was always tempered by an underlying feeling of apprehension. His unspoken demands for good performance and high marks, along with his punishments for misbehavior, lurked in their minds.

Although Karen was attentive, she always remained somewhat formal, never completely letting go. Rita Honroth, the children's close friend, recalls her impression that Karen "held court" with their little friends. For her, the children were supposed to behave in the "proper" way, to be generally seen but not heard, to speak only when it was "fitting."

Until his death, Uncle Berndt often came on weekends with his wife Ollie. He would join in the games and the children remember his vitality and spontaneity. Other weekend or dinner visitors included the original circle of young couples from Lankwitz and from the psychoanalytic group. Karl and Josine Muller-Braunschweig were part of both groups and were frequent guests. Karen visited them often, sometimes with the children. They were divorced in 1925 and a year later Karl married Ada Schott, also a child therapist. Eitingon, always more or less formal, was looked up to by the children as a father figure.

Simmel came fairly often, then less frequently after he opened his own private sanatorium on the Tegelsee in 1922, where Freud used to stay during Berlin visits in the later 1920's for rest and surcease from the pain of his cancer. Simmel was a witty, easygoing man. His quip when Karen asked him to repay a small loan she had given him was typical: "It is not enough for a woman to lend you money, she also has to have it back."

Hans Liebermann and his young wife, Lisa, and Sandor Rado and his wife, Emmy, also came for evening get-togethers. The children recall visiting the Rados' home as well, when his jovial, mercurial personality made a great impression on them. Abraham was an occasional guest, but seldom with the Muller-Braunschweigs. After his analysis, Karl apparently had also developed feelings of resentment toward Abraham, which, like Karen's, were related to some unresolved childhood conflicts which emerged during analysis, and so did not feel comfortable with him on social occasions.

Karen seemed to be more at ease and gayer with her guests when her husband was away on one of his business trips. And as Oskar was rising in the Stinnes organization, he was called upon to make more trips to neighboring cities. She was often uncomfortable with his friends, though she tried to give the impression that there was harmony between them.

Her mood was quite different on vacations. She loved the seashore and mountains and would eagerly plan their holidays from travel brochures months in advance. One favorite spot was the Hiddensee, a village on an island off the Baltic coast. Another was the Nordseebad Juist, on the North Sea coast. Generally she would go with the children and friends, without Oskar, though he sometimes joined them when his work permitted. During the early postwar years, they stayed in rooms rented from local fishermen, sharing their kitchen. After inflation they usually stayed in small room-and-board hotels. The children's memories of these summer vacations are still vivid. What fun it was to build their sand castles in the sand, to compare who had the biggest and the one that could best withstand the encroaching water. It was customary to rent a high straw chair for the summer, and build a sand wall around it for privacy. The chair was not comfortable to sit in, but it was a shield against the wind, and turned over, a protection against the rain. Karen's daughters also remember the picnics on long walks along the beaches, the clam-digging outings in the shallows and the berry-picking excursions among the dunes. These goodies, incidentally, also helped with the food bill during inflation, when the money sent by Oskar was worth so little.

During the summer of 1922, on a day outing to the island of Helgoland, a fierce storm blew up. First the children were almost blown off the cliffs they were climbing. Then on the boat ride back, while the children and all the other passengers were terribly seasick, Karen slept peacefully. When she awoke, she was unperturbed, unafraid and delighted at the "wonderful" trip. Perhaps her early sailing experiences with her father had inured her to the menace of wind and sea. Toughness, fearlessness and resiliency were qualities she prized.

During the summer of 1921 the family had their first vacation in the mountains, at Berchtesgaden. Here Karen found the ultimate expression of her love for nature and freedom. The mountains and the sea both gave her the same intense pleasure. The children recall long hikes through the fields, up the hills, along the cliffs, even when little Renate could not keep up and had to be dragged along. Once when she was going through a crying, whiny period, Biggi and Janne ganged up on her; they sang a song to tease her: "The sheep says 'baa,' Renate cries, we are full of joy and cheerfulness."* But the ridicule only added to the hurt. The crying finally stopped when Karen—and then the rest of the family—loudly imitated her, making her realize how silly it sounded. Karen often insisted that self-pity was useless and even destructive. The height of her joy during this vacation was a real mountain climb with a guide, up the Watzmann, one of the highest peaks in the region. This was usually considered

---

*"Das Merzschaf mächt, Die Naci schreit, Wir sind voll Lust, Und Heiterkeit."

a moderately difficult ascent. Later Karen was often to relate this achievement with pride and excitement.

One incident never forgotten by the Honroths occurred when the two families were together during the summer vacation of 1923, a short time after the death of Karen's brother. One day on the beach, she decided to go in for a swim alone. This was of no special import, as she was a good swimmer. But when she failed to return after over an hour, the others became anxious and swam out looking for her. Oskar finally found her, exhausted, clinging to a piling in deep water, still trying to decide whether to end her life or come in to shore. It was only after much pleading by all three that Karen was finally persuaded to allow them to pull her in to shore.

Hermine von Hug-Hellmuth, a young child psychoanalyst, was another friend who sometimes accompanied Karen on their summer vacations. Their preoccupation was mostly with problems of children and how psychoanalysis could—at least in theory—make them grow healthier and prevent later problems. Many of the analysts' children were sent to child analysts for even minor difficulties. It was the thing to do as part of the "good psychoanalytic upbringing" Karen often spoke of.

At age eleven, Janne—like Renate—went to Melanie Klein. Her experience typifies what was apparently the usual child analysis and the usual reaction of the child at that time. She would lie on the couch and relate the events that had occurred since the last session. When she mentioned enjoying playing ball, for example, there might be some interpretive attempt to equate the ball with the penis. Then for the last ten minutes the analyst would pronounce the "lesson" for the day, telling her what she was doing wrong and should not do. Little attention was paid to her real problems, such as her rivalry with Brigitte, her timidity, or her feeling that the others were being favored by her mother. Play therapy was not used at the time, though later on, when Renate went, it was tried experimentally. Janne felt that she got little out of the so-called analysis, not change nor understanding nor solace. It was more an unpleasant chore than anything else. For Renate, as we have seen, it was simply torture. Later Karen was to admit that her insistence on psychoanalysis for the children had been a big mistake.

But there were other activities that compensated for such unpleasantnesses. For instance, there were the trips to Grandma's house. Karen would put the girls on the train and someone would pick them up at the station. Oskar's parents—Grossfatti and Grossmutti—lived in a farmhouse in Hesse. His father had been a schoolteacher and a strict disciplinarian. Though he might have taken a stick to his two sons, as was traditional, the girls remember him as a kind and loving man. His wife had died shortly after Karen's mother, and he had married a woman considerably younger than himself.

The girls remember Grossmutti best of all. She is still living today in the town of Wolfenbüttel. The enormous kitchen with its big stove and coal box was the family center. Grossmutti lovingly taught them all she knew about cooking, sewing and homemaking. The cellar was a treasure house of stored produce from the farm, from which they would never come up without an apple or a piece of the ham that hung from the beams. She would make their favorite prune cookies in large sheets, which they would carry over to the local bakery to be baked in the community oven. When they were done, still warm, each would receive a big handful. They loved being tucked into a bed warmed by an old-fashioned hot-water bottle. During the war, produce from the farm helped the family to survive. The children recall Grossmutti as a warm, loving woman, with a great store of down-to-earth, intuitive human wisdom, even though she was not widely read or traveled. Karen did not see her often and may have been envious of the frank affection and close emotional ties the children obviously felt for her.

Toward the end of 1923, at the height of the inflation, Hugo Stinnes was still prospering from his foreign investments and lines of credit: Oskar was not. His own investments collapsed and his salary was worth less and less from one day to the next. Like thousands of others, he was ruined. He tried desperately to go into some other business, at one point, to invest—in a new movie company—by borrowing wherever he could. But to no avail. It was not a propitious time for new ventures.

Then, in 1924, a second misfortune occurred. While on a trip to Paris, Oskar took sick on the train and was hospitalized in Cologne with a form of encephalomeningitis. He remained there for about eight months in critical condition. At one point he gave himself up for lost. Now it was Karen's turn to plead with him, to encourage him to go on living—as he had done for her in the water off the beach.

Oskar did recover, but his personality had changed. He seemed broken in spirit, defeated; the feeling of failure obsessed him when he returned home. He needed to find some other occupation. He tried to promote inventions or business schemes, such as a round-the-world oceangoing showboat spurred on by unrealistic fantasies of the fortunes to be made. He tried a job with a wood products company. But he became argumentative, withdrawn and morose; he lost his friends. Because of his debts from the fruitless borrowing, his finances and Karen's were separated and he was eventually forced to declare bankruptcy. In 1925, the house and possessions had to be sold. It was a time of turmoil, travail and sadness for the entire family.

IX
BERLIN, 1925-1932:
MORITURI TE SALUTAMUS

"How many civilized men are fit for marriage? . . . The manliness complex in women and the corresponding insecurities in men are certainly typical manifestations of culture, at least in circles of the educated classes. The conclusion cannot be rejected that the civilized man of the present day has only a limited fitness for marriage. The actual course of most marriages makes the conclusion seem to be correct. We also have to remember the difficulties that have arisen out of the independence of women in today's marriage. Even with limitations of the capacity to love, a companionship is still possible if the partner adjusts to such limitations. However, this possibility, previously stronger when the woman was dependent, is becoming increasingly less since she too asserts her wishes and demands."
— *"Psychic Fitness or Unfitness for Marriage"*

The years from 1925 to 1929 were the golden era of Berlin. The Weimar Republic had finally stabilized the mark by pledging all its remaining gold reserves, lands and physical assets to secure the new currency—in effect, mortgaging the entire country. While this maneuver succeeded in reviving the economy, the years of runaway inflation had left deep scars. Thousands had been ruined (that many more had not was a testimony to the resourcefulness of Berliners).

To declare bankruptcy, as Oskar did, became so commonplace that many businessmen dispensed with the formality and simply announced to their creditors that they would be able to pay off ten or twenty percent of their debts, and started over from there. Hugo Stinnes died suddenly of a heart attack; his paper empire collapsed after his death and newer, and presumably sturdier cartels absorbed his enormous holdings.

The psychological scars left on Berliners by the years 1921 to 1924 took the form of uncertainty about and loss of trust in their economic, political and social institutions. It has been claimed that this period did more to change their traditional, tried-and-true middle-class morality than any other single set of circumstances in their history. It was as if the people wished to purge themselves of all restrictive mores. The revolution that Freud had been trying to bring about in the field of sexuality—both male and female—was now becoming a spontaneous social revolution. When the money that so many families had been saving for their daughters' dowries was wiped out, the entire traditional marriage system collapsed. Everyone began to speak of trial marriage, free love, the emancipation of women. Marriage itself began to be considered passé, bourgeois in a pejorative sense. These trends would assure Karen of a receptive audience for her ideas about marital problems.

A new social order sprang up in Berlin in which shallow living, amusement and a devil-take-tomorrow philosophy ruled. Everyone wanted to enjoy himself. As Otto Friedrich, that perceptive chronicler of the period, put it so well, the rituals of amusement became almost a religion of narcissistic self-indulgence. Prosperity had returned and money was plentiful, but the value of money had changed. Easy come, easy go; it was to be spent freely. The lesson everyone had learned was that money could not be counted on as a permanent source of security.

Cafés and cabarets thrived and catered to every taste. A kind of erotomania was rampant. Sexual expression, regardless of its form, became the keynote. There were homosexual cafés, transvestite cafés, topless or bottomless or totally nude cafés, pornographic "circus" cafés. Prostitution involving both men and women, of all ages, flourished. The perverse became the normal, the accepted. This freedom of expression exalted the body beautiful, with an emphasis on nudity. Nude dancing, *Schönheitstänze*, became the rage: in the cabarets and *Tanzbars*, in the frankly erotic style of Anita Berber and Josephine Baker; in theaters or at intimate private soirees, in the more esthetic style of Isadora Duncan. Thousands would go to the beaches or lakes to expose themselves to the supposedly healing sun's rays. There was probably more to this trend than just sexuality; it seemed to be a reaction against the uncertainty and chaos of the previous three years, from the economic ruin, the dying, the suffering of so many. However much it might have been a narcissistic phenomenon, and artificial to be sure, it was also a necessary defense, an affirmation of the vitality of being. If money, tradition, social habit, authority could offer no security, at least the tangible body and its sensations could be counted on.

But the emphasis on physical sensation was not only a defensive escape; it seemed to be also a search for heightened experience. The use of drugs, both narcotic and stimulant, reached almost epidemic proportions, and defined a veritable Berlin subculture. Cocaine, generally taken by sniffing, was the most popular drug. It was sold on street corners and in cafés, or even distributed to guests at some of the private, exclusive soirees. Morphine was also widely used, though it was usually initially taken by medical prescription for painful conditions. Many neuropsychiatrists prescribed it for the large numbers of ex-soldiers still suffering from their wartime experiences, or for the depression and sleeplessness of many chronically frustrated women. Addiction brought many patients to the Berlin clinic. It was particularly widespread among theatrical people, who needed to present a social façade for their work in spite of any painful inner feelings. But many young people used these drugs simply for the "kick," the high, it gave them.

Women had finally become "liberated," at least as sexual beings; but more often than not, this freedom had a driven quality to it. As Walter Nelson has recalled in *The Berliners*, his fascinating saga of Berlin, a new type of woman was becoming fashionable—the independent, even impudent and sardonic working-girl or showgirl "flapper" type. She had not only a beautiful body but also the quick intelligence—the"*Schnauze*," or big mouth—that men found so attractive. And she was going to prove it to them.

While every age group participated in this trend, the young were especially active. The vociferously enthusiastic reaction to Karen's lectures at the Humboldt University in 1925 was repeated at a second series in 1931. Many members of the youth movement became feminist activists. The universities were more crowded than ever during this period. Unfortunately, some of the youth groups, unaccustomed to the heady freedom, still needed and sought structure, authoritarian leadership. Many would thus become easy victims of any movement that offered some stability or at least direction. The tightly organized Communist and Nazi movements seemed to promise these and even more: hope and ideals.

During these five years of economic stability, the political situation also remained apparently stable. The Nazi party continued to grow, although very slowly; the number of Nazi deputies in the Reichstag actually fell. During this time the popularity of all "parties of discontent" decreased. National self-esteem rose with the Locarno Pact of 1925 and the acceptance of Germany into the League of Nations a year later. Until 1929, the Nazis were not a significant political force, especially in Berlin with its predominantly liberal majority. In his memoirs, Albert Speer reported that when Hitler appeared to speak in the city, he had no uniforms or fanfare to accompany him; not at first. He dressed soberly in business clothes and spoke in a low key. Until then most people were preoccupied with the good life. They either underestimated his power or, if they were aware of his excesses elsewhere, considered his group a sect of unruly fanatics, a product of abnormal times that would soon dissolve. When their brutalities could no longer be ignored, people did not speak of them. It was understood that they were repugnant to "decent" Germans, to the intellectuals, to responsible citizens. At first.

Karen was never politically minded. She had generally voted for the Social Democrats, a moderate pacifist party slightly to the left of center. Pacifism fulfilled a deep need of hers. Active conflict with others was repellent to her. She could not understand the strife, for instance, between the various analytic groups, and constantly sought a rapprochement. Nor could she understand the conflict between the others in the Berlin Institute and herself. "Why can't we be friends in spite of our differences?" she frequently asked her friends.

Some of her friends, such as Simmel, Bernfeld, Erich Fromm and to a radical extreme, Willi Reich, were more politically aware. They were mostly leftists, intellectual Communists or socialists rather than true political activists. Simmel was, in fact, president of the Society of Socialist Physicians. In 1928 that society held a debate on the relationship between Freudian and Marxist doctrines. It was generally felt that Marxism and psychoanalysis were compatible and could even complement each other, though a few members criticized Freudian theory for not giving sufficient weight to economic and material factors in the causality of emotional problems.

There were occasional discussions of these ideas in the Berlin Society or in the coffee houses after meetings. One of the candidate analysts at that time recalls one such soiree in a café when Karen and Annie Reich were present. The latter complained that the evening before her husband had expounded on his political views, and taken out his dissatisfactions on her—whereupon Karen had responded, "I wouldn't have taken that." This reaction illustrates her attitude in general. While she was probably aware of the troubled situation, she was less concerned with the political reality than with its effects on Annie Reich, and later, after 1929, with the effects of societal unrest on the individual in general.

During these golden, exciting years, Karen was often to be found in either of at least two coffee houses. One was the Café Grossenwahn (Café Egomania), where the analytic students and faculty gathered after their meetings. As some of the students still recall, they felt that they learned as much here as from any course, lecture or presentation. In the informal, free exchanges, ideas were thrown out, tossed around, discarded. The discussions ranged over most of the subjects currently of interest to the analytic world. The analysts would drop their formal professional reserve: Things could be said that would not have been permissible at scientific meetings or in classes. Nonorthodox analytic ideas could be expressed. Personal concerns could also be aired. Dr. Edith Weigert recalls one evening discussion on the possibility of finding some way of integrating Marxist and Freudian ideas.

Another coffee house Karen frequented was the well-known Romanishe Café on the Kurfürstendamm at the corner of Budapester and Tauentzien Streets, just across from the Kaiser Wilhelm Memorial Church. Its huge, barnlike interior, seating perhaps a thousand persons, had an atmosphere of slightly seedy splendor. Its tall blond doorman seemed to have unique personal criteria for designating those he would permit to enter. His decisions were not based solely on affluence or dress or familiarity or state of sobriety, since he admitted rich and poor, stylishly and shabbily dressed, regulars and unknowns through the revolving door. Perhaps it was some intuitive judgment, known only to his unconscious. In any case, Karen was accepted as a regular. The café was a meeting place for friends passing through town as well as a second home for many Berlin intellectuals. They were to be found coming in or out, sometimes seated alone in reverie or writing or simply observing the passing scene. More often, they gathered in heated groups, discussing, arguing, laughing, drinking. Each regular group had its own *Stammtisch*, a table staked out by tradition, where its members were automatically included in the conversations and debates. Those known as loners wandered from table to table, participating here or there, sometimes cadging a drink, a cup of coffee or a snack. Some were bohemians, living off others; some were established and well-known professionals or businessmen; some were simply the lost; some, the aspiring who hoped to be found. There were tables of artists, writers, poets and literati, theater people and dancers, film actors, philosophers and theologians, lawyers, psychiatrists and psychoanalysts. On the balcony, chess players and card players spent hours at their interminable games.

It was here, during these years, that Karen got to know some of the people in other fields who influenced her thinking. She frequented not only the psychoanalysts' *Stammtische* but also the artists', where Charles Hulbeck was known. She had previously met some of these through her friend Lissie Marx. The young Berlin artists were again in a ferment. Dada and expressionism were dead. Everyone was talking about the Bauhaus group, which moved from Weimar to Dessau in 1925. Although the school was relatively small, its influence was tremendous. Kandinsky, Klee, Feininger, Grosz, Ernst and Gropius all worked or taught there; the Bauhaus proclaimed "the polymorphous nature of art" and advocated the conscious interaction of painters, architects, sculptors and film makers. (The Nazis condemned all abstract art as "Bolshevist" and closed down the school in 1933. Most of the artists associated with it were forced to flee the country.)

Among the philosophy and theology students who frequented the Romanishe Café were young Paul Tillich and Heinrich Zimmer. Everyone was discussing Marxist philosophy and its compatibility with religion. The new existentialist ideas of Heidegger (1926) and then of Jaspers (1929), the antirationalist, anti-intellectual philosophy of Ludwig Klages (1928), the logical positivism of Rudolf Carnap and the symbolism of Ernst Cassirer (1929)—which emphasize the empirical source of knowledge—were all hotly debated at these gatherings. The tenets of Oriental philosophy came up for discussion too, as Zimmer was then gathering material for his book on Indian thought; even the psychoanalysts concerned themselves with these concepts at their meetings.

Karen was able to involve herself more intensely in all this activity after moving from the house in Dahlem. Early in 1926, the family took an apartment on the Steinplatz in central Berlin. This was probably a last attempt to keep the marriage together in something resembling their previous style of life. The apartment was an immense duplex, with many enormous rooms to accommodate all their furniture from the house. An upstairs room, led to by a narrow staircase, served as Karen's private workroom and den. Even the maid remained with them as a token of continuity and stability. But the attempt could not succeed; the harmony was spurious, the stability only superficial and shaky. Karen and Oskar were now too far apart, going separate ways. As mentioned, their financial condition had also deteriorated and the lovely furniture was soon repossessed by creditors.

Finally, later that same year, Karen and the three girls moved out with some few possessions into a small apartment at 38 Lutzowüferstrasse. It was around the corner from the Berlin Institute, on the famous Landwehrkanal, with the Berlin Zoo at the back, close by the Tiergarten Park. The move was the beginning of a new emotional life for Karen, even though her professional activity at the Institute was basically unchanged.

Biggi at fifteen was an aspiring actress. Karen, remembering her own short-lived but perhaps still smoldering acting aspirations, walked around reciting dramatic lines she still recalled from that earlier time. Nevertheless she insisted that Biggi have a consultation with a professional acting teacher to determine whether she had talent. Biggi, perhaps anxious about the outcome, promptly became "ill." Her mother the analyst, realizing that she was probably only trying to avoid the testing situation, arranged for her to see the well-known Austrian actress, Ilka Gruening, whose school accepted only a few students. Biggi was accepted for the drama school with the warning, "I only prepare you for your career; you have to fend for yourself." And fend she did!

Karen was not a stranger to the world of drama and film. It is not certain whether she had previously met Ilka Gruening, but she had certainly known of her and had access to her through her analytic friend, Hanns Sachs. In 1925, Dr. Neumann of the UFA film company had approached Karl Abraham and Hanns Sachs about producing a film to illustrate graphically the principles and mechanisms of psychoanalysis. Abraham had been lukewarm toward the idea, but had tried to persuade Freud to sponsor it. He believed that if they did not back it, other "wild analysts" would do so anyway. Freud was definitely against it. He considered film a poor medium for conveying the intricacies, subtleties and dynamisms of the unconscious. He thought it would end up as a cheap form of exploitation. Nevertheless, Abraham and Sachs cooperated with Neumann. Sachs, with his interest in art, became enthusiastic about the project to the point of turning into a film buff. He discussed it with many of his friends, including Karen. Eventually he even wrote a short monograph about it. After Abraham died, Sachs continued on with the film himself as supervisor and consultant. It is probable that Karen met the principals involved, including G. W. Pabst, Werner Krause and Ilka Gruening.

The film itself came out in 1926, at the time Biggi was going into the dramatic arts. Its themes were especially relevant to Karen's concerns— her marriage and impending separation—and to the issues she was writing about, namely marital disharmony, impotence and frigidity, childhood sibling rivalry and distorted relationships with parents. In the film, a fortyish married man hears that a childhood cousin, away for many years, is now returning home. He, his wife and this cousin had lived and played together as children. He now dreams that he stabs his wife. He then develops anxiety and a fear of knives, becomes impotent and uninterested in sex, and the marriage begins to break up. Undergoing psychoanalysis, he then recalls his childhood envy of this cousin (sibling) because of favored treatment by parent figures. He relives his present anger toward the cousin, reacting to the fear that the cousin might take away his wife. After recognizing his subconscious inhibitions, he then loses his symptoms, his sexuality becomes normal and the marriage is restored. Sachs proudly presented and commented on the film at the annual meeting of the German Psychoanalytic Society held that year on May 6, in celebration of Freud's seventieth birthday. Karen applauded loudly with the others. It was received with equal enthusiasm by the public in Germany and the United States. Sachs was well satisfied.

Biggi remained in Ilka Gruening's school for several years, maturing and changing. In her need to assert her independence, her already strong, dominating personality became even stronger. One of her favorite capers was to wear her mother's only dress coat without telling her, so Karen would have to go to meetings without it. Typically Biggi was volatile and temperamental. According to her sisters, for a while she was constantly "the good actress . . . playing as if everything around her was a stage setting. Living with her was like being near a volcano, you had to watch out for what was coming forth." Yet she could be, and was often, kind, caring and generous, as numerous acting friends later attested. It was she, for instance, who usually came to pick up her mother at the Institute after late classes. Karen seemed to have difficulty in dealing with this volatility, these changes in attitude and behavior. It was indeed a time of "Special Difficulties in Handling Young Girls," the title of a paper she presented in 1929.

After returning from the Quaker school, Janne was put into a private school to prepare her for high school. She entered high school at fourteen and graduated just before she reached the age of seventeen, at least two years younger than the other graduates. She was a quiet, intellectual student who got good grades, although she herself felt she generally knew too little to really deserve them. At the end of high school she decided to go on to the university.

It was little Renate who suffered most keenly from the move into the small apartment. Having been irrepressible and hyperactive as a child, she still needed space, freedom, nature, woods and trees. She recalls feeling as though she were in a strait jacket. After her miserable experiences in previous private schools, she was placed in still another one. The Spitzgart School believed in a structured environment without excessive discipline. It seemed to be the educational atmosphere she needed. But she continued to feel the same way: It taught "respectability and niceties while underneath was cheating and hypocrisies." Nevertheless, having Renate safely tucked away was a relief for Karen. However, it was not to be for long. Renate was mischievous and given to practical jokes— whether in school or on the rooftop of her apartment house. The school authorities finally complained of her misbehavior and she had to be taken out.

Karen then placed Renate in the famous Salem Boarding School on Lake Constance. Its motto was *Mens sana in corpore sano,* with emphasis on "trust, honesty and a good attitude toward life as more important than grades." The three years she spent there were to prove happy ones. Perhaps in part this was due to her own maturation between the ages of twelve and fifteen. She made a number of good friends here, including her husband-to-be. She returned to Berlin only twice yearly during this time, for the Christmas and Easter vacations.

That first winter of 1926–27 in the new apartment brought hardships. The rooms were heated separately, each by a great tiled coal stove. There was a shortage of coal, and not much money to buy what little could be found. Only Karen's office and waiting room could be heated adequately. The water pipes froze and the family had to go down into the street to obtain water from an old horse-watering pump.

In spring Karen's mood always changed from gray despondency to cheerful optimism with the warmer weather and burgeoning of the flowers she loved. The two-month summer vacation was the time for togetherness. From 1928 through 1931 Karen went to Austria or Switzerland and stayed in small mountain resort hotels, usually with Renate and Janne or Biggi. Karen's old friend Tutti sometimes joined them. It was also customary for one or two patients to accompany her and continue their analytic sessions during the summer. This was an accepted practice of many psychoanalysts at the time, especially during the economic depression when they could ill afford the loss of income, but were still reluctant to sacrifice a summer vacation.

Her daughters remember the joy of these vacations in the mountains. Every day they took an early morning hike or climb, following by a swim in a glacial lake or stream. On one occasion they went on a real ascent, roped together, with a professional guide. Crossing a huge glacier, Karen and the girls were exhilarated by the danger of falling into one of the ice crevasses.

Otherwise, Karen usually devoted the afternoons to work with a patient or writing. The girls would often go off exploring on their own.

The region around Lake Maggiore in the Swiss canton of Ticino became her favorite vacation spot: Lugano, Ascona, Locarno and the nearby Rhône Valley. In 1931, Oskar, who was living in the area at the time, interested Karen in a rambling old one-story farmhouse in the village of Roncco, on the mountainside behind Ascona. She apparently bought it sight unseen at his urging. Why she did so at this time, when she was just deciding to emigrate to America, is difficult to understand. Perhaps it was to retain a foothold in Europe—to know that a piece of the old world was still hers; to have a place to fall back on if things did not work out in America; to placate Oskar, who wished to use it in her absence? As a haven, for surcease, to escape from the pressures and hurlyburly of everyday living; as an island safe from the threat of events in her homeland?

High up on the mountainside, the house had a spectacular view. Below was the ever-changing multitinted Lake Maggiore and the subtropical Isola Grande. Across the lake rose the Monte Ceneri, and beyond, the majestic Grisons Alps. Just off to the left Ascona and Locarno glimmered in the sun. Still, it was a steep climb up the old stone steps from the lake shore after swimming. One could also take a taxi up the winding road or the *funiculaire,* which still left a considerable walk. Most of the time Karen walked. Renate and Biggi were assigned the task of buying the necessary furnishings to make the house livable. Unfortunately, Karen was to spend only a short vacation time here before leaving Europe.

Although she loved to walk, and even took a certain pride in it regardless of the difficulties, it was sometimes especially arduous for her. She had some impairment of her feet, probably hammertoes. In the spring of 1930 her toes were operated on, and walking became particularly painful. Thereafter she had to wear custom-made space shoes. This she resented, not so much for the handicap but for their looks: She would frequently remark on how ugly they were.

Appearance had never been of major importance to her, at least on the surface. But perhaps her indifference to her looks was a defensive reaction that belied her true feelings. Indeed, in many little ways she showed herself to be quite sensitive about her appearance. She could not, or would not, sew, probably because of lack of time, and she usually needed a dressmaker for her own and the girls' dresses. Her childhood feeling of not being pretty and the need to compensate through intelligence was constantly present, just below the surface. Of course, she did like a new dress and did try to please men at times. When male friends to whom she might be more or less sexually attracted visited, she would dress with special care. But she seemed—at least after her marriage—to be resigned to those inner feelings, to not being pretty. On one occasion, when Oskar complimented her on a "new" dress, she almost sadly replied that she had been wearing it already for two years. On another occasion, one of her adolescent daughters wanted a pretty new dress with short sleeves— somewhat daring for that time. When Karen demurred at first and her daughter angrily cried out that Karen was too old to appreciate the need for short sleeves, she felt acutely hurt. She did appreciate feminine beauty, looks and clothes, but had repressed the need within herself. Later, in New York, one of her outstanding traits was to be her rather plain appearance, her subdued, unadorned dresses of homespun fabric.

In 1930 Biggi had her big chance. During her three years in drama school she had felt discouraged at times and wished to stop. But Karen encouraged her to continue. Then Biggi decided to try for the coveted Reinhardt Prize for aspiring young actresses. She still recalls her anxiety at having to recite, feeling "afraid of my own voice"—a natural stage fright. Her mother could not accompany her to the tryout, so she went with her Aunt Ollie (Berndt's widow), surreptitiously wearing her mother's blue silk dress coat. She placed first out of seventy contestants. But when the publicity picture appeared in the newspaper, she had to cut it out hastily before Karen saw the coat.

The prize started her off on an outstanding career. She had already received a year's contract with the Würzburg Theater. Now the UFA film company immediately offered her a screen test, followed by a starring role in the film *Abschied* (*Good-by*). She then acted in six stage plays (September 1930 to May 1931) in Würzburg before returning to Berlin. Karen was waiting for her at the station. Biggi still had on her stage make-up, which she had been so proud of, but Karen angrily insisted she remove it, complaining, "What have you done to yourself?" Nevertheless, she was terribly happy and proud of her daughter's success.

The UFA wished to engage Biggi for a long film contract immediately, but to everyone's consternation, she refused the high salary. She wanted to stay in the theater first, to try many roles, to "liberate" herself as an actress. "Pictures do not run away," she said. Beginning with a success as Fanny in *Der Goldene Anka* (an adaptation of the Marcel Pagnol's *Marius*), Biggi entered her first season in Reinhardt's Deutsches Theater, under the director Heinz Hilpert.

In 1931 Janne entered the University of Freiburg to start her medical studies. This, too, was a step of which Karen was proud.

The year 1929 was the last euphoric year of the golden age of Berlin. Unemployment was negligible, wages were high, everyone could afford some luxuries, everyone could enjoy himself. If anyone had emotional problems, he could afford psychoanalysis.

However, this prosperity was largely artificial. It depended primarily on foreign investments and loans. Businessmen, corporations, city and state governments all borrowed to build and expand. Under the new Young Plan, the German government could, in effect, float loans from the

Allies to repay the reduced reparations to the same Allied governments. Most Berliners paid little attention to these facts of international finance and politics. They still wanted to play and indulge themselves.

The motion picture *The Blue Angel,* which appeared the following year, symbolized perfectly the trends of these times. The unemotional hedonism and irresponsibility of the heroine, played by the new star Marlene Dietrich, eventually destroys the traditionalism, orderliness, and intellectuality of the old order, represented by the Professor. The Professor is destroyed by his emotions, by his idealized, romantic vision of his tormentor.

During the spring of 1929 there were already ominous portents of economic difficulties. A series of strikes and lockouts in the key coal, iron and steel industries increased unemployment. Prices again began to rise, hinting at an oncoming inflationary trend. The Black Friday stock-market crash in New York did not concern most Berliners.

Then that winter the Great Depression struck Berlin. Foreign loans were called in for payment and credit contracted. Companies started laying off workers. There were fifteen thousand small business bankruptcies by the end of the year. Suicides became frequent; at least seven per week were officially listed. Many more were probably not even reported. The number of unemployed rose to 1.5 million in January 1930, to 2.5 million in February, of whom 750,000 were in Berlin. It was to peak at 6 million in mid 1932. The jobless stood miserably around in the streets, huddling together for warmth in official "shelters." Some moved into tent colonies in the forests around the city. They were dispirited and often despairing. Some were resigned, others were angry and demonstrated to show it. The police often had to intervene to prevent looting or the plundering of local farms. The last democratic government fell in 1931 with the resignation of Social-Democratic Chancellor Herman Müller. It was the end of the Weimar government, that noble experiment.

Many of these disenchanted, angry unemployed, "the uprooted and disinherited," turned for redress to the solutions they felt were offered by the extremist political parties, the Communists and the Nazis. Fewer turned to the left than to the right. The Communists did not have much appeal: They were scattered and not well organized; there was internal disagreement over issues of tactics and doctrine; and Moscow was contributing little help. The moderates could not compete with the strongarm tactics of the extremists. Nazi party membership rose from only 17,000 in 1926, to 120,000 in mid 1929, to over 200,000 in January 1930, and to about 400,000 one year later—though Hitler claimed a million. In the general election of September 1930, the Nazis won 6.5 million votes and doubled their representation in the Reichstag to over 100. Joseph Goebbels later was to write that he helped the party by "winning Berlin" and introducing National Socialism into the mainly lower-middle-class population there.

Until 1929, although violence had been occurring elsewhere, Berlin had remained relatively calm. But now it could no longer hold itself apart; in fact precisely because of its large leftist working-class population the violence was even greater. Now the storm troopers marched through the streets day and night, looking for fights, beating up anyone in their way— hecklers, Communists, Jews. Most of the violence at first took place in the working-class districts like Wedding or Neukölln.

It seems incredible that Karen, like many other analysts in the Berlin Society at that time, was unaware of these events all around her. Even the International Psychoanalytic Association had gone so far as to cancel their 1930 congress because of "serious internal difficulties" in Germany. But there is evidence that Karen showed a curious naiveté about such events. Years later, an analytic candidate, a mature Jewish refugee psychiatrist, was being interviewed by Karen for admission to the new Institute in New York. When she related some of the maltreatment, persecution and suffering that had been inflicted upon her, Karen was genuinely astonished and incredulous. "I can't believe that, I can't conceive of that happening, it's not possible," she said. And her next comment was, "I would not have let that happen to me . . . I would have done something about it."

Two explanations can be given for this apparent ignorance. First, the city was so large that most people rarely saw the vicious fights, which would occur quickly, be over in a few minutes, the participants having vanished. People would simply disappear; bodies would be found in the Landwehrkanal or patients would arrive at the hospitals with "accidental injuries."

Second, Karen may have known what was going on in a purely intellectual way, but since such events were so removed from her own experience, so foreign to her own daily life, they may not have registered in her consciousness. One can read in the newspaper about murders in some other part of the city, but unless they relate closely and emotionally to the reader's own feelings and sympathies, they will be passed over without making a significant impression, or forgotten. To put it in simpler terms, as is known to every psychoanalyst, we only know (see, remember) what we wish to know (see, remember).

It matters little whether we call this naiveté, ignorance, denial, noninvolvement, incomprehension, repression or forgetting. This type of lack of awareness is not unique to Karen. NonJews, or even Jews who have not similarly suffered or who cannot empathize with the sufferers, may have the same type of response.

But if Karen and many of her colleagues and students at the Berlin Institute were largely unaware of these events, some of the American analytic candidates who were also studying at the university did know about the situation. The Nazis wanted to use the universities as spearheads of their influence and power. They made great efforts to infiltrate young party cadres into the classes. Classes and student groups were quickly organized. German youth, especially the intellectuals, were a prime target for propaganda. Unfortunately, the previous organizations of the Youth Movement, combined with the natural rebelliousness and arrogance of the young, made them relatively easy to convert. Trained by the traditional authoritarian family organization, schools and youth groups to be obedient followers, they had repressed their own authoritarian tendencies. But now, during late adolescence, rebelling against this forced dependence and experiencing their emerging feelings of strength and omnipotence, they quickly admired and adopted the Nazi concepts. Here they could be both eager, obedient followers and dominating leaders. Many professors had always been conservative, nationalistic and latently anti-Semitic. Of course, there were some, students and professors, who resisted, especially if they were liberal or leftist—but not for long.

Dr. Morris Isenberg, now a distinguished psychoanalyst in Queens, New York, was there from 1930 to 1935. According to him, "The American students felt the danger hanging over, and there was talk about Hitler. Most Germans didn't take him seriously until 1932. The people at the Berlin Psychoanalytic weren't concerned. I talked to many, to Eitingon too. The *Ausländer Studentverein* [foreign student union] didn't care for Hitler. The German students were mostly upper-middle-class but they went over to him once he really got started. It wasn't a question of religion, but they were afraid of Communism, they didn't want to be told what to believe. Many went for Hitler, planning to become Communists later. Student groups of Social Democrats and Nazis fought each other, mostly in the law and economics faculties, not in the medical school. Once the *Denkmal* [war veterans memorial] was smeared with tar. The Nazi students said the leftists did it and there was a tremendous fight. When the book-burnings started, the medical students were too busy to go. When Einstein came to lecture, the Nazi students made fun even of him."

Did this affect the medical school at all? "In our classes, the Nazi students would give the Nazi salute and sit in front together. Some professors saluted also. Only a few were Jewish. Siegfried Bernfeld, from the Berlin Institute, taught at the Humbolt; he would make minor references to Freud. He spoke in Bonhoeffer's amphitheater. He was an impressive and effective speaker, and spoke of hope. When he spoke of theory, it was in practical and general terms. Bonhoeffer was very human, friendly and approachable, not like the other professors; he was suave, a gentleman. He seemed to be nicer to the foreigners than to his own assistants, whom he would bawl out. He tolerated psychoanalysis. From 1930 on, even the important Jewish professors couldn't teach in the university unless they were baptized. The famous obstetrician, Asheim-Zondek, was forced to work in a laboratory in the basement. Some Jewish professors could still teach in the university *Polikliniks* in the Moabit section."

And what about life outside the university and the institute? "Money was scarce after 1930. We had meat once a week. Welfare payments were cut from ninety to eighty marks a month. I managed to earn a little extra income by occasionally giving lectures in English to labor unions on current topics. The labor unions were very strong in Berlin until 1933. But it still was a swinging town. We went to night clubs for a dollar, there was great sexual freedom, even more than in Paris. A lot of homosexual bars, transvestites and prostitutes. The coffee houses were cheap. We would usually go to one to talk. The Femina was a more expensive one, four marks, most couldn't afford it. There were telephones on the tables to call any girl there. The least expensive was in the Am Zoo section. We would pick up a girlfriend near the clock under the elevated station. You could spend all evening over coffee for one mark.

"Student dueling was still admired and done but was frowned upon officially. The Berliners didn't take things seriously, they joked about everything. There were many political jokesters in the cafés, like the Scala. They were arrested later on or the café was closed. In March 1933, a law was passed that if four people or more congregated, it was suspicious and they could be arrested. The official Jewish boycott started in April. Then in June Hitler went after Catholics and later Protestants too."

Another student there at the time, Dr. Joseph Pisetski is now Psychiatric Director at the Veterans Hospital in the Bronx, New York, as well as a practicing psychoanalyst. He was in Berlin from 1931 until 1938 and also had contact with the Berlin Institute. He worked alongside Janne in their medical-school laboratories and they often discussed psychoanalysis. He recalls how proud she was of her mother, and how impressed he himself was by Karen's name and presence. His recollections of those first few years in Berlin add to the picture given by Dr. Isenberg.

"Berlin was one of the most advanced places, culturally, in the world. The theater—Reinhardt, Brecht—the wonderful movies, the philharmonic, the vaudeville. It was a ferment like you hardly saw anyplace else. We would go to the cafés, especially the Café Wien. We talked about psychoanalysis and the goings-on in our classes. I met many singers and entertainers in the billiard room there. The homosexual bars, we would go just for the hell of it. These bars enraged the Nazis, who were puritanical. Later [the Nazis] came into the classes too. Professor B. used to come in with a 'Heil Hitler'; he would mention the fatherland. Professor K. was democratic, but he couldn't talk to anyone. Most of the others were formal and distant. In the classes, sometimes the Nazi students would make speeches about political events. A lot of the students, mostly the German but even some American, went in for sports like wrestling and skiing. Most of us traveled around Europe during vacations."

Asked how he managed to stay so long, Dr. Pisetski replied, "I was on the periphery. They didn't bother me. I wanted to get a job later in the hospital but couldn't. Maybe because I was Jewish, maybe because I was American. I was able to work in neuropsychiatry, first in the Hufeland Hospital, then in the Charité. The old professor was thrown out and the new one used to greet the patients as *'alte Kampfer'*—old warriors. In 1932, people were getting frightened, people began to disappear. But among the students, if you weren't interested in politics or leftist, and kept your ideas to yourself, they didn't bother you."

Whether or not Karen was aware of the actual violent brutalities, it would have been impossible for her not to know of the Nazis' aims and tactics. They were discussed, at least in theoretical terms, at the meetings of the Berlin Society. Patients spoke of it in their analysis. Her daughters were seeing some evidence of it in their schools and work. By 1932, the situation was deteriorating rapidly. Most of Karen's friends were Jewish. There was ample reason for disquiet, identified as she was with psychoanalysis. This, combined with her personal frustrations and disillusionments, made her desire to leave understandable. Years later, she was to reveal in a newspaper interview that she was "outspokenly antifascist." This stance was not based on religious beliefs or purely political considerations. It was derived from her strong feelings about the sacredness of each individual's life and rights. "Democratic principles, in sharp contrast to fascist ideology, uphold the independence of the individual and his right to happiness." During the war, she would sometimes discuss the Nazis on social occasions and express her distaste for their philosophy and methods.

X
THE BERLIN
PSYCHOANALYTIC:
BEFORE THE FALL

"Cultural factors exert a powerful influence on women; such, in fact, that it is hard to see how any woman may escape becoming masochistic to some extent, from the effects of the culture alone without any appeal to contributory factors in the anatomo-physiological characteristics of women and their psychic effects. There may appear certain fixed ideologies concerning the "nature" of woman; that she is innately weak, emotional, enjoys dependence, is limited in capacities for independent work and autonomous thinking. It is obvious that these ideologies function not only to reconcile women to their subordinate role, but also to plant the belief that it represents a fulfillment they crave, or an ideal for which it is desirable to strive. The influence these ideologies exert is strengthened by the fact that women presenting the specified traits are more frequently chosen by men. In such social organizations, masochistic attitudes are favored in women while they are discouraged in men."
—*"The Problem of Feminine Masochism"*

By the end of 1925, Karen, now forty years old, was considered one of the senior members of the Berlin Institute, an important personage. When Eitingon reported on the clinic's progress during 1924 and 1925, he paid her tribute. After mentioning that about eighty controlled analyses had been carried out during this time, he emphasized that "certain members have given devoted help in grappling with this task, especially Boehm, Kempner and Karen Horney." The teaching work of the institute was facilitated by the formation of a training committee and the development of a formal curriculum. In February of that year this progress was celebrated by a gala affair in honor of the fifth anniversary of the clinic. Nevertheless, the issue of training analysis was to become a problem for the institute and a more personal *bête noire* for Karen herself.

Preoccupied with the tragedy and struggle in her personal life, she did not write or speak much at the Berlin Society during 1925. The Ninth International Congress, held at Bad Homburg in September 1925, was to have unforeseen and profound effects upon her. She did not speak herself, but three papers drew her special interest. Franz Alexander, in "Neurosis and the Total Personality," proposed a broadening of the psychoanalytic concept of the individual beyond the libido theory. It even hinted that the then new ego psychology would have to include more of the personality than it currently did—both temperamental and present situational factors. This more holistic approach impressed her and was soon to influence her thinking.

Groddeck also delivered a paper, "Psychoanalysis and the It," that did not present anything new but tried to clarify his previous views. This paper had a mixed reception. Abraham described it as "platitudinous and monotonous." On the other hand, as Carl Grossman later wrote, "his well-wishers still thought he was a great man and his antagonists were unchanged. . . . Some members were stimulated and enchanted by it." These included Ferenczi and especially Karen. But Groddeck was so disgusted by the majority reaction that he vowed he would never again speak to psychoanalysts, explaining, "They have so little understanding."

Freud did not attend that meeting, but he had written a paper which his daughter, Anna, presented. It was titled "Some Psychical Consequences of the Anatomical Distinctions between the Sexes" and was a landmark for him. Until this time he had said and written that he did not clearly understand female psychosexual development. Now he postulated a consistent theory. He now stated that "In girls the Oedipus complex is a secondary formation. The operations of the castration complex precede it and prepare for it. As regards the relation between the Oedipus and castration complexes, there is a fundamental contrast between the two sexes. Whereas in boys the Oedipus complex is destroyed by the castration complex, in girls it is made possible and led up to by the castration complex." Out of her resigned acceptance of this primary penis envy and awareness of castration—that is, of her femininity—the girl "develops, like a scar, a sense of inferiority." The logical conclusion was, therefore, that to be a woman automatically means to feel inferior.

This view was in direct disagreement with Karen's formulation in her 1924 paper. According to her, while a primary penis envy was postulated, it was less significant then a secondary, later castration complex that arose defensively out of the Oedipus complex.

In the final paragraph of his paper Freud clearly noted his disagreement with Karen while simultaneously complimenting her. It is suspected—as Zenia Flugel has recently suggested—that the compliment was a backhanded one, given for the sake of politeness.[1] Karen apparently did not take kindly to his disagreement. The exchange was to spark a controversy over feminine psychology that was not only intense but well known to everyone at the time. It has since become obscured. The main protagonists were Karen and Ernest Jones on one side, and Freud and several others on the other side.

At this same meeting, two other events also affected Karen. One involved Helene Deutsch, who presented a report on the progress of the Vienna Institute, which was thereupon officially recognized. A gifted thinker and one of the few other important women in the psychoanalytic movement, she, like Karen, was interested in feminine psychology and had recently written a book on the subject.[2] But, as she has explained in her autobiography,[3] because of her early background, her later personality and her proximity then to Freud, she clung to his views as the basis for her own ideas more closely than did Karen. When Freud in that same final paragraph referred to "the valuable and comprehensive studies . . . of Abraham, Horney and Deutsch," he was giving them equal recognition. It is more than possible that Karen felt a sense of rivalry with Deutsch that could only have been exacerbated by the subsequent events. Helene Deutsch, for her part, was not aware of any such feelings; she recalls a relationship only of mutual respect.

The second issue, that of training analysis, was discussed later at the meeting. It was proposed that a committee be set up to study the possibility of establishing an international authority on training, and of working out preliminary plans for a training program applicable to all member societies. Eitingon, who was recognized as the highest authority after Freud on analytic training, was appointed its chairman, with Helene Deutsch as a member. Whether or not Karen was on this preliminary committee is not definitely known. There is some indirect evidence that she was not—in spite of her having devoted so much effort, energy and time to this question in Berlin. This may have left her feeling additionally slighted.

As a result of these several events in combination, she left the meeting angry, challenged and determined to respond. The ideas she had begun to work through at the two previous meetings were continuing to germinate in her mind. By October, less than a month later, she was able to present her second paper on female sexuality to the society: "Reflections on the Masculinity Complex in Women."

In November Karen spoke at the Humboldt Hochschule to an audience of young women university students on "Certain Types of Women's Lives in Light of Psychoanalysis." The lecture was received with such enthusiasm and the crowd so great (over two hundred persons) that she repeated it several times in what finally became a series. Gertrude Termer—who later married the psychoanalyst Dr. Frederick Weiss and was to become Karen's close friend—was then a student in the audience. She can still remember the excitement and the image of Karen "looking somewhat like Käthe Kollwitz, Nordic and almost blonde, with rather strict features although not especially pretty . . . but strikingly earnest and passionate, seeming to enjoy every minute."

Most of the young women there were in the Youth Movement or some feminist organization. Although Karen was not a member and made it clear that she was speaking purely from the psychoanalytic point of view, they regarded her as an example of the liberated woman, a symbol, an ideal. They identified her and her ideas with their own aims.

By coincidence, Alfred Adler was giving a lecture course there at the same time. It was customary for the speakers to meet in the lounge over a cup of coffee and it was reported that Karen and Adler had some discussion. In one of her lectures she mentioned that she was skeptical of some of his ideas but not against them.

A short time later the Berlin group was shaken by a grievous loss, to some extent expected, yet nonetheless stunning when it occurred in reality. After a year's fluctuating illness, Karl Abraham died in January 1926 of a chronic pulmonary infection, septicemia and liver abscess. It was suspected that these were secondary infections upon an undiagnosed cancer.

Most of the Berlin group attended his funeral, including Karen. Of Freud's inner Committee, only Ferenczi, retiring Sachs and Jones were there. Freud himself was too ill to attend and Eitingon and Rank were out of the country.

After Abraham's death, at a special meeting of the Berlin Society at the end of January, new officers were elected. Eitingon was the first choice for president but he declined because of his desire to work primarily in the International Association. After much preliminary backstage discussion by the Committee members, Ernst Simmel was then officially nominated from the floor and elected president by the membership and Karen became secretary-treasurer. The Training Committee was re-elected. The name of the society, now numbering forty members, was officially changed to the German Psychoanalytic Association to permit the inclusion of other local psychoanalytic societies now being formed.

Because of the pressures in her personal life caused by her difficult financial situation and the need to sell the house, Karen changed her official address to her office on the Kaiserallee. Her emotional state during the period while she was writing this paper on feminine sexuality comes out clearly in a letter she wrote to Groddeck:

Dear Doctor Groddeck:

You showed such a friendly interest in my former work on the woman's castration complex that I hope you will enjoy reading my new and more elaborate work on the same topic. Particularly since I discuss problems which you were the first to raise.

However I have deviated from the theories which were accepted heretofore. Yet your own thinking is so original that you will have full understanding for corresponding thoughts of others, even if they represent a blow to male narcissism.

I originally wrote much more aggressively but since I am not a Groddeck—and my work is for the Festschrift *for Freud—I followed Eitingon's advice and "pulled my punches" [meine Steine etwas in Watte gewickelt].*

The Festschrift *will not be published until May, but since*

I shall go to Baden to the Psychotherapy Congress in the middle of April and I do want to talk to you about these questions before then, I am sending you a copy now.

With best regards,
Your Karen Horney

She was now aware of and openly admitting her rebellion. She could not know the implications of this path nor where it would lead. She wished to be more aggressive but couldn't, for both internal and external reasons. In her writing, as in her speech, she still lacked the "Groddeckian" quality of open assertiveness she so admired. She would continue to heed Eitingon's fatherly counsel. The significant question was: rebelling against whom and what? Then, at both the emotional and practical level, if her paper was to be in honor of Freud's birthday—if she still needed his support and that of his followers—it could not be too assertive a challenge. It was the same old conflict within her that she had experienced so often before, how to be aggressive yet friendly and loving at the same time. Unfortunately the birthday *Festschrift* was not published as she expected. That forthcoming issue of the *Zeitschrift* was given over to a tribute to Abraham. The paper was eventually published in the following issue and Karen did go to Baden-Baden.

Although Jones refers by name to a number of Abraham's analysands at the Berlin Institute in his moving eulogy to Abraham in the *Zeitschrift,* he does not mention Karen. Why this curious omission? Was it perhaps the beginning of an unconscious process of repression that was to become more and more evident with respect to her later on?

In 1925, Dr. Wladimir Eliasberg, a respected psychiatrist and psychotherapist in Munich, had the idea of setting up an organization of European psychiatrists with common medical interests. Its purpose was to be ecumenical: to bring together practitioners of clinical medicine, neurology, psychiatry and psychoanalysis on common scientific, theoretical and clinical grounds. Its basic philosophy was holistic. Following the principles of medical psychology, psychic man in his wholeness was considered more than the sum of his psychological parts. All the schools of psychoanalysis were to be represented, as it was felt that each could contribute something to the explanation of mental functioning. Leading practitioners throughout Europe were asked if they were interested in such an organization. A preliminary invitation was extended to a first Congress in Baden-Baden in April 1926.

Karen was indeed interested, and quickly became a member (number 289). Perhaps it was because such friends as Groddeck, Simmel, Harald Schultze-Henke and later Erich Fromm were also interested. Perhaps it represented a low-keyed manifestation of her rebellion. Perhaps it signified a bringing together of opposing forces, a resolution of conflict—the pacifism that was always so dear to her. She attended the first International Congress of Psychotherapy along with 537 other physicians from 7 countries.

Eliasberg became the first secretary-general and the prime mover of this Medical Society for Psychotherapy (Die allgemeine ärtztliche Gesellschaft für Psychotherapie). It was to meet each year for the next six years, until it was taken over by the Nazis in 1933. Although its founders hoped for stimulation and eventual recognition from the German Psychoanalytic Association, this was not to be forthcoming.

Through 1926 and 1927, probably because of her preoccupation with her family situation, Karen suspended her teaching at the institute. Following her separation, throughout 1927, she was more than usually active. Though no longer teaching, she remained intensely busy at the clinic and at the institute as screening and supervising analyst. With her separation, her practice became more necessary for her; she now was the sole breadwinner, responsible not only for herself but also for her three teen-age daughters.

She traveled much, wrote, and spoke at least six times that year. It was as if a heavy restraining load had been removed and now she felt liberated, free to expand, to fly. In retrospect, there was also a hectic, frenetic quality to all this activity, as if she were driven. Possibly this was an attempt to escape the emotional turmoil of her separation.

In November 1926, she gave a public lecture on "Critical Marriage Problems of the Present Day." The choice of this subject so soon after her separation was more than a simple coincidence; it could only have been an expression of her own problems. Three weeks later she was asked by her old friend, Iwan Bloch, to speak again at the Medical Society for Sexuality. She chose the same topic she had recently presented at the Berlin Society, "The Masculinity Complex of Women." In the audience at this meeting was Max Marcuse, one of a group of medical sexologists. He was writing a book on marriage and sexuality from the biological viewpoint. He asked Karen to submit any articles she might have on the subject. She submitted three, which were published in 1930.

From mid 1926 until 1930, the problem of lay analysis was to be of great concern for the Berlin group. It was brought to a head when Theodore Reik was sued by an aggrieved former patient, who charged that Reik was a quack and that his analysis had caused him psychological damage. Public opinion was stirred to the point that a German Association for the Suppression of Quackery was formed. Freud saw this as part of the general inclination of medicine to restrict the practice of psychoanalysis. He wished to defend Reik and, in his small book, *The Question of Lay Analysis*, came out in favor of lay analysts practicing analysis. But in his discussions with Eitingon and Jones, he admitted that he was in a dilemma. Ernest Jones explained in his biography of Freud that this position was not simply a reaction against the medical profession's hostility toward psychoanalysis, as is commonly claimed. In fact, Freud was concerned that a strictly medical application of psychoanalysis might severely restrict its application to other fields. Psychoanalysis would end up as a small subform of treatment, alongside hypnosis, in a psychiatric textbook. Freud knew of the dangers of allowing analysis to be practiced by persons without adequate professional training, whether physicians—the "wild analysts"—or nonmedical practitioners. When Ferenczi had proposed the establishment of an ancillary organization of nonmedical analysts, The Friends of Psychoanalysis, before the Bad Homburg meeting in 1925, the proposal was dropped after a preliminary consensus opposed it.

Eitingon wished to bring it up again at a special discussion group at the next International Congress in September 1927, at Innsbruck. He believed that the problem of lay analysis was part and parcel of the broader question of analytic training. Was medical training to be a prerequisite for the psychoanalyst-to-be? It was decided to hold a special preliminary meeting of the society to sound out the faculty on this question. Horney, Simmel, Alexander, Muller-Braunschweig, Sachs, Rado, Otto Fenichel and Eitingon participated.

Karen's statement was succinct and to the point. She approached it as she would an analysis, teasing out the various issues involved and exploring each one. She dismissed the attitude of the public and both the civil and medical authorities, that is, external politics, as an unavoidable given factor. They were mostly against psychoanalysis and had to be fought. As for the attitude of their own profession—internal politics—this question must be considered as part of the broader problem of training. What background was preferable for the analyst? She limited this term to the clinical practitioner who is actually practicing. Nonmedical persons like jurists or anthropologists could benefit from analytic training for scientific purposes. She believed that only a medical background—even though it might involve much training that would prove unnecessary—could best provide the required skill in observing the living human being, in dealing with the suffering patient. Only this could give the necessary feeling of responsibility toward others and encourage the will to heal. These were the same feelings she had expressed when working in the clinic in medical school and later at the Lankwitz.

Within medicine, only clinical neuropsychiatric training "brings so impressive an acquaintance with the use of symbolism and the mechanisms of projection and displacement. Besides it seems an advantage to learn other psychotherapeutic methods, not only to learn to mix them on occasion with the 'pure gold of analysis,' but to be able to judge what other possibilities there are for any special case."[4]

Several opinions, including hers, expressed in the various analytic societies were later selected for publication in the *Zeitschrift* as an official analytic position.

However, her actual behavior casts some doubt on whether this statement was as wholehearted and deeply felt as it might seem. She herself had decided to continue her own analysis with a nonmedical analyst, Hanns Sachs, after her disappointment with her medical analyst. She had also sent her children to Melanie Klein, a nonmedical analyst. Several other lay analysts, for instance, Hermine von Hug-Hellmuth and Ferenczi, were her close friends. These discrepancies raised a question as to her real feelings that was to assume great importance twenty years later, and that was never truly answered. Was her public attitude at odds with her private one? Was she simply trying to follow the accepted line?

Three weeks after the special meeting in Berlin, on February 20, 1927, Karen and many of the group journeyed to Hamburg for the next regular meeting of the German Psychoanalytic Association. Local analytic groups were now being formed, not only in Hamburg but in Frankfurt and Leipzig as well. The woman arriving in the city where she had grown up was certainly a contrast to the young girl who had left there twenty years before. Then she had been unsure of herself, uncertain of her future, yet adventurous and daring, alive in her dreams and illusions. Now she was sure of herself, knowledgeable and mature, respected and welcomed, yet inwardly beginning to feel the disillusionment she had written about. Some of the younger analysts she had analyzed or supervised in the insti-. tute were now practicing in Hamburg and were there to greet her.

The paper she presented there was drawn from the one she had prepared for Freud's seventieth birthday. It was mainly a clinical paper, focused on one aspect of feminine sexuality rather than on the general issue of development. Although it discussed inhibition in sexual expression, it related to the broader topic of inhibition in general. On reading it, one gets the impression that Karen may have been referring to the inner conflict she was now feeling, in light of her own recent driven expansiveness. Was she still feeling some inhibition within herself, a struggle surfacing in the form of the hectic traveling and the need to speak out at meetings?[5]

In April 1927, the second meeting of the Medical Society for Psychotherapy was held. Karen attended, although she did not present a paper. She did meet her old friends from the south, Groddeck and the Grotes. On her return to Berlin, she presented a report of the meeting to the Berlin Society.

But there apparently was little time for rest: the next International Congress was scheduled for September at Innsbruck and Karen wished to speak out there too.

That Congress was important to her for several reasons. First, several papers were devoted to the question of character from the analytic viewpoint. Sachs spoke on character formation, Willi Reich on character analysis and Paul Federn on narcissism and character. Their ideas followed the lead of Franz Alexander's psychoanalysis of the total personality, and like his views, were to exert a great influence upon Karen's thinking. Federn, in particular, introduced a new concept, that of "alienation from self." This he defined as a "transitory narcissistic psychosis" within each neurosis. He, in turn, cited the philosopher Husserl ("a lack of actuality") and the psychologist Pierre Janet ("loss of the sense of the real"). He described it as a clinical phenomenon caused by a withdrawal of libido from ego structures like the body image. In modified form, this concept was to be crucial to Karen's later theory.

Another reason the meeting was so important was that Karen found herself with a powerful ally in her disagreement with Freud. Ernest Jones presented his paper, "The Early Development of Female Sexuality." Not only did he cite Karen's work repeatedly but he supported her view that femininity was primary. He believed that vaginal awareness occurred much earlier than previously thought, as part of an overall consciousness of being a girl. But Karen could not see the backlash that would result from his imprimatur. Even though she had distinguished early, primary penis envy—relatively insignificant, according to her—from a secondary, more important defensive penis envy, the priority of her introduction of this distinction was to be lost. This lack of credit was payment, as it were, for his support. He introduced the new terms *pre-* and *postoedipal penis envy*. Thereafter, starting with Otto Fenichel's initial reference[6] in 1930, credit for this distinction was to be given to Jones and Horney's name was to disappear from the classical literature on this subject until its recent revival.

The meeting was also significant for Karen because of her presentation of her own paper, "The Problem of the Monogamous Ideal." She focused on an analytic explanation of why couples remain married after "love is no longer a living force," and why spouses seek extramarital satisfaction. Coming so soon after her own separation, this presentation must have had some relation to herself.

The final topic of discussion that attracted Karen's interest was that of training analysis. It was a controversial issue. As an introduction to the debate, Rado spoke on the structure of psychoanalytic training, Sachs on problems of training analysis, and Helene Deutsch on control analysis. Karen was thus passed over.

The previously constituted subcommittee (at Bad Homburg) had invited every constituent society to set up its own training committee and training program. In order to ensure that the different plans would address themselves to the same issues, a questionnaire had been distributed, along with suggested sample answers. Three problem areas had been identified: the educational prerequisites for the psychoanalyst, specifications for a total training program, and equivalent credit to be granted for partial training or transfer from another institute. The delicate issue of lay analysis was thus included in the first question. It had, in a sense, been shelved, but remained to be dealt with. The more fundamental but unexpressed point at issue was whether each society would be autonomous in determining qualifications for itself or subject to regulation by the international body. This issue posed the danger of a split in the organization: Freud favored laymen practicing analysis, whereas most members—including Eitingon and more particularly, the American societies—preferred that all analysts have a medical background.

Although a compromise could be reached by allowing for "equivalent preliminary training," leaving it purposely vague, Karen, apparently cynical, spoke up loudly. She insisted that the term "equivalent" applied to lay candidates would have to be more precisely defined. Therefore a new subcommittee was formed to clarify an acceptable scheme for training by the next meeting. Eitingon, the chairman of the committee, then named Rado, Muller-Braunschweig and Horney to it.

Although they could not know it at that time, the last point on the questionnaire—credit for training in other institutes—was to become a matter of professional life or death for most of the members, who would soon be forced to expatriate themselves.

As a closing gesture, Eitingon summarized the work of the Berlin clinic. Since the previous report, in 1924, 831 applications had been received for analysis and 264 analyses completed. At any one time during these three years, 85 analyses were in progress. This work was carried on by Eitingon and seven full-time assistants, ten senior students and fifteen voluntary members of the society, including Karen. She was carrying an average of three or four candidates in addition to screening almost every applicant.

At the beginning of 1928, the Berlin Institute moved to new and larger quarters at 10 Wiechmannstrasse. It had outgrown its previous home. Not only were more treatment offices provided but also a large conference room and a library. Ernst Freud again volunteered to take charge of the achitectural changes and interior decoration. The official inauguration ceremonies were scheduled to be held later, in September.

During 1928 and 1929, Karen's surge of activity continued, though in a slightly different way. While she did not travel around as much, she returned to her teaching at the institute. She taught courses on principles of analytic technique, workshops on technique (*Technisches Kolloquium*), and courses on psychoanalysis and gynecology and on sexual biology. Many practicing psychoanalysts today still recall her courses, especially the clinical ones, with special pleasure. She had a particular talent for showing the whole patient, for laying bare the essence of the person. One of her former students states that "the patient would come alive. She would often say that if you start with sexuality, with penis envy, you don't understand the person." When they compare her with the other teachers, they usually felt that Simmel, Sachs and Bernfeld were equally good, even superior in lecturing. Simmel, however, would come too quickly to theoretical infantile sexuality; the patient would not come alive. Sachs overemphasized transference. As an example, he would report that five patients in one morning all stated that he resembled their father. He would see what he wanted to, would project his own feelings onto everyone and so lose the uniqueness of the patient. Yet he was always pointing out that transference can distort observation. Bernfeld spoke beautifully and would often lead into other fields—philosophy or art.

Karen had a talent not only for clinical presentation but for simplifying difficult concepts and phenomena. She made subtleties easy to see and understand, even for the beginner. Several recall her in 1928 as being young and beautiful and lively. She made the courses lively as well. At times she held seminars in her office-apartment. Before or afterwards she might invite students to play Ping-Pong.

Yet even with her liveliness and occasional playfulness, she remained serious and reserved. Dr. Gustave Graber, now a respected and honored psychoanalyst practicing in Berne, was the oldest student in his class with Karen, fairly close to her age. He had formerly been a teacher himself, became interested in educational psychology and wished to become a child analyst. He still retains a vivid image of Karen, "slim, in a beige or brown dress, with a medallion on a chain. She spoke in an even voice (*ausgeglichen*), not with force . . . but always interesting and it affected you. We would remain after the class and carry on long discussions about the psychology of women or the destructive instinct, which Freud was just writing about." This was in 1930 and 1931. Because of his Swiss background and his previous experience—he had been psychoanalyzed in 1916 and had already written several books on child development—Karen seemed to feel an affinity and respect for him. After leaving the institute, he continued to carry on a correspondence with her. These letters were lost when the Nazis seized his personal papers.

As well as returning to teaching, Karen now began to participate more actively in presentations at the society's meetings. Until 1928—at least as Dr. Edith Weigert remembers her at meetings—she "was never outgoing or ostentatious; I think she withdrew. She was never officially rejected, like some of the others. She never protested . . . was more withdrawn . . ." But during 1928 something in her seemed to change; she became more sure of herself, more assertive. She entered forcefully into the discussions of nearly every paper: "Race and Psychology" (Roheim), "Repressed Memories" (Sachs), "Conditions of Practice" (Simmel), "The Death Instinct" (Alexander), "Ego Psychology" (Reik), "Organ Neuroses" (Schultze-Henke), "Transference," "Psychology of Religion" (Raknes), "Social Milieu and Neurosis" (Bernfeld), to cite but a few. However, except for one brief communication, she did not present any papers of her own at these Berlin meetings. It was as if her attention was turned outward toward others more than toward herself. Her own creative energies seemed to be lying fallow. Perhaps, too, she was still harboring some anger at the reception accorded her last paper on the masculinity complex, and still needed time to work it through. Her daughter recalls that at about this time, the large picture of Freud that had been hanging on her wall was taken down and disappeared, though Karen gave no explanation.

In March, apparently on Karen's recommendation, Erich Fromm was invited to speak at the meeting. His topic was the psychoanalysis of lower-middle-class persons, in keeping with his sociological orientation.

Fromm was born in Frankfurt in 1900 and was then entering upon his fruitful career, destined to make him one of the world's outstanding thinkers and writers. He had studied at Frankfurt, Munich and Heidelberg, where he received his doctorate in 1922. As part of his psychoanalytic training at the Berlin Institute from 1923 to 24, he had been analyzed by Sachs; it was there that he met Karen, fifteen years his senior. They had apparently felt a mutual attraction. He seemed able to combine opposing attitudes in his personality. On one hand he retained a conservative, traditional streak, as evidenced, for instance in his interest in the rabbinical, Judaic tradition of his family. During intimate social gatherings he might sing traditional Jewish songs with gusto, or tell Jewish jokes. On the other hand, he also showed maverick, iconoclastic tendencies in his leftist views, rebelling against the social status quo. It may have been this quality, of which Karen had her share, that attracted her, or his ability to encompass his contradictory inner drives. Indeed his attempt to reconcile opposites was one hallmark of his theories, for instance the contradictions between inner psychic and external social forces, between psychoanalysis and Marxism, between love of life (biophilia) and love of death (necrophilia). As for him, he could well have experienced her in the same way other students in his class did: She represented a caring, understanding, yet at the same time strong mother figure. After returning to Frankfurt, he and his wife, Frieda Fromm-Reichman, became active in organizing a group of South German analysts—including Groddeck, Kurt Landauer, Heinrich Meng and Ernst Schneider—into the Frankfurt Psychoanalytic Institute. At the same time he was teaching at that university's Institute for Social Research. He and Karen were to meet each other again in America years later, and to remain friends for the next fifteen years. They were to influence one another on an intellectual level as well, although they brought very different backgrounds to the ideas they shared.

In April 1928 Horney attended the next Congress of the Medical Society for Psychotherapy at Baden-Baden. Schultze-Henke and Simmel accompanied her, and she again encountered her friend Groddeck. That now much-discussed topic, character development, was the overall theme of the meeting. Although she did not present a paper, she participated in a panel discussion on "Psychotherapeutic Thought in Today's Medicine." She was the only Freudian analyst on the panel; the others were either nonanalysts or analysts from different schools.

That September, on her return from her vacation, the new quarters of the Berlin clinic were inaugurated. Eitingon reported that 104 analyses were then going on; there were 25 new students. Karen's old friend Karl Muller-Braunschweig spoke of the possibilities and increased scope of the clinic in the future. The special invited guest, Anna Freud, praised the clinic's newly expanded work, and expressed a fervent wish for its continuation. Freud himself was in Berlin but could not be present. He was staying at the Tegelsee sanatorium for a rest, suffering extreme pain from his oral cancer.

Even though Karen may have felt excluded from these proceedings by not being asked to speak—in spite of her having worked so assiduously at the clinic—it did not affect her participation in the society's meetings. During the rest of that year she continued to take an active part in almost every discussion of the papers presented.

The year 1929 was to be eventful for other reasons. In February, Otto Fenichel presented a paper at the society on the "Pregenital Antecedents of the Oedipal Complex," published in 1930. He agreed with both Freud and Karen on various differing points, apparently trying to mediate between them. He disagreed with Freud's and Jeanne Lampl-de Groot's formulation of the girl's preoedipal condition as a castrated masculinity. This was the paper in which Fenichel adopted Jones's terminology, *pre-* and *postoedipal penis envy*, ignoring Karen's earlier work on these phenomena as well as her terminology, primary and secondary penis envy.

But the disagreement was soon to be heightened.

During her usual summer vacation, Karen again attended the annual Psychotherapy Congress. This year the theme was the obsessional (compulsive) neuroses (*Zwangsneurose*). On July 31 she gave a paper on the "Clinical Psychoanalysis of the Obsessional Neurosis." It was reportedly well received. Alexander was there also from Berlin and spoke on "Neurosis and the Total Personality." The expansion of the classical theory was becoming more and more his personal interest. Erwin Strauss, then an analytic candidate at the Berlin Institute, was already showing his interest in phenomenology, a field in which he was to become a recognized authority. His paper was entitled "Compulsiveness and Space." Although Karen was familiar with Alexander's ideas, having discussed them with him at meetings, Strauss's were new and intriguing to her. It was probably the basis for her inviting him to the get-togethers she was planning to hold in her home. Among the others she met there was Stekel, one of the first analysts to deviate from Freud's theories.

After this meeting, Karen had little time to rest. The eleventh International Psychoanalytic Congress was being held the following month, at Oxford this time. Most of the Berlin group wanted to go and they were in a good mood. Their English hosts did their best to keep up this mood by arranging a program of sightseeing through castles, museums and landmarks.

Then Helene Deutsch presented a paper on "Feminine Masochism in Its Relation to Frigidity." Although she did credit Karen with an "illuminating" previous description of the "flight from femininity," she then disagreed with her. Following Freud's line, she felt that the Oedipus complex was initiated by the preexisting castration complex. This rebuff may have added to Karen's bitterness.

Then the issue of training analysis and, more particularly, lay analysis, was a source of further disquiet. Many non-German analysts had resented that Eitingon had appointed only Berlin members—Rado, Muller-Braunschweig and Horney—to the Training Committee. While it may have been Eitingon's administrative error, it redounded as a criticism upon these three. Several constituent societies had simply ignored the questionnaire, since the appended suggestions had been interpreted as subtle coercion. So the committee ignominiously had to admit its failure to reach any conclusion. A new one was then appointed, with Jones as chairman and members drawn from different societies.

Karen's mood by the end of the meeting was quite different from what it had been at the beginning. In a treasured, candid home movie taken of the arriving members by Dr. Sandor Lorand, Karen appears cheerful, buoyant, almost gay as she greets the others. But in the closing photograph of the group, she looks preoccupied and distant, with a wry, almost severe smile. Her position in this photograph could be an indication of her stature in the psychoanalytic world. She is seated in the front center, flanked by Abraham, A. A. Brill, Eitingon, Anna Freud and Marie Bonaparte. Anna Freud recalls Karen from this meeting. She, herself, felt like a young newcomer there while Karen was generally considered a senior, experienced authority, toward whom she felt a certain slight awe.

After her return to Berlin in October, Karen presented a brief communication to a meeting of the Berlin Society, "On Special Difficulties in Handling Young Girls." It is not known whether she was treating any adolescent girls at the time in her practice. But her own daughters were now thirteen, sixteen and eighteen, and passing through some of the typical difficulties of adolescence. This was the only paper she presented during these two years at the society.

On the other hand, she was devoting more time than ever to the institute during these years. The number of candidates was increasing during 1928 and 1929, and now included a number of Americans. At the Oxford meeting, Eitingon had reported that 115 analyses were then being conducted (compared with 85 in 1927), including 26 training analyses. Many of the candidates recall Karen vividly from this time.

Ray Gosline and George Daniels were two of the Americans. Daniels was to have contact with Karen later in the New York Psychoanalytic Institute, but was then still the eager young student applying for admission.

Appearing for his screening interview with her, he found the institute "humming with activity." Karen received him in her private office. To him she seemed like a key figure and appeared well accepted there. She "emanated importance and self-assurance. She looked solid and well-framed without being large or overweight. . . . She had bobbed hair, · slightly tinged with gray and was dressed plainly and modestly . . . not at all modishly. She was very dynamic and spoke up quickly instead of being reticent and waiting, sensing my own uncomfortable hesitation. She seemed to be a kindly person, but very incisive and certain of her own ideas." Her first question was "Are you neurotic?" When he answered that he thought he was not, she was apparently quite pleased, smiled, and the rest of the interview went along easily. He felt that he was accepted and left with a good feeling.

Some of the others who passed through during this time and whom she was to meet later in this country included Erwin Straus, William Silverberg and Fritz Perls.

Perls had been briefly analyzed and then supervised by Karen. He felt she was the one person he could completely trust. In 1930, after having been in a second analysis with Jeno Harnik, Perls felt too disturbed and despairing to continue with him; he considered Harnik too passive in his classical analytic approach to cope with his serious distress. He again turned to Karen for advice. She replied, "The only analyst I think could get through to you would be Wilhelm Reich." And so he continued on what he was to call his analytic pilgrimage. He admitted to finding Reich "vital, alive and vital." Later, though, after his flight to America, in reviewing all his experiences with psychoanalysts, he reminisced that he got "from Reich, brazenness; from Horney, human involvement without terminology."[7]

By the winter of 1929, the great world-wide economic collapse and depression began to affect Berlin. The small world of the institute could not remain insulated for long. The number of candidates slackened through 1930, especially the foreign students and more particularly the Americans. Private practice also fell off, especially psychoanalytic patients. Fortunately, Karen had retained an interest in her patients' medical problems, so she could treat enough patients to pay her bills; yet she too passed through a most difficult period. Eitingon's American financial resources dried up, so for the first time he found himself unable to sustain the clinic as he had been doing for so long. The rest of the attending staff were asked to contribute as much as they could. Even Freud—as Jones has described—was obliged to reduce his patient load to three psychoanalytic patients, partly because of his infirmity, partly because of the economic situation. By 1931 Simmel's Tegelsee sanatorium—the hope for a purely psychoanalytic facility—was forced to close its doors.

Yet the institute was feeling the pinch for still another reason. The problem of training analysis was not simply a semantic issue, at least in Berlin; it was a bread-and-butter problem. At least three or four newer psychoanalytic groups had arisen in the city. Many nontraditionally trained practitioners, who called themselves psychoanalysts—the "wild analysts" of ten years before—were beginning to treat patients.

In February 1930, the tenth anniversary of the institute was celebrated as a gala event. Eitingon spoke on his "Reminiscences on the History of Psychoanalysis." Rado was selected to present "The Work of the Clinic." Karen was again bypassed and it seemed as though Rado had become, after Eitingon, the leader of the clinic organization. Perhaps this was a result of the differences in their personalities.

Both were highly intelligent and thoughtful. Both were ambitious, but manifested it in different ways. Whereas Karen was more reserved and self-effacing, only recently having become more affirmative, Rado was frankly outgoing and pushy, more outspoken, even brash. She was slower in expressing her thoughts, turning them over in her mind; he was more impulsive, spontaneous and open. Others have reported that when they were together in a room, you could sense the tension between them. True, when he was given the task of writing up for publication the clinic's work of that decade, he assigned specific aspects of it to each of the members involved, including Karen.[8] Freud himself wrote an introduction to the publication in tribute to the institute's accomplishments.

But the outstanding event of the year, at least in terms of its fateful impact on the group, did not even occur on European soil. By one of those curious turns of fate, it was to determine the future life of several members, including Karen. An American Association for Mental Health was being formed to promote mass mental health. Following the appeals of that unsung pioneer, Clifford Beers, himself a former mental patient, its founders meant to draw professionals other than psychiatrists into the movement. The association decided to hold their first international congress in Washington during the coming year. Financed by wealthy private individuals (this was still before the Depression), they wished to invite the outstanding European psychoanalysts. Nine German analysts were invited to attend and present papers, all expenses paid, including Alexander, Rado, Rank and Horney. She could not make the trip at the time. Rado relates that when he received his invitation, the money situation being what it was, he thought it was a practical joke and threw it into the wastebasket. It was only shortly afterward, when Alexander called to say that the offer was bona fide, that he went to retrieve it. Alexander, more adventuresome, immediately wrote back his acceptance.

The meeting itself was significant not so much for its scientific content—more a potpourri of reports on the status of various mental health trends than anything original—as for the ambitiousness of its goals, its ecumenical spirit and the number of participants. Instead of the thousand anticipated, thirty-five hundred came, representing every helping profession. One European analyst commented that it was typically American in its style and grandeur.

Alexander has described in his autobiography[9] how he was approached at the meeting about coming to Chicago to organize a psychoanalytic institute at the university, with himself as professor of psychiatry. Several factors contributed to this choice of Alexander, both then, in 1930, and again in 1931, after the first year's unsuccessful trial. Alexander was then perhaps the foremost training analyst of young candidates. Lionel Blitzsten, the young but influential Chicago psychiatrist, had been analyzed by him for a short time in 1927. Alfred Stern, one of the early advocates of the new analytic institute, had also been analyzed by him. Harry Stack Sullivan, then beginning his psychiatric career, though not a member of the institute, was still an influential voice in Chicago. He had previously met Alexander in Berlin and had been most impressed. With so many favorable opinions, Alexander had been the logical preference.

One particular evening discussion with Alexander about schizophrenia, the subject that interested Sullivan most, stood out in his mind. He had felt excited by Alexander's knowledgeable statements all evening, until later, when he had realized that it had been he, himself, who had done most of the talking.

Upon his return to Berlin from Washington, Alexander called Helene

Deutsch to tell her the news and ask if she might possibly be interested in joining him as his assistant. Marie Briehl, in her office at the moment of the call, recalls Deutsch replying that she was not interested then. Because of this, Karen was later offered the position, an offer which was to change her life.

At a special meeting in January 1930, the German Psychoanalytic Association voted to disclaim any responsibility or support for the Medical Society for Psychotherapy. This amounted to a censure, not only of the organization itself, but more pointedly of those Berlin analysts who had been involved in it. The ostensible reason was the ill-defined attitude the latter group was taking toward psychoanalysis. In fact, they did accept as members not only Freudian analysts but "deviants" as well—Jungians, Adlerians, Stekelians and unaffiliated therapists. Simmel, the president of the Berlin group, who read the announcement, was himself interested in the psychotherapy group. Karen was against the disclaimer, since of all the Berlin members, with the possible exception of Ferenczi, she was perhaps the most involved in the psychotherapy society. She not only attended most of their meetings and presented papers but was as well known to that group as to the Psychoanalytic Association. She did not feel that those who did not follow the strict psychoanalytic line should be excluded. She maintained that even though they differed, they could still be friends and work together.

This pronouncement, however, was not a deterrent for her, or for Simmel or Ferenczi, all three, admirers of Groddeck. They attended the next meeting of the Medical Society for Psychotherapy in April at Baden-Baden, along with Schultze-Henke and Arthur Kronfeld from Berlin. The theme of the congress was again the obsessional-compulsive neuroses. Karen presented an important paper, "The Specific Problem of the Obsessional Neurosis in Light of Psychoanalysis." Interestingly enough, the special lead paper at this meeting was "The Psychotherapeutic System of the Oriental: Yoga in Light of Psychoanalysis." Although Karen was already interested in philosophy, this subject had a special effect upon her. Eastern philosophy and psychology were to preoccupy her intensely later in her life.

In her paper, she disagreed with the generally accepted notion that the compulsive repetition of thoughts or actions was the specific characteristic of these compulsion neuroses alone; it existed in other conditions as well, she said, like the stereotyped, repetitious patterns of schizophrenia. She also disagreed with Freud's concept of "repetition compulsion" as its dynamic basis, noting that this was only a hypothesis, even for him. She cautioned against the acceptance of this hypothesis as proven, which would cover up real gaps in knowledge and block the path to further insight. She pointed out that although anxiety is present in these conditions, it is also not specific. What is significant is that it seldom appears in manifest form. The presence of strong underlying destructive or aggressive tendencies is equally important. In hysteria these can be discharged through abnormal movements or sensations or paralyses, thereby affording relief from the underlying impulses. In the compulsive patient, such actions are blocked and the patient remains overinvolved with his thought processes alone. He must restrict real activity because of the intensity of the dangerous destructive impulses. As a result, wishing and thinking become greatly intensified, and to the patient, acquire a magic power. Rational intellectual insight is thus powerless against this state.

She went on to define the predominant and perhaps most specific problem of the obsessional-compulsive neurosis as this magical power of thought, existing alongside an otherwise rational intellect. Thoughts and impulses seem like reality. By rigid control alone the patient feels he can prevent the action, which is in itself originating from the power of his thought. Compulsion, then, is really only a secondary reactive symptom, rather than the primary cause.

Horney warned that therapy is more difficult in such cases than with the hysterical neurosis. There the patient's feelings and motives are in the foreground; the analyst can interpret them effectively because of the patient's reason. The compulsive, however, dissociates his reason from his emotions. Not only are his inner feelings foreign to him but he needs his compulsive reasoning as a defense. He will describe thoughts that he will destroy others, but when you point out that such impulses are aggressive, he will not be aware of this feeling.

Paul Lussheimer, then a young psychiatrist from Mannheim, recalls how enthusiastically this paper was received at the meeting. He had met Karen first at the Berlin Institute while he was interning in Bonhoeffer's neuropsychiatric service in 1928. He again saw her at these Baden meetings, where he had been introduced to her by a surgeon. He was amazed at the number of nonpsychoanalytic physicians who knew her. According to him, "She emanated warmth . . . was kind and friendly . . . but still had her own determined way of doing things. She gave a beautiful lecture and received great applause."

In the audience were several members of the Leipzig group, who were then preparing a seminar on culture and medical psychology for the coming semester (1930–31). The course was intended to consider Freud's *Civilization and Its Discontents* from the philosophical, religious and psychoanalytic viewpoints. Karen and her younger friend Arthur Kronfeld—originally from Leipzig but then working at the Berlin Institute—were invited from the Berlin group to participate.

After the Baden meeting, a number of the participants, including Karen and Simmel and possibly Fromm, gathered at Groddeck's house to socialize. Among other things, they discussed Freud and his state of health, and whether he might accept an invitation to visit Baden for a rest. But no formal invitation was ever sent.

On her return to Berlin, Karen found that Alexander was preparing to leave for Chicago. He was the first to go. Until now, the members of the group had felt little threat from the political situation. In fact, just the year before, Alexander had moved his office from downtown Berlin, over a theater, into a newly bought house in the suburbs, intending to settle down more permanently. Apparently he and Karen discussed the question of moving to the United States. According to her daughter, Karen mentioned coming here in mid 1931.

In 1930, no meeting of the International Psychoanalytic Association was scheduled. However, several local societies—or subsections of the German Psychoanalytic Association—outside Berlin had recently been formed and wished to meet with their Berlin colleagues. A meeting of German analysts was especially indicated in view of the recent disavowal of the Medical Society for Psychotherapy by the Berlin group. So a meeting of the German Psychoanalytic Association was held in Dresden in September. Most of the Berlin group attended, including Karen. Most of the South German analysts went also; among them were Fromm and Groddeck.

In his keynote address, Eitingon seemed to find it necessary to defend psychoanalysis against some of the criticisms then being leveled against it. His paper was thus titled "On Newer Criticisms of the Methodology of

Psychoanalysis: Some Observations on Today's Intellectual Attitudes." It was apparently directed against those who wished to emphasize the importance of social factors. Fromm spoke, in support of his usual orientation, on "The Application of Psychoanalysis to Sociology." Karl Muller-Braunschweig also picked a related topic: "Psychoanalysis and a World-View: Pride [Hubris] in the Domination [Hegemonie] of Thought and Will." Karen herself spoke on "Distrust Between the Sexes." She was again preoccupied by and returning to the subject of marital difficulties.

The final paper, which must have been of special interest to Karen, was by her friend Groddeck. He insightfully discussed the misadventures of Struwelpeter, the disobedient child whom she used to read about when she was younger.

In December of 1930, Rado also received an offer from Dr. A. A. Brill, whom he had met during the Washington meeting, to come to New York and organize a training institute modeled on the Berlin Institute. He relates that his decision to accept was based on an increasing awareness of the impending dangerous situation. He already recognized the considerable inroads of the Nazi organization into the lower house of the German Parliament and foresaw that they would take over within a short time. This was the beginning of the exodus.

As well as continuing her active participation in discussions at the Berlin Society and teaching during these two years (1930–31), Karen organized a kind of social and clinical group to meet every month in her home. It included colleagues of different theoretical persuasions—Freudians, Adlerians, existentialists—and both senior members and students. Occasionally they met at the homes of others. Among those who came more regularly were Schultze-Henke, Fritz Kunkel, Arthur Kronfeld and Arthur Gruenthal. Alexander and Edith Jacobson sat in from time to time. Erwin Straus and Eric Wittkower, still young students, attended irregularly. They still remember the pleasant social atmosphere, so accepting, and how honored they felt to be invited. Discussion ranged over the entire gamut of interests, psychoanalytic and otherwise, theoretical and clinical. For Karen it was something like the debates she had so enjoyed in medical school and with her Lankwitz friends. Other members of the society also dropped in, but most seemed deterred by a subtle disapproval on the part of some senior members of the institute of such interdisciplinary colloquies.

In January 1931, Karen presented a paper on "The Negative Therapeutic Reaction" at the society. At the same time, she resigned her position as secretary-treasurer. In retrospect it appears that she was already loosening her ties with the institute in preparation for her departure.

That March she took another step toward independence from the current analytic doctrine. She presented a paper, "On the Death Instinct," that was critical of Freud's concept of aggression and destructiveness as an innate, instinctual drive. Wilhelm Reich spoke on the same subject. With his leftist leanings, he attributed individual destructiveness to capitalism and other economic inequities and to the social injustices that derived from them. Therese Benedek, in a third paper, defended Freud. She believed that anxiety was due to the "perception of liberated death instinct" through "instinct diffusion within and against the self." Her conclusion was that the "study of the dynamics of instincts may substantiate [Freud's] speculations."[10]

Karen's remarks here were a condensation of her lecture at the Leipzig course. The latter was officially titled "Culture and Aggression—Some Thoughts and Objections to Freud's Death Instinct and Destruction Instinct."[11]

She made a distinction between those ideas of Freud which were based on his "ingenious though subjective speculative imagination" and those derived from his experiences and observations of patients. The existence of unconscious hostile, aggressive and destructive drives was an example of the former. He postulated that these could give rise to anxiety or guilt or chronic failure. While she accepted the existence of feelings like hostility or aggressiveness, she did not believe they were derived from a death or destructive instinct. She felt that such emotions or attitudes could arise either as constructive and life-preserving—the mother fighting for her child—or as a reaction to frustrations, insults or previous anxieties. For her man is not innately evil or destructive. While he is not basically "good" either, he does have a need for self-expansion, a will to live. Whereas the culture may require some curbs on instinctual impulses, excessive or threatening restraints can transform the healthier sexual or aggressive drives into destructive ones. Such unacceptable restrictions could be the product of cultural factors like lack of economic security or unfavorable social pressures on the woman, or of emotional factors like attitudes of parents toward the child.

Here Karen is not only taking issue with some of Freud's basic tenets, she is also striking out in an entirely new direction she was to follow subsequently. This is her first paper applying her own tentatively modified psychoanalytic notions to sociology and social issues. Of course these had been discussed during her presentation on the death instinct before the society. Obviously she was influenced, in part, by her attitude toward her own religious background and by her discussions with Karl Muller-Braunschweig and his ideas about religion and morality. The works of religious philosophers like Kierkegaard were well known to her. In addition, she was exposed at that time to several other influences. The Oriental philosophies were being called to her attention both by the paper at the recent Medical Society for Psychotherapy meeting and by her discussions with her young friend, Heinrich Zimmer, a student of Indian philosophy. Paul Tillich, the young leftist minister, also took part at times in these discussions, and his views probably had an impact on her as well. He was to remain a lifelong friend of hers.

And finally, the then recently published book of Albert Schweitzer, *The Philosophy of Civilization* (Part II), apparently influenced her thought. In his previous work, *The Quest for the Historical Jesus,* the great physician-theologian-philosopher-musician had almost echoed the message that Karen had proclaimed in her teen-age diary about the nature of Jesus. As a living human being, he represented the essence of God in every individual. This concept would certainly have drawn her to Schweitzer's works. In *The Philosophy of Civilization,* he considered humanistic religious ethics and morality; some of his ideas are similar to those Karen was to apply to the individual in her later theory. For instance, he discussed the will to live as the highest form of knowledge. This is contrasted with cognitive knowledge, which is "from the outside and forever remains incomplete," whereas "the knowledge derived from my will to live is direct and takes me back to the mysterious movement of life as it is in itself. . . . The essential nature of the will to live is the determination to live itself to the full. It carries the impulse to realize itself in the highest possible perfection . . . an imaginative force determined by ideals." This is the life force which had freed Karen from her inner dungeon when she was eighteen, which she had made the highest goal of her medical studies and which she was now positing as a basic tendency in every human being—in contrast to Freud's death instinct. For Schweitzer, "everything

. . . which can be brought under the description of material and spiritual maintenance or promotion of human life" is moral and good. Everything in human relations that leads to "material or spiritual destruction or obstruction of human life" and development, is bad and immoral. In modified form, this was to become Karen's philosophy, embodied in her evolutionary theory of morality.

Aside from the contents of Karen's paper on Freud's *Civilization and Its Discontents,* the spirit of this presentation is impressive and most revealing. It contrasts with Freud's pessimism about the inevitable lot of mankind and society, driven by innate destructiveness to strife and war unless such instincts could be curbed or sublimated. Her spirit was optimistic yet realistic. She was not a Pollyanna however: Man is not necessarily "good" by nature but he can grow constructively if those obstructive tendencies created by other individuals or society can be undermined, prevented. This can be done both for the individual—in cases of neurosis—and for society.

In April 1931, not long after her return from Leipzig, Karen was saddened by the death of her old, much-loved friend, Hans Liebermann. He was eulogized by Eitingon as "an artistic soul, a man who loved flowers and beautiful things." But his long affliction had taken its toll; he had required pain-killing drugs and had become addicted. He finally died of kidney failure and uremia. The loss was an extremely painful and grievous one for Karen, the third close friend to die in three months. Armine Loofs, a man whom she had liked and admired in the analytic group, and Josine Muller-Braunschweig, the divorced first wife of Karl Muller-Braunschweig, had both died young, suddenly and unexpectedly. Josine's death was especially upsetting. Karen had known her since their college days in Freiburg. Josine had followed Karen through the Urban and the Lankwitz hospitals. They had shared their intimate experiences as young marrieds and then had worked together at the Berlin Institute. Josine's death may have contributed to her decision to leave Berlin.

The sixth Congress of the Medical Society for Psychotherapy was being held that year in May, again in Dresden. Karen wished to attend perhaps just to be with her friends, since she did not present any official paper. Simmel accompanied her. There were to be two themes this time: the relationship between somatotherapy and psychotherapy, and dream psychology. The latter topic was apparently chosen partly in tribute to Freud's seventy-fifth birthday. Simmel spoke on "The Influence of the Soma on the Psyche." Karen was interested in this in relation to female hormones and their effect upon development. Another paper, more controversial from the analytic point of view, was presented by Jung. He spoke on "Symbolism in Dreams" and in life as well. He disagreed with Freud's focus on unconscious sexuality in dream interpretation and wished to extend the symbolic meaning of dreams to collective and archetypal elements. For Karen, perhaps the most significant statement at the meeting was a discussion by her friend Paul Tillich of the relationship of psychotherapy to religion.

During all these months Karen had been mulling over and developing some new ideas on the old issue of feminine sexuality. The differences between hers and Jones's position on the one hand, and that of Helene Deutsch, Lampl-de Groot, Fenichel and Freud on the other, remained unsettled. Karen apparently felt the need to respond to Fenichel's 1930 paper, "Antecedents of the Oedipus Complex," and Deutsch's paper, "Female Masochism." The problem now was whether the little girl's earliest belief that she was a disappointed (castrated) boy was a normal developmental phase (primary phallic) or a secondary defensive reaction against oedipal conflict and the wish for a child (deutero- or secondary phallic). Or, on the contrary, was the girl's femininity—including her awareness of a vagina and wish for motherhood—primary and normal rather than being derived from castration or oedipal feelings?

At the beginning of 1931, Groddeck had sent Karen a paper of his exploring the possibility of an inherent bisexuality. This view could imply that the child had the potential for experiencing itself, from the beginning, as complete: the boy as a complete male with a penis, and the girl as a complete female with a vagina rather than only as a penis-possessing or penis-lacking, frustrated boy. In April she wrote him:

> My Dear Doctor Groddeck:
> I am anxious to thank you for the paper re bisexuality. It happens to coincide with my own train of thoughts which now are occupying my mind in connection with my own work. These are a critique of Freud's concepts of the devel-

opment of the woman. Incidentally, do you know Wind-
huis's writings on bisexuality? He shows the importance of
the concept of bisexuality among primitive tribes.

Best regards to you and your wife,
Your Karen Horney

Furthermore I would like to discuss all these problems with
you personally. Perhaps I will drop in to see you at the
beginning of my summer journey.

This new train of thought could also suggest to Karen that the roots of the
fear of the opposite sex lay in the denied awareness of that other sex in
oneself. Jones came to the same conclusion somewhat later when he
pointed out that both sexes could only reach maturity by overcoming such
a fear.[12] Assuming this was so, was there any difference between the fear
of the opposite sex felt by men and that felt by women? This was the
problem to which Karen was now turning her attention.

Groddeck soon replied to her, in August:

Dear Doctor Horney:

I regret that you were not able to come to Baden. We
would have both been glad to see you here.

Thank you for your paper.* You know I think highly of
your opinions on the role of the woman. I hope a more elab-
orate explanatory paper will follow soon. It would avoid the
false use of your authority by people who would still like to
explain everything by the idea of the "cry for a child"
[Schrei nach dem Kinde]. That would really harm your just
cause.

I was surprised that you put so much credence in the
physiological research into the effects of ovaries and cor-
pus luteum. However that doesn't matter as long as the
premenstrual disturbances are finally closely examined.

I hope to see you here. However you will find someone
who is busy with things far removed from analysis. But
based on analysis, you can build a bridge to every problem.

Sincerely,
Your Groddeck

---

* This apparently refers to her recent paper, "The Distrust Between the Sexes."

In addition to making a distinction between the fear felt by each sex for the other, Karen was still trying to explain differences in psychological development partly on the basis of physical or hormonal factors. This was the area to which Simmel had addressed himself at the Dresden meeting. She had indeed been influenced by his ideas.

By the end of the year she had organized her thoughts into a paper with the imposing title "The Dread of Women—Observations on the Specific Difference in the Dread Felt by Men and by Women Respectively for the Opposite Sex"[13] and sent it in to the *Zeitschrift*. But Karen was unable to present her ideas to the International Association in person; it was the next Congress, scheduled to be held in September at Interlaken, in Switzerland, that was to be abruptly cancelled because of "the serious internal situation in Germany, the duration and extent of which cannot be predicted." (In fact, by mid 1931, the exodus was underway. First Alexander and Rado, then Sachs left for Boston in September.)

Another reason for Karen's haste in publishing was the appearance of Freud's second important paper on female sexuality in the *Zeitschrift* in October, in which he reaffirmed his previous views, which he spelled out in greater detail. He further specifically agreed with the ideas of Fenichel, Lampl-de Groot and Helene Deutsch, adding that the latter two "as women analysts . . . had been able to apprehend the facts with greater ease and clarity because they had the advantage of being suitable mother substitutes in the transference situation with their patients" while he himself had "not succeeded in unravelling any cases completely." This last statement appears to be an admission of his difficulty in understanding women and that his conclusions were more theoretical than based on his usual precise clinical observation—a point which Karen had previously brought up. And was not Karen, too, a woman and a "mother substitute"? Yet she disagreed with these other women.

Freud does mention her contention that he had exaggerated the importance of primary penis envy, noting her belief that a secondary form develops to avoid the girl's impulses toward her father. These claims he rejects. He also curtly dismisses Jones's objections.

Significantly, he qualifies these disagreements and defends himself in a notable and telling, though often overlooked, footnote: "It is to be anticipated that male analysts with feminist sympathies and our women analysts will disagree with what I have said here. They will hardly fail to object that such notions have their origin in man's 'masculinity complex' and are meant to justify his innate propensity to disparage and suppress women. The opponents of those who reason thus will think it quite comprehensible that members of the female sex should refuse to accept what appears to gainsay their eagerly coveted equality with men . . ."[14]

Since these were ideas that Karen had often expressed in her various papers, this paper is the closest he ever came to an overt polemical argument with her.

At this same time (October 1931) she presented a paper to the Berlin Society entitled "Critical Thoughts on the Phallic Phase." Whether this critique was a response to his paper or simply the result of her own developing train of thought is difficult to know. Freud did mention that "the bisexual disposition . . . characteristic of human beings manifests itself much more plainly in the female than in the male." He also stressed the importance of the clitoris—the female organ homologous to the penis— and the virtual "nonexistence" of the vagina until puberty. In light of Karen's subsequent concern with both these ideas, it could be assumed that she reacted strongly to his statements and attitudes.

During the latter half of 1931 and through 1932, in spite of the departure of several members and the unfavorable economic situation, the institute and clinic continued to function as usual, at least to all appearances. Students continued to arrive at about the same rate, even a few from America.

Martin Grotjahn, now a prominent psychoanalyst in Los Angeles, still remembers Karen from his classes and especially from his initial interview. Anxiously facing her in her office, he recalls that "she looked at me with a curious silence, sitting there at her cluttered desk and waiting. I had some doubts whether she would take kindly to my attempts to bring some order to the corner of her desk next to me." Yet she had a kindly twinkle in her eye and he quickly felt at ease. "She was an impressive and beautiful woman towards whom one developed an almost immediate deep confidence. She seemed to be an all-understanding Mother Earth. She offered a place of rest in the turmoil of those times."

The turmoil was indeed being felt. In November, Fenichel presented a paper, "On Social Anxiety," echoing the concern if not fear of the more socially aware members. During these months, Karen was a discussant of this paper and many others. These included such varied titles as "The Masochistic Character" (Willi Reich), "Alcoholism," "The Unconscious in

[138]

Art" (Groddeck), "The Psychic Functions of Sexual Activity" (Schmide-berg), "Hartmann's Theory of Sexuality" (Gero), "Sadism in Women" (Jacobson), "Erotogeneity and Object Libido" (Landmark), "Religious Sublimation" (Kluge), and "The Girl's Early Discovery of the Vagina" (Boehm).

After the discussions at the meetings, everyone would stand around before going for the real discussion session in one of their favorite coffee houses. At this time, Brigitte, Karen's eldest daughter, was already an es-tablished actress. As Grotjahn recalls, "We all waited secretly for the great moment when she appeared to call for her mother to drive her home. The girl was of such beauty that nobody wanted to miss her. To see both women together was unforgettable."

It was a standing joke among the analytic students that they could rec-ognize those in analysis with Karen: They had a peculiar mannerism, a tic, which looked as though they were picking invisible insects from their clothes. When one looked more closely, however, the imaginary insect turned out to be cat hairs, picked up from Karen's analytic couch, which her two cats liked to sleep on while it was still warm from a patient's body.

While Medardi Boss, another student of that group and now a distin-guished Swiss analyst, also remembers Karen as a "charming, full-blos-somed woman," he found her somewhat aloof, both at meetings and in analytic work. It was a time of economic depression, unemployment and insecurity, which he discussed with her often. She seemed well aware of what was happening, according to him, and thought that Germany was heading for deep trouble. At times she would ask if he could pay her in Swiss francs, to be left in a Swiss bank, which she could draw upon when she was there.

By the end of 1931, Franz Alexander was returning to Chicago after a first disappointing year there, followed by a year at the Judge Baker Foundation Clinic in Boston. As the Psychoanalytic Department of the University of Chicago Medical School had not succeeded, he had been asked to set up an independent Chicago Psychoanalytic Institute. He knew he would need a reputable assistant director and teacher and he had suggested Karen, whom he liked and respected. In mid 1931, the board of trustees of the new institute had contacted her. Its new president, Alfred Stern, had come to Berlin to interview her and had been favorably impressed. As soon as Alexander knew definitely, he called Karen long-distance and asked if she would accept the appointment, for a three-year period. She agreed to begin in September 1932. Stern sent her an official letter of appointment a short time later so that she could apply for the required visas.

After she made this momentous decision, Karen appeared to have mixed feelings about it, as her daughter Renate recalls. This was understandable. On the one hand she was saddened and subdued, even somewhat frightened by the unknown future. It meant leaving her friends, her practice, the institute, the clinic. Her daughters were finally settling down and enjoying their school and work, each after having gone through a period of adolescent turbulence.

Nevertheless, her separation from her husband was still recent. She wished to leave behind the aftermath of the break, its emotional effects on her, on her daughters, on her practice. The decision also meant leaving behind much else that was unpleasant. She was to some extent disillusioned with her psychoanalytic circle. She felt that in spite of her differences with Freud, she should be able to remain on friendly terms with everyone. She simply could not understand why anyone could feel resentment when she disagreed about theoretical ideas. Indeed, in February, she, Felix Boehm, Bernfeld and Hugo Staub had been named by the society as a public speaking committee, to address the general public. Three weeks later, following intense audience reactions to lectures they had given, there had been a debate in the society questioning their propriety. The issue had been raised of how much such controversy promoted the aims of the group, whether in public or within the society. This constituted an implied notice to the four to avoid criticism and controversial issues. In addition, Karen had continued her active involvement with the Medical Society for Psychotherapy in spite of official disapproval.

And finally, the external situation in Berlin was deteriorating rapidly. Even though Karen was not Jewish, and so not directly threatened, most of her friends were. Psychoanalysis itself was soon to be considered a "Jewish psychology." Jung, on taking over the presidency of the Medical Society for Psychotherapy with the authorization of the Nazis in 1933, was to declare that "the factual differences between German and Jewish psychology, long known to intelligent people, can no longer be denied and that can only be helpful to science."[15] Everyone connected with psychoanalysis would soon be suspect, and they were feeling the pressure even then. In fact, however reluctantly, the members could not help becoming aware of the political situation. In June 1932 there was a general discussion at the society on "Political Points of View and Psychoanalysis." This was followed a week later by a discussion on "Problems of Group Psychology and the Economic Crisis." The conclusion of the debate was that "the Nazi movement shows that the family environment of the lower-middle class causes their radical tendencies to take the direction of political reaction rather than revolution. Analysis of the effective content of racial theory shows that 'Nordic' is equated with 'pure, asexual,' while 'alien' equals 'something sensual, base, animal.' "

If these were negative motives for her decision, things to distance herself from, there were also positive factors. The new position offered a challenge, an adventure, an opportunity for independent thinking and teaching. It carried a possible academic medical appointment, which had been improbable in Berlin, where the university was unfavorably disposed toward psychoanalysis. Obviously Karen did not know the true situation in Chicago and complete details of all the disappointments Alexander had suffered.

Although the issue of female sexuality was apparently closed, as far as Freud was concerned, with the publication of his 1931 paper, it was not for Karen. During the spring of 1932 she continued to develop her arguments on the primacy of femininity in the little girl. This focused on whether the little girl really was aware of her vagina. As far back as 1926, Josine Muller-Braunschweig had written a paper asking what the development of the little girl would be if her attention was forcibly called to the existence of her vagina by extrinsic causes. She presented such a case, a child who had had vaginal pinworms. Then in January 1932, Boehm had presented to the society his clinical observations proving that discovery of the vagina occurs earlier and more often than was commonly supposed.

Karen drew all these ideas together into her next paper, entitled "The Denial of the Vagina—a Contribution to the Question of the Specific Genital Anxiety of Women."[16] She argued that girls do have early awareness of their vaginal sensations which is then repressed because of anxiety. "An undiscovered vagina is a denied vagina."

This was to be the last of her papers on female infantile sexuality. Although she continued to be preoccupied with the problems of women, it was no longer in reaction to Freud's ideas. Hereafter her interest was prompted by her experiences in the New World.

Freud was never to modify his views. In 1937 he wrote, "When we have reached the wish for a penis and the masculine protest, we have penetrated all the psychological strata and reached 'bedrock' and our task is accomplished. The repudiation of femininity must surely be a biological fact, part of the great riddle of sex." His pessimistic tone was evident when he further noted that "Ferenczi was asking a great deal when he laid it down as a principle that in every successful analysis these two complexes must have been resolved."[17] Here he admitted that he did not understand women yet, neither completely nor even as well as he understood men.

In 1938, in his last book, he commented, "We shall not be very surprised if a woman analyst who has not been sufficiently convinced of her own desire for a penis also fails to assign adequate importance to that factor in her patients."[18] This may have been a last pointed reference to Karen.

Karen soon became immersed in the difficulties of preparing for her forthcoming trip to America, about which she wrote Groddeck in June 1932. She wished to see him to say good-by before she left. He was still recovering from what seems to have been a stroke during the winter of 1931. His emotional state probably contributed to this condition. Always the idealistic, innovative maverick—unrealistically so at times—he had become convinced that he could cure Hitler of his anti-Semitic paranoia. He had planned to visit the Führer for this "therapeutic" purpose, but his family and friends dissuaded him from his dangerous enterprise. Unable to carry it out, feeling helpless against what was happening in the country, he had become tense, depressed and even somewhat paranoid himself.[19]

En route to England, Karen could only spend a few hours with him in Baden-Baden between trains on the night of July 22, and she did not wish to tire him excessively. (It had been arranged that Renate would go directly to Hamburg in August to board the steamer; Karen was going to England first for a brief vacation, and would catch the boat at Southampton.) It was the last time Karen was to see Groddeck. For her, sadly, this friendship was one of the splendid things she was leaving behind.

XI
FEMININE PSYCHOLOGY: PROUD TO BE A WOMAN

"The conclusion that half the human race is discontented with the sex assigned to it and can overcome this discontent only in favorable circumstances . . . is decidedly unsatisfying, not only to feminine narcissism but also to biological science."

—*"On the Genesis of the Castration Complex in Women"*

"I, as a woman, ask in amazement, and what about motherhood? And the blissful consciousness of bearing a new life within oneself? And the joy when it finally makes its appearance and one holds it for the first time in one's arms? And the deep pleasurable feeling of satisfaction in suckling it and the happiness of the whole period when the infant needs her care?"

—*"The Flight from Womanhood"*

Karen began her first paper (1923)[1] on the psychology of women by questioning Abraham's reformulation of Freud's basic concept of penis envy. His analysis was that, coveting the missing penis, all women must experience either passive castration fantasies or active desires for revenge against the favored male. Instead of this anatomically-based, therefore immutable and inevitable explanation she postulated three partial causes for the attitudes supposedly related to penis envy. One was urethral eroticism—the desire to urinate like a man. This male ability, when overvalued narcissistically, may give rise in girls to feelings of being at a disadvantage. Secondly, a scoptophilic drive—the ability of the boy to see his genitals, while they are hidden for the girl—can add to such feelings. And thirdly, since the male can touch his genitals, he can so satisfy the desire to masturbate. This is not possible for the girl; therefore her onanistic wishes must be suppressed. Thus, even though the penis-envy complex is typical of the little girl, it is not a primary phenomenon.

She felt that the various feelings resulting from this complex, during each girl's development, could cast light on its true source. In some cases, the girl passed from a narcissistic desire for a penis to a desire for a man (who represented the father) by means of identification with her mother; or to a desire for a child. In such patients, there might be fantasies of rape or love by the father, denied in reality. These could become the basis for neurotic feelings of chronic disappointment, for difficulties in grasping reality, for unhappy relations with parents, or finally for an obsessional need for a child. Such deep motives can be elucidated only after the original "masculinity-complex" phenomena—feelings of revenge against men, repudiation of feminine functions, unconscious homosexual trends—have been penetrated by psychoanalysis. The homosexual tendency can result from a shift from identification with the mother to identification with the father, often with vacillation between the two.

In order for this type of identification to occur, the girl's fantasies about her relations with her father would have had to be initially extremely strong. They would have had to involve an early and strong sexual attachment to him, then residual feelings of anger against him for the imagined deprivation (or incest), and guilt resulting from the fantasies. One conclusion she drew was that this complex of unconscious emotions, namely "wounded womanhood," must therefore precede and give rise to penis envy, with its feelings of having been deprived of the penis (castration).

Another conclusion was that at maturity, a great part of sexual life, especially as regards creative ability, becomes the responsibility of the woman. This notion was to lead Karen into her later, more developed point of view.

By the time her second paper (written in 1924, published in 1926)[2] was ready, a new Freudian term had been coined: the phallic phase. According to this concept, only the penis—or the clitoris in the girl—was of dynamic importance in determining psychosexual development. A regressive fixation on its psychogenic meaning could occur at any of the significant changes in the woman's life, such as puberty, first sexual intercourse, pregnancy or the birth of a child. This phase would have to be successfully traversed for further normal development to occur.

Karen challenged this traditional analytic view. She pointed out that it was based upon, and measured by, the boy's view of female development. It was also conceived by male analysts. And finally, the standards habitually used for evaluating civilization have always been masculine. Given this bias, the psychology of women has always been subjectively viewed according to men's relations with women. It represents a "deposit of the desires and disappointments of men." Yet women have adapted themselves to these wishes as if this male-based interpretation represented their true nature.

Since, as one example, the analytic meaning of coitus has been described as a "desire to return to the womb," then only men would be able to experience any real pleasure or fulfillment from it. The woman must therefore, in this view, content herself with only "compensatory devices" such as masochistic pleasurable feelings. Karen felt that motherhood was not simply a burden imposed on women by the victorious man. Pregnancy, birth, nursing, motherhood all have intense positive values and can generate pleasurable feelings in the woman. If these functions do become a handicap, it is only because of the social struggle involved. In fact, the man's need for creative achievement in certain masculine fields could well express a compensatory effort for his small role in creating the baby.

In Freud's view, the woman's tender attachment for a man (father) and wish for a child arose only through penis envy. While Karen agreed on the ubiquity of the little girl's envy, related to the lack of the penis, she now based it on the three partial instinctive drives she had previously described: urethral eroticism, scoptophilia and onanism. It was not a basic instinct in itself. This she designated as primary penis envy.

However, to explain the attitudes observed clinically in adult women toward men—hostility, depreciation, revenge, inferiority feelings, flight from feminine functions, hypochondriasis—she postulated another dynamic mechanism. This was the fear of vaginal injury, derived in turn from unconscious oedipal (incestuous) wishes. To escape such fear and anxiety, "the girl takes refuge in a fictitious male role." While this saves her from her unconscious feminine desires, it inevitably brings with it feelings of inferiority, since she is now measuring herself against standards and values foreign to her own biological nature.

It is only as a result of these early oedipal phenomena, namely the early attraction of the little girl to the opposite sex, that she turns a libidinal interest toward the penis. The woman was, according to Karen, a female first and a disappointed male second. She called this secondary penis envy and considered it perhaps even more significant than the primary type. Freud's male-type castration anxiety was thus really a feminine genital anxiety. Karen's formulation could thus be schematized as the following sequence of psychosexual events: awareness of femininity first, then oedipal wishes, then fear of vaginal injury (castration anxiety), then assumption of a male role (masculinity complex), and finally inferiority feelings.

But in addition to these biologically determined, unconscious factors, Karen believed that the actual social condition of women contributed to feelings of inferiority. Not only is the woman constantly taught that men are superior—a constant stimulation to her masculinity complex—but in today's male-oriented society, she cannot achieve satisfying substitute outlets to express it. The "flight from womanhood," as she called the total attitude of the woman, is thus a combination of psychic and social factors. But of course there is reason to be proud to be a woman. Indeed, observations of many men in analysis demonstrated an intense envy for such creative female functions as childbearing and motherhood.

Although her third paper in 1926[3] was focused on a specific clinical subject—frigidity and the inhibitions accompanying it—it still ranged over a broad spectrum of female psychological functions and developed previous ideas.

She opened with a cautionary note that sexual frigidity could not be considered a "normal" condition of women in modern civilization. Nor could it be seen pessimistically as a serious illness in itself. It is always a symptom of some underlying psychological disturbance and always accompanied by other clinical impairments, even though the woman may superficially appear to be otherwise healthy and effective. These can consist of characterological difficulties; of disturbances in menstruation, pregnancy or nursing; of chronic anxiety; or of poor emotional relationships with men.

Such symptoms would indicate a rejection of the feminine role, the "masculinity complex," even though the woman might not consciously reject sex itself. While she may resent and disparage men, she will also envy them and consider them superior. Feeling herself wronged, discriminated against, she perceives her female virtues as inadequate or negative. She may make claims on others or on life for compensation. In dreams or fantasies, her sexual organs are pictured as incomplete or damaged, sometimes leading to gynecological or other physical symptoms.

To explain these phenomena, Karen reiterated the psychosexual developmental concepts she had evolved in her previous papers. However, she now expressed these more in terms of actual, empirical factors than in theoretical terms. The transition from early narcissistic penis envy to the later normal object-libidinal desire for a man and child can be blocked by multiple home conditions. For instance, early favoritism toward a brother, parental concealment of and taboos on sexual interests, observation of parental sexual intercourse, brutality of a father and/or illness of a mother associated with sexual activity, punishment for masturbation can all contribute to fear of feminine impulses. (It is to be noted how these factors were similar to early conditions in her own life.) They add to the guilt arising from earlier unconscious attachment to the father; this can be additionally threatening if religious prohibitions have been present (where God equals the father). The later, secondary masculinity complex or penis envy creates a vicious cycle. It intensifies in turn the inhibition and leads to the other symptoms.

External, cultural factors, like education, custom, or social needs, can also contribute to a distorted development. The greater social value placed on the male adds a contemptible quality to being feminine. The split made by men between sexual and romantic "love" relationships can also create inhibitions in the woman, who must then repress one aspect of her emotional expression.

In this paper, Karen was beginning to turn more toward a characterological view of psychic function, stressing attitudes, subjective experiences and reality factors. Although she still was using Freudian terms, she was beginning to reinterpret them.

In her fourth paper, "The Dread of Women" (written in 1931, published in 1932),[4] Karen continued to develop her previous thesis that each sex had ambivalent feelings toward the other: a hostile, disparaging attitude combined with an envious admiration. The negative feelings of the male—dread, anxiety, fear—for the female were especially important and required elaboration.

History is replete with instances of this dread, ranging from the Biblical taboo on the menstruating woman through the belief in the demonic possession of witches to male analytic patients' overt or symbolically expressed fear of sexual intercourse. Freud had qualified this as a castration anxiety, a fear of the father. While she agreed that such a dread often did exist, even though it could be denied or disguised as an excessive adoration of women, she disagreed about its causes. She felt that a fear of the father was less important than a straightforward fear of vaginal penetration. This fear of the female genitals was present from early childhood. In support of this notion, she cited the boy's normal infantile curiosity, the evidence found in children's sexual games, the instinctive search for an opening to complement his phallus, the fantasies boys usually have—and the fear or anxiety that arises from such activities. This, according to her, was related to the unconscious desire for the mother, for "the mystery of motherhood."

More specifically, within this general feeling, the dread can result from a fear of the mother's prohibitions or of her punishment for the anger contained in his impulses; or from a fear of being derided or rejected for his small, inadequate penis. The true nature of this dread is thus not castration but the threat to his masculine self-esteem. It differs from the little girl's fear of the male (father) in that she instinctively perceives the vagina as too small for the phallus. Her dread is of destruction of her genitals; it is physical. However, one must not automatically equate "male" impulses with "sadistic" and "female" with "masochistic." This would be an unwaranted generalization.

The threat to self-esteem associated with fear of the female can have several consequences for later male development. With his attention (libido) turned back to his own penis, a phase of heightened phallic narcissism now follows, equivalent to Freud's phallic phase. This restores his self-esteem. He thereby believes his penis should be larger, may feel anxiety about its size and have to go on proving its potency. Perhaps male ambition, the need to achieve and the need to conquer women are an expression of this drive. Another result could be the man's tendency to debase the woman, to lower her self-respect and so maintain his own sense of superiority. A superior woman would be too great a threat to his masculine pride. This was her answer to Freud's explanation of why men so often chose infantile, uneducated, hysterical spouses, or used prostitutes for their sexual needs. According to him, the desire for an inferior woman results when the two currents of the erotic instinct, tenderness and sensuality, fail to fuse into one. Tenderness can then be felt for a woman of equal status or ability, sensuality for one of lower status. Sexual relations are possible only with a woman who is inferior to his idealized "pure" mother; they would otherwise be impossible due to the unconscious idea of incest. The debased woman can be rescued and elevated in fantasy. In so doing, he is thus carrying out his unconscious oedipal wish to possess the mother and identify with his father.

In this paper Karen is continuing to turn to noninstinctual attitudes to explain these phenomena, sometimes in combination with her own original interpretations of the instinctual factors proposed by Freud. Significant, too, is her reasoned, logical analysis of such attitudes as, for instance, self-esteem and pride. This ability to sort out complex emotions and attitudes into simpler components, applicable clinically, was to become the hallmark of her later work.

"The Denial of the Vagina,"[5] her fifth paper on female psychology (1933), continues to develop the theme of the primacy of the little girl's femininity over penis envy. After reviewing Freud's latest ideas on feminine psychosexual development, she noted that if accepted without qualification, they would inevitably lead to certain specific consequences for the woman's adult psychic life. If Freud's theories were correct, then the "masculine trend" of even a normal woman would make it difficult for her to accept the phases of her development as a woman. Consequently, a high incidence of homosexuality would be predicted and the desire for motherhood would be only "secondary and substitutive," remote from any true instinctual need. Woman's overall reaction to life would be largely determined by her "strong subterranean resentment." Since Karen had found no clinical evidence for any of these deductions, she was forced to disagree with some of the basic tenets of Freud's theory of infantile sexuality.

In particular, she had observed that signs of early masculinity (penis envy) were not generally found in young girls. On the contrary, little girls usually exhibit "spontaneous feminine coquetry" or maternal solicitude by age two. Little boys often wish to have breasts or children. Even though children might admire some sexual traits and behavior of the other sex, they still behave on the whole as their own sex typically does. But if an inherent bisexuality is assumed, it would explain the child's uncertain psychological attitude toward his or her own sexual role—which usually becomes firmer only with later conditioning and the finding of love objects.

The important conclusion to be drawn was that vaginal awareness was present in a girl's earliest childhood. This was based on Karen's observations of little girls' vaginal masturbation or cases of extrinsic vaginal irritation. In adult patients, these infantile experiences are usually repressed, but the patients then show evidence of disturbed vaginal sensibility. For instance, there may be a high vaginal sensitivity to masturbation along with anxiety, vaginal spasm or pain, or frigidity in coitus.

In addition, the frequent occurrence of rape fantasies or dreams, accompanied by anxiety, in childhood before there is knowledge of coitus, suggests some kind of awareness or "instinctive knowledge" of vaginal function. Early masturbation or sexual games could also create anxiety, through the fear that the child has injured herself by making a hole in her body. Finally, if women's anxiety over later masturbation is truly related to the unconscious idea of sexual relations with the father, it would also require a previous childhood knowledge of the nature of the vagina.

The conclusion is that sensitivity in and awareness of the vagina is significant from the beginning, but that libido is deflected from it because of anxiety. This anxiety results from the girl's dread of its destruction by the man (father); from feelings of physical vulnerability derived from seeing menstruation or birth; from fear of her own hostile impulses and possible retaliation; and from her inability to verify her physical wholeness visually (whereas the boy can see his penis).

Because of these factors the fiction is long maintained that the vagina does not exist. For Karen, "behind the failure to discover the vagina is a denial of its existence." Everything connected with the vagina—knowledge of its existence, sensations in it, instinctual impulses related to it, even memories of vaginal masturbation—must be repressed from consciousness. Vaginal sensations are transferred to the more visible clitoris and the masculine sexual role is preferred. This view was the reverse of Freud's contention that only clitoral sensations were early and primary, justifying the phallic phase for girls. With such a specifically feminine, primary vaginal sexuality, she believed that the concept of primary penis envy with the strength postulated by Freud would be hard to retain.

Karen's last relevant papers on feminine psychology were written after her arrival in the United States. The new sociocultural conditions she encountered here made a strong impression on her, evidenced in several of her papers on other subjects. As far as the psychology of women was concerned, she had already begun to turn from a purely biological toward a more sociological approach. In America this emphasis became even more pronounced.

In "The Problem of Feminine Masochism,"[6] she challenged several current views on why women unconsciously seek masochistic satisfaction in their sex life. She denied that it was inherent in their "essential female nature" or a necessary consequence of their anatomical structure. If so, by extension, women would also have nonsexual masochistic character trends more frequently than men. She pointed out that these assumptions had been based upon the hypothesis of feminine penis envy and the masculinity complex (the desire to be masculine). It maintained that "active-sadistic libido for the clitoris is deflected inward masochistically." The girl's discovery of the lack of a pleasure-giving penis would deny her satisfaction from her own sexual activities; she could henceforth only derive pleasure from suffering.

Karen disagreed that suffering and the "bloody tragedy" of illness, accidents and pain are the fundamental lot of women. To believe this would simply follow the psychoanalytic errors of generalizing culture-limited concepts like the Oedipus complex, and of failing to distinguish between pathological (neurotic) and normal phenomena. She clearly showed that such symptoms in women result only from special social circumstances. Furthermore, still another distinction must be made in using the clinical concept of masochism—namely, between sexual masochism and moral or attitudinal masochism.

It has been clinically observed that many masochistic trends provide reassurance against fears or grant atonement for sins. Or they promise the attainment of otherwise unachievable goals, or permit the hostile manipulation of others. These dynamic trends can be symptomatically expressed in various ways: as the direct inhibition or denial of fears; as the renunciation of action or goals; as exaggerated optimism; as excessive expectations of others, especially for love or sexual satisfaction, with frequent disappointment; and as feelings of incompetence, humiliation, martyrdom or exploitation. All these feelings are usually accompanied by lowered self-esteem, inferiority complexes and suffering. They produce, in turn, an aversion to all forms of competitiveness and aggression.

In various combinations, such symptoms might be expected as a reaction to various cultural influences on the woman. These might include the blocking of outlets for emotional expansiveness and free sexuality, the restriction of childbearing as a source of self-esteem, the lower status and the economic dependency of women, and the surplus of marriageable females. Even some traditional psychoanalytic doctrines, holding to the alleged inferiority of women, could contribute to the same symptoms. While innate female biological attributes—lesser physical strength, menstruation, being passive and penetrated during coitus—need not have masochistic connotations in themselves, they can lead to or be interpreted as such.

Karen's conclusion was that no woman need be prey to masochistic tendencies, either by virtue of simply being female or by living in today's society, unless she already has neurotic needs to satisfy through masochistic suffering.

In this paper her emphasis on social factors far outweighs that given to instinct and biology. More significant, however, is the notion now emerging of psychodynamic forces and attitudes, both intrapsychic and interpersonal. These are seen to arise as a product of infantile as well as later ongoing dynamic factors. While admitting the possible traumatic influence of childhood events, she questions why early pathological emotional reactions should be "lastingly . . . maintained throughout life" and become the only way of seeking satisfaction. Her answer is that they continue "to be supported by various dynamically important drives," arising in later life as a result of later experience.

In her 1934 paper, "Personality Changes in Female Adolescents,"[7] she focused her ideas about feminine psychosexual development on pubertal girls. She first described four kinds of personality change occurring with the onset of menstruation, in response to conflict. These included, briefly, an aversion to sex with an intense interest in substitute activities; a total absorption in sexuality, with a loss of interest in work; interpersonal detachment, with inhibition in both sex and work; and homosexuality. In spite of their clinical differences, there are common personality factors which relate these four types. All feel an insecurity about their femininity. All hold conflicting attitudes toward men and a partly unconscious destructive hostility toward other women. This results in a relative incapacity to truly love anyone. All have strong defensive feelings about masturbation. Although such feelings begin in adolescence, they continue into adulthood.

These common underlying psychological attitudes come out during psychoanalysis and are turned toward the woman analyst. For example, the woman's guilt or fear about masturbation may be related to her fear of hostile feelings toward another female (originally her mother). In part, such feelings could have been a reaction to real rejection in childhood. But more often they are the result of guilt over unconscious aggressive fantasies, with fear of retaliation. All these women are thus constantly competitive or antagonistic to other women. This attitude can spill over into their relations with men as well. It produces more conflict at puberty, when there is increased sexual desire in opposition to feelings of fear.

These four different types of behavior represent varying solutions to the early anxiety and conflicts the child develops in its attitudes toward its parents. Attitudes like aggressive competitiveness or clinging dependency, or withdrawal later become character traits. Then by shifting the competitiveness into a striving for perfection in another field of activity, the first type can avoid the sexual competition with other females for men. The second type clings to men for love, admiration, sexual satisfaction. She does not withdraw from rivalry with other women, but, in effect, seeks out men for allies. With the third solution, instead of the emotional investment of the other types, there is a stunting or restricting of emotionality: "Don't get involved and you won't get hurt." The fourth solution consists of a reaction-formation: The hostile competitiveness is replaced by its opposite, a love for other women. Yet the underlying feeling often emerges in dreams.

Symptomatic attitudes like these, which are still maintained by underlying anxiety in the adult, can express themselves in a pure form, can be mixed, or may follow one another. They must be recognized to be treated. For severe cases, psychoanalysis is required.

Karen's closing sentence expresses a sentiment that was to become more pronounced—albeit more controversial—as she grew older: "We must not forget, however, that life may be the best therapist." This was to become the cornerstone of her more fully elaborated later theory. The individual has the potential and the innate urge to grow throughout life. This includes the constructive tendency to heal oneself. It is also significant that she always refers to herself as a psychoanalyst and to her method of treatment as psychoanalysis, in spite of these revisions and reinterpretations of classical Freudian theory. Two such newer ideas were introduced here. One was the concept of basic conflict in the child resulting from contradictory relations to the parents. This concept was still not clearly developed at this point. The second was the notion of solutions to conflict—as contrasted with Freudian defense mechanisms—consisting of the development of dynamic attitudes to overcome preceding anxiety that results from this basic conflict.

Two final papers, written in 1934 and 1936, merit inclusion among Karen's works on feminine psychology. From their titles, "The Overvaluation of Love"[8] and the "Neurotic Need for Love,"[9] both would seem to deal with the same subject. But the differences in approach, methodology and spirit between the two papers show a notable evolution in her thinking even during these two years.

In the former paper, at the outset she seems to focus on certain problems of the modern woman in today's "patriarchal" society. As she observed in her practice, many women tend to have a compulsively overvalued longing to "love a man and to be loved." Her opening statement in this connection is a memorable commentary on the woman's social role: "Woman's efforts to achieve independence and enlargement of her field of activities are continually met with a skepticism which insists that such efforts should be made only in the face of economic necessity, and that they run counter to her inherent character and natural tendencies. Accordingly, all efforts of this sort are said to be without any vital significance for women, whose every thought should center upon the male or motherhood."

However, on closer analysis she sees the explanatory and determining factors underlying woman's attitudes as deriving from instinctual (libidinal) and infantile drives. There is thus an interweaving of biological and sociological, of childhood and on-going adult experiences.

Characteristically, all these women had difficulty in establishing good, durable relations with men, showed inhibitions in their work along with an impoverishment of their other interests, and feared being abnormal. Possessed by the idea that they must have a man, they pursued men. But failing to satisfy this need, they usually ended up feeling inferior, inadequate, ugly, or anxious. As defenses against such feelings, they often overemphasized their dress and appearance, denied or feared any dependency needs, and in some cases developed compulsive drives for achievement which might have been projected onto their male partner—if they found one. They often felt intense rivalry with other women, with a need to triumph and unconscious aggressiveness, sometimes motivated in turn by unconscious homosexual tendencies.

This paper, in brief, would seem to be an elaboration and refinement of her previous paper on adolescent girls. It qualifies the four different types of solutions to conflict and applies them to adult women seen in clinical analytic practice. Here is to be found the beginning of the holistic-dynamic view that was to become so characteristic of Karen's more fully developed theories. The individual and society, internal and external, present and past influences are all mutually interacting and cannot be easily separated in determining the final common pathway of symptoms and personality.

In "The Neurotic Need for Love," there is an even greater emphasis on current psychosocial factors. The fundamental question is raised as to whether there can be a direct repetitive relation between any infantile instinctive drive and a later adult attitude. A definite distinction can and must be made between the two. Thus, one can distinguish between libidinal and nonlibidinal love, between healthy or spontaneous and neurotic or compulsive love, between erotic and sexual love. Unhealthy developmental attitudes acquired in infancy must be sustained by dynamically important drives of later life if they are to cause neurotic symptoms in adulthood. This paper begins the development of her final theory of neurosis.

In sum, Karen's contributions to feminine psychology were made over a thirteen-year period (1923–36) of eventful transition in her life. Initially she took issue with the tenets of Freudian psychology, which had quickly won general acceptance (at least by Freud's disciples). These described female development from a male-oriented, phallocentric viewpoint, and seemed to give the woman an inferior status. Although her behavioral observations were similar to Freud's, she ascribed them to different psychological causes and later partly to cultural factors. She stressed the positive aspects of femininity. As her ideas developed, she put increasing emphasis on interpersonal attitudes and on social influences in determining the woman's feelings, relations and role.

From the methodological viewpoint, she pointed out the need to distinguish between healthy and neurotic traits. She also made a clear differentiation between infantile influences as initiators of developmental distortions of personality, and later on-going dynamic factors required to maintain such neurotic patterns. She applied the principles of the scientific method to her reasoning, stressed the difference between hypothesis and fact, called attention to the limited applicability of the single case study to the broader group, and warned of the danger of unwarranted generalizations. She indicated the need to lay bare the complex underlying psychic processes giving rise to any specific symptom, whether somatic or characterological. But she cautioned that amelioration of the symptom following interpretative uncovering of its apparent emotional roots did not necessarily prove a specific cause-effect relation.

XII
ON MARITAL PROBLEMS

"For some time I have been asking myself with growing astonishment why there has as yet been no thorough analytical exposition of the problems of marriage, although assuredly every single analyst would have a great deal to say on the subject. . . . Perhaps (I said to myself) the whole question touches us too closely to form an attractive object of scientific curiosity and ambition. But it is also possible that it is not the problems but the conflicts that touch us too closely, lie too near to some of the deepest roots of our most intimate personal experience."
—*"The Problem of the Monogamous Ideal"*

Karen's writings on marital problems included six papers published between 1927 and 1932.* In "Psychic Fitness or Unfitness for Marriage,"[1] she began by considering the preliminary conditions for marriage: What emotional demands does the marital state impose on the partners and what qualities of personality are necessary to fulfil them? The "ability to love," as such, is too vague to explain difficulties. Marriage must be considered as both a sexual and an emotional relationship. Overt sexual disturbances which would make an individual actually unfit for marriage can easily be discerned by the physician (aversion to sex, for example, or sexual promiscuity), particularly in extreme cases. But the intermediate gradations between "normality" and "pathology" are more difficult to recognize; they are dependent on psychic attitudes toward the partner, which in turn result from psychosexual development.

The man may show a split between his sexual and loving emotions (the *"Spaltung im Liebesleben"* described by Freud). Thus, he may adore the woman but have inadequate sexual relations. In such a case, he may be emotionally fit for marriage, but the woman will have to make do with less sex; or the reverse may be true. The impact of this disturbance on the

* Other papers have dealt with the man-woman relation, like "The Dread of Women," but in a more general fashion, not limited to marriage.

marriage will depend on her attitude. If she also needs either less love or less sex, difficulties need not arise. If she has intense needs that her husband cannot fulfil, the partners will be incompatible, particularly if she is so revered by the husband that he regards her as untouchable and unapproachable by other men. Such a man will feel contempt for other women.

A man's unconscious homosexuality can also be a problem. If only partial and well sublimated into friendships or business activities, this tendency will not preclude a good marriage, especially if the wife's love requirements are small. In such cases, marriage may keep the man from even becoming aware of his homosexuality. The emotional bond will act as a compensation for the suppressed sexuality. At times, in overreaction to the lack of sex, the man may encourage the woman to have affairs; or by projection of his own repressed attitudes onto her, he may believe she is unfaithful or homosexual herself.

A third difficulty for the husband can be excessive narcissistic self-love. Here intemperate masturbation may be one result. Or it can be sublimated into a hobby, like collecting, or into business activities.

The extent of these various limitations will ultimately depend on the degree of preexisting "hate between the sexes" or even the "readiness to hate." This can follow a childhood envy of the opposite sex, based either on a "masculinity complex" in a woman, on insecurity about one's own sex (the feminine man or masculine woman), or on a fear of sexuality. At worst, marriage will be out of the question. If these traits are less pronounced, marriage is then possible, although conflicts over domination and submission will inevitably ensue. These cases run the gamut from simple deviations in psychosexual development to actual neuroses.

In some instances, marriage can alleviate the neurosis, particularly when it is a result of previous inadequate sexual satisfaction or a reaction to some recent traumatic experience. More often, marriage can precipitate neurosis even in relatively healthy persons.

The duration of the marriage bond is normally threatening to some unstable persons. Living together stirs up conflicts. A need for new love-objects can arise from the same factors that led to the marriage in the first place, or from disappointments in the relationship. However, the reverse can also be true, namely a stable but unhappy marriage, especially when the person finds psychic peculiarities similar to his own in the partner.

For example, mutual hostility may be compensated for by a stronger positive emotional bond. Or mutual identification based on common interests—children, household, economics, mental traits—can have the same result.

In her second paper, "On Psychic Determinants in the Choice of Mates,"[2] she took up the childhood factors that unconsciously motivate a person's selection. She still believed that infantile drives did not differ from later ones. Although the principles of the Oedipus complex were valid, their expression could be manifold, hidden or devious. The conscious explanation of one's choice could be quite different from the unconscious reason. If a displacement of the libidinal tie to the parent of the opposite sex occurs, the person may seek a much older mate. If the normal pubertal liberation from parental ties occurs later in the marriage, then marital infidelity may take place.

Unconscious rivalry may be operative in the person who chooses a previously or still married person as a partner: He is out to best the earlier mate. If such competition is frightening, however, the person may recoil from such a marriage. This competitiveness can be the result of childhood rivalry with a sibling.

Sometimes it is not the real parent that is sought unconsciously, but an idealized image of the parent. The man may seek a madonna figure or a virgin. This image may include traits which originally caused him to suffer as a child. The real mate may be adored or given nonexistent qualities in fantasy.

Where a split between the sexual and the emotional occurs, the chosen mate may be idealized abstractly but physical sex will be sought outside the marriage. Or a known "bad" woman will be chosen, with intent to "save" her. And when there is an inner uncertainty about the person's own sexuality, he or she may find security either in feeling superior to and more important than the mate or in making the partner more vital and stronger and then leaning upon him or her.

Unconscious homosexual drives can lead a person to seek a mate with idealized attributes of the parent of the same sex.

Such instinct-driven motives can operate even in marriages of convenience or arranged marriages. If they do not determine the initial choice, they emerge soon afterward. Nevertheless, accidental forces can play a significant role, as in the man who marries several women of entirely different personalities. This may occur when the man is a "Don Juan" type, searching for something he is unconsciously fixated on but cannot find. Then the true, objective qualities of the mate are entirely ignored. Or finally, it can occur when there are multiple, polymorphous fixations in the past, only incompletely represented in each spouse.

The third paper of this group is entitled "The Psychic Roots of Some Typical Marriage Conflicts."[3] In it, Karen pointed out that it was unproductive to try to understand severe marital conflicts simply on the basis of how the two personalities fit together. Secondly, sexual difficulties alone were less significant than "psychic impulses." Certainly the initial infatuation leading to marriage is usually due to the need for release from sexual tension. But sexual drives can then be transformed into "objective" erotic attitudes which can be either positive, e.g., tenderness, devotion, care, or negative, producing conflicts.

For instance, some unconscious attitudes can be sublimated: The marriage can then be ruined by excessive withdrawal into work, thereby frustrating the spouse. The same drives can be displaced into emerging "polygamous desires." If these are admitted, they can lead to extreme jealousy, followed by the desire for revenge. Even if the infidelity is only imagined, due to unconscious projection, the same result can follow. And through suppression, these attitudes can lead to regressive earlier-stage libidinal symptoms like compulsive eating or preoccupation with money. Other neurotic symptoms can also result, all unconsciously used to inflict pain on the spouse. Even latent homosexual tendencies can become overt.

As well as evoking sublimation or regression, the marital bond can be experienced as a restriction or duty. This will sometimes lead to revolt, in fact against the restriction, but directed against the spouse. Or it can lead to the assumption of a parental restraining role by one partner toward the other. Often such a role comes out more intensely at the time of the marriage of the children. The wife then assumes characteristics of either her mother or her father, although not necessarily those of her actual parent, but rather the characteristics of an idealized or degraded image of the parent. The difference between the neurotic and the healthy marriage lies precisely in this degree of the spouse's identification with or separation from his or her parents.

The question must be asked why people still marry despite frequent misfortunes or frustrations. The answer is that people have unreasonable expectations of happiness—based on infantile fantasies. The parental relation is idealized in memory; this ideal is sought in the marriage. The unconscious incestuous relationship is also sought, but the taboo against it is equally strong. The evolution of any marriage thus corresponds to the evolution of the oedipal situation, based on the entire preceding psychosexual development.

In 1927, at the tenth International Psychoanalytic Congress, Karen spoke on "The Problem of the Monogamous Ideal."[4] She first roughly summarizes her previous three papers, emphasizing the threat to marital relations arising from the id in the form of unconscious infantile expectations of the idealized parent that must lead to disillusionment with the spouse, and from the superego in the form of the incest taboo. She then goes on to describe the ways in which the ego deals with these psychic conditions. The love that a partner expects to feel for his spouse can be overestimated; unconsciously it becomes a sin not to love. The suffering felt by the wife—whether in the form of sacrifices that she feels are demanded by the family, or as slavery to the spouse—is used to justify continuing the marriage. A certain pride—neurotic, of course—is taken in being the martyr. But then secret hostility arises to alienate the partner and drive him to seek outlets elsewhere. The stimulated polygamous desires of one spouse then come into conflict with the ideal of monogamy of the other.

One marital partner generally makes a claim on the other to renounce all outside attachments. This is the first time Karen mentions such "claims," which later were to be elaborated on as part of her theory. The origin of such a desire to possess and monopolize is ambivalent love-hate feelings. These are derived from infantile oral incorporative needs as well as from the child's frustration and hatred toward the parent who cannot be possessed. Wounded narcissism also enters into it, since the inevitable frustration wounds one's pride: later this becomes a question of prestige. In some cases, anal-sadistic elements play a role, when the spouse is regarded as a chattel that can be lost.

Such claims are always reinforced through the sanctions of tradition and law regarding marriage, which usually weigh more heavily on the woman. Punishment for infidelity has always been severer for the woman. In addition, even though marriage licenses sexual intercourse, this act is psychologically more significant for the woman since she alone can conceive—a function from which the man is largely removed. Consequently, an unfaithful wife, especially an obsessional personality type, will feel a greater burden of guilt than an unfaithful husband.

Two years later, Karen presented a paper entitled "The Distrust Between the Sexes" to the German Woman's Medical Society.[5] The question she asked was why an atmosphere of suspicion and distrust so often exists between spouses.

One reason she proposed was the intensity of dimly felt emotions, the passion and ecstasy to which the lover is tempted to surrender. Since these feelings, with their implications of limitlessness and loss of self, are so frightening, the person becomes cautious and reserved. An intense need for love also carries excessive unconscious wishes and longings for happiness. Expectations of what the partner should be or do are often contradictory. These can only lead to disappointment and resentment, since what is taken for true love is only the overvalued expectations. Alongside love, however, always lies a repressed destructive hostility. This is derived from childhood: in reaction to the fear of parental rejection if sexual desires are expressed, in reaction to being relegated to second place alongside a favored sibling, in reaction to the child's own anger and hostility against the parents. Such pent-up anger and aggression can only be expressed in fantasies; they are the source of early anxiety.

The man often unconsciously fears the woman because of the imagined "magic powers" related to her sexual functions (the true meaning of castration anxiety), so he must keep her subjugated. He feels contempt for her as a sexual being at the same time that he adores and idealizes her "pure" nonsexual motherliness. The patriarchal society and the supremacy of the male have always been traditionally advocated as a result of such attitudes. Still another contributory factor is that the male is more dependent sexually on the woman because of her greater role in childbearing. His interest in keeping her dependent is therefore greater.

Finally, since marriage offers the greatest possibility of durable happiness, one tends to overlook the equally strong possibility of the emergence of these destructive attitudes which are also inherent in marriage.

This paper was notable for its frequent references to social patterns in different cultures, as they showed a historic bias in favor of maleness. Karen was beginning to emphasize the role of cultural influences, as opposed to the previous stress laid on instinctual factors.

Her final paper on this subject, "On Problems of Marriage,"[6] was, in effect, a summing up of all her previous ideas. She opened with a poignant question that merits quoting: "Why are good marriages so rare? . . . Can it be that the institution of marriage cannot be reconciled with certain facts of human existence? Is marriage perhaps only an illusion, about to disappear, or is modern man particularly incapable of giving it substance? Are we admitting to its failure or to our own when we condemn it? Why is marriage so often the death of love? . . . On the surface the problem appears to be very simple—and very hopeless."

One "subterranean" general cause she proposed was the discrepancy between a spouse's real imperfections and limitations and the illusory unconscious expectations or claims. Another was the conflict caused by contradictory expectations, one or both of which might be unconscious. Still a third was the chronic hatred or distrust connected with relations between the sexes.

In describing many clinical examples of how these conflicts could express themselves, she reviewed much of her previous work. Her newer thoughts focused more specifically first on the male and then on the female contributions to marital problems. The husband can see his wife mainly as a source of prohibitions, just as his mother was. Or he can respond to his image of her as the asexual saint or the harlot, with consequent inhibition or contempt. Or he can fear that he will not be able to fulfil her demands, and as a result develop an extreme sensitivity to humiliation when his pride is hurt.

The wife can bring a degree of frigidity to the marriage, indicating some deep hostility or an inability to really love. This can be derived from a childhood fear of sex or motherhood. Sometimes this basic attitude manifests itself as a compulsive competitiveness with the man, or as a rejection of her feminine functions, such as childbearing. Thus, the arrival of a child can start marital conflicts.

In closing, she cautioned that such problems could not be solved either by admonitions about renouncing needs or about duty, or by advocating unlimited freedom. But some could be alleviated by working on unrealistic expectations and finding a balance between freedom and renunciation, between acceptance and change. This article prepared the way for more detailed examination of the personality traits that give rise to domination, submission, neurotic claims and neurotic conflicts, a central concern in her later work.

XIII
THE NEW LAND: CHICAGO

"The greater freedom from dogmatic beliefs I found in this country alleviated the obligation of taking psychoanalytical theories for granted, and gave me the courage to proceed along the lines which I considered right. Furthermore, acquaintance with a culture which in many ways is different from the European taught me to realize that many neurotic conflicts are ultimately determined by cultural conditions."
—*New Ways in Psychoanalysis*

As the Statue of Liberty loomed up to the left in the early morning mist, and the brick and glass mountains and canyons of Manhattan glistened in the sun off to the right, Karen stood silently with Renate, meditating at the rail. It was an end and a beginning. Here was the land she had dreamed of in her games with Tutti. It was the land where, as she had imagined and had read, even the lowliest, even the Indians, could live with dignity. Where the noble chief Winnetou would dispense justice wisely and for all. She had even envisaged herself coming here when she was twenty, with her first love, to start a different life. And, as for thousands before her, the statue stood there welcoming, promising liberty for the "storm-tossed and homeless." The voyage on the *Hamburg* had been long and tedious, enlivened only by the walks around the deck. She had been impatient.

Karen passed the immigration and customs examination without hitch. She had impeccable sponsors and a good position waiting for her. Besides, up until 1932 the influx of immigrant refugees, especially the intellectuals and professionals, was still relatively small. The great wave of the late thirties was yet to come. Nevertheless she still resented all the administrative, bureaucratic procedures. She found them demeaning and humiliating, as she was later to indicate to Rita Honroth, when she was passing through the same routine.

[165]

Although they were met on the dock by Emmy and Sandor Rado, who tried to be as kind as possible, Renate recalls—through the eyes of her delightfully impressionable adolescent sensibility—the "really frightening impact of the first moments on land, with the taxi ride through the narrow busy streets, between those terrifying high buildings. We finally emerged on Central Park and were taken to the most luxurious hotel we had ever seen. We stood there lost, like Alice in Wonderland, in a high-ceilinged gilded lobby. Elegant bellboys were everywhere. We entered gilded elevators which took us to our deluxe suite overlooking the park and the massive, overwhelming city. After the days of nothing but blue sky and the serenity of the immense expanse of the ocean, the onslaught of these new bewildering impressions was almost more than we could master."

This initial anxiety was compounded by the differences in customs Karen continued to encounter. It became a veritable "culture shock" for a while. Their first cocktail party, set up for them in New York shortly after their arrival, left Karen confused and angry, as she confided to her daughter. Everyone standing around "speaking at the same time about nothing, with nobody listening to anyone else," bewildered her. She was annoyed, in addition, by everyone addressing her as "Karen." How dare they! Why, in Germany it could take many years to get to that point of familiarity, and even then, only after permission was officially requested and granted. Her English was fair and readily comprehensible, but it was still more the stilted, book-learned than conversational language. Renate recalls how ashamed she felt of her mother's English, even though her own was no better, if not actually worse.

But New York was only a passing-through experience. A now unremembered friend—either Rado or someone sent from the Psychoanalytic Institute—was driving them to Chicago. They were told that New York, with its crowds, skyscrapers and sooty air, was not truly America. The real America would be seen in the countryside and the mountains they would cross en route. However, both Karen and Renate were amused by the Adirondacks. These were not mountains; compared to the Alps they had just left, they were hills.

For the first few weeks, their initiation to Chicago only added to the disillusionment. It was still the tail-end of the Prohibition era, with its gangland feuds. During their first night in the Hotel Windermere, a gang shooting took place there. Karen quickly learned that violence was not an exclusive feature of Germany; it was part of human nature everywhere. As part of their introduction, a tour of the city was arranged, including its famous—and malodorous—stockyards and slaughterhouses. After it was over, Karen and Renate were so disgusted and nauseated that they could not eat meat for some time.

Since the Chicago Psychoanalytic Institute was downtown, they quickly decided to live on the North Side, nearby. Karen found a rather elegant furnished apartment overlooking Lincoln Park. The panoramic view was apparently a necessity for her, here and later in her New York office and in her summer homes. The big problem, however, was the high rent. Karen had arrived almost without funds; she did not even have the minimum balance required to open a bank account. When she expressed concern, Renate convinced her to be expansive, to take a chance and forget the expense. Renate, herself, soon entered the progressive Francis Parker High School near the park. But Karen's reactions in this situation evinced the conflicts she was experiencing in the clash of her previous values with those she was finding in the United States. The opulence of the hotel in New York and now the elegance of the apartment in Chicago dazzled, delighted and dismayed her. She felt it contradicted the basic simple tastes and naturalness she was used to and preferred. She was outraged when a colleague asked her how much money she earned after her first day of work at the institute. She angrily felt that everyone was too interested in material things.

The difference in social values also kindled her own inner conflicts. The luxury and opulence stood for ostentation, exhibitionism and expansiveness, which contradicted with her instinct toward self-effacement. What she saw as materialism, an overemphasis on the importance of money, may have conflicted with her pride in her simplicity and in her freedom from the thrall of possessions. Then too, a concern about money was vulgar; intellectual and esthetic values were more important. Yet one may question how much repression and self-deception was involved. After all, she had had fine furniture, possessions and money for a time in Berlin. And her later acceptance of these values was to come quite easily. In fact such a change was one of the things that impressed Margaret Mead about Karen. Karen's appearance at their first meeting in 1932 was striking. "She looked like a 'typical' Viennese intellectual . . . a studiously neglected appearance, no makeup, a plain dress. But the next time I saw

her in New York, she looked elegant, with an expensive hat and dress."
This was an example of the shift in her values over a period of some six
years.

Perhaps equally important to Karen's first reactions was the fact that
people spoke so openly about such things as income with characteristic
American directness, candor and informality. In Europe, such matters
were personal and intimate, not to be publicly bruited about but to be
reserved for the family and close friends. This openness would take some
getting used to.

The fledgling Chicago Psychoanalytic Institute was still in a precarious
state. In fact, psychoanalysis itself was just beginning to be recognized
outside New York City as a worthy field of study. As Ernest Jones wrote,
"The struggle for recognition was particularly severe [in America] and it
was not easy to win new adherents. In 1925, there was only one analyst
west of New York, Lionel Blitzsten in Chicago."

After finishing his residency and a short stint in the army, Blitzsten had
practiced and taught neurology at Northwestern University until 1921.
Dissatisfied with what he felt to be the inadequacy of neuropsychiatry, he
became interested in psychoanalysis. Following the path of so many
young American students, he made the pilgrimage to Freud in Vienna.
Unable to obtain the master for his analysis, he had to be satisfied with
Otto Rank, with whom he had the usual few months' analysis. In addition,
he attended several meetings of the Vienna and Berlin Psychoanalytic
Societies, and the psychiatric clinics in Berlin and London. As he met
many of the important analysts there, it is possible, though not certain,
that he met Karen at this time. On his return to Chicago in 1923, he
began to practice both neurology and psychoanalysis, which he actively
advocated. But his chief in neurology, Dr. Hugh Patrick, was against analysis, so Blitzsten left. He joined the Children's Mental Hygiene Clinic at
Michael Reese Hospital in Chicago, along with Harry Levey and George
Mohr, all equally interested in analysis. In 1927, he decided that he
needed further analytic training. He was analyzed by Alexander in Berlin
for almost a year. This time he attended Karen's courses—in fact was
probably supervised by her—and got to know her fairly well.

In 1928 he began to practice psychoanalysis in Chicago as one of the
first members of the American Psychoanalytic Association there. Specialists in other fields referred patients to him for analytic treatment and he

soon attracted a circle of colleagues into psychoanalysis, a number of whom went for their own analyses to other cities or to Europe. On their return, he then referred patients to them and provided supervision. In 1930, this group included Thomas French, Helen MacLean, Margaret Gerard, Leo Bartemeier and Karl Menninger, all of whom were to become analytically-oriented psychiatrists. That year they formed the Chicago Psychoanalytic Society, with Blitzsten as its first president.

However, Blitzsten was not suited for administrative work or an organizational position. He was a poor public speaker. For the same reason his formal, didactic courses at the university had been considered dull. His forte was teaching in small intimate groups, whether at the bedside on his rounds or in workshop discussions. Since the university was still antagonistic to teaching psychoanalysis, several students asked him to be "at home" one evening a week to discuss patients from the analytic viewpoint. So began the famous Monday-evening "Blitzsten Seminars," which were to be responsible for the analytic orientation of several generations of psychiatrists. Among this first group of young colleagues were Robert Knight, Sigmund Lebensohn, Robert Tidd, Robert Morse, Henry Brosin, Ralph Crowley and Douglass Orr. They were sometimes known as SOB's (Sons of Blitzsten). Although their attendance at these extracurricular meetings was not forbidden by the university, it was discreetly discouraged.

The arrival of Franz Alexander at the University of Chicago in 1930 introduced another element into the situation. In his partly autobiographical account, he has related how this first year was a "formal defeat," a "failure of the experiment with psychoanalysis," almost confirming Freud's severe reservations. He felt this was primarily due to the initial hostility of the medical faculty. In contrast, the social science and law faculties and students welcomed his psychoanalytic material. He was not even assigned a lecture room in the medical faculty until near the end of his year—but it was too late. At the time, analysis was not approved by the lay public either. It became a cult among the avant-garde and intelligentsia, a fashionable thing to do, but it was still underground. But in a short time its popularity was to grow. Those who were analyzed spread the gospel. These included several on the administrative board of the university.

The committee that called Alexander back from Boston in 1931, after a year at the Judge Baker Guidance Center, to organize the new independent Psychoanalytic Institute, was a private, nonmedical one. He therefore believed that his first task at the institute was to improve relations with and gain acceptance from the medical profession. This aim led to his concentration on research, especially into psychosomatic conditions, and on ways of shortening analytic therapy for medical patients. Such a direction had to lead perforce to a deemphasis of the classical Freudian theory and training principles, even though initially Alexander tried to model the institute on the Berlin one.

As the institute opened, Alexander and Blitzsten were the only two qualified to do training analyses; Thomas French qualified shortly afterward. A number of the Blitzsten-trained young analysts were assigned to teach theory courses and seminars. The Chicago Psychoanalytic Society became one of the three original member societies of the American Psychoanalytic Association, toward which it was to remain oriented. Actually, in 1935, the American Association was to become a federation of local societies, including the New York, Washington, Chicago and then the Boston groups. In a very short time, the Chicago Institute had more candidates than it could handle.

At the twelfth International Psychoanalytic Congress in Wiesbaden in 1932, Alexander reported on the progress of the institute. He explained that the clinic would provide ample clinical material. Grants from the board of trustees would provide payment of the instructors who had no private practice and those working in the clinic only a few hours daily. The problematic question he raised was that of cooperation with nonanalyst instructors. Jones, Eitingon and Ferenczi were all against having nonanalytic specialists work there; occasional cooperation with medical instructors would be preferable. Brill and Eitingon were both appointed to the institute's advisory board.

Karen was not present at this Congress, which was the first she had missed in a long time. It took place in September, just after she had left for Chicago. Significantly, the attendance was lower than usual, with fifty-nine members and about sixty guests present. Eitingon spoke in his introductory address of the "distress and exigencies of the times . . . the meeting is being held in Germany in view of the economic distress elsewhere." It was to be the last one.

The atmosphere in the Chicago Institute was at first all amity and cooperation—at least on the surface. When Karen arrived, the interplay of forces among Alexander, Blitzsten and herself was balanced, but apparently required little to shift into disequilibrium and dissension. She honestly intended to side with and support Alexander. She began immediately to work with candidates in training, to supervise others and to teach. Two courses were assigned to her: psychoanalytic technique and feminine psychology.

Karen soon found her way to the Blitzsten Seminars, which pleasantly impressed her. She quickly became friends with Blitzsten. Here she found the same exciting atmosphere as in her Berlin analytic evenings. People really talked with one another, openly agreed or disagreed and still remained friends. Lay students interested in sociology and psychology attended at times along with the medical students and analytic candidates. The meetings were held in different homes, sometimes going on until three in the morning, and even then people were reluctant to leave. Karen soon found that though they were all so interested in psychoanalysis, there was a subtle suspicion of its German origins and tone. To be more accepted it would have to be somehow modified, Americanized. Otherwise there would be resistance to it, at least among those who had not been trained abroad.

Both at these meetings, and at the institute, the other analysts treated her with deference. Several of them had trained in Berlin and attended her courses there. She was the senior analyst there and in spite of her position as Alexander's assistant director, considered the most experienced and the most knowledgeable. (She was in fact six years older than Alexander.)

For the first few months, aside from her work, Karen was preoccupied with preparing for her State Board Examinations, which would cover all the basic sciences as well as clinical subjects. She spent her evenings studying, even taking her medical tomes to bed to read until early morning. To add to the difficulty, now it all had to be done in English. She felt overburdened, discouraged, depressed. The other analysts and their wives tried to be helpful and supportive, especially Dorothy Blitzsten; the two saw a great deal of each other in Chicago and later in New York. Karen managed to pass the examination that winter. Indeed, she was astonished that everyone had been so kind and understanding. With that weight off her mind, she felt freed again to devote herself to her clinical work, her teaching and her writing.

Her daughter Renate was having her own problems of adjustment that had to be dealt with during this period. After the freedom and self-determination of her previous Swiss boarding school, she was finding this American high school too restrictive. For instance, she could not run freely in a tight bloomer gym costume. And then, the new sexual mores were so different here, even disturbing. In Europe, boy-girl relationships could be deep, even intimate and loving, but they were based solely on feelings of camaraderie, without any sexual implications. Here the boys seemed to want to neck or pet immediately. Karen, in spite of all her knowledge of sexual development, had never really enlightened her daughter. Her expertise had been more theoretical than practical. Renate felt homesick, a great nostalgia for the old ways. Even though both were going through such a trying experience, they had not confided in each other. Each was afraid of upsetting the other. Perhaps Karen's constraint about speaking of such matters was also partly due to her reserve about personal, intimate, emotionally charged questions—much as she had felt about money matters after her arrival. She had a strong need to separate her formal public self from her private self, a trait that many friends were to notice. Karen and Renate finally decided that they would have to return to Berlin for a vacation visit that very next summer.

After her examinations, Karen needed to celebrate. Why not hold a cocktail party like the one she had seen in New York—even though she had then thought it to be one of those detestable American customs devised only for torturing people. Her first party in her home turned out to be a big success. Most of the group at the Chicago Institute came. She needed liquor but none could be bought; this was still during Prohibition. So she simply sent Renate to the local pharmacy to obtain some on a prescription for medicinal alcohol. Renate recalls with amusement how she made the cocktails by mixing the alcohol with whatever juices she could find in the house. At least everyone drank the concoction and no one complained.

As soon as she could, Karen again turned to her writing. Because of her course on feminine psychology, she was asked to present a paper before the winter meeting of the Chicago Society of Obstetrics and Gynecology. The topic was "Psychogenic Factors in Functional Female Disorders."[1] In her presentation she pointed out how the various functional disturbances

1. Captain Berndt Wackels,
Karen's father.
(*Courtesy B. Swarzenski.*)

2. Clotilde van Ronzelen, "Sonni,"
Karen's mother.
(*Courtesy B. Swarzenski.*)

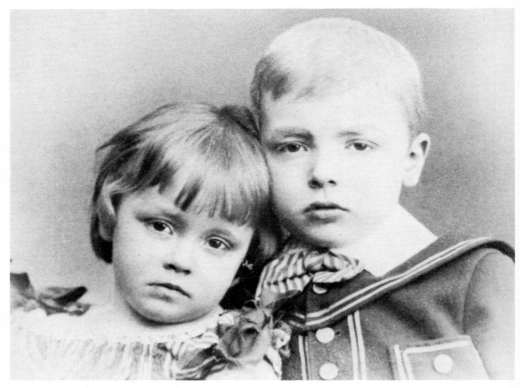

3. Karen, age 4, and her brother Berndt, age 8. (*Courtesy R. Patterson.*)

4. On the steps of Blankenese where Karen played. (*Courtesy Krögersbuch-und-Verlagdruckeri, Hamburg-Blankenese.*)

5. The schoolyard of the Blankenese Elementary School, circa 1890, which Karen attended. (*Courtesy Krögersbuch-und-Verlagdruckeri, Hamburg-Blankenese.*)

5

4

6. Sketch of Karen, about age 15. (*Courtesy B. Swarzenski.*)

7. The all-male pathology lecture class of Professor Virchow, Berlin University, circa 1890. Karen was one of the first women to study medicine there.

8. Old Street in the University district of Freiburg, circa 1905, near where Karen lived.

7

8

9. Karen with classmates after their *Physikum* exam, 1908. (*Courtesy B. Swarzenski.*)

10. Karen and Oskar with Brigitte and Marianne, 1913. (*Courtesy M. Eckardt.*)

11. Dr. Karl Abraham, Karen's
analyst, circa 1912.
(*Courtesy F. Weiss.*)

12. Dr. Hanns Sachs, Karen's
second analyst, circa 1914.
(*Courtesy F. Weiss.*)

13. Marianne, Brigitte, and Renate in front of Zehlendorf house, 1919.
(*Courtesy R. Patterson.*)

14   15

16. Karen with psychoanalytic friends in Wiesbaden, 1925. Karen is second from left, with Ida and Louis Grote and Hans Liebermann at right. (*Courtesy B. Swarzenski.*)

17

18

14. Dr. Georg Groddeck, Karen's
friend and mentor, 1924.
*(Courtesy Mme. Margaret
Honegger.)*

15. Dr. Carl Muller-
Braunschweig, circa 1945.
(Courtesy E. Newspiel.)

17. Brigitte at about age 21.
(Courtesy B. Swarzenski.)

18. Marianne at about age 20.
(Courtesy M. Eckardt.)

19. Renate at about age 19.
(Courtesy R. Patterson.)

19

20. Part of the analytic group at the Oxford Congress, 1929. (*Courtesy G. Daniels.*)

1. F. Alexander, 2. G. Zilboorg, 3. G. Daniels, 4. R. Gosselin, 5. Emmy Rado,
6. K. Lewin, 7. A. Healy, 8. R. Spitz, 9. E. Sharpe, 10. Mrs. Liebermann, 11. S. Rado,
12. J. van Ophuijsen, 13. S. Ferenczi, 14. A. Brill, 15. Mrs. Alexander, 16. Karen
Horney, 17. Marie Bonaparte, 18. M. Eitingon, 19. A. Freud, 20. E. Jones,
21. L. Jekels, 22. E. Simmel, 23. O. Fenichel, 24. H. Sachs, 25. R. Loewenstein,
26. H. Nunberg

21. Paul Tillich in a photograph inscribed for Karen. (*Photo by Elli Marcus.*)

22. Karen in New York, 1936.
(*Courtesy J. Sullivan.*)

23. Harry Stack Sullivan.
(*Courtesy Dr. Otto Will.*)

22

23

24. Erich Fromm. (*Courtesy Dr. J. Schimel and the William Alanson White Institute.*)

25. Karen at age 60 in 1945.
(*Courtesy G. Lederer-Eckardt.*)

26. Weekend at Fire Island.
Clockwise from top left: Alex
Gralnick, B. van Bank, Mrs.
Daniel Lipshitz, Joseph Furst,
Harold Kelman, Karen, Muriel
Ivimey, Herta Seideman.
(*Courtesy B. van Bark.*)

25

26

27

28

27. Karen with Butschy, circa 1948. (*Courtesy American Institute for Psychoanalysis.*)

28. Karen, Brigitte, and Katherine Crane in Japan, 1951. (*Courtesy Dr. Akahisa Kondo.*)

29. Karen in Cuernavaca, 1950. (*Courtesy B. Swarzenski.*)

30. Daisetz Suzuki and Karen, in rear, with Cornelius Crane, left, and Joseph DiMartino, during their trip to Japan in 1951. (*Courtesy B. Swarzenski.*)

29

30

31. Karen in the garden of temple in Kyoto, 1951. (*Courtesy Dr. Akahisa Kondo.*)

of the woman's reproductive system—dysmenorrhea, frigidity, vaginismus, menorrhagia, fear of masturbation or pregnancy—could be related to various unconscious emotional attitudes or conflicts.

What is significant about this paper is the number of caveats it brings up. For one, she cautions that there is no direct or specific relation between any simple emotion and any particular symptom. There are always many complex historical causes at different levels of consciousness which can be uncovered only by psychoanalysis. Second, no simple experimental situation can reveal the true nature of such symptoms. Third, even if the symptom is ameliorated by uncovering its apparent psychic roots, this does not necessarily substantiate a cause-effect relation. The change could result from some adventitious therapeutic effect, like suggestion. And finally, the scientific method of testing must be applied to validate any assumed results. This meant that several psychoanalysts, using the same analytic method of free association on similar patients, would have to arrive at the same effects.

Why was she emphasizing these methodological issues now in such a cautionary manner? Alexander was promoting his psychosomatic research project at the time. He was considering the problem of the broad and complex mind-body relation in terms of a direct connection between specific attitudes and somatic symptoms in particular patients. Karen had often warned against unwarranted generalizations in her previous papers: One must stick to the immediate clinical evidence and to the patient under observation. Each patient was an individual case, presenting a unique web of interrelating factors. More specifically, however, she was probably expressing her feelings about Alexander's proposals, indirectly disagreeing, as was her wont.

In December, over the Christmas vacation, Karen and most of the Chicago group journeyed to Washington for the annual meeting of the American Psychoanalytic Association. It was her first participation in a meeting of this organization. Many of the members knew her personally from the Berlin Society. Even the younger ones knew her by name, since her article "The Denial of the Vagina" had, by coincidence, just appeared in English in the *International Journal of Psychoanalysis*.

She presented a paper there on "The Problem of Feminine Masochism."[2] The theme she expressed was basically a continuation of her oft-repeated message: Women are not sexually or socially masochistic, are not doomed to suffer, because of their inherent nature or physique. When they are suffering, it is because of either special neurotic attitudes they have developed or contemporary social conditions.

More important, though, she became better acquainted with members of the Washington group, who were soon to play a significant role in her future life. Harry Sullivan, Clara Thompson, Billy Silverberg, Bernard Robbins and Ernest Hadley were all there. A few of these had previously been candidates in Berlin and had attended her courses. She again met Rado, now Director of Education at the New York Institute, whom she had only met briefly during her passage through New York, and Brill, too, whom she had last seen in Oxford in 1929.

She had met Sullivan previously in Chicago. Although he had settled in Washington in 1923 while working at the Sheppard-Pratt Hospital, he had become friends with Edward Sapir, the anthropologist, and Harold Lasswell, the sociologist, at the University of Chicago in 1928. Thereafter he often visited with them and was influenced by their thinking. He had also attended Blitzsten's seminars and the two had become close friends. During the ensuing years, they were in frequent communication, supported each other's positions, referred patients to each other and shared ideas. Personally they were alike in some ways and quite dissimilar in others. Both could be amusing and witty when they wished. They were both often sarcastic, even acerbic, with those who disagreed with them on the basis of pretensions. Yet they invariably showed great respect for their patients, and great sensitivity; both had an uncanny gift for arriving at seemingly incredible insights based on the slightest diagnostic clues. Both men had the ability to mobilize opinion and to attract a circle of followers, although Sullivan seemed to enjoy formal organizational activity (and the attendant power struggles) in which Blitzsten was sometimes reluctant to engage without Sullivan's prompting. Blitzsten seemed to need to have friends around him more than Sullivan, who was a more private person, a tireless speaker and a prolific writer with a distinctively circuitous, archaic and often impenetrable personal style.

Following this 1932 meeting, which Blitzsten did not attend, Sullivan wrote him a long letter in his typical style, commenting on the acrimony and factionalism that had gone on behind the scenes. He believed that some of the Alexander-New York-Boston axis (as contrasted with the Blitzsten-Washington-Baltimore axis) were *principally occupied in the spinning of a dense scholastic web that will give them the position of illuminati by isolating them as a foreign language group from the eroding influences of fair criticism on the level of the psychiatric herd. This is so utterly at variance with my conception of the course of human progress, and particularly of the fertilization of psychiatry by psychoanalysis, that I take real pleasure in cutting the fabric away.*

Karen became friends with Sullivan as well as Blitzsten; she was to meet him later again in New York, where he had established his private practice in 1931.

The trouble in paradise began within a year after Alexander initiated his new thrust toward briefer psychoanalytic therapy, and psychosomatic research. Some of his staff began to question his emphases, Blitzsten among them. He objected to the short-term focus on presenting symptoms instead of the conventional unravelling of underlying childhood factors. He disagreed with the use of supervising analysts who were not yet officially accredited, even though they might have had some experience. He disapproved of the assignment of candidates to the treatment of research patients from the clinic; he believed this required more experienced therapists. And he opposed the inclusion of a lay board member in discussions of candidates' personal histories. This violated professional ethics and personal privacy. Karen basically agreed with Blitzsten's views.

This disagreement led eventually to such an uncomfortable atmosphere that Blitzsten appealed to the American Psychoanalytic Association in protest. Drs. Oberndorf and Kubie were sent to look into the matter. They decided in favor of Blitzsten's position, whereupon Alexander agreed to modify the new practices. He still needed the backing of the American parent body. In effect, this constituted a censure. But the Chicago Institute was privately funded and his individual stature was such that within a short time he began to ignore their recommendations, whereupon Blitzsten resigned from the institute. However, he continued to do training analyses and supervisions, and to see Alexander at Chicago Society meetings. There was no official split, as Blitzsten did not have the temperament to organize a dissident group.

Karen was in a difficult situation. Even though she personally objected to the revisions proposed by Alexander, she still had to work as his subordinate at the institute. She apparently tried not to become involved in this factional struggle; some described her as aloof. It was reported that she rarely spoke up even in mild protest, at least not at first.

It was an ironic situation. Alexander had met with Freud before coming to the United States. The latter had feared that psychoanalysis would be watered down or corrupted to make it more palatable to the American medical profession. Alexander thus bore the responsibility of maintaining the purity of analysis. Now he was being accused of revisionism. Blitzsten, an innovator in using analytic techniques to treat psychosis, and Karen, who had challenged established analytic concepts, were cast in the role of conservatives and traditionalists. This incongruity could be explained by the distinctions they each made between theory and practice to justify their positions. Alexander believed he was upholding traditional psychoanalysis; he was only modifying the technique. Karen felt that even though she questioned some theoretical concepts, she was still a true psychoanalyst in practice. This distinction was to become an issue later in New York.

At the spring meeting of the American Orthopsychiatric Association in Chicago, Karen decided to take the opportunity to present a paper on "Conflicts in Mother-Child Relationships."[3] It was at this time that her daughter was going through such a difficult period of adjustment. Karen, herself trying painfully to adjust to a new culture, caught in the rivalries and internal political pressures at the institute, would certainly have had difficulty in handling Renate's problems. Although the paper mentions other cases she treated, much in it could have referred to her own unconscious attitudes, of which she had considerable awareness by now. She notes in her conclusions that a mother's early conflicts with her own parents can lead to related conflicts with her children.

One conclusion may have been particularly relevant to Karen's current relationship with Renate. Childhood fears related to experiences with one's parents can lead to "an immense but vague feeling of insecurity" regarding one's own children. Especially "in this country. . . . Parents . . . are in terror of being disapproved of by their own children, afraid that their own conduct, their drinking, smoking, sexual relations, will be criticized by the children. Or they worry incessantly about whether they are giving the children the proper education and training. The reason is a secret sense of guilt with regard to the children, and leads either to overindulgence in order to avoid their disapproval, or to open hostility."

When Karen had met the analysts in the Washington group at the last meeting of the American Association, she had been asked if she would speak before their society. In April 1933, she finally addressed them on "A Frequent Disturbance in Female Love-life." Although the manuscript of this presentation has been lost, presumably it also dealt with the subject of female masochism, an elaboration of the material she had presented at the American Association. A month later, in May, she gave a talk on the same subject before the Chicago Society.

With the coming of summer, Renate returned to Berlin—by freighter, to economize. Karen followed a month later on a regular steamer. Many changes had occurred during their year away. Biggi had become famous after winning her prize and was now acting on the stage. Marianne was finishing her preclinical years in the University of Berlin Medical School. She had been accepted at the University of Chicago School of Medicine for her last two clinical years, and was looking forward to the change. The two girls were living in a small apartment which their good-natured housekeeper, Frau Böse ("Mrs. Anger"), struggled to keep in order, waiting for the day when Marianne would leave.

On meeting with Boehm, Schultz-Henke, Muller-Braunschweig and many other old friends in the psychoanalytic group, Karen found little cause for comfort. Both the economic and political situations had worsened. Several other analysts had either left or were preparing to leave: Hanns Sachs to Boston, Eitingon to Jerusalem, Simmel to California.

Hitler had become Chancellor in January 1933. In February the Reichstag building went up in flames. This served as justification for the suspension of constitutional guarantees of civil liberties, with imposition of the death penalty for disturbance of the peace. In the last democratic election, in March, even though the Nazis gained votes—largely through intimidation—they still fell far short of the majority needed to govern legally. But Hitler persuaded the Catholic Centrists to vote with the Nazis for his Enabling Act by making promises of favored treatment which he quickly repudiated afterward. He so became the legal absolute ruler of the country in spite of his relative lack of popular support. In April, all

Jews, leftists, liberals and republicans were purged from the civil service. This involved the universities first, then through added decrees, the arts, theater, film industry and the press.

One such order forbade any Jew to be on the council of any scientific organization, including the Berlin Psychoanalytic Society. After consultation with Freud, Boehm agreed to replace Eitingon as president. It was not yet forbidden to practice psychoanalysis, but everyone knew this was the ultimate intention of the authorities. They realized this change of presidents now would never prevent the Nazis from outlawing that "decadent Jewish science," but why hasten it by giving them a pretext? So the organization continued to function, with fifty-six members (seven residing abroad) and thirty candidates. Some anti-analytic physicians of the Charité even took advantage of this opportunity to issue an indictment of the Berlin Society and the practice of psychoanalysis.

In May, students in many university towns staged public book-burnings to symbolize a "burning of the un-German spirit." In Berlin, five thousand students marched five miles along the streets singing Nazi songs, carrying Nazi flags behind cars loaded with books. They had built a huge pyre in front of the Opera House on which they burned thousands of condemned books, including most psychoanalytic ones, while Nazi officials looked on and applauded.

The destruction of Freud's books was symbolically aimed at the theoretical roots of his work. When he learned of this, he reacted typically with a black witticism: "What progress we are making. In the Middle Ages they would have burnt me; nowadays they are content with burning my books." Perhaps it was fortunate that he could not have foreseen the ovens in the death camps only a few years later.

Even Karen's favorite organization, the Medical Society for Psychotherapy, was taken over in June by the Nazis. It was permitted to function under their aegis as the International General Medical Society for Psychotherapy. To remain a member everyone had to agree to subscribe to the principles of the "German National Revolution" and to read *Mein Kampf*. This would then have to serve as the basis for any further psychiatric work. Faced with such restrictions, Ernst Kretschmer, then president, resigned. The society's seventh congress, scheduled to have been held in Vienna in April, was cancelled. Carl Jung then agreed to take over in June as both president and editor of their *Psychotherapy Journal*. His sub-

sequent role is controversial. His infamous remarks distinguishing between Aryan and Jewish psychology—apparently including psychoanalysis—have been taken to indicate an anti-Semitic bias. Jung himself
was later to deny this, claiming that his intention was really to save as
much as possible of the movement. In any event, Jungian analysis remained untouched during the Nazi regime.

A few months later, after Karen's departure, the Nazis began to put
pressure on her friends to exclude all Jews as members, if they wished to
continue to exist. In December the Berlin Society convened a special
meeting, with Ernest Jones presiding. To forestall repeated threats by the
regime to dissolve the society, the few remaining Jewish members "volun-
tarily" offered their resignations.

In August, after Marianne had passed her *Physikum*, she, Renate and
Karen left for Paris. They spent several days there, living in an apartment
in Montmartre provided by a friend of Marianne. Paris did not appear to
have its usual gay, carefree atmosphere. It seemed shabby and gray, even
in the usually lighthearted Left Bank student quarter. Perhaps it was the
weather, perhaps their mood. They were concerned as much about the
situation they had left behind as by the one to which they were returning.

Back in Chicago in September 1933, they found a larger apartment on
Lake Shore Drive. It was high up, overlooking the lake. Spray from the
waves splashed the windows on stormy days. The girls often went swimming from the rocks in front of the building, to the astonishment of the
doorman and passers-by. With a new elderly German housekeeper, the atmosphere of their apartment was more reminiscent of their old home.
The Blitzstens lived around the corner.

Karen's mood lightened, her spirits rose. Perhaps the events she had
witnessed in Berlin had weakened her attachment to her previous life and
roots. She may have felt now that she had to accept these newer values,
even if strange. She could not go home again; she could not return to the
past. Besides, did she not have her two daughters with her? Another
event that must certainly have pleased her and made the situation easier
was the arrival of Erich Fromm as a guest lecturer at the University of
Chicago. She had probably been instrumental in securing the appointment for him. During his stay there he visited Karen often and met many
of the local psychoanalysts and sociologists.

Karen's home soon became a center of social activity, soirees and discussions. The Blitzstens well recall the "analytic weekends" and lunches or dinners at each other's homes. Among the guests who took part were Karl Menninger, Leo Bartemeier, Harold Lasswell, Fromm and others. Karen is remembered as witty, loquacious and scholarly. And yet, in spite of her vitality and almost constant humor, she was not "juicy" or anecdotal, like Sullivan or Blitzsten. They talked about children and schools and education, about political events in Europe and America, about analytic ideas and the role of women. On one occasion, with Blitzsten and Alexander present, Karen admitted that her disagreement with Freud largely concerned his ideas about women. Alexander mentioned Freud's "instinctive" politeness to them; Blitzsten countered that no one ever heard much of Mrs. Freud. They all felt that women were slighted in his theories.

The war had not yet broken out, but serious trouble was obviously brewing. Karen, seemingly intent on not taking sides, remarked, "One side is as bad as the other, what difference does it make?" She was glad to be out of it, and immediately brought up her concern for Brigitte.

Nevertheless, the effect of these friendships and discussions was so stimulating for her that she decided it was time to be adventuresome and splurge. The best way to be truly American was to have a car. So they bought a used car. But first it was necessary to learn to drive. The girls learned easily and quickly. For Karen it was another matter. She had some inherent block either in understanding directions or in following the rules and regulations of the road. Renate suspected that she wished to treat the car like a patient rather than a mechanical object. It should itself know what to do rather than having to be directed. After many lessons from her daughters and some near-misses with other cars, she considered herself ready, an adequate driver. She liked to drive and did so with abandon and apparent disregard for the limitations of reality. Woe unto anyone who had the misfortune to be a passenger with her.

During 1933, Marianne enjoyed her work in the medical school. Even Renate was coming to appreciate her school more. Her English had improved tremendously, the black gym uniforms were no longer required, and she made several good friends. She even shared the lead role in the school's graduation play, *Cradle Song*, with her best friend, Celeste Holm. Whatever the merits of the play itself, it was an exhilarating experience for her and fun for Karen. All three were fast becoming acculturated, or at least learning to understand American ways.

Karen's attitude at the Chicago Institute also changed during this time. The development was similar to that which had occurred at the Berlin Society. She became more outspoken and assertive. Alexander was to note that even though he had previously recognized her as "one of the most independent, skeptical and questioning thinkers of the Berlin group" and had been deeply impressed by "the outstanding clarity of her thought and by her theoretical approach from clinical observations," he now found that their relationship was becoming "neither productive nor congenial." He referred to her "polemic ardor," which was to say, her tendency to express herself forcefully. Apparently he felt this was excessive, since she would "involve herself in controversy even where her ideas were not only a confirmation of Freud's views, but where they represented a valuable contribution to existing knowledge." To him, this was evidence of an intense "resentment against Freud, which expressed itself in her attempt to discredit some of his most fundamental contributions, with the ambitious goal of revising the whole psychoanalytic doctrine." However, he believed that this was "a task for which she was not fully prepared,"[4] a belief he apparently imparted to her. It was this opinion, that she was overreaching her real abilities, which hurt her—or her pride—the most, and which was soon to move her toward systematizing her ideas. Some of her other critics at the institute thought that she was becoming arrogant in her indignation at some of Alexander's ideas.

As recalled by several students there, her course and her clinical seminars in psychoanalytic technique (which she gave in 1933) were exciting and innovative. They combined the old and the new. She continued to use such classical concepts as transference, unconscious oedipal feelings and defenses against them, death wishes, castration anxiety, and oral or anal needs. In combination with these, she introduced newer interpersonal and culturally oriented defensive stances like unemotionality, intellectualization, seeming obedience and compliance, propitiating attitudes and needs for superiority. In her technique, she would start analyzing the more conscious, on-going attitudes and gradually penetrate to the deeper, earlier childhood ones, always emphasizing the need to seek each and all intermediate attitudes responsible for the preceding one. Resistances had to be analyzed—or at least worked on—first. Behavior manifested toward the analyst had to be considered first in terms of unconscious present feelings toward others. Only then could they be seen in terms of infantile attitudes toward parents, now being transferred onto the analyst. Rules for terminating the analysis could be clearly defined: No ideal end-point was to be sought after, the patient would go on analyzing himself after official termination

In addition, she and Alexander cochaired weekly case-discussion meetings with the candidates. As in Berlin, the students here were impressed by the clarity and logic of her expositions, her ability to lay bare a patient's complex personality and sort it out into simpler, related attitudes, needs, feelings and ideas. This was most helpful to the young analysts-to-be, who were still insecure and needed definite rules to follow. But what impressed them most was her bearing: In spite of her outwardly calm expression, she seemed to radiate an infectious enthusiasm that stimulated them.

In the late fall of 1933, Karen spoke at the Chicago Society on "Misuses of Psychoanalysis in Daily Practice."[5] Then in December, without much rest, she and Blitzsten went to the winter meeting of the American Psychoanalytic Association in Washington. Her previous paper on feminine masochism had caused discussion since then, and she was asked to speak on the topic again, to elaborate on some of her ideas. At the business meeting, she was appointed to the Committee on Membership Regulations, which would draft the rules to be applied to all future American psychoanalytic societies (along with Blitzsten, Rado, William Silverberg, Abraham Kardiner and Sullivan) and to the Committee on Establishment and Certification (of local societies). To be once again in the company of her friends from Washington did her much good, and gave her a feeling of support in the situation with Alexander. She was also asked if she would consider teaching at the Washington-Baltimore Institute during the coming year. This would mean commuting once monthly for perhaps six months. She would be officially named to the teaching faculty. She agreed.

On their return to Chicago, she and Blitzsten spent one meeting of the Chicago Society in January reporting on the Washington meeting. Then Karen was off again. That same month she was invited to speak before a special combined meeting of the New York Neurological Society and the Section of Neurology and Psychiatry of the Academy of Medicine. Her presentation was an expanded version of her previous talk in Chicago: "Concepts and Misconcepts of the Psychoanalytic Method." Here she reiterated some of the methodological points she usually covered in her courses on technique. The focus was primarily upon the concept and technique of free association, one of the major therapeutic tools prescribed for psychoanalysis.

As free association had been originally defined and practiced by Freud, it was intended to provide access to the patient's unconscious thoughts. By interpreting themes derived from the patient's uncensored utterances, the analyst could, at least in principle, relate present attitudes to early sexual feelings or identifications with the parents. Karen felt this was a misconception, for several reasons. The patient might unconsciously distort the facts, presenting only selected aspects. Or he might distort his feelings and emotions out of the need for self-deception. Or he might be consciously controlling his speech and emotions. Or he might verbalize impersonally without relating to thoughts he was bringing out. The analyst's interpretations could also be too vague or arbitrary if based on theoretical assumptions about infantile relationships.

However, this procedure could be rendered clearer and more precise. The patient's emotional reactions during the sessions could reveal more about his attitudes or psychic trends than his verbal communications. Visible reactions toward the analyst could explain his present attitudes toward others with greater certainty than they could those from the distant past. To try to explain a person's present attitudes immediately in terms of presumed infantile relations is to leave out all the intermediate life situations and attitudinal links in his developmental chain. Besides, intense interpersonal reactions occurring during the analysis could impede fruitful analytic work. These must therefore be understood in terms of their immediate underlying motives and emotional causes; only then could their infantile roots be elucidated.

Karen then demonstrated how each defensive reaction, feeling or attitude exhibited during the analysis could result from some specific preexisting and deeper attitude, which in turn was determined by still another deeper one, and so forth. In principle, the process of each psychoanalysis—although different from any other—could be unraveled according to a diagrammed schema, one factor leading to another. The personality was envisaged somewhat like an onion, with each layer being peeled off until one arrived at the deepest core emotion.

Although she admitted this was an oversimplification both of the personality and of the psychoanalytic process, the principle was nonetheless valid. It was her attempt to apply the rigorous precision of the scientific method to what had generally been a somewhat subjective, perhaps vague procedure. Even Dr. Bernard Sachs, the New York neurologist and foe of psychoanalysis, was able to say in his discussion of the several presentations that hers was one analytic paper he could accept. It was both clinical and scientific.

Indeed this was a significant paper for Karen. It was the first of the rare occasions on which she defined technique and thereby challenged a cherished and basic tenet of Freudian practice. Freud had introduced this free-associative method as a sine qua non of analysis, after abandoning his previous method of hypnosis.

Equally important, she was now modifying several theoretical concepts. She was placing the primary focus of attention on the patient's present attitudes and later life experiences as the causes of neurosis. She did not completely abandon the infantile oedipal feelings, but these receded into a place of secondary importance. This issue was to become of crucial significance for her later on. That she did not totally disavow the Oedipus complex would be taken by some supporters as evidence that she was still a Freudian analyst. On the other hand, Ernest Jones was soon to say that her method of analyzing the personality from the outside in, so to speak, was a reversal of the true Freudian perspective, namely to work from the inside instinctual core to the surface. In addition, here she expanded the concept of "unconscious" and its corollary, unconscious motivation and determinism. Instead of *the* unconscious, a repository of infantile attitudes or events, it now became unconscious functioning in a broader—albeit still deterministic—sense.

This presentation was her introduction to the New York community of physicians, psychiatrists and psychoanalysts. Though she could not have foreseen it then, it was to influence her future professional life and status. It also highlighted the incongruity of her position vis-à-vis Alexander in Chicago, inasmuch as she had been teaching these ideas at the Chicago Institute. On the one hand they were in keeping with his demands for shorter psychoanalytic methods and his scientific approach. But on the other, they challenged traditional psychoanalytic theories, a major issue with him.

In February, she gave her paper on female masochism again before the Chicago Society. It was evidently a provocative subject, and everyone wished to say something about it. Partly as a result, she and Blitzsten were invited later that spring to speak at the Menninger Clinic in Topeka.

Karl Menninger, one of the few midwestern psychiatrists, had become converted to psychoanalysis at the famous 1930 meeting of the American Association for Mental Health. He had been analyzed by Alexander and had completed his training at the Chicago Institute. When he returned home, he intended to build his father's small clinic into a major psychoanalytically oriented center. His inviting prominent members of the Chicago faculty was part of this plan. Besides, he had become a good friend of Karen's during his stay in Chicago, and a frequent visitor at her social evenings, as well as almost a regular at Blitzsten's seminars. These Monday-night meetings had, by the end of 1934, become so popular and well attended that they were no longer the intimate seminar workshops he had originally intended.

By this time, the friction and increasing strain between Karen and Alexander was affecting her. She was objecting to his proposals more openly than before. He was irritated by some of her ideas and innovations. Blitzsten suspected that part of the problem may have been her need to dominate and consequent difficulty in accepting a subordinate position. Alexander was to write that he himself felt their differences to be mainly professional, a result of the extent to which she wished to revise the classical theories. "Hers was a revolutionary approach which implied the repudiation of so many of Freud's fundamental concepts."[6] He saw this, specifically, as being too "antibiological and antigenetic." By contrast, he considered himself more evolutionary, preferring slower change. Significantly enough, he too was to be included in the same company of "Neo-Freudians" as Karen not long afterwards. It was inevitable that he notice the cultural differences that had struck Karen, and upon which she had based her own newer thinking. As he put it, "The psychoanalytic material was different here from that of Europe." In this country he found "the freshness of a youthful world, deeply involved in the problems of adolescence, full of energy, unsure of itself, hectically competitive, always on trial." These attitudes contrasted with the European "regressive mentality of a disillusioned, tired old man, living on the forced vigor of a second childhood." Like Karen, he "recognized the need for re-evaluation of cultural factors in personality development," and shared her views "concerning certain gaps in traditional psychoanalytic formulations."[7]

In spite of these differences and even after she left Chicago, he was to remain friends with her. At meetings thereafter, they were often seen together. In 1950, at a luncheon interval, Alexander remarked rather sadly to Frederick Weiss, his former Berlin analysand, that he was only then really appreciating her viewpoint. It had taken a long time!

By September 1934, Karen's two-year preliminary contract with the Chicago Institute would be terminating. The decision had to be made whether to continue or not. Karen was disheartened. Her daughter remembers the distress she felt each morning at the ordeal of having to face the difficult situation with Alexander. She had come with high hopes. Perhaps they had been illusions. Was Alexander right when he claimed that she was only a rebel rather than a truly creative innovator, that she "did have excellent critical faculties but did not supply anything substantially new and valid for what she tried to destroy."[8] This opinion continued to rankle her.

Yet Karen would have stayed on anyway, in spite of everything. She still needed the money to finish putting her two daughters through school. She could not afford to give up the job and salary, the only security she had in this strange new country. Besides, quitting would mean leaving her daughters. She would be totally alone, alien. She was almost fifty; wasn't this too old to start all over again? On the other hand, there was something alluring, exciting about the prospect of being free again. She had such a strong desire to develop her own ideas, to disprove Alexander's remarks. It was a frightening dilemma!

Talking it over with her daughters, she was finally persuaded to leave her security once more and take the step. They would manage with very little. It would be not only good for her, but absolutely necessary. She had so much to do yet. So she decided to sell the car after her short vacation and go to New York to be on her own. Perhaps now she could make still another beginning!

At the thirteenth International Congress in Lucerne, at the end of August, Alexander startled the membership by announcing that the partnership between him and Karen was dissolved as of that date.

XIV
NEW YORK:
MOVING UPWARD

"My desire to make a critical re-evaluation of psychoanalytic
theories had its origin in a dissatisfaction with therapeutic
results. I found that almost every patient offered problems
for which our accepted psychoanalytic knowledge offered
no solution and which therefore remained unsolved.

My purpose is not to show what is wrong with psychoanalysis, but, through eliminating the debatable elements, to
enable psychoanalysis to develop to the height of its potentialities. . . . I do not expect them to accept my formulations in their entirety, for they are neither complete nor
final. Nor are they meant to be the beginning of a new psychoanalytical 'school.' "

—*New Ways in Psychoanalysis*

In August of 1934, Karen found her first New York home: the Surrey
Hotel, on Seventy-sixth Street just off Madison Avenue. The hotel itself,
more residential than transient, was rather elegant without being too expensive, with its canopied entrance, its doorman, and its overstuffed
leather sofas in the small, wood-paneled lobby. Elegant perhaps, but
more conservative and dignified than modern or flamboyant. "Distinguished" would be a more appropriate term. And she would be able to
see patients here without their feeling overwhelmed by its opulence—as
she had felt in her first New York hotel experience—or depressed by any
hint of shabbiness. The fairly tall building, of some fourteen floors, ended
the street of low brown- and graystone houses like an exclamation point at
the end of a sentence. Many of those three- and four-story houses still had
the stone stairway leading up to the first floor, and their baroque sculpted
stone ornaments around the roof edge and windows. All in all, the street
gave one a reassuring feeling of substance and solidity, of traditional
middle-class conservatism. It was reminiscent of many similar streets in

Berlin. From her upper-floor window, looking over and beyond the roofs of the adjacent low buildings, Karen could see the greenery of Central Park a block away. Not much of a view, not the overlook toward Lake Maggiore or Lake Michigan or even Lincoln Park, but a glimpse of nature nonetheless. And close enough for a leisurely walk. Besides, it was centrally located. The Psychoanalytic Institute and all her friends were close by. Sullivan was soon to move to Sixty-fourth Street, Fromm lived on Sixty-sixth and Clara Thompson on Eighty-third.

Thompson had returned to New York in 1933 after a two-year psychoanalysis with Ferenczi in Budapest. She had turned to him for her training, first in 1928, at Sullivan's urging; he had been impressed by Ferenczi's learning during the latter's visit to the United States in 1926. As one of the first organizers of the Washington-Baltimore Psychoanalytic Society, Thompson had been its first president. Along with Sullivan and Silverberg and then with Karen, she continued to commute to Washington until 1939 to teach there. By temperament and personality, the two women were similar in some ways but quite different in others. One colleague who knew them both at this time commented that even though both had needs for leadership, domination and prestige, Karen was more like "a Brunnhilde . . . in her carriage, dignity, forcefulness and charisma. She fascinated and at the same time frightened many of the students. Clara was more tender, encouraging and emotionally involved." Both seemed to have felt disadvantaged as a woman in a masculine world. Thompson's interest, like Horney's, remained particularly focused on the psychology of women. She, too, constantly affirmed their ability and rights, without being a militant feminist.

She was a quiet woman, who sometimes used to refer to herself as the "silent Swede." Like Karen, she had a most perceptive clinical acumen and was a dedicated humanistic analyst. She also was a most independent individual who would speak up readily and could not be easily intimidated. The two became fast friends in 1934 within their little circle. Karen persuaded Thompson to become a member of the New York Psychoanalytic in 1935.

Karen was barely settled in when she was terribly saddened by a letter, probably from Karl Muller-Braunschweig, announcing the death of her dear friend, Groddeck. He had meant so much to her that she needed to write Frau Groddeck at once:

[188]

My Dear Frau Groddeck:

Because I was constantly traveling, I only now received the news of your husband's death. I am deeply shocked. I felt Dr. Groddeck was one of the few analysts who was a complete human being [ein ganzer Mensch], strong, courageous and warm. It was painful to me that I could not establish a closer rapport with him, even though I was really seeking it. Those analysts whom I respected and liked, formed in some way an attachment to him too: Liebermann, Loofs, Ferenczi, Eitingon and Fromm.

I would also like to express one more thought, even though it may sound indiscreet—I had the strong feeling that you understood, in a wonderful way, how to support and protect him exactly as he needed it. I believe that was a great accomplishment, and it was for a man who was really worth it.

With heartfelt sympathy,
Your Karen Horney

How much this letter tells about Karen, she who complained that women in general were denigrated, were relegated to an inferior position by men and male society. Here she is praising the feminine and wifely role of helpmeet and assistant, in the self-effacing woman Frau Groddeck was known to be. Karen, too, had deep needs to be self-effacing and loved; perhaps she too would have wished to be dependent upon and taken care of by a strong and dominating protector.

In professional circles in New York, Karen's reputation had preceded her. The favorable impression she had made as an astute clinician at the New York Academy of Medicine the previous January now rebounded upon her. She was greeted warmly at the New York Psychoanalytic Society. She was one of the first notable, recognized German-speaking Freudian analysts to arrive—along with Rado and Sandor Lorand, who had already been in New York for some time. Most of the faculty and members had met her at psychoanalytic meetings and some had attended her courses or been supervised by her in Berlin. At this time, most of the Americans there were still sympathetic to the plight of the immigrants. They considered Karen a refugee, though in fact she had not been forced to flee, being neither Jewish nor political. She did not consider herself one.

At the New York Institute, she was assigned to teach a course of clinical conferences. She also began to be referred candidates-in-training for analysis and supervision. In addition, other analysts as well as nonanalytic physicians began to send her patients. One of her first nonmedical sources of referrals, with which she had been in touch right after her arrival, was the United Jewish Aid Society, soon to become the Jewish Family Service. They were seeking psychiatric consultants on a volunteer panel to help and supervise their social-work staff. Most of their patients were refugees. Rose Landers, then its director, recalls how Karen was "approachable, understanding and helpful to both the social workers and patients. She seemed so down to earth, able to meet patients on their level. They felt at home with her and peaceful. She was dynamic and full of life. Our social workers all worshipped her."

Karen gave a short talk to their workers on "The Restricted Applications of Psychoanalysis to Social Work."[1] In it she sketched out her conception of what constituted a neurosis. Three groups of factors combined to give rise to neurosis. The first is an infantile fear-anxiety state occurring when a parent's neurotic attitudes cause intimidation or frustration of the child's instinctive needs. This basic state also includes rebellious hostility repressed from awareness. The second is later-developed character trends, needed as defenses against the original repressed but still frightening attitudes. These later trends restrict, inhibit and narrow the person's lifestyle. The third is an actual conflict situation in the present that causes the hitherto adequately repressed impulses to emerge into awareness. These generate acute neurotic symptoms. Given such a neurotic character structure, the effectiveness of any therapeutic intervention will be inversely proportional to the previous duration of the illness; will depend on the intensity of the actual traumatic situation; will vary with the extensiveness of the neurotic inhibitions. The severity of the neurosis can be estimated empirically, based on the degree of impairment the patient suffers in his sex life, in his work and in his relations, in his flexibility in handling money, and in the paralyzing effect of his inhibitions.

Karen proposed professional limitations as guidelines for the social worker. Resolution of a severe neurosis cannot be brought about except by psychoanalysis. Even so, some symptomatic improvement can be produced when the present conflict situation is relatively important compared to the underlying neurotic state. In such cases, care must be taken not to stir up the deeper anxieties or touch on the major defense attitudes. The less severe neurosis can be helped a great deal by uncovering the actual conflict situation and then relating it to the symptom dynamically. While social-work therapy will help specific situations, the main task will "naturally be to let the patients themselves see their problems."

While a personal analysis is not mandatory for every social worker, it is essential when disturbing personal character difficulties interfere with his or her therapeutic work. The application of analytic principles by social workers "has to be definitely different from the usual analytic technique."

This little-known paper was a milestone in the development of Karen's thought, not so much for its subject matter but as a transition point between two approaches to psychology. It was her first attempt at systematizing, her first reference to the "neurotic structure of a life." It was written just after her breach with Alexander. His charges that she wished only to revise, without having anything to put in place of what she would destroy, must have struck home. Now she was, wittingly or unwittingly, beginning to create her own theory.

Within six months her practice schedule was filled. Her worries about earning a living on her own had been groundless. Some analysts practicing today recall seeing her for supervision at her hotel suite.

By the winter of 1934–35, she began her lecture-discussion courses at the Washington-Baltimore Institute, as she had agreed to do. She was officially named Lecturer with the Professorial rank in Psychoanalysis. From then on, through 1935 and 1936, she commuted almost every month, alternating between the Shoreham Hotel in Washington and the Lord Baltimore Hotel in Baltimore. Her course was titled "Some Fundamental Problems of the Psychoanalytic Method." Following the same format as in Chicago, she covered the topics of transference, the patient's reactions, the analyst's personality, the technique of interpretation, working through, and interventions other than interpretations.

True to their promise, after their mother's departure, her two daughters moved into a tiny and inexpensive but homey apartment on the North Side, close to the University of Chicago campus. Both seemed to be finding themselves and loved their college work. In fact the two girls jointly managed to buy an old Ford with a rumble seat. As Renate recalls, the rides with their friends in this jalopy were the high points that "wonderful year." Marianne, much like Karen, found special joy in her clinical casework, in human contact. Karen's various analytic colleagues and students—the Blitzstens, Leon Saul, even Alexander—looked in on her and took an interest in her progress. Other students in her class remember her as rather shy and gentle, extremely bright, a serious student and hard worker, "a person who knew what she was doing." So much so that she was often assigned to present patients to other medical students as a teacher. (She graduated from medical school at the unusually early age of twenty-two; she herself felt she was too young, that she lacked maturity.) Karen, proud of her daughters, came to visit them over the Christmas vacation of 1934.

At the beginning of the summer of 1935, Renate dropped out of school to return to Berlin—by freighter again. She was impatient to marry her boyfriend, with whom she had become engaged by correspondence. Although Karen had not foreseen this decision, she simply acknowledged it without objection or show of surprise, and wished Renate good luck. She confided to her friend Dorothy Blitzsten that she would have preferred her daughter to continue her schooling and was not happy at her leaving. Whether this sang-froid was a positive attitude of noninterference, a desire to encourage her daughter's self-reliance, a feeling of silent resentment, or an attitude of detachment and indifference is difficult to determine.

In May 1935, she was officially elected a member of the New York Psychoanalytic Society. Incidentally, by a curious coincidence, she was still listed at the time as a "Member, Residing Abroad" of the Berlin Psychoanalytic Society (until 1937). This could have occurred because of difficulties with the mails, but in any event it kept her informed of psychoanalytic events and facilitated her participation in the Berlin programs.

Later in May she spoke at the annual meeting of American Psychoanalytic Association. This time her topic was "Certain Reservations to the Concept of Psychic Bisexuality,"[2] reminiscent of discussions she had had with Groddeck. Now it was reconsidered in the new context of her present concern with "moral" masochism. While she did not question the existence of an inherent predisposition to bisexuality, she called attention to the uncertainty of scope and function of such a predisposition in development. She pointed out that the characteristics of the other sex are often adopted as screens for sado-masochistic drives. In such patients, the underlying masochism constitutes the primary dynamics, rather than the apparent bisexual wishes. The main therapeutic focus should be on these deeper trends. In this paper, too, while retaining some of the instinctual motivations of the Freudian theory, she was reversing the causal sequence usually attributed to them.

The next three years, from 1936 to 1939, were good ones for Karen. In a photograph taken by Sullivan in the winter of 1936, she appears younger than her fifty years, with a vigorous and determined look on her face. Gertrude Lederer, who soon was to become her lifelong confidante and Marianne's mother-in-law, recalls her first brief encounter with Karen at this time on Times Square. "She was bare-headed and white-haired . . . a square solid appearance and so darkly tanned that I seriously thought she had dark skin by nature. She was dressed in something very colorful, looking like an Indian. But I was fascinated by her eyes that looked deep into you, even though only in passing. It was a face one could never forget." These were prosperous years for Karen as well. The Great Depression was practically over and people could better afford psychoanalysis. She was receiving more referrals than she could handle and was in turn referring them to colleagues. Socially her life was active and full. Sullivan had organized a small group in 1930 with the three other Washingtonians that began to meet weekly for dinner and informal discussion. Since Prohibition was still in effect, they would gather in a speakeasy. He whimsically named this group the Zodiac Club. Each of the participants was given a fanciful animal name, supposedly representative of his personality. Sullivan was a horse, Thompson a puma, Silverberg a gazelle, Edward Shipley an okapi, Jimmy Sullivan (Harry's stepson) a seahorse. When Karen joined in 1934 she became a water buffalo. Sullivan was not only fond of using symbols, but also quite impressed by cultural factors, especially after his contacts with Edward Sapir, the cultural anthropologist. In this respect his views and Karen's were similar. The horses head, in particular, had a very personal symbolic meaning for him, derived from two sources. It represented the Chinese symbol of eternal life. It also harked back to the Irish folk tale about the "West Wind, the horse who runs with the earth into the future." It was thereby associated with all the stories he so loved from his childhood.

After the end of Prohibition, the group met in a restaurant, usually followed by a late evening at one of their homes. These meetings were, for Karen, reminiscent of her college and informal professional gatherings in Berlin. The discussions were free and far-ranging, animated and sometimes heated, of psychoanalysis, politics, philosophy, art, religion. Karen is remembered as having been, more often than not, rather taciturn at these discussions. She was not anecdotal like Sullivan. The others often had to draw her into the conversation. This was especially noticeable when recent psychoanalytic movements in this country were mentioned with which she may have felt unfamiliar. She was more vocal about European events and experiences—especially after a good meal and a few drinks. But they were also struck by her reserve about her own ideas on psychoanalysis. She seemed to be particularly reticent—or secretive— about discussing her current work with the group, as if she feared her ideas would be stolen from her. It was often difficult to get her personal opinion. She gave the impression that she needed to control whatever she might say, to put her own copyright upon it.

The Blitzstens came in from Chicago fairly often. The happy evenings with the various members of the Zodiac were a continuation of their socializing in Chicago. Among others who joined them on occasion were Hortense Powdermaker, a friend who was interested in cultural psychoanalysis, Randolph Paul and Jerome Frank, two lawyer friends, and Margaret Bourke-White, the photographer, as well as other people from the stage or ballet. There was much partying for a while. Dorothy felt that Karen stood out not only as "attractive, well-dressed and sophisticated, with a slightly European air," but as having a special joie de vivre and a tremendous vitality. The small social circle was described as "a group of unconventional people doing conventional things. We all had our idiosyncracies. Karen and Silverberg were the most conventional among us." For a while Karen and Sullivan were particularly friendly and seemed to have much in common. They often would go, before or after the Zodiac get-togethers, to jazz concerts, the theater, or night-spots like the Blue Angel. However, this relationship appeared to cool after he moved to Sixty-Fourth Street.

Erich Fromm was another of these friends, even though he was not an official member of the Zodiac circle. After completing his lectureship in Chicago, he had come to New York, where, in addition to his private practice, he was working at the International Institute of Social Research at Columbia University. He often dined or visited with Karen. Above all, though, they influenced each other's thinking profoundly. One of the group felt that Karen learned sociology from Fromm and he psychoanalysis from her.

As the situation worsened in Europe, other German or Austrian analysts who had known Karen appeared in New York. Many sought her out for advice or simply for friendship. Some remained in New York, others moved on to different cities.

Edith Weigert, for instance, filled Karen in on the events occurring in both the Berlin and Vienna psychoanalytic communities. In 1938, she had just come to the United States after a five-year sojourn in Turkey, having hoped vainly for the demise of Hitler. She brought greetings from Eitingon in Jerusalem, where he had organized a new psychoanalytic society. She was then seeking analytic connections in Washington, where she planned to settle. Karen referred her to Sullivan. She advised Edith to compliment him, since he was a highly sensitive man and susceptible to flattery.

Another visitor was Robert Fleiss, who often discussed therapeutic problems with her, both in her home and at the New York Institute. In his analyses, he often tended to worry excessively about his patients' families. In one such informal discussion at the institute, in which Karen participated, someone remarked that she seemed to know how deep to go, when not to get too close to the patient during the analytic relationship. Her advice to him—and to several other analysts taking part—was that it was sometimes wiser to pay less attention to the traditional sexual problems. She had a special ability to activate others and therefore always gathered a small circle of listeners. Those around her noted that she seemed to be different from the other immigrant analysts. She never appeared sad at having been displaced and having lost her country, never felt uprooted. On the contrary, she generally appeared to be satisfied with her lot, enjoying life in New York. One colleague invented a term to describe her: *"verglückt"* (happy-go-lucky). However, some questioned whether her attitude and the advice she gave might not have betrayed an unwillingness to discuss her own personal emotional problems, an avoidance.

Another old analytic friend who visited her a few times was Wilhelm Reich. Karen had known him fairly well for some time in Berlin. A dissatisfied Marxist, he was also interested in the relation of the social structure to the individual. But his position was too radical for her. She had participated in the discussion of his paper at the Berlin Society in 1932; it had been one of the few psychopolitical papers presented there. On that occasion, he had shouted that German fascism was an inevitable consequence of their patriarchal, authoritarian family system. His view was that Marxism was not psychological enough, and Freudian psychoanalysis was not sociological enough. Yet simply adding them together would not suffice; he had to create a new synthesis. She did not agree either with his theory of sexual stasis—the damming up of sexual energy by incomplete orgasmic release—as the cause of neurosis. She could accept that unresolved emotional conflict could affect the sex life, but in the broader sense, more through total sexual relationships rather than simply through orgasmic potency. She agreed only partially with his idea that the body was the major fixation point for the energy inhibited by neurotic conflicts. His concept of "character armor" was too pat for her. Certainly she accepted that many somatic symptoms, including muscle tension, were caused by conflict, even as Groddeck and Simmel had insisted. In fact, during her analytic work, she would often send the patient to a physiotherapist for concurrent exercise, dance therapy, relaxation work or massage, especially after she again met Else Durham and Gertrude Lederer in New York, both practicing this type of therapy.

In 1933, Reich published *The Mass Psychology of Fascism*. Shortly afterward, in his book *Character Analysis*, he had emphasized the need for analysis of the total character structure, particularly referring to behavior traits used as a defense against repressed needs or attitudes. For the Freudians, this constituted primarily an analysis of resistances, later to be considered "ego analysis," but it was nevertheless a definite advance over the earlier Freudian concepts. Karen also advocated the general notion of analyzing "resistances first" in her courses, but she differed over what constituted such resistance. Reich had, for all practical purposes, broken from the official psychoanalytic movement in 1934. The final break had occurred over his interpretation of the masochistic character—the same issue that Karen was so interested in. To some extent their views coincided here. Instead of seeing Freud's self-destructive urge ("driven by the death instinct") as responsible, he attributed it to an "anguished cry for love."

These questions offered them considerable common grounds for discussion. Later, in his autobiography, Reich was to complain that Karen had "stolen" some of his ideas for her own, although without his most important elements, "without sex, without bioenergy, without libido, without anything."[3] Karen openly acknowledged her debt to him for his stimulation and for his stress on the need to analyze the neurotic defensive character traits. In point of fact, none of his ideas did appear in her theories as such. The concepts of the need to analyze the total personality (character analysis) had been previously advanced by others—Alexander and Paul Federn, for example—besides Reich. Karen herself had been moving in this direction for at least seven years. Furthermore, her notion of analyzing defensive characterological resistances whenever they occurred, before exposing new conflicts, had also been presented several years before.

Otto Rank, too, returned from his stay in Paris at the end of 1934 to face the ambiguous, if not outright hostile, attitudes of his former Freudian colleagues. He visited Karen to discuss this situation, with which she was certainly familiar and would have sympathized. He invited her to participate in a series of lectures he was putting together at the New York School of Social Work on "The Organization of the Self." She suggested other speakers who could contribute: Kurt Koffka, the Gestalt psychologist, and Ruth Benedict, as a socio-ethnologist.

Rank, in turn, sympathized with Karen's disagreement with Freud on the question of female sexuality, which would have coincided with his own rebellious stance. He had written to his secretary in 1933, in response to a comment she had made about women in psychoanalysis, ". . . together with other phenomena in the world (for example, Karen Horney, who is now in Chicago), it seems to me this is the natural revenge of women against the 'masculinizing psychology.' Karen Horney is the closest and simplest example, because she does it openly. In that sense it was a very clever move of Alexander to bring her to Chicago, first of all to get the chestnuts out of the fire without harming his own fingers thereby. Freud is trying his best to accept these things, evidenced by his article on feminine sexuality."[4]

However, after the appearance in 1937 of Karen's first book, *The Neurotic Personality of Our Time*, Rank's attitude apparently changed. This was shown in an anecdote related in his biography. One of his patients, who had been "Freudized" for four years, brought in Karen Horney's book. "He [the patient] asked whether I [Rank] had read it. I said no. Then he said I didn't have to. I had said all of it in the last fifteen years."

While Karen disagreed with many of Rank's ideas, she found some of them most congenial. In particular, she liked his emphasis on the importance of spontaneous emotional experience, both as a healthy attribute of the child and as a necessary prerequisite for real awareness during analysis. She was often to cite this in her later books. Also, his description of the internal conflict and dualisms involved in the creative process was to influence her own thought. His concept of "the inherent striving after totality which forces [the person] in the direction of surrender to life" was close to her own later notion of self-realization.

Among her nonanalytic friends of this period, none was to be closer to her or to have more of an influence on her than her "Dear Paulus," the name she insisted on calling Paul Tillich. He had arrived in New York only a few months before her, invited to join the faculties of Columbia, the "university-in-exile"—the New School for Social Research—and the Union Theological Seminary. He had chosen the latter. He had been forced to flee Germany as a liberal after being dismissed from his professorship in philosophy at Frankfurt because of his criticism of the Nazi regime. As a Religious Socialist—a movement he had helped to found—he had long opposed the regime for their "brutal ideology of force," and had recently published an indictment of their program. During his five-year stay in Frankfurt, he had met a number of people known to Karen also: Kurt Goldstein, the psychiatrist, Max Wertheimer, the Gestalt psychologist, Karl Mannheim, Max Horkheimer, Theodore Adorno, Max Marcuse and Fromm, all sociologists. Karen was to meet these men again during her work at the New School, and their ideas influenced her own.

She quickly renewed her close friendship with both Hannah and Paul Tillich, exchanging visits with them both in the city and later when they moved to the Hamptons. Occasionally they would dine out or go to the theater or an art museum together. As Hannah has related in her autobiography, at times Karen's psychological counsel helped them through difficult moments. More significantly, perhaps, Karen absorbed many of Tillich's ideas during their discussions. Yet it was not one-sided; in his subsequent theological works, he took over some of her ideas, giving them a religious relevance. And how they both liked to discuss! Tillich was an articulate man, with a toweringly brilliant intellect covering many fields of erudition. But his was not an ivory-tower intellectualism. He was also a warm, emotional and expressive person. He enjoyed the isolation needed to think and write; he also enjoyed human contact, drew people toward him and could be witty, charming, urbane and seductive with women. An intense, all-embracing curiosity combined with an insatiable lust for living constantly drew him into experiencing everything new he could find. When he first arrived in America, he and his wife wandered all over the city to taste, touch and see all that was different. His was, all told, a complex, multifaceted personality.

In some ways his philosophy resembled that of Schweitzer, by whom both he and Karen had been influenced. Although he was a romantic idealist in the tradition of Fichte and Schelling, he believed in the "repudiation of every social Utopia." Perfection was thus unattainable. He felt that theology is, and must be, involved with culture, and must explain its problems, i.e., must be "apologetic." The theologian must be committed, must be directed by "immediate experience of something ultimate in value and being of which one can become intuitively aware." He blamed other religious philosophies for their lack of involvement with society. For him, culture was the spiritual creativity manifest in every area of life. It consisted of meanings one supplies that are conditioned by society and its restrictions; religion, of meanings that are personal, subjective and not conditioned by society. Bourgeois, capitalist society—meaning chiefly the Nazi regime he had just left—was irrational, demonic and profane. "It has lost its ultimate reference, its center of meaning, its spiritual substance." To introduce rational clarity would banish the demons and might introduce God, but would deny the holy as transcendental. It would still be secular. The technical mentality tends to secularize, brings about a loss of reverence for nature and eventually reduces the individual to a machine.

He maintained that theology, the science of religion, consisted of a polar, dialectic relationship between "the Yes and the No." Grace is a Gestalt, unifying the two. To accept one without the other is unproductive. Life is a process of actualizing potentials, whether in the organic, psychological, spiritual or historical dimension. The historical differs from the others in that it would include the element of fulfillment as well and implies a process in a particular direction. The individual is the bearer of history, the reality in which history occurs.

These were some of the concepts he had expressed before 1940, the early period of his contact with Karen. The relevance of these concepts to her theory is evident. Attention to the culture, the role of historical development, actualization of one's potential, the need to be involved (in therapy) all appeared. As their relationship continued into the period when both were creating their most significant work, each gave to and took from the other. Tillich later became both more of an existentialist and more interested in individual psychology—probably as a result of Karen's influence. Thus he paralleled her definition of neurosis in his own definition of man's existential situation: "man experiences his present situation in terms of disruption, conflict, self-destruction, meaninglessness and despair in all the realms of his life . . . he seeks reality to overcome the estrangement of existence. In such estrangement, he is cut off from what he is."[5] But Tillich's philosophical theology became an existential ontology, while Karen's theories remained rooted in empirical and observable human attitudes.

These years were good, too, in that Karen's mind was at its most active and productive.

In the fall of 1935, Karen met Dr. Clara Meyer through a mutual physician friend. Dr. Meyer was not only an enthusiast of psychoanalysis but was also the Dean of the New School for Social Research in New York. The school was famous for its innovative, forward-looking program of adult education, often on controversial topics. It had always favored psychoanalytic speakers, as they generally drew a large audience. Alfred Adler, Otto Rank, Sandor Ferenczi, Fritz Wittels and Sandor Lorand had all been guest lecturers and had proven tremendously popular. Karen was asked if she would be interested in presenting her ideas in a series of lectures. She accepted eagerly. It would be an opportunity for her not only to develop her views while preparing the lectures but also to reach a wider audience than otherwise possible. Besides, she probably would get some referrals from a type of person best suited for analysis, the highly motivated intellectual. And not least of all, it would be a step in the direction she had long desired, toward a possible professorship. True, the New School was not a university, but no one could tell where it might lead.

Her invitation was facilitated now by a project of the New School's president, Dr. Alvin Johnson, to help refugee European intellectuals.

This charitable and dedicated humanitarian saw what was to come in Europe and the plight many refugees would find themselves in on arriving here. As he himself has explained in a later letter to Mrs. Laura Fermi, wife of the famous physicist—themselves both refugees—he made extreme efforts to find places for as many as possible in famous American universities. When he soon discovered that many universities could not, or would not, accept refugee scholars, he conceived the idea of a "university-in-exile." This would be a complex of universities with separate professional faculties—law, medicine,,engineering, arts, physical sciences—in various places and would be supported by funds from charitable foundations. The Faculty of Social Sciences was to be at the New School in New York. He had to drop this grand project when other emergency committees were formed, with easier access to the great foundations. But the New School faculty remained active and became famous. As one result of his efforts, over one hundred European scholars were gainfully resettled here. Another result was the gradual change in academia's attitude toward the foreign scholar and toward scholarship itself. The foreign scholar became more accepted and scholarship became more recognized in this country as a cosmopolitan rather than a merely American activity.

A third result was the fruitful collaboration that ensued among Horney, Johnson and Dean Meyer. Not only did Karen continue to teach lecture courses at the New School as long as her energy permitted, but her colleagues—refugee and American, psychoanalyst and sociologist—did so as well. This relationship developed into an official affiliation between the New School and the new American Institute for Psychoanalysis from the time it was formed in 1942 until today. Karen was often consulted thereafter on the appointment of other professionals to the New School faculty and her recommendation was responsible for placing a number of them there.

A final and perhaps fortuitous result of her relation to this school was that the psychoanalysis associated with her name came to be considered more a social than a medical science. Johnson himself stated that "what the imported scholars brought us was moderation of our own extreme Freudian doctrine rather than more Freudianism." This would certainly have applied to Karen. But while she encouraged this identification of her ideas with the social sciences at this early stage of her New York career, she later was to question the wisdom of this rapprochement. Then she still needed professional recognition, was seeking a wider public audience and was feeling the effects of Fromm's influence. A few years later, she was to experience a conflict about whether her brand of analysis was more socio-cultural or medical.

Her first course, starting in September 1935, was entitled "Culture and Neurosis." The lecture hall was packed and the response of the audience was as enthusiastic as it had been when she had spoken on feminine psy-chology at the Humboldt Hochschule ten years earlier. Such an audience response was to become a hallmark of her lectures.

This lecture series had two felicitous, far-reaching consequences. One was the publication of an article with the same title, containing a summary of the initial lectures. A second result was her being asked by the pub-lisher Walter Norton to set forth an expanded version of the course in a book.

In the article "Culture and Neurosis,"[6] the influence of Fromm's purer sociocultural approach is evident. Karen is here confronting the issue of "whether and to what extent neuroses are moulded by cultural processes in essentially the same way as 'normal' character formation is determined by these influences." The existence of a neurosis is determined not by the presence of typical symptoms but by underlying conflicting character traits. And the fundamental conflict—that is, the basic conflict of the child in its relations with its parents, continued on into adulthood—always revolved around the issue of competition and rivalry. As a neurotic drive, competitiveness differs from the similar normal trait in three ways. First, it involves an indiscriminate self-comparing and having to surpass others when no such real need exists. Second, the ambition is directed toward grandiose aims, often in fantasy, without adequate efforts to achieve them. The demands to attain them are so rigid that any falling short is experi-enced as failure. Third, an intense hostility is involved in relating to the imagined competitors. This engenders an automatic fear of retaliation.

As a result, such a neurotic has a fear both of success and of failure. It is safer to recoil from competition. This can be brought about by inhibitions, self-checking, self-belittling—all experienced as a painful sense of inferior-ity.

Anxiety can occur in such competitive neurotics when a "boundless craving" for affection or recognition exists simultaneously. The anxiety feeds on itself; it can lead to hostility toward others, which brings a fear of retaliation that leads to greater anxiety, all forming a kind of vicious circle. Both of the above attitudes toward success can be generated in the child by neurotic parents' demands and expectations which he must adopt or imitate to gain their affection. However, specific cultural influences can also favor the appearance of such anxiety-driven competitiveness. For example, the culture puts a premium on competition and winning—in work, family relations, and love—to the extent that these can replace similar healthy responses. We also preach that success will follow from extreme competitiveness but few having such ambitiousness do achieve success, whereas those with the opposite traits often attain it. Furthermore, this confusion is enhanced by a double standard of morality: Aggressive competitiveness is needed for success but one should also be unselfish and giving at the same time.

Although this article was Karen's most notable departure from Freudian theory to date, it went largely unnoticed. It did follow the same direction she had been generally taking since 1934, with more emphasis on the interplay between on-going dynamic attitudes. Until now she had always admitted that at the deepest level of motivation, at the core of the onion, lay repressed infantile psychosexual relations with the parents, however secondary they might be. Now any such infantile attitudes were not required to explain the neurosis. The later developed personality, with its inner conflicts and unconscious motives, stood by itself as an explanation. True, these began in reaction to unhealthy parental attitudes, but the latter were almost incidental. Another departure was the deemphasis of generally accepted neurotic symptoms as criteria for illness. The symptom-neurosis was replaced by the character-neurosis.

The question that must be raised is why Karen chose to discuss now, out of all possibilities, the particular traits of competitiveness, ambition and aggressiveness. Possibly she was referring to the rivalry she had felt with Alexander and the frustration of her ambitions in Chicago. As she had been in New York six months, possibly she was feeling the strain of having to subsist there, of having to build a practice in competition with other analysts. This would conflict, of course, with her loneliness and need for friendship, love and approval.

In November 1935, Karen was able to interrupt her busy schedule of practice, lectures and teaching in both New York and Washington to present her first paper at the New York Psychoanalytic Society. After all, she was teaching at the institute and needed to make herself known personally to the younger candidates. Its title was "The Problem of the Negative Therapeutic Reaction."[7] Basically it dealt with the same material she had discussed in her first two lectures at the New School. "We must consider the role of competitiveness, rivalry and ambition in the entire make-up." The material was treated here more technically, more from the purely psychoanalytic viewpoint. It was introduced in relation to the question of why patients may react to a good, appropriate interpretation by becoming worse, angry, disparaging, negative. According to her, the analyst's knowledge is experienced as superiority; the patient's competitiveness is stimulated and he must retaliate. His excessive expectations of perfection in himself, and then his reactive, intense disparaging hostility come out. Secondly, the process of becoming aware of his flaws is experienced as a blow to his narcissism, with resulting humiliation. He must respond by humiliating the analyst. Thirdly, the short-lived relief of symptoms which is usually felt, and which is usually interpreted as progress in analysis, must be immediately squelched by discouragement. Thus the negative reaction is really an expression of the fear of success. Fourthly, when guilt feelings are also present, the interpretation can be experienced as an accusation. The patient reacts often by trying to prove the analyst wrong. And finally, the remark can be felt as a rejection, since the patient also needs the analyst's affection. "These people are constantly wavering between rivalry and affection."

Karen pointed out that although these two attitudes are infantile ones, similar attitudes in the adult are "not direct repetitions or revivals of infantile attitudes, but have been changed in quality and quantity by the consequences which have developed out of the early experiences. . . . It is needless to say—and I say it only because misunderstandings have arisen—that this procedure does not mean that I attribute less importance to childhood experiences than any other analyst. These are of fundamental importance since they determine the direction of the individual's development. In fact, memories pertinent to the present situation do arise if the upper layers are carefully worked through."

This is the first time she admitted openly that there were "misunderstandings" on the part of her more orthodox colleagues. They were still minor. But she needed to reassure everyone that she was not hostile. Her own need for acceptance and affection was showing through.

In December 1935, Karen returned to Berlin over the holidays to see her daughters. Renate had gotten married several months before, after a series of tragicomic mishaps involving posting public betrothal banns in Chicago three months beforehand, when the censor would not allow such notices to pass through the mails (the engagement was finally announced on radio, published in a newspaper and transmitted via the embassy); procuring of witnesses at the last moment; getting rid of the ubiquitous SS guards at the local city hall; and, for Renate, facing her serious, most proper and conservative in-laws in their splendid house. Karen enjoyed being with her daughters. Brigitte was now a well-known actress, playing a lead role in a Berlin theater. One night Karen attended the play. As mother of the leading lady, she was seated in the box ordinarily reserved for VIP's. In the audience it was whispered that she must be an important party functionary.

She also took the occasion to present a paper, again on "The Negative Therapeutic Reaction," before the Berlin Psychoanalytic Society. She was still considered an overseas member, returning for a visit. The society was functioning as an independent organization then, though it was evident to everyone that its days were numbered. All branches of science were being forced to fall in line and conform to the Nazi *Weltanschauung*, a process of subjecting all organizations to direct governmental control. Less than half the members of three years before were still present. The number of candidates had fallen to eighteen. The recently passed Nuremberg Laws not only deprived all Jews of their German citizenship, relegating them to the status of "subjects," but also excluded them from public and private employment, for instance in the hospitals. Many were without means of earning a living, even though they were not officially forbidden to practice medicine until 1938. Members could still practice psychoanalysis in their private offices, using Freudian terms. Felix Boehm, Karl Muller-Braunschweig, Werner Kemper and Harald Schultze-Henke were still teaching these concepts in courses and seminars. Only Freudian analytic concepts were objectionable to the Nazis, not only because Freud and most Freudian practitioners were Jewish, but also because the misunderstood emphasis on sexuality made it offensive to them. They also resented the use of the couch as undignified. Schultze-Henke was beginning to introduce a new terminology for some of the original Freudian terms: desmology, desmolysis (for analysis) and family complex (for

Oedipus complex), among others. This may have represented an attempt to circumvent the Nazi prohibition and preserve Freud's concepts even though without their original names. Or it could have been a preparatory basis for his own neopsychoanalytic views, which were published in 1940. Karen was influenced by some of his ideas that were either discussed at this time or later in his book, *The Inhibited Human Being*.

On her return to New York, Karen again seriously took up her writing on the new book. As she had little time from her work with patients, she got into the habit of rising about five A.M. to write before seeing her first one. Time, which had always been in short supply, was now becoming a precious commodity. She was helped by two people: her secretary, Marie Levy, and Ernst Schachtel. The former listened, discussed, typed, edited, retyped. The latter would read articles relevant to the topic she was writing about, and then discuss them with her. This was an invaluable time-saver for her.

Schachtel had met Karen at the beginning of 1936 through Fromm. He had originally studied law in Berlin and Heidelberg, then had practiced until the Nazi takeover in 1933. As a refugee first in England, then in Geneva, he had edited a book, *Authority and the Family*, under the sponsorship of Fromm, Horkheimer and Marcuse, all of the Frankfurt School of Sociology. His wife, a psychologist, had turned his interest toward that field. After his arrival in New York, he had completed the psychoanalysis begun in Berlin. Karen had helped him obtain a position at the New School, teaching a course on Rorshach testing, which he also did privately. She further sent him patients when he was starting his own private practice.

In 1936 Karen was also concerned about Renate's situation. Her daughter and son-in-law wished to return to the United States, but he needed a definite offer of a job. Karen made efforts to find him one connected with film-making, possibly as an assistant director. But her desire to see her daughter was so great that at the beginning of her summer vacation, in late June 1936, she again traveled to Berlin for a short visit. This time it was also to celebrate the arrival of her first granddaughter, Kaya—her own first baby nickname. Renate had prepared a special dinner for her arrival. Rushing to the airport, they found that her plane had arrived early—but there was no sign of Karen. Worried, they rushed back home, thinking she might have taken a cab. Finally, after three hours, she called from downtown; she had first gone to see her orthopedist about her feet, had had her hair set and done other shopping chores. Now, she blithely explained, with these needs attended to, she would feel free. Was it simply a disregard for time and agreed-upon arrangements, or a disregard for the feelings of others? As Renate recalls, "Time was always precious to her and sentimental she was not!" This type of disregard, however, was to be noticed later by many who had dealings with her. But Karen was somewhat reassured that Renate was well, and promised to continue her attempts to bring them here.

She continued that summer vacation in Cuernavaca, Mexico. She finished the manuscript and sent it to Norton. He suggested several changes, in the first chapters in particular. Karen wrote him that she too was making changes, such as adding a section on anxiety and hostility. The title had been changed from *Culture and Neurosis* to *The Neurotic Personality of Our Time*. The changes rendered the structure of the book more consistent with the title and internally as well.

In answer to his question as to whom the book was primarily addressed, Karen wrote an explicit reply: to psychiatrists, psychoanalysts, psychosociologists and social workers. "It contains quite a few *new* contributions to the subject of neurosis, such as the concept of anxiety with its liberation from biological grounds, the generation of anxiety from repressed hostility, the neurotic need for affection as anxiety-conditioned, the striving for success and power as anxiety-conditioned, an attempt at the solution of the problem of masochism." She had already asked the opinion of a number of socio-ethnologists, including Ruth Benedict, Margaret Mead, John Dollard and Harold Lasswell. Their response had been uniformly enthusiastic. They welcomed the book as supplying psychological data they could work with. Her friend Alvin Johnson recommended a professional editor to smooth out the book, Elizabeth Todd. She worked thereafter with Karen on her other writings and gave her much help.

After sending off her signed contract, Karen spent the last weeks of August in a Mexican town called Isla del Borreos, just resting. This region seemed to hold a special fascination for her. The lush, colorful vegetation, the lakes, the ancient Indian pyramids seemed to provide both stimulation and tranquillity. While the scenery was not as picturesque or as grandiose as the Alps, it had a different charm. It was a place of contrasts. On the one hand the atmosphere was laden with the spirit of a rich and time-less past, with the wisdom of the ancient Indian priests. Philosophical meditation, soul-searching and mysticism fitted in perfectly. On the other, the local people showed an intrinsic oneness with the earth, an acceptance of the here-and-now. The unhurried pace of life was soothing— once you could accept the policy of *mañana*, tomorrow, the unchanging status quo. It provided a natural counterpoint to the lush, rapid growth of vegetation, evidence of nature's creativity. This region held the same fascination for other analysts. Hanns Sachs used to vacation there as well.

That fall Karen moved from the Surrey Hotel to the Essex House, a residential hotel at 160 Central Park South. Although this was more expensive and opulent, Karen felt she could now afford it. With the book contract signed and a definite date scheduled for its appearance, it is understandable that she would have felt self-confident, even expansive. Here at last she had her view overlooking the park. The rest of the year was spent, in addition to her usual hectic activity, in polishing the manuscript. It had been agreed that the publication date would be in the spring of 1937. Many details still remained to be worked out in meetings with Norton, and Karen established a friendly relationship with him that lasted until her death.

She also recommended to him that he consider publishing Fromm's book on character and culture, which he was still working upon at the time. She described this book in preliminary form as one "which deals with the relationship between culture and personality structure. Dealing with the normal personality, the book represents in a certain sense a parallel to mine. Dr. Fromm tries to put psychoanalytical theory on a sociological basis, in contrast to the physiological and biological foundation which we find with Freud." Unfortunately, nothing came of this recommendation.

Her course of clinical conferences at the New York Institute was being well attended. In addition, she was assigned a new course of lectures at the New School for the coming spring semester of 1937. As its title she chose "Open Questions in Psychoanalysis."

In December 1936, over the Christmas holiday, she again returned to Berlin, where she was scheduled to present another paper. This time she

found many changes in the psychoanalytic situation. The German Psychoanalytic Association had in May been permitted to continue to exist only
as a branch of the International General Medical Society for Psychotherapy. (In November 1938, it was finally dissolved officially.) Under
pressure from the authorities, its members had had to vote to resign from
the International Psychoanalytic. The Berlin Institute was now a section of
the Nazi-authorized German Institute for Psychological Research and Psychotherapy—popularly known as the Reichsinstitut or Goerings-Institut.
Its new director was Dr. Matthias Heinrich Goering, an eighth cousin of
Deputy Führer Hermann Goering. This new institute, taking over the
building of the former one, was divided into three sections: *Arbeitsgruppe*
A, Freudian; *Arbeitsgruppe* B, Schultze-Henkian; *Arbeitsgruppe* C,
Jungian. Although separate programs were scheduled for each group, in
practice most of the members attended all meetings.

In July 1936, Dr. Goering had laid down the rules that must be followed if the psychoanalytic group was to continue to function. He promised it considerable freedom if it remained within these regulations.
Lectures would be allowed, training analyses forbidden. Goering or his
wife would have to attend all lectures to verify that no Freudian technical
terms were being used.

Frau Goering had initially been opposed to psychoanalysis. But she un-
derwent an analysis with Kemper and thereafter felt quite positive about
it. Dr. Goering, himself, was a rather easy-going, kindly and friendly
man, modest in his tastes and clothes. Although he had been a member of
a rightist war-veterans group when younger, this outlook had been tempered by his religious upbringing. Previously a rather obscure practitioner, he had written little and spoken little; he was not too articulate.
Goering's major—perhaps only—qualification for this new position was his
name. However, it was thanks to him and this name that psychoanalysis
and its practitioners were to be saved from greater havoc during the rest
of the Nazi regime. Several still-living analysts have described how his
warning saved various members of the group.[8] At the end of the war he
was picked up by the Russians and, possibly because of his name, sent to
a camp in the Soviet Union. There he died in obscurity.

While in Berlin, Karen stayed with Ada and Karl Muller-Braunschweig.
At their home she met some of the other analysts, including Kemper. He
accompanied her to the meeting. The little group discussed the situation

of psychoanalysis and of their mutual analytic friends under the new regime. The paper she presented was "On The Neurotic Need for Love" (*Über das neurotische Liebesdürfnis*). Basically it was a condensation of the three corresponding chapters in her first book. At this meeting, listed as *Arbeitsgruppe* A, representatives of nonFreudian analytic views—Adlerians, Jungians, Schultze-Henkians—were also present. Karen is reported to have remarked that such cross-fertilization of analytic ideas could be useful. Her paper was received with enthusiasm. That it was even permitted indicated that its terms were not considered Freudian. Goering personally found the presentation so interesting that he requested a copy of the book for further discussion. Upon her return here, Karen had a copy forwarded to him.

During this visit, she also consulted a lawyer to begin the necessary legal arrangements for a divorce. During the intervening ten years, Karen, officially separated from Oskar, had apparently never been disturbed by the lack of an official divorce. Whether she saw him during her visits to Berlin is not known. Why she had waited this long is a matter for speculation. In any event, the German courts being as disorganized as they were during this period, her final divorce papers did not come through until two years later, in 1939.

When Karen's book came out in the spring of 1937, its reception was mixed. This was to be expected. Reviews were most favorable among the sociologists like Ruth Benedict, Harry Bone and Harold Lasswell. Psychoanalysts of culturalist views were also positive about it. Clara Thompson, for example wrote, "Because of the difference of accent in the approach to the problem of neurosis from the usual psychoanalytical one, she tends to diverge from strict Freudian theories at some points. . . . In short, the author views the whole situation from a cultural angle, whereas Freud seeks a biological foundation. The points of view, of course, do not necessarily exclude each other. The book will certainly arouse controversy in analytical circles. . . . If there are analysts who believe that the words of Freud must not be questioned, they will find some 'heresy' in this book. To the person, however, who welcomes constant seeking after new truth and the testing and re-examining of old ideas in the light of new points of view, this book will be a stimulus, whether he agrees altogether with its theories or not."

Among the most orthodox analysts, Ernest Jones, who had always supported Karen, wrote the review for the *International Journal of Psychoanalysis*. To his credit he remained as scrupulously objective as possible, without polemics or even any value judgments. He simply picked up Karen's theme of the importance of cultural factors, noting that she "deprecated what she considers Freud's exaggerated views on biological factors. . . . What really recedes into the background is infantile sexuality." He first called attention to Karen's notion that a reaction like "the Oedipus complex is not as common as Freud assumes . . . is artificially generated from the atmosphere in which the child grows up . . . is not the origin of the neurosis but itself the neurotic formation, and is the expression of the desire for reassurance." He answered that "This observation is a dangerous half-truth." To assume that oedipal sexual impulses were called forth and even generated by anxiety did not make them less sexual. "To draw a contrary inference is equivalent to emptying the baby with the bath."

The responses of the members of the New York Institute varied. A few felt strongly critical about the deviation from Freud. Most believed her views were not too threatening and could be accommodated either within the classical framework or as an extension of ego psychology. Besides, Karen was not alone in moving in this direction. Abraham Kardiner, a respected and authoritative analyst of the "modern" American outlook, had also recently come out with a culturally oriented book, *The Individual in Society*. He was an ethnological analyst who arrived at his similar ideas about the importance of the cultural factors through a study of behavior and customs of various primitive tribal groups. His view carried weight because he had been analyzed by Freud himself. Paul Federn, for instance, seems to have been favorably enough impressed by Karen's book to offer to try to have it published in Switzerland, where he was supposed to have some influence. Even though Karen may have been troubled somewhat by the criticisms, she was now too flushed by her feeling of achievement to take them especially seriously. Thus, in response to a critical letter received from one analyst, she wrote Norton, "He expects a magic formula as a solution to the whole problem of neurosis and is thus incapable of appreciating it when he gets something of value."

The book elicited reactions in Berlin as well, where she had sent copies to her friends. In October a full regular meeting of the Goerings-Institut was devoted to its discussion.

By early 1937, Karen was already beginning work on the first chapters of her second book. As it would be drawn from her new course at the New School, its title initially was to have been the same, *Open Questions in Psychoanalysis*. In May, in addition to her regular courses in Washington and Baltimore, she gave a special presentation before the Psychoanalytic Society there on "The Problem of Anxiety." This was basically drawn from the similar chapter in her book. The audience reaction was lively, with spirited discussion, and generally favorable. Here she related anxiety to hostility, regardless of whether it occurred in young children or adults—a distinction which was soon to become quite significant. According to this view, conflicts between opposing dynamic attitudes in the adult were as important as those involving infantile psychosexual impulses in causing anxiety.

Marianne's progress also gave her cause for happiness at this time. After graduation in 1936 from medical school, Marianne served her internship at Billings Hospital with distinction. While there, she became aware of her lack of knowledge of psychiatry and decided to enter that specialty. It was not surprising, her mother being who she was. She left Chicago in June 1937 to become a resident in psychiatry at Cornell's noted Payne-Whitney Clinic in New York. Shortly afterward, on the recommendation of her mother, who considered him an able psychoanalyst, she entered her personal training analysis with Erich Fromm.

Karen's summer break that year was spent with the Schachtels and Fromm at Lake Tahoe. It was partly a working vacation for her. The Sierras were not the Alps, but their serene beauty could still provide the impetus for creative writing. On her return, she was assigned in addition to her regular clinical conferences at the New York Institute an extra course, "On Narcissistic Phenomena."

To finish the year, over the Christmas holidays, Karen returned once more to Berlin, this time by boat. She was feeling more worried than usual about Renate and the baby. Renate had written that the food situation had become difficult since the last visit, with shortages of several foods, especially fats. After landing at Hamburg, Karen arrived waving excitedly from the train at the Berlin station. She carried two mysterious, heavy yet fragile valises; they were the reason she had come by boat. She insisted on carrying them herself, allowing no one else to touch them. The following morning, when Renate come down, there under the Christmas tree lay a dozen pints of whipping cream and about ten pounds of butter. This was her gift to the little family.

The two happy weeks passed too swiftly. Brigitte was working in films. Although she was not interested in politics, she had had to adapt to the restrictive situation in the film industry if she wished to work. And at this time, her work and career were her major concerns. But she could not remain indifferent to the events occurring all around her.

Shortly after the accession of Hitler to power in January 1933, Goebbels was appointed Minister of Propaganda. Films had always been his personal hobby. As he recorded in his diary, he made a distinction between the artistic and the political possibilities of film. Contradicting him, however, Hitler stated in April that the two could not be separated. All movies would have to be instruments of propaganda. But he did not reckon with the group of artists he was dealing with. By June, after the notorious Aryan Clause was issued, all the film companies had begun to discharge Jews. This applied to all new films; those already made with Jewish actors or producers could still be shown (until 1937). A month later, a Reich Chamber of Culture was created, to which everyone working in any cultural organization had to belong. A special film board controlled the movie industry. By 1934, although the government continued to pressure the industry, most of the company officials remained cool to the Nazis, since they had extensive foreign connections, and subtly counteracted the directives of the authorities. Most of the actors, directors and writers felt contempt for the regime. But that year, the office of *Filmdramaturg* was created, representing the state, with responsibility for direct supervision of all film-making, including censorship.

By 1935, all the Jewish actors and actresses had left and a few non-Jewish ones as well. Many capable performers stayed on, however. "By 1936," it was reported, "the film colony of the Reich was virtually formed, a stock company which was to continue almost unchanged until 1945. . . . The women stayed out of politics whenever possible, with one or two exceptions."[9] (After the war, of some fifty members, about six were considered to have cooperated with the Nazis.) Then in 1936 all criticism of film and drama was officially prohibited; any reporting could only be descriptive, without value judgments.

After her film debut in 1930 and her subsequent year in Würzburg,

Biggi played for several years on the stage in the Deutsche Theater, the Lessing-Theater and the Volksbühne. She became a star—at least in the German-speaking countries—in the 1934 film *Love, Death and the Devil.* In it she sang a song which, according to one critic, "she rendered with élan, sensuality and sentimentality. She has turned out to be, as far as possible, a successor to Marlene Dietrich."[10] Biggi did not want the fixed, long-term film contracts she was offered. In keeping with her need for change, she did not want to be type cast; she wished the freedom to fly, to liberate herself through many different roles. Nor did she wish to live the limited life-style of a star; she wanted to live life to the fullest, in whatever form it came. So full of life was she that one commentator called her "a girl with whom you could steal horses," who would try anything. Within three years, by the time of Karen's last visit, she had played in some seven films, all quite different, all hits.

In her acting, she combined an intense emotional expressiveness with tremendous self-discipline and self-control. One critic later saw in her an "erotic radiation" which made her "as unique as Dietrich or Marilyn Monroe."[11] Karen once related that she saw much of her own mother's dominating personality in Biggi. Yet, however much Biggi might have needed to have her own way, beneath this patina lay a basic—even at times excessive—empathy for those who were troubled or anxious—even perhaps a certain timidity. It was said that she could not say no to anyone who asked a favor. Around the film colony, she was known as a soft touch who would give or lend money to anyone who asked. Thus, even though she was often earning a top salary, she seldom managed to save, in spite of her modest style of living.

While in Berlin this last time at the end of 1937, Karen wanted to speak to and meet with her analytic friends. It was possibly dangerous to telephone them, as Renate suspected the phones would be tapped. "Everyone felt the eye of the Gestapo was watching." This would be especially true for psychoanalysts, engaged in a forbidden "non-Aryan" profession. But Karen simply had to visit some of them. She was saddened to learn what was happening in the field.

Karl Muller-Braunschweig had remained a constant admirer of Freud. Unfortunately, as his son recalls, his "reductionistic" focus on Freudian ideas had narrowed his own fertile and manifold interests in art, theology, psychology and science. Nevertheless he still remained a "strange mixture of vitality and great sensitivity," along with a sometimes excessive certainty and arrogance about his opinions. These were traits in some ways similar to Karen's at that time. Like so many German intellectuals, he had hoped for a quick end to the Nazi regime, without fully recognizing its dangers and excesses. He simply could not understand many of its features.

At this time, in 1937, Muller-Braunschweig was rather depressed. The inevitable future of Freud, foreseeable since 1933, had already strongly affected him. He was not noticeably cheered by Karen's visit. His young son, Hans, now a well-known psychologist, recalls her as "a friendly woman, who explained the functions of a steam-engine . . . in a way which grasped well the importance (real and symbolic) those technical things had for us. She had anyway, a good contact with us children." In addition, Karen wanted to know from Karl how her book was being received in Germany. She wished to discuss possible prospects for having it translated and published in a German edition.

The atmosphere in Berlin in 1937 was much different from that of her last two visits. Nineteen thirty-six had been exceptional. Since both the winter and summer Olympics were then being held there, the authorities had taken great pains to conceal all evidence of their terroristic activities. The city was beautified and scrubbed clean. All anti-Semitic signs were taken down, and it was forbidden to write the usual scurrilous defacing slogans on stores. The streets were bedecked with international flags. Thousands of visitors were welcomed. Berlin was to be a showcase of harmony, acceptance and enthusiasm for the new and greater Reich. In the winter Olympics, two token Jewish athletes had even been permitted to participate on the German team.

But with the departure of the visiting throngs and the pomp and circumstance, the oppressive restrictions were intensified. The terror of the Gestapo and SS reigned unchecked. Everything they did was now legal. The country was an absolute police state.

Psychoanalysis, at least in the Berlin offices of the few still practicing it, had "gone underground." It had become a curious kind of therapy, full of duplicity, evasions, double messages and double-entendres, the meanings of which had to be interpreted by patient and analyst alike to be understood. Several analysts have described how cryptic messages were divulged and passed on to warn and so save someone threatened. The patient, in revealing possibly incriminating personal material of a political nature, put himself at the mercy of the analyst. The analyst, hearing such information without reporting it, rendered himself an accomplice, equally culpable. Medical ethics, personal secrecy and privileged communication could scarcely withstand police interrogation, torture and the threat of the concentration camp. The doctor-patient relationship was thus complicated by their artificial alliance against the authorities. Each had to wrestle with his conscience. All were fearful, yet courageous.

In spite of such circumstances, analytic teaching was continuing. The Freudian, Jungian and Adlerian analysts rotated in conducting classes. In addition to their courses at the Goerings-Institut, Muller-Braunschweig and Schultze-Henke were conducting forbidden case-seminars in secret at their homes. A new polyclinic had been organized under Kemper as director. Patients were being treated there even under the existing conditions. Curiously, too, the number of analytic candidates increased that year. A spirit of camaraderie and cordiality grew among analysts of the different theoretical schools, as if to reinforce one another against the external danger. Few—perhaps 5 percent—were actually party members. Although the Goerings, themselves, were initially Nazis and formally remained so, they proved remarkably liberal and autonomous, acting under the terrible pressure only when absolutely necessary. They were even reported to have helped in the efforts to save some of the others.

Only a short while later, after the occupation of Austria in March 1938, Muller-Braunschweig was invited to come to Vienna to "act as a sort of caretaker of the Psychoanalytic Institute" there. According to Jones in his biography of Freud, Karl "arrived from Berlin, accompanied by a Nazi Commissar with the purpose of liquidating the psychoanalytic situation." Fortunately, the entire Viennese psychoanalytic community, as well as Freud's family, had previously decided to flee if possible; the future seat of the Society would be wherever Freud would settle.[12] According to his son, Muller-Braunschweig had accepted this task "only after long hesitation, in the hope of rescuing as much as possible." Even so, when he had arrived at the Vienna Institute, and gone through the rooms with Anna, his sadness over what was happening was most evident. Somewhat later, he wrote a letter to her in an attempt to console her. This letter fell into the hands of the Gestapo, whereupon he was called to their headquarters and interrogated. He was insulted as a "friend of the Jews" and forbidden to teach or publish, although he was still allowed to practice. All this added to his depression. It also placed an additional burden upon and pall over his family.

The departure of Freud in June from Vienna did not change the confused state of psychoanalysis in Berlin. The situation in the two cities was different. As Edith Weigert has pithily put it, "In Berlin it was serious but not catastrophic; in Vienna it was catastrophic but not serious."

While she was there, Karen was greatly impressed by all the activity taking place in spite of the horrible external situation. This time she was glad to leave, although still worried about Renate. From the steamer *Europa,* on her way home, she wrote Norton to suggest another title for the new book: *A Personal Outlook on Psychoanalysis.* She felt this preferable because it covered both the critical and constructive aspects. A philosophical reason was that "all we can say about anything, and all that is worth saying, is after all something personal, versus 'external truth.' " But this was not yet to be the final title.

At the scientific session of the New York Psychoanalytic Society meeting in January 1938, Karen spoke again on "The Problem of Neurotic Anxiety." Apparently she felt that either some venting of feelings on the subject or further explanation of her position was needed. The paper was a reprise of the previous one in Washington, but its reception was quite different. It was discussed by Lawrence Kubie, Bernard Robbins, Adolph Stern, Sandor Rado and Fritz Wittels. In this topic lay the nub of her difference with the classical concepts. Her emphasis on the significance of cultural factors was not the crucial criticism; that could even be incorporated into the framework of ego theory with a little stretching. More important was her deemphasis of infantile psychosexuality, as Ernest Jones had noted, with its replacement by on-going dynamic adult attitudes as the cause for anxiety. The paper was both criticized and defended. Kubie recalls that he tried to conciliate and minimize the differences of opinion. In her response, Karen reiterated the point she had made in her previous paper there on the negative therapeutic reaction. She insisted on the great importance she still attached to infantile reactions, repeating that she did not neglect them. Yet in the wake of her recent book and the official criticism of it, the doubt still remained in the minds of many there that she rejected infantile sexuality.

By March 1938 she had submitted to Norton two other suggestions for the new book title: *New Goals* and *New Ways in Psychoanalysis.* Either of these would better express the book's purpose—to present a critical evaluation of psychoanalysis which contained contributions of her own—while making it clear that she did not want to found a new school but to build on the foundations Freud had laid.

One incident at this time illustrates Karen's special type of naiveté. In March, Rita Honroth arrived in New York on the steamer *Hamburg*. Karen had provided the affidavits of financial responsibility for her (as she also did later for Rita's sister). After going through the immigration procedures, Rita was detained at Ellis Island. Because she was listed as an "unattached female," without money or legitimate means of support, it was questioned whether she might be in the United States for "immoral purposes"—especially since her sponsor was another unmarried woman who lived in a hotel (the Essex House at the time). In desperation, Rita called Karen. Busy with patients that morning, Karen sent her secretary Marie Levy. Useless! In fact, the appearance of another young woman, a stranger and not a relative, only added to the doubt. Karen would have to come herself. The following day, she appeared at the hearing, furious at having to cancel her appointments and disrupt her day. The attitudes of the immigration judges only added insult to injury. Didn't they know who she was! How could they question her truthfulness! Didn't they recognize a responsible person when they saw one! But she soon had to sweep aside her injured pride when she saw the serious atmosphere of the hearing. There was a very real danger: Rita could easily be deported back to certain death. Realizing this, she changed her attitude quickly to a more reasonable, concerned and helpful one. It was a lesson she never quite forgot.

Karen not only helped Rita find a small furnished apartment, but also supported her—and her young husband, who followed three months later—for the next eighteen months, until they could both take their State Board Medical Examinations and find work.

Rita found Karen "warm, friendly and interested in our progress. She was full of that singular, breathless, child-like wondering quality that at least appeared as a thorough enjoyment of life. She had a way of responding with a delighted, laughing *ja-ja* as an affirmation of her being 'with it.' It was, in part, the way of appearing 'cheerfully masterful' often observed in psychoanalysts. It also had a special quality and sound that gave the impression that life somehow still had all the wonders and surprises it might hold for a child. It also gave the deceptive impression of simplicity and na- iveté, as does her writing. There was about Karen, for me, an aura of earthiness, timelessness and strength—analogous to the German 'Ur-mut- ter'—that exerted a strong spell. Her preference for handcrafted materials and furniture in vibrant colors seemed a perfect expression of her self. It was a strange mixture of simple tastes and peasant woman's shrewdness with the high-bred sophistication of the affluent intellectual."

All during this time, Karen permitted the struggling young couple to use her hotel apartment when she was away on vacations.

Her own living habits showed the same curious admixture of expansive luxury with rigorous frugality and self-denial. Occasionally, with company coming, she would have the hotel service prepare a sumptuous meal. The rest of the time she lived and ate quite simply. To avoid the loss of time entailed in cooking and kitchen chores, she would often prepare a huge casserole that could last many days, even though it meant eating the same food at every meal. One favorite recipe was a kind of pudding made of dried mixed fruits and bread, baked in the oven. Although it tasted good, it required a cast-iron digestive system when it was almost the exclusive fare.

Many of her friends of this period well recall this hotel apartment. Kardiner remembers lively evenings there with John Dollard and Erich Fromm. It was still Karen's "sociological" period. She had bought a small roulette wheel and one of their favorite parlor games was to play roulette for pennies. Sometimes she would ask Fromm to sing. He sang Hassidic songs, recalled from his early training in Hebrew school, in a beautiful, soulful voice.

That summer Karen took her vacation in France and Switzerland. She was increasingly disturbed about Renate. Her daughter could no longer tolerate the severe regimentation, the oppressive restrictions and constant surveillance. She had become fearful and guarded. Perhaps rebelling within, she had also become lax in carrying out the many obligatory duties required of every German citizen, sometimes even forgetting to make the Hitler salute. If this was noticed by her neighbors, it could become dan- gerous. She simply had to leave Germany. She arranged to meet Karen at the house in Switzerland to make some plans. As she was not a Jewish ref- ugee, an immigrant visa was not possible. The normal quota was filled for many years. The attempts Karen had made to find her son-in-law a film position had thus far been unsuccessful. Only a tourist visa remained within the realm of possibility. With the optimism and determination of youth, they would find a way to leave.

And so they did. Renate's husband, a film photographer, offered to look into a color photography process used only in America for his company. They gave him an official assignment. Armed with these letters, he and Renate were granted a passport for themselves and their child. To their surprise, the issuing immigration clerk, after the first usual official warnings spoken in a loud voice, sympathetically whispered, "And don't come back."

In November 1938, just after Hitler's invasion of Czechoslovakia, they boarded the steamer on a cold gray morning. The atmosphere was chilling—physically and emotionally—frightening and uncertain. Would someone stop them at the last moment? Would the ship even be permitted to sail? They had had to leave all their belongings behind in their apartment. Only one suitcase each for immediately necessary clothes, and ten marks apiece, were permitted to anyone leaving the country. On arriving at the Statue of Liberty, Renate reflected on how different it was from the previous time, over six years before. Now she was a mother, taking the place Karen had been in then, probably experiencing the same feelings her mother had had.

Karen was joyfully awaiting them on the pier. They could only remain in America for one month. During this time Renate reached a greater understanding, a new and closer rapport with her mother. Karen found that her daughter had lost much of her tomboyish exuberance and spontaneity as a result of the difficult experience of living in Germany. Yet out of the same crucible had come a greater maturity and self-reliance. Karen tried to use every influence, to pull as many strings as she could, to obtain permission for them to stay permanently. Her naturalization papers as an American citizen had come through by now. But it was to no avail. In the end, encouraged by a former schoolfriend who had immigrated to Mexico, and whom Renate had contacted, they were able to find a haven in Mexico City.

Although Karen had practically finished the manuscript of the second book by November and had sent it to the editor, she continued to make extensive revisions for several months. She was still doubtful about the title: She wrote that perhaps *New Aims* would be better than *New Goals*. In the end, of course, she accepted *New Ways*. Her choice of title for the next lecture course at the New School may have indicated some of the difficulties she was having in her daily living. In 1938 it was "Problems of Everyday Life" and for the winter semester 1938–39, "Applying Psychoanalysis to One's Self and Environment."

In the spring of 1939 she contracted for an office-apartment in a new high-rise building being constructed at 240 Central Park South. The architect happened to be the brother of her friend Clara Meyer, the New School dean, who had told her of the opportunity. On the architect's recommendation and advice, she was also able to purchase a parcel of land at Croton-on-Hudson, for a summer cottage. Although she claimed to have little acumen for business dealings, a "poor business head," as she was fond of saying, she certainly managed to discover where to turn for help!

By 1939, the trickle of refugee professionals was beginning to become a torrent. While the members of the American Psychoanalytic Association wished to help these unfortunates, it also realized that their accreditation and absorption into the American mainstream could present a problem. Besides, with the events occurring in Europe, the situation of the International Psychoanalytic Association was precarious. In June 1938, the American Association declared itself, in effect, no longer subject to decisions of the International Association and no longer represented on the international Training Committee. This meant that hereafter the American Association, now autonomous, would set up its own requirements for training, would no longer accept membership in a European society as an automatic qualification, and would not honor the member-at-large status for analysts living in the United States. So the center of gravity of the psychoanalytic world shifted west.

At the same time, the various refugee-aid committees—the National Committee for Resettlement of Foreign Physicians, the American Council for Emigrés in the Professions, among others—were actively trying to help with jobs or money. A similar Emergency Committee on Relief and Immigration was formed by the American Association and the New York Psychoanalytic Society. Although Kubie asked her, Karen did not join this committee, a decision that did not endear her to its organizers. They could not understand her stance. On the other hand, without their knowledge, she did much to help a number of the refugees she knew personally. She sent numerous affidavits of support and money to Europe during the next two or three years, as well as after the war. She also sent many food and clothing packages. In fact, in 1939 she actively campaigned for a refugee-aid bill, calling or writing her friends and politicians. She wrote Norton:

> *A bill has recently been presented by Robert Wagner in the Senate and Edith Rogers of Massachusetts in the House, which will make possible the admission into this country of 10,000 German refugee children—half Jewish, half Gentile—in 1939 and 1940. This will give an opportunity to the thousands of children, whose parents beg to have them admitted anywhere, even though it means separation from them, because of the physical danger and moral degradation to which they are subjected each day, to come to this country and live a normal life, where they may have relationships with foster parents and contacts in school and community.*
>
> *It is important that outstanding people approach their Senators and Representatives, indicating their desire as human beings to secure passage of this Bill.*
>
> *As I am very much interested in this movement, I am writing to ask you to send a letter or telegram, and to get as many of your friends as you can to do likewise.*
>
>

With kind greetings,
Karen Horney

This letter tells much about her and raises questions as well. Why the reluctance to participate officially in helping refugee analysts, alongside her obvious feeling for the unfortunates she knew personally or for children? Perhaps it had to do with some deep-seated resentment she unconsciously harbored toward anyone connected with Freud. Perhaps it was an unspoken resentment toward her critics in the New York Society. Perhaps she could only sympathize when she was personally involved. The plight of her daughter Renate was still a fresh wound. In this message she was also revealing that she was aware of the dangers, terrors and suffering—even if only in a distant, indirect way—experienced under the Nazi regime.

The influx of these refugee analysts into the New York Institute and Society created a new situation there. Most of them were Viennese, students or colleagues of Freud, deeply devoted to him and committed to following his ideas strictly. These included, among others, such prominent names as Bela Mittelmann, Ludwig Jekels, Johann van Ophuijsen, Paul Federn, Herman Nunberg, Kurt Lewin, Fritz Wittels, Annie Reich, Robert Fleiss, Henry and Yela Lowenfeld. Their attitudes, and especially their votes, influenced policy. The traditional German authoritarianism of their background began to manifest itself in stricter training standards, greater insistence on adherence to orthodox theory and rejection of any deviation, more attention to the hierarchical organization of institutes, and in the creation of close-knit inner circles—in short, in less liberalism and more conservatism.

These arrivals and the influence they exerted created tension, even a certain friction, with their younger American colleagues in the institute— even with some of the previous European newcomers. Their old-world traditionalism clashed with American modernism. Alexander stated it well in a later letter, written when he himself was being considered a "revisionist":

> *It is difficult to evaluate the influence of these European analysts in general terms. The majority propagated a conservative orientation and had an aversion to further experimentation and revision of theory and practice. Their influence was beneficial inasmuch as it introduced and preserved the original concepts and contributed to [the] making of psychoanalysis a respected specialty within psychiatry. . . .*
>
> *While Rado and I tried to introduce a more progressive spirit into the training of psychoanalysts, with less indoctrination and a more critical point of view, the other psychoanalytic Institutes (with the exception of those in Philadelphia and Washington) became more and more conservative in their orientation, mainly interested in strict organization of professional standards and training. At the*

*beginning this was desirable, but later it became an impedi-
ment to further development.*[13]

These conditions aggravated the factionalism and "power politics" already present not only in New York but in the American Psychoanalytic Association as well. Here it became indeed a complex factional and interpersonal situation, with many stresses and strains.

This, then, was the climate in the late spring of 1939, when Karen's second book was published. Its impact spread and grew from a ripple to a wave.

XV
THE NEUROTIC
PERSONALITY
OF OUR TIME

This first version of Horney's theory focused on the nature of the neurotic personality within the context of its cultural milieu. She maintained that there was no universal "normal" human nature in absolute terms, nor any typical neurosis. Many examples from different cultures show that what will be considered neurotic depends on cultural norms. Approved standards vary not only according to culture but also according to period, class and even sex. Deviation from any defined normal, however, is not sufficient by itself to define neurosis. Both social (cultural) and medical (psychological) factors are operative, without either being primary or decisive.

More specifically, the definition of neurosis must include four broad characteristics. First, the person's reactions are rigid and inappropriate to the expected cultural pattern. Second, there results a discrepancy between his potentials and accomplishments. Third, he exhibits anxieties (or fears) that are different from and more intense than those of the culture. The defenses against these anxieties produce suffering and impairment of the capacity to live to the fullest. And fourth, there exist partly unconscious emotional conflicts for which solutions are automatically sought. Although conflict between personal strivings and social pressures is a necessary component, this is not enough either; it can lead only to the suppression of the strivings or to realistic suffering from their frustration. What is essential is that such conflicts in turn generate anxiety. Attempts to allay the anxiety then lead to additional contradictory but equally necessary defensive measures. However, the mere *presence* of these conflicting tendencies is not sufficient, either, to constitute a neurosis unless they deviate from similar normal tendencies in the culture, are sharper and thus more injurious to the personality, and the means of resolving them less satisfying.

[225]

Neurosis cannot be defined in terms of special symptoms experienced, since these can be absent or unrecognized. Symptoms can also be removed without resulting in a cure of the condition. Although the manifest symptoms of character neuroses can differ in each case, the dynamic processes and conflicts are similar in all. They involve five areas of function: needing and giving love or approval; self-evaluation; self-assertive attitudes; aggression; and sexuality.

To understand these conflicts, it is necessary to understand the nature of anxiety. It differs from fear in being inappropriate to the situation in which it arises. Since it thus seems irrational, the person feels helpless with it. But it is appropriate to the personal meaning of the situation. It can manifest itself in many ways: as intense and torturous; as partially or totally outside awareness; as a special fear; as a physical symptom. It is a complex emotion, always part of a more comprehensive attitudinal problem. Anxiety usually has as content some specific underlying feeling—anger, hate, love—that the person may not catch as it passes. In this culture, a few major defensive means of escaping anxiety are predominant. One is rationalization, or finding convenient reasons to explain it. Another means is conscious or unconscious denial. When conscious, this can simply involve doing the things that are frightening. A third defense is to narcotize the anxiety with alcohol or drugs or by some distracting activity like work, socializing or sex. Direct avoidance of anxiety-producing situations is still another defense. This last can operate unconsciously through inhibitions in the various activities that usually produce anxiety.

In principle, anxiety can result when the discovery or carrying out of any driven impulse would bring about the violation of any other equally vital interest, need or impulse. Hostile impulses are one of the most important forms of emotion that produce anxiety in both the child and the adult. The typical means of keeping anger or rage from awareness—repression, dissociation or projection—are usually ineffective. Keeping the anger "encapsulated" in an unconscious form only allows it to build up. Pretending that it is others who are really hostile only makes one feel more threatened. Besides, this only causes more reactive hostility, more repression, more anxiety—a vicious cycle with each emotion building on the other.

Every neurosis begins in childhood. Although understanding the neurosis is impossible without tracing it back to its infantile conditions, a one-sided emphasis on childhood situations as causes of the adult neurosis will be equally ineffective. The concept that the adult relives infantile experiences as they originally occurred—"compulsive repetition"—is rejected. The basic soil for all neuroses is an atmosphere that lacks genuine parental warmth or affection for the child. The parents' attitudes may be camouflaged as part of their own neuroses or may be expressed toward the child in frank rejective behavior. Such attitudes can include preference for a sibling, unjust punishment, smothering overprotection, sexual seductiveness, ridicule or scornful rejection, unfulfilled promises, impossible or contradictory expectations, denigration of the child's needs, wishes or interests. Although the child may experience sibling rivalry or the classical type of oedipal relation to parents, they are neither instinctive, universal nor necessarily present. They can only be produced by the family atmosphere in which the child grows.

All these rejective attitudes from parents will tend to generate hostile protest in the child. But the child's hostility must be repressed. This is so because of its helplessness and need for the parents, its fear of their anger or intimidation, its fear of losing their love, and its feelings of guilt at expressing hostility. The resulting "basic anxiety" is a feeling of being small, helpless or lonely in a potentially hostile world. There is usually little awareness of the repressed hostility or hatred. However, these may subsequently crystallize into character traits. These various emotions are not the neurosis itself, but they form the nutritive soil out of which it develops when they are later influenced by social factors.

In our culture, four major ways of allaying this basic anxiety (of achieving security) are current. These are methods of relating to others; they are referred to almost interchangeably as attitudes, strivings, needs, wishes, tendencies, drives or desires, so that their precise psychological nature is not certain. They are: seeking affection, submissiveness to rules or people, gaining power, and withdrawal. While these may be normal tendencies in our culture, they become neurotic when motivated by underlying anxiety or insecurity. Then they provide reassurance.

In this case, they take on certain characteristics. They assume a driven, compulsive quality, whereby the person's happiness or very existence is felt to depend on satisfaction of the need. They become indiscriminate and overgeneralized. Usually two exist at the same time, and the clash between incompatible tendencies forms the "dynamically central conflicts" of the neurosis. Each need may take many forms and may give rise to other secondary attitudes required for its satisfaction, such as demands on others.

The neurotic need for love can be clearly distinguished from genuine love through its deeper purpose: to relieve anxiety. It is thus self-centered. In reality it is a clinging to, a need for, a using of, the other person. The neurotic generally has an incapacity for love and an inability to accept it when received. He feels unlovable, distrusts the giver; this is often due to hostile feelings mixed into his attitudes.

The object of this need may be a constant single other person, like a spouse. Or it may simply be any other indifferent person, or a group. The need usually gives rise to compulsive compliance with others' wishes and self-abnegation. An accompanying need for approval can be intense. Yet the person resents this dependency on others without being able to break it. It is sought after with a greed that may correspond to the "oral" trait of classical psychoanalysis.

This neurotic need for affection is also insatiable. It can therefore produce a fear of losing the affection when received. The result is often exaggerated jealousy or the demand for unconditional and exclusive love. The intensity of this need also renders the neurotic hypersensitive to rebuff, therefore fearful of rejection by others. Easily humiliated, he becomes subject to rage reactions. To avoid these, he will easily develop inhibitions of various kinds. In connection with this type of reaction, a typical vicious circle of emotions can occur, whereby such a need can build on itself by creating new, secondary anxieties. Thus, a need for love, when rebuffed, may cause reactive hostility which must be repressed and so generates increased anxiety, which in turn increases the need for love to relieve it, and so forth.

Three different evolutions of this need for love may occur. The development of a constant, indiscriminate craving for any affection is one. A withdrawal from contact with others plus the use of impersonal activities to obtain it is another. Third is the development of an attitude of cynicism, with disbelief in any possibility of receiving affection.

The neurotic can use various techniques to obtain love that involve unconscious appeals and demands on others. For instance, there may be a demand for love in return for love given (bribery), in return for suffering experienced (pity), in return for sacrifices performed (justice), or through indirect threats (reproaches or arousal of guilt).

One frequent symptom of this need for affection is an increased desire for sex. This observation disagrees with Freud's notion that sexual frustration, "dissatisfied libido," is the basis for love. Tenderness would be only a sublimated sexual drive. However, many of the supposedly sexual attitudes will be found to be expressions of anxiety. These include indiscriminate sexual activity, bisexual choice of partners, increase in sexual desire accompanying rising anxiety, and changes in sexual impulses toward the analyst during analysis. Sexual behavior is thus determined by neurosis and compulsive needs rather than the other way around.

The neurotic striving for power, also motivated by anxiety, can be divided into three forms. The form taken will depend on its aims, the fears it reassures against, and the trend of its underlying hostility. First is the striving for power itself, which reassures against the feeling of helplessness or insignificance. It will express itself as a need to dominate, control, have one's way and be right. Second is ambition, the striving for prestige, admiration and success. These reassure against the fear of humiliation. They result in a further need to impress and then to disparage others. Third is the need for possessions to reassure against the fear of impoverishment or dependence. A resulting secondary need is to exploit or deprive others.

Neurotic competitiveness is a specific and special manifestation of this quest. It differs from similar attitudes normal in our culture in several ways. It is indiscriminate, constantly raising comparisons with others. It is aimed toward excessive ambitions which provide the feeling of being exceptional and unique. Therefore, there must inevitably arise feelings of disappointment no matter what is accomplished; it is never enough. The power of neurotic competitiveness is maintained by intense underlying hostility toward others, with a deep desire to frustrate and defeat them. Because of this deeper emotion, it constitutes an area of special neurotic conflict, even, for instance, in the analysis. There exist both a fear of success (which can bring possible threatening loss of affection) and fear of failure (which threatens possible humiliation). In sexual relations, this state can play a great role. Sometimes the man's need to degrade the partner may be disguised by a brittle feeling of admiration, a desire to put her on a pedestal. Or the husband who was first wanted when failing and weak may be rebuffed after succeeding.

Because competition is so threatening, the recoil from competitiveness is as significant a symptom as the need for it. Inhibitions, feelings of inferiority, self-belittling, real failures, and a discrepancy between potentials and achievement can all result from this conflict.

Because awareness of the discrepancy between exaggeratedly ambitious goals and reality is so painful, the neurotic may substitute grandiose fantasies about himself for the reality. These differ from both normal and psychotic types of similar notions. The normal person can accept his as fantasies, can even laugh at them. The psychotic, unaware of reality, believes his. The neurotic lies between the two and fluctuates from one extreme to the other—especially when his self-esteem is hurt by some failure.

Neurotic guilt feelings, with their accompanying conscious and unconscious self-recriminations, differ from genuine guilt. They are the expression of anxiety or fears—more precisely, the fear of disapproval or criticism, or the fear of the exposure of pretenses or a façade. The neurotic fears that he really might have a lack of assertiveness, weakness, hostility or unwillingness to change in spite of his appearance of strength. It is easier to accuse oneself than to confront others. And if faults are expediently accepted without actually doing anything about them, there is no real need to change.

What has been called masochism can thus be interpreted as a defensive need for suffering, contrasted with true suffering. It aims first at cloaking the underlying demands, self-accusations, and needs to dominate. The neurotic can, by suffering, achieve these ends; it is a kind of secondary gain. Second, it is part of a drive toward self-oblivion and self-abandonment. This means getting rid not only of the doubts, limitations and fears that are part of normal human existence, but also of the specifically neurotic conflicts, otherwise insoluble and accompanied by intense suffering. These dionysian tendencies provide hope of relief without danger of real self-elimination. It furnishes some satisfaction, however poor, in "losing the self in something greater."

This initial version of her theory was her first attempt to bring together the fragmentary ideas she had thus far presented in her various papers into a cohesive and internally consistent explanation of why and how people became neurotic. While it was only a partial rather than the complete revision of the whole psychoanalytic doctrine Alexander had implied, it was an ambitious project nonetheless. Her clinical experience had demonstrated the importance of childhood experiences in initiating neurotic development; that she could not deny. Yet she wished to repudiate the Freudian emphasis on infantile instinctive urges and the psychosexual relationships derived from them as the source of neurotic conflicts. In their place she would substitute cultural factors as equally significant. At the same time, these alone did not suffice to explain all the neurotic phenomena, as Fromm maintained. The delicate question was how to allow for the effects of sociocultural influence while at the same time postulating intrapsychic mechanisms to explain neurosis. In fact her explanation of how external, cultural factors relate to internal forces and emotions has remained since then one of the least clear aspects of her theory. There is certainly evidence that at this point she was still trying to straddle the fence: to convince her orthodox colleagues that she had not completely rejected infantile sexuality and her culturalist friends that she agreed with them also. Her rebellious break was not yet complete.

XVI
THE FIRST SCHISM

After Karen finished the manuscript of *New Ways in Psychoanalysis,* a curious change occurred in her personality. Whereas previously she had attended the New York Society meetings only infrequently, she now came to and actively participated in almost every one. Some of the informal discussions were even a bit comically emotional. She and another senior female analyst had one such debate over the interpretation of a dream about two women, one undressed and the other clothed. It ended in a shouting match about whether their actions represented feelings related to penis envy or social deprivation. Karen is officially listed as discussing various papers in at least seven meetings between March 1939 and May 1940. These include such diverse topics as "The Significance of Choice of Analyst" (Thompson), "The Repetition Compulsion" (Kubie), "Studies of Gastric Ulcers" (Mittelmann), "Homosexuality" (Robbins) and "Psychology of Urticaria" (Saul) among others.

What could have been the reasons for such a change? Perhaps it was simply a question of time: Having needed all her available time to write, she had had none for professional meetings. But this is an oversimplification; it was more a question of psychic energy. Having devoted her creative energy so intensely to her recent book, she seemed to have run down her psychic battery. She had run out of ideas to write about. Now she needed a period of rest or of recharging through outside stimulation. She found it by directing her still intense curiosity and interest outward, to the work of others. This shift from inner to outer focus had occurred twice before at the Berlin Society.

Perhaps, though, there was still another factor involved. This participation indicated a change from a passive and self-effacing attitude to a more active and expansive one. The clue to this change can be found in a short paper she wrote around this time, "Can You Take a Stand?" [1]

This is one of the few papers that she clearly indicates refers to herself. It relates to her attitudes not only toward her critics in the society and institute but also toward the Nazis. It sheds light on her apparent indifference to their terrorist practices, a stance that was criticized by some and incomprehensible to others. In the paper, she mentions that she was amazed to be called "wishy-washy" for not making a definite value judgment or taking a stand toward those who were obviously offensive and hurtful. She had felt what she considered a laudable pride in being objective and tolerant, able to see both the good and the bad. *"Tout comprendre, c'est tout pardonner."* But she had now come to realize that this pride was neurotic and irrational, that these explanations were excuses. Both in herself and in the patients she cited, the true motives were deeper feelings: a fear of others and a distrust of one's own self. Such feelings arise in a child very early in reaction to its parents. The child's feeling of not mattering can result from her sense of not being acceptable unless she "uncritically adores one parent or fulfils their ambitions for her or becomes subservient to the demands of a self-sacrificing mother." This description could well have been applicable to her own attitudes toward her parents.

As a result, she continued, such a person is easily swayed by any inviting ideology that gives a sense of security and guidance, be it leftist or fascist. She loses her own initiative and evaluates herself largely in terms of what others think of her. Karen's statement about dictatorship is a notable one, which she repeated in public interviews and which has often been quoted. These "traits may be agreeable in relation to the immediate environment, but seen from a broader point of view, they constitute a danger. It is people with these traits who succumb most easily to Fascist propaganda. Fascist ideology promises to fulfil all their needs. The individual in the Fascist state is not supposed to stand up for his own wishes, rights, judgments. He can forget about his own weakness by adoring the leader. His ego is bolstered up by being submerged in the greater unity of race and nation. Democratic principles are in sharp contrast to Fascist ideology. Democratic principles uphold the independence and strength of the individual and assert his right to happiness. It is important that everyone convinced of the value of Democracy should do his utmost to strengthen self-confidence and will power, and to develop individual capacity for forming judgments and making decisions."

The reaction to her second book, *New Ways in Psychoanalysis*, followed quickly after its publication during the summer of 1939. The "official" reviews appeared in the fall. The one in the *International Journal of Psychoanalysis* by Auguste Stärcke but approved by Jones, was relatively kind. There were no personal judgments of Karen, or polemics. While the reviewer pointed out the areas of Freudian theory Karen rejected—the libido theory, Oedipus complex, death instinct, repetition compulsion and superego—he attributed this to a more basic rejection of the instinctual and psychosexual source of mental functioning. Regarding Karen's modifications of therapy, the reviewer focused on her holistic, characterological view; on her emphasis on the present; and on the greater activity she advocated for the analyst. In summing up, he found that she did not "stray too far from a reasonably analytic attitude to the patient. . . . On the whole, Dr. Horney does not lead us so far astray from the field of orthodox analysis as she wishes to make out. As far as positive contributions go, there should not be much difficulty in introducing a number of them into the regular body of psychoanalytic knowledge without disturbing its existing structure to any great extent." This was conciliatory indeed.

The second review, by Otto Fenichel, was published both in German in the *Zeitschrift* and in the American *Psychoanalytic Quarterly*. It was a scathing response, in which Karen was criticized for not understanding Freud at all. Characterizing her disagreements as "attacks" and listing the questioned areas as "offensive" to her, he then criticized her for not admitting that what she retained was not psychoanalysis at all. While he agreed that analysis had not yet sufficiently considered social factors, he cautioned against accepting Karen's theory as a new sociological psychoanalysis.

Further reaction simmered closer to home. In October, Karen presented her views at a regular meeting of the New York Society in a paper with the long title "The Emphasis on Genesis in Freud's Thinking; the Influence of the Genetic Viewpoint on Therapy and Practice, Its Value and Debatable Aspects." This was the most direct confrontation yet, as it focused on the nuclear issue, the relative importance of on-going dynamic factors versus infantile psychosexual ones. The paper was discussed by Lorand, Thompson, Ludwig Jekels, Kardiner, Gregory Zilboorg, Lewin and Federn. The discussion was so heated and so many wished to speak that a second evening a month later was devoted to it. This time Carl Binger, Harmon Ephron, Mittelman, Kubie, David Levy, Robbins, John Millet and Wittels joined the previous group in discussing the paper.

Karen had some defenders among the younger and more socially minded analysts and those who were personally friendly to her. But the general tenor of the discussion was critical and hostile. Kubie, as moderator, recalls that he and others, as far as he knew, felt no personal animosity toward Karen. He tried to keep the discussion impersonal and at the level of issues alone.

She was seated in the audience this evening, with her friends the Lowenfelds, both analysts, with whom she had come. As she heard the criticisms, she at one point turned red and tears came to her eyes. She turned to Yela Lowenfeld and remarked, "I don't see why we can't have different opinions and still be friends." She had expressed similar feelings at the disputes in Berlin ten years before. This was the only time she is reported to have openly wept in public.

The distinction between theory and practice was one of the important issues raised on the floor. Once when she was being condemned for theoretical points, Lorand asked her directly how she would treat a patient with unresolved feelings toward a father figure, a typical oedipal case. When Karen described her method of handling it, he exclaimed in her defense that he still considered her a Freudian analyst in spite of her theoretical differences.

The position of Zilboorg, stated shortly afterwards in a paper on "The Fundamental Conflict with Psychoanalysis,"[2] exemplified the view of the opposition to Karen. "When the person's instinctual life becomes a serious hindrance to the serenity of his conclusions, the current superficial conflicts, if unduly stressed, enable him to hold himself at the greatest possible distance . . . and he avoids the discomfort involved in 'looking at himself.' This is particularly and explicitly the characteristic of the views recently evolved by Karen Horney." Her emphasis on present attitudinal conflicts was thus seen as a means of avoiding deeper instinctual conflicts, both in herself and in people in general.

In the fall of 1939, Karen asked for a new course, "A Critical Evaluation of Certain Psychoanalytic Concepts," which would cover the same subjects discussed in her book. At the same time, the overall New York Institute curriculum was divided into three distinct yearly sections—junior, intermediate and senior. Courses were either required for each year or elective in the senior year. Whether this reorganization was in any way related to Karen's situation was to become an issue. Her course was permitted but was made an elective in spite of her request that it be required for all students. The official explanation was that the younger candidates would not be ready for exposure to such "deviationist" ideas before being well grounded in the traditional Freudian concepts. Karen felt this to be a rebuke. According to the institute's later official statement, it was not intended as one. The two events were simply coincidental. The student survey and curriculum change had been arranged previously.

In January 1940, Karen finally moved into her new office-apartment. Though not large, it was comfortable. The combined living-waiting room was furnished in a rather casual style, with much of the coarse-textured material she so liked in evidence, and many bright-colored cushions. Along the walls were the books she loved. A little table for patients waiting held only one magazine, *Gourmet*. Her office overlooked the park from the twenty-fourth floor. Seated at her desk, she could see far across the lakes and trees to the skyscrapers on the opposite side. They reminded her of the high, distant mountains she so loved. A second door permitted easy egress for the patient who might not wish to go again through the waiting room. It led into a cubicle which then opened into the bedroom. The bedroom itself contained a little refrigerator and table so that Karen would not have to go into the kitchen for snacks.

In spite of the negative reception they gave her book, Karen continued to attend the New York Society's meetings through 1940. Many of the members did not bear her any personal antagonism, or so they claimed. Others were cold. She moved closer to the more liberal, social-minded members, those who sympathized with and supported her views, even if they did not agree with them. These included her friends from the Zodiac group. (As Sullivan had returned to Washington at the end of 1938, the Zodiac Club was no longer officially in existence, but the remaining members continued to socialize.)

Among her friends outside the New York Society were Fromm, Margaret Mead, Ruth Benedict, John Dollard and a growing number of New School associates. They spent long convivial evenings, perhaps once a week, discussing cultural issues. Margaret Mead remembers how they debated the difference between "individual" traits and those repeated by different individuals in one culture. This distinction was to become a key concept in Fromm's thought. On another occasion, they focused on certain customs of American Indians, which by coincidence, several patients had brought up. That evening, by further coincidence, Karen had come upon the statue of a wooden Indian on her way home. They questioned whether the Indian could be a symbol, a Jungian archetype.

By this time, many other refugee friends of Karen's were arriving. They too entered into her social life. Paul Lussheimer, the young Mannheim psychiatrist with whom she had become friends at the Medical Psychotherapy meetings, was one of these. The Lussheimers, the Lowenfelds and the Tillichs formed a social group who would often get together on weekends. Ernest and Anna Schachtel, Fromm and Karen formed another circle. They not only met on weekends but spent part of several summer vacations together. Paul Kempner, her banker friend from Berlin, arrived with his wife. Then came Erich Maria Remarque, the writer, who had his summer home in Switzerland next to hers. These formed still another circle, often with the Tillichs. Karen's social life was full, with gatherings and invitations to one home or another, or dining out.

One memorable evening, Remarque took the group to his hotel restaurant to meet his friend, Salvador Dali. Beforehand, they all drank well to the occasion; when they arrived, they were all more or less tipsy. When Dali came in, Karen and Tillich were absolutely unable to speak to him. They just stood there and giggled, while Remarque and Hannah Tillich tried to start a conversation. Dali finally walked out, understandably in something of a huff.

In June 1939, Marianne completed her residency in psychiatry and became a staff member of the Payne-Whitney Clinic. Her evident clinical ability resulted in her appointment as an instructor at the Cornell Medical School. Her training analysis was progressing apace. As was to be expected, she was changing from her previously rather shy, subdued and inhibited self to a more outgoing, self-expressive and independent person. As a natural part of the process, she began to vent her feelings—partly against her mother for real or imagined deprivations or slights. Just as naturally, her analyst suppported her striving for inner freedom. But this delicate, transferential situation was to have unforeseen effects.

During the two years from 1939 to 1941, Karen was continuing her analyses and supervision of candidates at the New York Institute. Gradually she was attracting an increasingly larger group who wished to work with her. In part this may have been because of the intellectual appeal of her new ideas. Some were more receptive to them than others. It may also have been due to the clarity of her presentations and expositions. Too, it may have had to do with her personal qualities. At fifty-five, she was still an attractive woman, with the same distinctly felt charm that had been attributed to her at the Berlin Institute. Several of her students described it in analytic terms as a countertransferential effect; perhaps it corresponded to Brigitte's "erotic radiation." Her popularity and the demand for her supervision was later attributed, in an official report of the Psychoanalytic Institute, to "an unscientific tendency to form cliques around the persons of individual instructors and to reject the ideas of others. . . . some students remained almost entirely under a single theoretical point of view. . . . The relationship between teacher and student was being used to gather together a band of disciples." The implication was that Karen and her liberal group had some self-serving motive for holding on to students which was injurious to their training.

In addition to her theories and her influence on students, a third controversial issue arose during 1940. A number of candidates who were ready to graduate except for their final papers found their theses rejected on grounds of "not being analytic enough." They were asked to rewrite them in a more acceptable form, meaning more in conformity with orthodox concepts, less couched in Horney's or Kardiner's ideas. Of the fourteen whose theses were rejected, eleven finally accepted the additional work and three demurred. While the official report was to claim that only these three were associated with the "dissident" group, in fact all fourteen were.

The society was prey to complex factionalism at this time. Besides the "Horneyites," there was a second dissatisfied group, with which some of the fourteen students were allied. This group included Abraham Kardiner, Rado, George Daniels, David Levy, Carl Binger and others. They were later to break away to form their own psychoanalytic institute. Some of the then orthodox members have even claimed that Karen was not the real target of the critical feeling that was seemingly directed against her. In fact, it was aimed more at Rado, because of both the new adaptational theory he was beginning to formulate and teach and his dictatorial handling of the Educational Committee. A vain attempt was made to unite these two groups. A special meeting between Karen and Rado was arranged at Sarah Kelman's home, with Kardiner present, in order to try to reconcile them. But the same tension that had existed between them since the Berlin days intruded now. Rado was apparently unwilling to make up, even though Karen would have been willing to do so. He hardly spoke at the meeting. Kardiner himself relates that he felt reluctant to "entrust his destiny" to Karen. He believed he would have a more promising opportunity with Rado, who had previously supported his anthropological teaching at the New York Institute. He and Karen felt no personal animosity toward each other, spoke freely, and in fact, felt strong ties of friendship. But each was evidently disappointed in the other's lack of support.

During 1940 Karen and her friends saw in the three issues proof of an unfair discrimination against them and the students working with them. They complained of intimidating tactics, of rigid dogmatism in teaching and of violation of academic freedom. Many protests were made to the Executive Council, the Board of Directors and the total membership at meetings. At times the debate was acrimonious. Some of the "dissident" students have since related how they were unofficially pressured to select more "acceptable" analysts or courses lest they jeopardize their chances for graduation or membership in the society. Some received "friendly" phone calls from orthodox senior analysts advising them to "do what was right." These practices were verified by the answers given to a questionnaire submitted to all the students in February 1941 by David Levy.

By March, tension and recrimination was so high that sixteen of the dissatisfied members began to meet at the homes of Robbins and Thompson to discuss the situation.

On April 29, at the annual business meeting of the society, after the new officers were nominated, Levy presented the results of his student questionnaire. Then, following a vociferous debate, with Zilboorg leading the attack and Robbins the defense, Karen was disqualified as an instructor. Two versions of this action have been given. The official version claimed that only her status as an instructor was changed, limiting her to teaching third-year students. Karen's own version states that she was removed as a training analyst. The grounds: that she was disturbing the students. The vote: 24 to 7, with 29 abstaining. The reason for the large abstention was two-fold. Some of Karen's German-speaking colleagues, though they disagreed with her position, were still friendly and sympathized with her, and could not bring themselves to reject her unequivocally. In addition, a number of the dissidents were preparing to leave the society and could neither vote against her in good conscience nor vote for her without revealing their own intentions prematurely.

The dramatic moment that followed the vote has never been forgotten by those who were there. In a dead silence, Karen rose, and with great dignity, her head high, slowly walked out. Thereupon Thompson, Robbins, Ephron and Sarah Kelman rose and followed her out. They all went to a bar for a few drinks. And then they marched jubilantly down the street, arm in arm, following Thompson's lead in singing Karen's favorite spiritual: "Go down, Moses, Way down in Egypt land, Tell old Pharaoh, to let my people go"—the song celebrating the liberation of the Jews from Egyptian tyranny.

Three days later, the group sent an official letter of resignation to the Secretary of the Society:

> *For the last few years it has become gradually more apparent that the scientific integrity of the New York Psychoanalytic Society has steadily deteriorated. Reverence for dogma has replaced free inquiry; academic freedom has been abrogated; students have been intimidated; scientific sessions have degenerated into political machinations.*
>
> *When an instructor and training analyst is disqualified solely because of scientific convictions, any hopes we may have harbored for improvement in the politics of the Society have been dispelled.*
>
> *We are interested only in the scientific advancement of psychoanalysis in keeping with the courageous spirit of its founder, Sigmund Freud. This obviously cannot be achieved within the framework of the New York Psychoanalytic Society as it is now constituted.*
>
> *Under the circumstances we have no alternative but to resign, however much we may regret the necessity for this action.*
>
> *Yours very truly,*

A copy was also sent to the American Psychoanalytic Association. In the covering letter of explanation, they stressed that this was not a personal matter, even though attempts had been made to convert it into one for political reasons. It was a question of scientific integrity and development. They further cited the effects upon the students, and referred to the questionnaire of David Levy, who was then President of the American Association. They assumed that their membership in the parent body was automatically terminated as well, since they had resigned from the local member society. Their plan to form a new psychoanalytic association, which they hoped would have a national scope, added to this assumption, since one could not belong to two rival psychoanalytic associations at the same time. Yet they closed with the "hope that our work on behalf of our science will, within the next few years, warrant our again being incorporated into the American Psychoanalytic Association." Karen did not wish to break with the association and at the next meeting, in May, tried to prevent it, though in vain.

During the next six weeks, at almost weekly meetings of the group in various homes, plans for the new organization were discussed, committees were set up to work on a constitution and a temporary executive council nominated. Karen was authorized to enter into negotiations with her friend Alvin Johnson regarding possible affiliation with the New School. Silverberg, still an official member of the Washington-Baltimore group, joined the new group at once. He was nominated for president. Fromm seems to have been involved also, but whether he attended these meetings is not known; his name is not mentioned in any of the documents of this time. He had been a member-at-large of the American Association, but had lost that status when the category had been eliminated. Apparently he had never been informed of this, and found out, to his surprise, only several years later.

In May, the annual meeting of the American Association was held in Richmond, Virginia. Although Karen made a statement of her reasons for resigning at the general meeting, the question of her membership was tabled by the chairman, Adolph Stern from New York. The grounds were that the New York Psychoanalytic Society had not yet acted upon it. Then in the Executive Council a motion was made that it was inconsistent with the constitution to belong to both the American Psychoanalytic Association and the new association. This was carried by a close split vote, with considerable influence exerted by the councillor from New York. Silverberg, as an invited guest, presented the view of the new group, though without much force. The importance of this decision to him can be imagined, since he had just been nominated for president of the American Association, a position he would presumably have to renounce unless he intended to resign from the new group. He lost the election by one vote—a vote which, had it gone otherwise, could have so added to his influence that it could have changed the council's decision and thereby changed the course of Karen's life.

Finally, at the meeting of the Council on Professional Training, which Karen attended as she was a member, it was officially decided that

> the problem of psychoanalytic training, especially in relation to the didactic analysis and supervised analysis, was to teach the candidate what is accepted as basic Freudian psychoanalysis and not what any individual may consider his interpretation or his deviation from Freudian analysis to be. All such moot points of view have a place in the curriculum of each Institute as special courses of a graduate nature, but have no place in the preliminary basic training of the candidate.

This supported the position of the New York Society. And so the new organization was excluded from the main body of accepted "classical" psychoanalysts and stood on its own, alone.

The fourteen candidates, having now completed their training and graduated, sent in their own joint resignation in June. They all immediately applied for, and received, membership in the new Association for the Advancement of Psychoanalysis. The name expressed the forward-looking spirit of its members, the view that psychoanalysis was not yet definitive and would be creatively developed further. The new name for the training arm of the association was chosen in June, the American Institute for Psychoanalysis.

To conclude the history of the schism, the five original founders soon sent out a circular letter to every member of the American Psychoanalytic Association, giving the reasons for their resignation. Addressing themselves primarily to the issue of psychoanalytic education, they distinguished between two concepts of psychoanalysis. One conceived of analysis as "certain concepts and techniques . . . handed down by Freud, or the 'classical' form." The other conceived of it as "still in an experimental stage of its development, full of uncertainties, full of problems, to which anything approaching final and conclusive answers is still to be sought"; this was the "nonclassical" form. Practitioners of the latter, the new group, felt that the decision should be left to the student as to which group of ideas he should be exposed to first. They accused the New York Society of believing that "scientific issues may legitimately be decided through possession of political power." The new group wished "to create a new center for psychoanalytic work, devoted to truly liberal and scientific principles in training, investigation and discussion."

Finally, in November, the New York Society felt obliged to issue a statement on its own behalf and in its own defense. It objected to the name of the new institute as misleading, in that it implied a national scope. In point of fact, the new group did wish such a broad scope, and it initially attracted members from Chicago, Washington, Baltimore and Philadelphia in addition to New York. Then the statement scored the various claims of the new group as having been founded in protest against the "scientific dogmatism entrenched behind political power" within the New York Society. It denied the three issues Karen had protested against since 1940, and claimed no violation of academic freedom. On the contrary, it accused the dissident group of the same type of violation in attempting to "maintain an exclusive influence on the education of a small group of students."

However, this statement in self-defense rendered itself questionable by failing to foresee the new development that took place shortly afterward but which had already been brewing and was an open secret. This was the withdrawal from the New York Society of a second group of dissidents in June 1942. Fourteen members were involved, and significantly not all were American "modernists"; but at least three were German-speaking analysts. The historical account of the soon-to-be-formed Columbia Psychoanalytic Clinic describes the atmosphere of the New York Society in terms similar to those used by the first group:

> For several years . . . a great deal of dissension and dissatisfaction had been going on with a considerable number of members of the New York Psychoanalytic Society, first from the rigidity being shown in demanding that candidates for membership conform to orthodox standards, and the generally stifling atmosphere of the meetings of

the Society itself. . . . Dr. Rado was constantly working for higher academic standards in training and introducing new ideas in his reformulation of Freudian psychoanalysis. He also had repeatedly pointed out the limitations of having an Educational Committee under the political influence of a Society. His stand led to considerable resentment from official quarters.

The events of the last winter and spring were of such a nature as to give us a distaste for further participation in the affairs of the Society. For several years there has been an atmosphere of bickering, slander and gossip, in which none of us has felt that we could function profitably.

It has been stated by some that we are innocents who have been led . . . by certain ambitious, self-seeking and troublesome individuals. We do not admit this allegation. We are clearly aware of undercurrents of rivalry and disharmony in the Society and of certain distortions of fact. We have never regarded the issue of so-called "Academic Freedom" as Simon-pure. Other members have voiced their conviction that we are good riddance because we are not "true believers." That is a matter of opinion.[3]

Fortunately, the organizers of this second group were able to avoid the fate that befell Karen, ostracism from the classical psychoanalytic world. By negotiating with the American Psychoanalytic Association before resigning completely, they were able to effect a change in the constitution and have themselves accepted as an official, accredited member society.

XVII
THE NEW ORGANIZATION: HOPES, DREAMS AND ILLUSIONS

Karen was excited, they were all excited about the new organization. For her, though, it was a mixed emotion. Now that she had taken a stand, expressed and acted on her hostility, the inevitable reaction set in. The pendulum swung to the opposite side: She felt she needed others. So that summer (1941), instead of taking her vacation alone, traveling or in a summer resort, she spent part of July with the Schachtels and Fromm in their house on Monhegan Island in Maine. She needed their companionship and emotional support.

August was spent in her now finished summer cottage in Croton, which had been built to her specifications by Herbert Meyer. She needed the time to work on the manuscript of her third book, *Self-Analysis*. Seated in front of the huge picture window, with the view of the Hudson River and the valley beyond, she had an ideal place to work. This book was to be based on the course on self-analysis that she had given at the New School the previous winter. Her interest in the issue was an outgrowth of her contacts with the social workers at both the Jewish Family Service and the New School. In her 1934 paper for them, she had emphasized that although the concepts of psychoanalysis might be helpful to them in their work, there was a distinct difference between its use by the trained analyst and its use by the nonanalyst. In her lecture course during the winter/spring semesters of 1939–1940, "Applying Psychoanalysis to Oneself and Environment," she had focused on the use of "factual psychoanalytic knowledge by teachers, social workers and laymen in an effort to aid others . . . in making an adjustment to their environment." She had discussed the conscious and unconscious motivations of nonprofessionals analyzing friends, while stressing that analysis was a dangerous tool. The material she had presented included the possibilities and difficulties of self-analysis. The reaction to this course had been immensely enthusiastic. She decided she would elaborate on these ideas and began to organize her notes for a new book.

Besides, at a personal level, she was always questioning her own motives and reactions. The situation at the New York Society had certainly been disturbing to her. The realization of how she had failed to take a stand and her subsequent change was indeed an insight. It was an example of her own attempts at self-analysis. And yet, in spite of these she was apparently unaware of the further inner changes that were taking place in her attitudes. The manifest swings she was experiencing were perhaps the immediate cause for her interest in this subject. She had written to Norton in late summer of 1940 that her "interest in writing has reawakened indeed. This time it is about self-analysis, the idea being to combat the defeatist belief that one must necessarily go to an analyst in order to understand and remove neurotic disturbances. I should like to encourage people to the effect that they can do a good bit of analysis themselves . . ."

Another sign in 1941 of her "reawakening" was her added teaching at the New School. In the winter she gave two further courses: a "Seminar in Psychology" with Max Wertheimer, her psychologist friend from Berlin, and Hans Speier, also a refugee. She had recommended them for appointment to the faculty. She also taught the course on "Types of Personality." This was a study of various types of personality structure, as outlined by Freud, Jung, Adler and herself. It discussed various characters depicted in literature, an interest derived from her own omnivorous reading. Then in the spring of 1941, together with the same psychologists, she gave a second seminar on "Power, Domination and Freedom." There could have been no doubt that she was drawn to these topics by the situation in the Society and her reactions to it.

The first meeting of the new Association was held in September 1941 at the New York Academy of Medicine. Silverberg was president and Thompson, vice-president. Harold Kelman, one of the fourteen whose final paper had been rejected, was secretary. Stephen Jewitt, the head of the psychiatry department at the New York Medical College, was treasurer. He was soon to play an important role in the evolution of the group. The Association did not elect Karen president for several reasons.

As she had been the center of controversy, they wished to avoid drawing the attention of the outside world to her again by putting her in such a position. They also wanted to emphasize the eclecticism of the new group, that it was not formed around her ideas. Silverberg was a highly respected and honored member of the classical analytic community. His connection with the Washington group gave the appearance of a broader geographical scope. They hoped to draw analysts from elsewhere in the country.

But perhaps as important as these political reasons were Karen's personal feelings. Overt and direct exercise of power was not congenial to her personality; it conflicted too much with her self-effacing tendencies. While she certainly possessed needs for leadership and prestige, these could only be expressed indirectly, from behind the throne, so to speak. She manifested them not by exerting direct domination but simply by the mere force of her presence, her charisma, the unspoken authority of her being. She seemed usually to be unaware of her effect on others; when she could sense it, she struggled with it. It was not due to haughtiness or an attitude of superiority. The energy behind these needs was more directly invested in her intellectual work, her theory and eventually in the means of perpetuating it—namely, in the organization itself. She was not interested in being a "political" or organizational leader and so left this to others. This aversion to official leadership may have been what she referred to in her book as a recoil from competition. This aversion was to be significant in explaining some of the later difficulties of the group. And so she became dean, concerned mainly with course curriculum, teaching and candidates.

At first, twenty-one analysts made up the membership, including six from Washington, Detroit and Chicago. As was to be expected, Marianne joined as a candidate. Both Sullivan and Fromm were recommended for honorary membership by Thompson and Karen respectively. Sullivan accepted; Fromm was unwilling to accept at that time. The honorary status would only acknowledge his contribution to an allied science; it would not recognize his standing as a psychoanalyst. Why the "honorary" at all? he wanted to know. Why not a regular member? Had he not been involved in the formation of the new group from its inception? He would join only if he were allowed to train and supervise analytic candidates. At a special meeting in November, this was granted him, although a minority voted against it as committing the Association to the principle of lay analysis.

There is much question as to Karen's attitudes toward this issue, especially at this point. Publicly opposed to lay analysis, she contradicted herself in both her previous and present personal behavior. She had even referred her daughter for treatment to Fromm, whom she liked and trusted. According to him, she was not opposed to lay analysis, at least in her personal exchanges with him. She often joked about her previous statements and never expressed an opinion against the nonmedical practice of analysis. In any event, at this time the matter remained in limbo, temporarily bypassed in the euphoria of the new venture.

In his speech at that first meeting, Silverberg was optimistic, hopeful and idealistic. Perhaps overly so. He dedicated himself and the organization to the "firm conviction in the worth and dignity of the human individual: the belief that human beings in social situations should and, if fairly well adjusted, can have a fundamental liking and respect for one another, that each of us should and can acknowledge a fundamental validity in the other, and hereby acknowledges that the other has certain rights which all must respect . . ." He criticized those who had not hesitated to use power and force to silence dissenters and so denied the freedom of thought and communication so necessary for any valid science. He was being a prophet of a sort when he pointed out that the insistence on this freedom was all they had in common and the only justification for the group. Otherwise they represented many divergences and differences of opinion. He solemnly hoped that this principle and faith might never be compromised. Alas, he was being utopian in failing to allow for the human foibles of the members. At this same meeting, Karen launched the monthly scientific conferences with her presentation on "Psychoanalysis and Self-Development."

The first two years were halcyon. Courses were given at the Institute itself in a rented apartment, at the Flower-Fifth Avenue Hospital under the auspices of the postgraduate division of the New York Medical College, and at the New School. Monthly scientific lectures were given at the Academy of Medicine by members or by invited guest speakers. To counterbalance the formality of these presentations, monthly informal "interval" meetings of the students were held at the Institute, where free back-and-forth discussion could take place on topics of personal concern. Every senior member was teaching.

All exerted themselves, but perhaps nobody worked as prodigiously as

Karen. She was giving lectures on the "Structure of Neurosis" at the hospital, a series on "Psychoanalytic Technique" at the Institute, another on "Fundamental Problems in Psychoanalysis" with Thompson at the New School, along with a seminar series on "Personality and Culture" with Ephron, Fromm and Lasswell, her friend from Chicago. She did all this in addition to screening new student applicants, attending regular meetings with the faculty about courses, and presenting or discussing papers at the Association meetings. She was also working on her third book and seeing private patients. At the monthly scientific meetings during this period, Karen invited such friends to speak as Ruth Benedict, Abraham Kardiner, Abraham Maslow and even Alexander from Chicago.

Most of these meetings were important, even outstanding statements in their own right. But it was not only the speakers and subjects that were significant, even though many did come to hear the special guests. These were certainly not the usual psychoanalytic conferences. Some indefinable spirit of enthusiasm, even fervor, animated the audience, which included not only Association members and analytic students but professionals from related fields, analytic patients and simply interested laymen as well. The students felt excited, stimulated, with a strong desire to learn. These were venturesome, pioneering, ground-breaking days, and the new approach to psychoanalysis carried it beyond its usual scholarly limits.

For instance, there was one meeting especially vividly recalled today. Fromm was to be the speaker and Ruth Benedict to head the discussion. Suddenly, without previous notice, Sullivan rose to the podium. His first remark, "I am a schizophrenic," drew an audible gasp from the audience, which was followed by a round of applause. Karen applauded especially loudly. When asked about this at the close of the meeting, she replied that she had particularly applauded Sullivan's courage in self-revelation, whether true or not. It was the same type of frankness she had admired in Groddeck twenty years before and which she continued to prize. Yet here was another contradiction. She admired it, often demanded it in others but was angered by the frankness and openness she found in Chicago, and was herself reserved about her own intimate feelings or ideas.

In May 1942, the Association held its first annual meeting in Boston, in conjunction with that of the American Psychiatric Association. It was a gala affair, both scientific and social, in honor of the group's first successful year. The morning session was devoted to a panel discussion of the socio-psychological "Implication of Destructiveness." A parallel could be drawn between this topic and Karen's at the Leipzig meeting ten years earlier. True, the contexts of each were different. Then, in her paper on "*Der Kampf in der Kultur*," Karen had been presaging the advent of the Hitlerian nightmare. But insofar as she emphasized the human element, the psychological factors that first permitted and then had to fight against destructive trends were not dissimilar. The other members of the panel included her (still) friend Alexander, Daniel Schneider, Alexander Martin and finally Abe Maslow—who was to create his own psychology later, based in part on Karen's ideas.

That afternoon Silverberg compared those religions that see man as innately sinful with Freud's view of the individual as basically destructive, driven by a death instinct. He felt that neither was tenable or compatible with Karen's view of the person as self-healing and growing in a constructive direction. For him, the present world crisis represented the struggle between believers in these two contradictory philosophies.

Karen spoke on "The Role of Unconscious Arrogance in Neurosis." She had come to realize the importance of neurotic pride as part of the "illusion of having superior moral qualities." She had first broached this in her 1938–39 course on "Neurosis and its Relation to Moral Problems." Now this emotion was coming more into focus in her theory as a central factor in the neurotic structure, responsible for self-blame and self-contempt, and therefore for depression, and, in the final analysis, for masochism itself.

Clara Thompson also spoke on the topic of "Penis Envy in Women"[1]—that old subject of disagreement between Horney and Freud. She insisted that a new and more accurate meaning must now be given to that term. The Freudians used it in a biological-sexual sense. She felt it also had a nonsexual, competitive, therefore social and interpersonal, sense, with connotations of a superior-inferior, privileged-underprivileged hierarchy. Social factors could also contribute to an overemphasis on the penis, like parents' attitudes toward the sex of their child, with preference for a boy and rejection of a girl. In the "type of warfare which so often goes on between men and women," the penis could become a symbol of male conquest of the female. Its lack and resulting envy, would be felt more intensely by those women who already feel inadequate. While it is true that Thompson was a feminist, having already published several papers on related themes, one might question why she chose this paper at this time. It could have suggested some underlying feeling of rivalry between her and Horney, as was suggested by some of the participants there.

No such feelings were manifested in the evening at the dinner and dance. All was harmony and gaiety. Karen danced with most of the men there, students and faculty alike. She seemed to be enjoying herself wholeheartedly and was the belle of the ball.

In June 1942 her third book, *Self-Analysis,* was published. Its title was deceptive for several reasons. For one, it implied that the book was a do-it-yourself guide for a person wishing to analyze himself without professional help. It was not, or at least could only serve as one to a very limited extent, "with a question mark." For another, it also must be seen in the context of her theory: It presents certain changes in her view of the neurotic character structure. While these were only to be tentative, at the time they showed the evolution of her thought, a change of emphasis and her groping toward a better systematization. For instance, the two broad neurotic trends—here also termed needs, drives, wishes or strivings—described in "The Neurotic Personality" are now subdivided into ten distinct, more limited trends. Each could reinforce another similar trend or enter into conflict with a contradictory trend.

A third reason for its ambiguity was that the title was a double-entendre. It referred not only to Karen's patients but also to herself. While she wrote that the main patient cited, Clare, was an actual woman treated, she confided to her secretary that it was a composite. Some of the historical facts could well have been derived from her own life, and the attitudes related to her own personality. In other words, she was continuing, consciously or unconsciously, with her own self-analysis. The main trends selected for analysis in this "patient" were compulsive self-effacing ones: needs for affection and love, need for a partner. These were seen to conflict with repressed ambitious drives. The resulting symptoms included a loss of awareness of her own spontaneous wishes, which she had acknowledged as her own in her recent admittedly personal paper, "Can You Take a Stand?" Also included were inhibitions in work, which she had just spoken of in a newspaper interview.

During this period, the war was having an impact on everyone, though perhaps Karen was more sensitive to it than others in spite of her efforts to remain above it. Biggi was still at the center of the enemy camp, perhaps dangerously so. Renate had been emotionally hurt by the conflict. If she was now safely out of it, she still was separated from Karen by the circumstances. And even though Karen felt distaste for the Nazi principles and methods, she did not feel the hatred that the persecuted German Jews did who came here as refugees The inner conflict she felt rendered her hypersensitive. As part of the war-effort, the Association's War-Efforts Committee issued a series of war bulletins, based in part on panel discussions at the New School in March and November 1942. Karen contributed two of these. In one, "The Understanding of Individual Panic,"[2] she pointed out that panic reactions to emergency situations usually result from the triggering of preexisting anxiety. But, she warned, prophylaxis and therapy in these cases would best be aimed at the group, since the individual in this state is not amenable to reason.

The second brief paper was more personally significant to her: "Children in Wartime." It brought back her reminiscences from the First World War. She knew from personal experience how children suffer. "A child understands war in terms of his own home. War means that brother is away in the army, or that father is working on the swing shift and sleeps all day, or that mother is working in a defense plant and is not at home as she used to be. Alterations of the stability of family life and everyday routine are upheavals which are a disturbing force to children of all ages. A physical desertion of the child as a result of war has its emotional counterpart of deprivation and neglect. The full force of these events will be felt—not now—but in years to come. Mothers try heroically to keep things as much 'like home' as possible. In trying to do so, they overtax their own endurance and necessarily develop certain unintentional resentments toward their children, adding to the anxieties they are trying to allay. This is frequently seen where the mother feels she must be both mother and father to the child."[3]

The children! This was a serious concern to her—even as she had campaigned for the German and Jewish children. Had not her youngest daughter suffered, and was she not even now forced to live in an alien country, far away? Perhaps this still rankled. And there was Biggi, who in spite of her success, was still living in the eye of the maelstrom.

In 1941, Biggi had married a handsome young cameraman. As reported in *Film News*, while her marriage was a surprise, her choice was considered typical of her independent and unconventional personality. She could have had any prestigious, eligible movie-star or wealthy business-man. But she chose an average man. By the end of 1942, she had played in some twenty-odd movies and was one of the best-known and hardest-working actresses in the movie colony. This small group was close-knit; everyone in it knew everyone else. Until then it had been relatively favored by the regime—namely Goebbels—and its members permitted a fairly free existence, provided they worked within the regulations imposed. They reciprocated by cooperating, generally accepting his choice of films, but resisting his policies when they could—with some few exceptions. Although many of the films produced carried some subtle or not-so-subtle propaganda message, usually glorifying some aspect of German life, only about six were maliciously anti-Semitic or vicious, not counting the obviously slanted, out-and-out war documentaries. This easy-going relationship existed until the Gottschalk affair in late 1941.

Joachim Gottschalk was one of the most charming, famous, and above all, popular male stars in films. Sometimes called the "Frederic March of Germany," he was becoming a national institution. Except for one thing. He was married to a Jewish woman. Although Goebbels had been willing to overlook even that in view of the actor's popularity, the situation became intolerable when she began to attend official functions. He gave Gottschalk an ultimatum to divorce her; she and their child would be spared, sent out of the country. Biggi had worked in at least three films with Gottschalk. She was his good friend, liked and admired him, and he turned to her for help. She and Gustav Knuth, his best friend, both advised the divorce immediately, to save the Gottschalks' lives. When Joachim pleaded that he could not separate from his wife, Biggi flew to Zurich to find work for him there in the theater headed by Emil Oprecht. She returned to Berlin while her proposal was still being considered. But too late. When the Gestapo came to take Gottschalk, he and his wife had killed their child and committed suicide.

Few actors dared to attend his funeral. Biggi was one of the six who did, a courageous and daring act, perhaps quite dangerous for her. After this tragedy there was almost a revolt of the film community; they became completely alienated from Goebbels and the regime. Some even spoke openly against the authorities. Friends warned Biggi to be cautious. Her personality seemed to change. She became subdued, laughed less; yet few of her friends knew how she really felt.

Then in 1942 she suffered a relapse of the tuberculosis she had had as a child, this time in her knee. Apparently with special permission because of her public stature, she was allowed to go to Davos in Switzerland for treatment. How much Karen was aware of the Gottschalk affair is not known. Official versions were released in the international press, but details could not be written through the censor. She said nothing of it, even to those closest to her. Karen did learn of Biggi's illness through letters from Switzerland and was much disturbed by the news. She pleaded with her daughter not to return to Berlin, to no avail. During these two years it was a weighty burden she carried, in addition to the others, though few, if any, of her friends were aware of it.

Changes were also taking place in Marianne's life during this time. Toward the end of 1940, Gertrude Lederer-Eckardt, then a physiotherapist at the Payne-Whitney Clinic, had invited the residents to her home for tea. There Marianne met her son; it was love at first sight. They were married about a year later. Gertrude had long been interested in psychoanalysis and was curious about the famous psychoanalyst, Karen Horney. Karen was then suffering lower back pain and needed special massage and exercise. Gertrude became her physiotherapist. Soon she was being referred other patients and colleagues by Karen.

A humorous anecdote is recalled about their second meeting. Gertrude's nickname was Truebel, often mispronounced in English as "Trouble." A publisher's party was to be held for Karen, to feature her second book. Karen's editor, Elizabeth Todd, who had known Gertrude at the New School, asked, "And should I invite Trouble?" Karen, astonished, replied, "Why will we be inviting trouble? Will we be drinking too much?" It finally dawned on her that they were speaking of her daughter's mother-in-law to be.

Shortly afterward, Karen's previous part-time secretary, Marie Levy, had to leave. Gertrude offered to do the typing. This developed into an almost full-time position that was to last for the next twelve years. In addition to being her physiotherapist, nurse, secretary and typist, Gertrude became her social secretary, real-estate agent, accountant and banker, card partner, trouble-shooter, sounding board and, above all, her intimate friend and confidante.

How this relationship became so durable for so long is a striking comment on Karen's personality. The two women got along so well because the needs and attitudes of each seemed to complement the other's. Gertrude kept herself out of Karen's professional world. They generally agreed before any discussion as to what role Gertrude was to take: whether she was to remain a silent listener, a sounding board, or whether she was to participate, answer back, criticize and argue. Both had a keen sense of humor, so when there were disagreements, they could easily transcend and laugh at them. Each knew she was simultaneously depending upon and using the other and each enjoyed it. In a way it was similar to Karen's adolescent relationship with Tutti. And in the end, Karen liked to be taken care of, even pampered. She sensed that she was being loved not for her stature or reputation but for herself. Doing things for Karen also fulfilled Gertrude's needs. Where Karen might be too analytical, too intellectual, Gertrude was down to earth. Where Karen might be impulsive or superficial, Gertrude was cautious and reasoned.

By the end of 1942 the Association and Institute had grown impressively, to thirty-four members and twenty-nine candidates-in-training. Among the latter were a number of German refugees whom Karen had known in Berlin. Two of these were to be of special importance in Karen's remaining years and in the evoluton of the group: Richard Hulbeck, the exuberant ex-Dadaist, and another former social rebel, Frederick Weiss.

These two, along with Paul Lussheimer and Erich Remarque, had much in common. They and their wives met in each other's homes for dinner or in Karen's apartment. Occasionally, Tillich and Reinhold Niebuhr joined them. Their intellectual interests coincided: art, the theater, literature, philosophy and the social situation, especially when they spoke of Germany as compared to America. Hitler and the Nazis were discussed too, though less as a political than as a social phenomenon. They all remember the atmosphere of *Gemütlichkeit;* Karen as the genial and hospitable hostess, her fat German housekeeper, Mrs. Strauss, outdoing herself with the food. Karen loved good wine, especially from the Rhineland, and all varieties of cheese, local and imported. Hulbeck was at his best expounding his views on art, on the decadence of modern painting and its significance as an expression of man's present psychic state. He mourned the eclipse of Dada, which he really felt had never died. He was also quite knowledgeable about literature: Thomas Mann, Jules Romains and André Gide were close personal friends, and he often recounted his impressions of them and their work. Lussheimer often held forth on social

conditions in Europe and the United States. He had worked in social welfare clinics for the underprivileged, for school children, for alcoholics and
addicts. The influence of social conditions on health—the role of nutrition
and sports—was of concern to him. Remarque was concerned about the
conditions of the refugees. They, themselves, were all refugees, even
Karen in a certain sense. He was organizing his ideas in preparation for a
book, based partly on his own experiences in France. His attitude toward
Karen was quite different from the others'. They respected her, a feeling
tinged with awe. Tillich was friendly and warm, and on her level, but also
looked up to her. Remarque was also warm and liked her, but he alone
was masterful with her. His favorite expression for her was "little goose."
She seemed to like this attitude of his.

During this period, Karen had been dabbling in oil painting. She asked
Hulbeck to give her weekly lessons in the small studio he had set up in
his apartment. As he recalled, "She was really interested and enjoyed it
. . . though her painting was realistic and conservative. She had difficulty
with the abstract. When we tried to work on objective painting, I had difficulty in reaching her; she couldn't grasp it. Even then, she definitely
had talent and great intelligence."

As the months passed, he began to get the impression that she "became
more of a friend than a pupil. I felt the whole business of art lessons was
an attempt to find closeness to someone. She needed someone, I had the
feeling she was frustrated. Her daughter, Brigitte, was in Germany and
Marianne was preoccupied with her new marriage. She seemed to have
no one really close, like family. She gave the impression of being at some
personal turning point . . . between Fromm's ideologies and existentialism—though she never used that word. Something like the idea that
life wasn't really the outcome of your relationships with your parents but
of your ability to handle it without neurotic symptoms. She was looking
for a man companion who could reach her high standards. It was hard for
many men to approach her because of that."

Hulbeck had always been interested in philosophy and would readily
embark on long discussions. He had turned to existentialism, like so many
other intellectuals, out of despair over the chaos and death caused by war.
Now he felt that the social and economic structure, psychological systems,
even art, resulted from man's existential "state of being." Picasso's multiple perspective, the cubists' fragmentation, the futurists' constant move-

ment all gave evidence of the world's frenetic, disjointed, chopped-up, inauthentic existence. Modern art had become interested in the abstract, had turned away from the human figure to portray mathematical lines or machines, was preoccupied with the "objective" and the "structural" rather than with reality, because of man's loss of certainty about himself and his identity. Minimal art was empty because man felt empty. The emphasis on form and pure color bespoke man's search for stimulation and heightened awareness.

He and Karen discussed this intertwining of philosophy and art during their painting lessons. As he relates, "I wanted philosophical discussion, she was more practical and basically analytical. We both felt that the German people were really idealistic, with their romanticism and great philosophical works, but that this was destroyed by the present regime and the war. I spoke of this disaster of idealism and then the upcoming of life itself again. In the search, one can discover the chance problem: anything can happen at any time. The irrationality of life. For her this was only a jump to the neurotic Idealized Image of self, escape from the fears you can avoid. With strength to resist the unforeseen, you can continue to live."

To further the public education goals of the Association for the Advancement of Psychoanalysis, an Auxiliary Council—generally known as ACAAP—was formed in March 1942. It consisted of members' current or former analytic patients or simply well-wishers interested in psychoanalysis. While the idea for ACAAP initially originated with Karen, the first impetus came from Sarah Kelman, one of the original five who had resigned from the New York Society. Although the efforts of the ACAAP to popularize Karen's ideas were of mutual benefit, it added to the burden of the members who had to address them monthly.

A second ACAAP function was fund-raising. Money was needed for a permanent home, a building which could house not only the administrative offices and teaching facilities but also a new psychoanalytic clinic. Karen's hopes to see psychoanalysis practiced in a clinic had been frustrated by her involvement with the Berlin and Chicago clinics and, unfortunately, she was not to see this project successfully carried through. Preliminary plans for the clinic were drawn up by Harold Kelman, chairman of a clinic committee (along with Karen and Silverberg). They were sent to the members in December.

After terminating an analysis, Karen often continued a social relationship with her former patients. They also often became members of the ACAAP. One of these friends was Elizabeth Lancaster. One evening she and her husband invited Karen to a political dinner in honor of President Roosevelt. They were seated at a table with a group of Russian diplomats. After the President addressed the meeting, Karen was able to meet and greet him personally. It was noticed that she seemed singularly unimpressed, in contrast to most of the others there. Asked about this, she half shrugged and replied that meeting him was of no special interest to her. On the other hand, she seemed much more impressed with the Russians and extremely curious about their exotic country. She remained with these new-found acquaintances most of the evening, questioning them and discussing conditions in the Soviet Union. We can only speculate about this reaction. Was it that the trappings of greatness or public stature did not really appeal to her? Or was it pride, a defensive "sour-grapes" feeling against some painful envy, that inhibited her? This type of defensive reaction was later to be described in her theory.

Another similar relationship was with Cornelius Crane and his wife, Katherine. Originally from Boston, he was a wealthy manufacturer of such mundane necessities as bathroom fixtures. His family still maintained an estate at Ipswich, near Boston, with an eighty-room house, known as Crane's Castle. The mansion was perched high on a hill but he himself lived in a small house on the grounds. One of Karen's favorite "sports" there was to go rolling down the sand dunes nearby. She was often invited to social evenings, both there and in the Crane apartment in New York. The servants there got to know her well; they whispered that she must have some magic power because of the way she could influence Crane and members of the family. Crane was an avid orientalist, a knowing connoisseur and collector of Japanese art, interested in Eastern philosophy. It was through him that Karen first heard of and then met Daisetz Suzuki, the well-known Zen Buddhist philosopher and sage. He was, during the ensuing years, to exert a deep influence on her.

Still another memorable event of this year, happily recalled today by many analysts, was the annual students' party held in Karen's Westchester home. The candidates put on skits impersonating and lampooning some of their former instructors at the New York Institute. One of them learnedly discussed the scientific meaning of the "Oy" as a psychological entity.

They sang old-time songs; Gershwin's "It Ain't Necessarily So" was the theme song. They danced and Karen joined in. Some felt that she was having difficulty in really "letting down her hair," that her basic tendency was still to remain aloof. But everybody had a good time.

During these two years, at least five newborn baby daughters of candidates' wives were named after Karen. Her affection and concern toward these young mothers and babies were shown either by personal visits to their homes or hospital, or by a personal letter. Walter Bonime, one of the students and a close friend of Marianne, for instance, remembers such a visit one Sunday morning. He and his wife were busy with diapers and household chores. Karen immediately swept into the kitchen and cooked the eggs for brunch, serving them with grace, motherly attention and *Gemütlichkeit*. In a photograph Bonime treasures, Karen the godmother is seen cradling little Karen Bonime in her arms, perhaps a little gingerly, with a rapt, tender expression on her face.

As 1942 drew to its close, so too did the honeymoon period of the Association. Until then they had felt united as much by the ideal of absolute professional freedom as by the need for a common bond against an external threat. It had been much like the competitive siblings in a family surrounded by hostile neighbors. By 1943, the previously submerged interpersonal strains began to surface. Precisely who and what were responsible, whether the differences were ideological or personal, is difficult to pin down. As is to be expected, each of the persons involved has given his own version.

XVIII
PERSONALITIES AND
MORE SCHISMS
(1943-1945)

The problem of Fromm's status, dormant until then, flared up in January 1943. A number of students asked that he be permitted to teach a "technical" seminar in view of his stimulating clinical presentations. "Technical" referred to a clinical course dealing with patients rather than theoretical ideas. The 1941 resolution allowed only the latter type of course. However, in point of fact, during his New School courses on both social factors and dreams, his introduction of clinical examples had been accepted as consistent with his personal clinical experience.

Unable to accept this proposal, as it would officially sanction lay analysis, the Faculty Council suggested a compromise: a New School course on theoretical fundamentals, limited only to Institute candidates. Fromm refused this as demeaning to his standing as a clinical psychoanalyst. He felt he would not be on a par with the other instructors. For him, analysis was as much a social science as a medical one. When this was reported at the March membership meeting, Thompson, then president, appointed a committee to study the question and report back at a special meeting. She chose Frances Arkin, Belle Beaumont, Judd Marmor and Silverberg—none of whom was in the so-called Horney group—to avoid any possible claim of power politics. Fromm advised this committee that he would resign if he could not teach technical seminars. The committee recommended that his teaching privileges be revoked. During the discussion at the special April meeting in Janet Rioch's home, the point was also raised that the New York Medical College would not permit a lay person on its faculty. The committee's recommendation was accepted by a vote of eleven to four.

The ideological issue was lay analysis, as both Karen and Fromm later stated. Was it the real issue?

During this interval there were signs of the impending trouble. At the

March "interval" meeting, Janet Rioch spoke on "Growth and Development of a Group." She traced the development of a religious group that had undergone many splits and variations in its dogma. An obvious reference to the possible outcome of the current situation, it was both a warning and a plea for unity.

At the same special April meeting, Thompson presented her version of the situation. She believed that the three issues officially raised did not touch the real question; they were "red herrings." She pointed out that although the medical school would not allow a layman on its own faculty, it would not have jurisdiction over the Institute faculty. Fromm could therefore be included if desired. Since Fromm had been permitted to analyze and supervise candidates without exception, to refuse him technical/clinical courses was contradictory. Finally, to believe that the acceptance of a lay analyst would endorse lay analysis in general was spurious. Several other analytic institutes had such lay members and were still recognized by the American Association.

She believed that the real basic issue was either political or personal. Later she was to include herself in this controversy, maintaining that neither she nor Fromm had been receiving candidates in referral for some time. It was personal, she claimed, inasmuch as Fromm's presence on the staff was only desirable as long as his personal reputation enhanced the prestige of the Institute. When Fromm's growing fame began to overshadow that of the Institute, he was no longer wanted. She may have been referring to the rise in his stature after the publication of his book *Escape from Freedom* at the end of 1941, or to his immense popularity with the students. It could also have been political, she said, in that three different ideologies existed—Fromm's, Sullivan's and Horney's—each with its own group of adherents. Rivalries or "power politics" had arisen among them. The "Horney Group," she claimed, was particularly eager to extend its power and influence at the expense of the opposition. She compared the current situation with that in the New York Institute two years before. Karen was accused of practicing the same discrimination she had then objected to, with the same violation of academic freedom.

The official statement, issued three weeks later, rebutted these claims, presenting the various resolutions in exact detail. It denied any violation of academic freedom by emphasizing the fact that everyone was teaching. Others were teaching even more hours than Karen. It reiterated that the question of lay analysis was the basis for this dispute rather than any personal feelings.

The situation at this point recalls the famous story of judgment of the Rabbi of Minsk. When each opponent in a heated argument presented his case to the Rabbi, he judged both of them right. When a bystander objected that with diametrically contradictory arguments, each could not be right, the Rabbi replied, "And you too are right, my friend." The same was true in this case, as the two sides were speaking on different levels, which neither was willing to see or to admit.

At the close of that meeting, Thompson and Rioch—along with Sullivan, who had remained silently in the background during the meeting— joined Fromm in resigning. It is claimed that Sullivan was happy at this outcome because he could now organize his long-sought-after New York branch of the Washington group. The four out-of-town members soon followed: Benjamin Weininger, James Moloney, Marjorie Jarvis and Blitzsten.

Two weeks later, Karen, Robbins and Silverberg presented their case to a special meeting of the students. Robbins clarified the medical school's opposition to the presence of a layman on the faculty. For him, even at this point, good relations with the medical school and the medical profession outweighed any possible benefit to the Institute itself. Silverberg stressed the lay-analysis question. He related his experiences with the American Association. Their present attitude was to exclude from membership societies with lay members. Karen emphatically denied any feeling of resentment or antagonism toward Fromm. Ruth Moulton, now a distinguished analyst in New York but then the young president of the student body, quaking in her nervousness, presented her doubts about their version of the situation. She was later complimented on her "hair-raising frankness."

All the students were indeed confused; most had divided allegiances. They felt they had the most to lose by the schism, namely the services of different outstanding teachers. The youthful idealists felt deceived at the betrayal of their expectations. They were pained to see their idols' feet of clay, to see the flaws in their supposedly omniscient parent figures. Some felt they still really did not know the real issues behind the split. Others believed that if the students remained united and determined, they held enough power to force the two groups together again. One noted that both Thompson and Karen had seemed "obviously scared at the violence of the students' reactions and would go a long way to compromise."

One candidate, Dr. Ralph Rosenberg, wrote

The faculty has little to gain by the split and its accompanying mud-slinging.

We do not know the actual issues. Academic freedom cannot be the issue, for Horney is as tolerant of other opinions as any human being can be. Lay-analysis cannot be the issue, for Fromm has offered to compromise his position to suit the medical situation.

I suggest that the students invite the Fromm and Horney groups to discuss their differences in the presence of the students, and that we do our best to throw oil on the troubled waters.

This will first enable the students to discover the actual issues at stake. Second, our presence will restrain the combatants, prevent too much hair-pulling, and foster an atmosphere of compromise.

In effect, I feel we children should get together and spank our unruly parents for their childish behavior.

P.S. We should act promptly before they get too set in their incompatibility.

> *Sincerely,*
> *Ralph*

But this suggestion could not be carried out. As he had feared, it came too late. Three of the students also resigned. As was to be expected, most followed their personal analysts.

With all the accusations and denials, one wonders what Karen's feelings and position really were in this situation. Undoubtedly she felt torn, with much emotional conflict. She was publicly committed against lay analysis, privately not opposed to it. She was being subjected to a great deal of pressure: from Silverberg, whom she respected and needed, to uphold the medical nature of analysis; from her younger colleagues, Robbins and especially Kelman, to seek medical affiliation and start a clinic. Both were ambitious and hoped to play a more significant role in any such new setup. Kelman, seeking to advance his leadership role in the Institute, consciously or unconsciously would have been against anyone who could possibly interfere. In addition, he may have been vying with the others for the favored attention and affection of Karen.

Against this weighed her long-standing, intimate friendship with Fromm. She denied any feelings of anger or competitiveness. Had she not even tried to promote the publication of his first book? However, she seems to have felt some deeper rivalry. At one meeting, when she mentioned his book, by an unconscious slip of the tongue she referred to him as Dr. Freud—which she laughingly corrected. Nevertheless, the feeling had leaked out and was significant to many who heard it. Within the group she recoiled from leadership by direct domination through power. Yet she needed the prestige that derived from her theories. As long as Fromm's ideology "complemented" her own—as she had explained to Norton—they would have been acceptable to her. If, instead, they competed, she could have experienced some personal threat. This was to occur later with Kelman. One conflict now was to be the leader she was expected to be, while at the same time going along with, appeasing the others.

Beyond this, perhaps other personal motives were involved. As Marianne was progressing and growing and freeing herself from her own inhibitions, she naturally experienced some resentment or rebellion against her mother. For her, the split was also a more personal conflict. She was torn between Fromm, her analyst, and Karen, her mother, who expected her loyalty. Karen began to blame Fromm for Marianne's attitudes, even though he had overtly discouraged Marianne from taking action on any of the feelings or impulses emerging during her analysis. She seemed to forget her own analytic awareness that such sentiments were part of every successful analysis, and that they generally were projections of rebellion against inner restrictions which did not refer to actual situations or real persons, present or past. In any event, there had been a cooling off of Karen's relations with Fromm for some time before the actual split. He had complained of feeling unwanted by the group; she had complained of his lack of interest and of feeling hurt. He confided to Paul Lussheimer, visiting socially on the night before he received the registered letter advising him of the Institute's vote—in effect his dismissal—that there were personal relationships involved.

A paper Fromm wrote just at the time of the schism could, perhaps, shed some light on his relations with Karen. Its title: "Sex and Character."[1] That he even chose this topic, out of keeping with his other concerns at this time, is suggestive of its relevance. He contradicted the views of liberal, pure culturalist analysts—like Karen—who claimed that social factors alone produced characterological male-female differences. He insisted that biological differences between the sexes do cause such disparities, although social factors could modify them. Every relationship between a man and a woman involves both sexual need and interdependence, as well as difference and potential antagonism. The man's basic fear is of failing, sexually and socially. His defense is a wish for prestige, a craving to prove himself. But in so doing, he must compete with others, women as well as men. As a result of this need for prestige, the man develops first, a "typical male vanity" that colors all his activity. Second, he becomes hypersensitive to the woman's ridicule. Here his defense is to dominate and overpower her.

Whereas the man's primary fear is of not succeeding, the woman's is of being dependent on the man. The woman needs attractiveness and so develops a typical "female vanity" about her looks. Where the man's chief expression of his hostility lies in his power, both physical (sexual) and social, the woman's is in her ability to ridicule, to undermine. Against the woman's ability to bear children as a strength, the man must prove his productivity through his reasoning ability.

He emphasized that these sexually rooted attitudinal differences were present not only in neurotics, but also in normal persons. They did not provide a basis either for casting men and women in different social roles or for inequalities in political and economic status or for relegating either sex to a superior or inferior position.

With such emotional conflicts going on within her and around her, it could not have been a coincidence that Karen chose as the subject of her fall 1943 New School lecture series "Integration of the Personality in Psychoanalysis." In her summary description of the material, she wrote, "Contradictory goals in essential matters mar social and individual life equally. [My] purpose is to show the consequences for the personality of basic unsolved conflicts and the difficulties opposing a solution." This was to become the basis for her next book, *Our Inner Conflicts*, which she was already beginning to compose in her mind. In the introduction, she was to note that this book grew out of her experience not only with her patients, but with herself as well. "A crescendo of observations opened my eyes to the significance of such conflicts."

Other clues to Karen's feelings were revealed in two brief papers she presented to the ACAAP in the spring of 1943. In "Goals of Psychoanalysis," she decried the feeling of hatred for one's enemies and quoted the Bible in support. It was not enough simply to resolve conflicts, not enough to remove the obvious neurotic trend and permit expression of the repressed attitudes. This would carry the danger that, for example, a previously dependent, submissive person would simply become a hostile, aggressive one, with cravings for power and prestige. "Another analyst had told her of a patient" who was now healthy because the patient had given up short-lived affairs with successive partners. She felt that both the submissive-turned-aggressive person and the reformed promiscuous person remained just as neurotic as before, with "solutions that were not solutions." Instead, positive, constructive attitudes must emerge, like the desire to do creative work.

Then in "Some Personal Remarks—Why I Love Psychoanalysis," she compared her feelings to those of a "sailor who speaks of his boat. He knows its deficiencies and its assets and loves it regardless of any faults it may have." She loved psychoanalysis because of the almost esthetic pleasure one found in doing a good piece of analytic work, for instance, with a dream. She also loved it because of the satisfaction it gave in helping to heal another person. But aside from these intellectual and therapeutic pleasures was a third, recently discovered reason. This was its value in helping one to grow. One could develop at any age, not only when one was young.

In both of these short papers, Karen was apparently referring to the changes she had been experiencing in herself during her passage through the difficult period of the schism. She was now coming to terms with herself.

During the Christmas vacation of 1943, she was able to detach herself from affairs of the Association. On Sanibel Island, Florida, she relaxed in the sun and went swimming. She also turned more toward her new hobby. She began to paint more concertedly. She realized she was only a novice, but she enjoyed it immensely, as she wrote Norton from Florida. A while previously at a luncheon meeting, he had suggested to her a book on sex and neurosis. She now had thought it over and agreed: "Considering the importance of the subject, I should like this book to be a really good one. I should like this all the more since I feel responsible for our analytic group, and the book will, so to speak, be a collective work of the group." She suggested Robbins and Kelman as co-editors; she considered Kelman to have a talent for organizing. She herself would contribute two or three sections. The group was then giving a course on the subject at the New School. The various instructors—Ephron, Beaumont, Robbins, Marmor—could write on their special areas of expertise. This project, however, was never to materialize.

With the departure of Thompson, Fromm, Sullivan and Blitzsten, her friendship with each of them, the pleasant days, party evenings and close relationships of the previous years were ended. But how could she simply cut them out of her life? In truth, the break was not entirely free of sentiment; she later confided to Gertrude that she was saddened and had felt pushed into behaving the way she did. And yet it was felt by several of her friends that she did have that capacity. She could drop friends for some slight, without remorse or regret and without looking back. Some called her fickle in her friendships. Perhaps this tendency was still a residual defensive neurotic trait. It acted as a detachment, needed to avoid the easily hurt pride or loneliness felt after separation. At that time it could also have been a constructive change, such as she had described in her recent paper. She had obtained some insight and resolution of a neurotic need in her previous relations with those friends, coming to terms with her compulsive need for them. Perhaps it was a need for reassurance through their affection. Perhaps it was an awareness that the previous "partying" with them had been a form of neurotic "shallow living" she was to describe in her forthcoming book. In any event, her ability to cut old ties involved a degree of insensitivity to other people's feelings that was at odds with her otherwise keen understanding of motives.

Following Thompson's tenure, Robbins became the third president of the Association. In his presidential survey, he optimistically spoke of finding a "phenomenal growth during the previous two years. The training school has proved a profound success and the quantity and quality of those enrolled has exceeded our fondest expectations." It was significant, in light of later developments, that he stressed the good relations with the medical college that he was hoping for. Attendance at the Academy Scientific meetings was excellent. The number of members was now twenty-two, with thirty candidates-in-training. But further trouble was brewing.

Negotiations with the New York Medical College had been carried on all through the previous year. After the issuance of the prospectus for the proposed clinic at the hospital, Kelman had been named as its prospective director in June 1943. Although Jewitt had previously accepted it, in August he rejected the proposal. The medical school would not accept the Institute—or its clinic—as an already organized unit. Karen had constantly insisted that above all, the unity of the Institute must be preserved. That was the only way to retain its autonomy in determining courses and staff, and thereby to foster its high standards of training. Her bitter experience with the Chicago Institute, where policies had been set by its lay board, had sensitized her to the dangers of having nonmedical considerations imposed. It was felt that Jewitt wished not only to have analytic lectures and personal analyses given to under-graduate medical students, but also to take over the analytic training program in full. The members of the Association would become part of the psychiatric department. That in itself would not be so bad. But to what extent college supervision and authority would apply was not yet clear. As the meetings of the executive and faculty councils went on during the last months of 1943, a sense of divisiveness within the group became evident. Some of the members, more conservative, seemed to be fearful; they continued to raise objections over apparently minor points. Again and again clarifications were demanded of Jewitt. Other members, more impatient, wished to proceed with the affiliation, which they considered a unique opportunity, at once and worry about problems later on. Silverberg believed that psychoanalytic education was, in any event, better in a medical school than in a private institute. Details could be worked out later once it was a *fait accompli.*

Jewitt, who attended some of these meetings, became aware of this division of opinion. He interpreted the councils' holding back, the unnecessary questions, as a reluctance to join analysis with medicine. This was what Karen was to be accused of later, in effect, a contradiction of her previous stance with Fromm. Such a charge was definitely not true. She desired the affiliation, but that desire had to be weighed against her fear of what could happen to her beloved theory and the Institute.

In fact, later in January, she wrote to Jewitt to correct the impression he had expressed, denying that they had a "resistance against tying up the teaching of psychoanalysis too closely with medicine." Shortly afterward, he made clear that no lay analysts could be admitted to his faculty. But he granted that no appointments would be made by his department without permission of the Institute. At one point, Kelman objected that teaching analysis to nonanalytic physicians might lead to the danger of having improperly trained persons practicing analysis. In February Jewitt replied that he had no further "blueprints"; that the difficulty lay in trying to make satisfactory arrangements with a whole group already organized into an institute; that he would henceforth deal directly with the individuals involved. A few days later, the six interested members resigned to join the Medical Faculty.

Jewitt's about-face and the ensuing resignations occurred so suddenly and with so little warning that Karen was taken by surprise. Certainly she had been aware of the difference of opinion among the members and its crystallization into opposing groups. But she had not foreseen its being acted upon. In retrospect there had been preliminary rumblings. The previous December, she had moderated a discussion at a special interval meeting of the students on "The Psychological Difficulties in Our Group." There she had pleaded for harmony and unity. It was again her familiar attitude "we can have differences but still remain friends," which she had seen disproved so often. At the next interval meeting in January, Harmon Ephron presented his "Thoughts on the Conformity Principle." He protested expectations that they all follow the demand for unity, which he interpreted as conformity.

This new loss was a heavy blow for Karen. She felt deep despair. At one point she told Kelman that she was thinking of giving up the whole thing, quitting the Institute and devoting herself only to clinical practice. His encouragement and determination did much to sustain her. With Silverberg went most of her hopes for an eventual reconciliation with the American Psychoanalytic Association. Robbins was an equally great disappointment. As one of her former, most promising analysands, he had become a "favorite son." He had influenced her in the Fromm affair, and she had respected his opinion. With him, though, the break was not complete. In spite of his official resignation, he continued to work with his Institute analysands and supervisees, and to maintain friendly relations with her. In fact, in September she was continuing to suggest to Norton the new book by her colleagues, in which Robbins prominently featured. And in October, in a letter to Marianne, he still referred to the Institute in friendly terms, as "our group," as if he had never left. Rapport continued after the split to the extent that candidates who so wished were permitted to take courses in the break-away institute and given appropriate credit.

Some of the remaining members, who felt loyalty to Karen, were nevertheless disappointed and even angered by the failure of the Institute to associate more closely with medicine. They were impatient and urged Karen to find other means of strengthening their relations with the medical profession. Alexander Martin was one of these. In reply to his urgings, Karen wrote him:

> *Dear Alec:*
>
> *What is at stake are differences in policy concerning the medical profession. You have always felt we should make a more close and direct approach to the medical profession. We others feel that at this point we have to put all our energies into our own growth. We feel also that as soon as we are over our worst growing pains—in one or two years—we will definitely participate: in psychiatric conventions, giving courses to physicians, etc. The difference is not one of principle but of timing.*
>
> *You have lent your support to many valuable psychiatric enterprises. You do believe that we give a serious and valuable training to psychiatrists. You do essentially believe in the philosophy we stand for.*
>
> *I know you are very decent and fair and that you have a good feeling of loyalty. You may disagree, you may be angry at us. But believe me, your [non-support] now when we are struggling so hard, would mean another demoralizing blow . . . This group is part of my life work.*
>
> *As ever,*
> *Karen*

The remaining members had to fill in for those who left. By mid 1944, there were only thirteen members in the Association, five of whom were still in military service. Now Karen had to turn to the newer and younger members not only for their help in running the organization but for friendship as well. One of these was Harold Kelman, who became the new president of the Association.

Her relationship with him was a complex one, which was to play a significant role not only in her own life but also in the subsequent development of the Institute after her death.

Twenty-one years her junior, he had admired her almost to the point of adulation and had taken three supervisions with her—rather than the usual one—at the New York Institute. She had supported and encouraged him, especially when his final paper had been rejected. And in turn, he had been one of the student activists who promoted the schism. He had emulated her and had become the staunchest exponent of her theory. Perhaps he initially came to see her as a substitute mother figure, as so many other younger candidates admitted to feeling about her.

After his medical education at Harvard, he had entered psychiatry via neuropathology and neurology at Columbia's Psychiatric Institute. His fellow residents at Montefiore Hospital still recall him as extremely bright, but rather secretive, not relating well to the others, a loner. When he was chief psychiatrist at the Marine Hospital on Staten Island, his former residents remember him as extremely demanding, perfectionistic and authoritarian, but a good organizer of his service. His rapid rise in the new Association was a heady experience for such a relatively young man. It could only have resulted from, and further whetted, his existing driven need for prestige and power. During the period of uncertainty and schism, his compulsive perfectionism and arduous work did much to keep the Association and Institute going. He was as demanding of himself as of others. To what extent these attitudes influenced Karen and had a direct impact on the other members—even antagonizing or alienating some—can only be surmised. Where Karen could not assume a direct dominating or commanding position, she could delegate that role to him. His organizational talents could serve her aims; her prestige and public appeal could further his. In effect, each personality complemented the other; they needed and used each other, fortunately to the advantage of the group.

During the war years, Karen divided her vacations between her summer home in New York and visits to her daughter in Mexico. She did not keep the Croton house—built to her specifications by Herbert Meyer—very long, only two years. Even though it was comfortable, with its enormous fireplace and view of the valley, it had a major defect. There was no place to swim. Without swimming, summer was just no vacation. So in the spring of 1942, she and Getrude Lederer set out for Fire Island to find a "little shack" close to the ocean. While trudging across the dunes with an agent to see his choice, they came across a large beach house for sale at the water's edge. Though it was too expensive and too large, with eight guest rooms, it was her dream house. She bought it fully furnished the next day. She spent only part of two summers there and soon discovered its disadvantages. Friends and students flocked in on weekends, allowing her no rest. The beach was overcrowded with other vacationers; the house was unheatable and therefore chilly on cold mornings; and it was inaccessible after September, when the ferry stopped. So she again looked and found another smaller house at Wildwood Hills on Long Island's South Shore. High up on a bluff, it overlooked the beach, with 132 often-counted steps going down to the water's edge. This one had a fireplace for heating and a garden for planting; a German neighbor who took care of repairs and provided them with fresh vegetables. Karen and Gertrude planted two pine trees, named Philemon and Baucis, which grew prodigiously during the almost five years she owned the house. Here, with Gertrude, she could paint or garden or walk along the beach or play her beloved games of canasta or just sun herself on a deck-chair. Whenever she moved, the previous house was immediately forgotten and never mentioned again. (It was Gertrude's task to dispose of them.) This easy separation and nonattachment was similar to the attitude she had toward the old friends she could drop so easily. She bought and sold these houses the way someone else might dispose of a used dress, without regard for the large sums of money, the time and effort to make it livable or any apparent emotional attachment.

Besides needing the surcease from work, she also wanted to see her daughter each year over the summer or Christmas vacation. Her trips back and forth were adventures in themselves because of plane priorities. She was "bumped" several times, stranded in cities along the way and had to take the train. One such incident was described in her last book. The first few times it had happened, she had been furiously indignant that "they" dared to do it to her. After she began to rationalize that maybe it was for the best and maybe the plane would crash, she suddenly felt like laughing. The anger disappeared. She became aware of the unconscious claims she had been making: to be treated as an exception to the rule and to have special care from Providence. With this realization, she was able to enjoy even the uncomfortable train ride and sightseeing in the Texas towns where she found herself. This bit of self-analysis was typical of her, an example of the method she advocated in her last book.

Her visits were also adventures. The fascination she felt for everything different and exotic was enhanced by her intense curiosity, the same attitude she had toward her own inner experiences. All the sights and scenes and people intrigued her. From the colorful vegetation to the tranquil lakes, from the local market to a local wedding, from the museums to the ancient ruins, she rushed to take them all in. She was like a child at a circus. It was typical that immediately on arriving, she would have a list of things to be done, purchases to be made, chores left over, special food or wine to be procured. For instance, she would bring several watches to be repaired; why they would be left until then when they could be taken care of more easily at home, was a mystery. A certain wine would have to be bought; red wine in tea was supposed to be an effective antidote for the "turistas," the visitors' diarrhea. During her stay in 1940, Karen discovered the Yucatan, a region of jungle and mountains that lured her back several times thereafter.

She seemed to have an apparently unlimited energy and needed to be doing something constantly. Renate was kept busy with her mother—touring, sightseeing, shopping, playing cards for black beans. Perhaps her driven quality during these years was a reaction to the anxiety-provoking events in the Association. She needed time to unwind.

During the summer of 1944 Renate and Karen rented a house just outside Cuernavaca, with a beautiful view of the valley from the patio. Karen was then occupied in working on her book *Inner Conflicts*. She spent much of her time writing, and only then seemed able to relax. By that time, Renate had two more children: a daughter born in 1940 and a son in 1943. As a grandmother, Karen was rather strict and insistent on "good manners," but tender nonetheless. One of her greatest pleasures was to take the three children to a *feria* or carnival and ride on the merry-go-round with them. Her painting was also becoming a special joy by now. She would seat herself in view of some special sight—a church, tree or vista—set up her easel and paint, sometimes as long as there was enough light. Often she would be surrounded by a group of gaping children.

The final title of the book she was working on was not yet definite. In August 1944 she wrote Norton to suggest as a title *Artificial and Real Harmony*. She also continued to encourage him to publish the joint book on sex and neurosis, in spite of the fact that several of the proposed contributors had already left the Association. A week later, still dissatisfied, she proposed another change, *Genuine* for *Real* Harmony. It was only a month later, after her return, that the final version was settled on.

Her intense curiosity and spirit of enquiry led her in still another new direction in psychoanalysis at this time. One of her supervisees, Alexander Wolf—today a well-known authority on group therapy—was then trying to develop methods of group psychoanalysis. This was as yet a new and unproven type of treatment that promised to bring analysis to a larger number of patients. He was being drafted at the end of 1943 and needed some colleagues to take over his groups. When he discussed it with Karen, she offered to take over one group; Robbins took over another. Although she accepted it as a challenge, it proved to be particularly difficult. For her the problem was straightforward: How could the ideas and techniques of one-to-one analysis be applied to several persons at once, in her group only women. It should be simply an individual analysis multiplied by six. Her theoretical concepts were applicable; the dynamics of each patient's attitudes and emotional changes could be understood. The relationship between her and each woman patient could be clearly sketched out.

But beyond these theoretical notions, she ran into difficulties. Each patient was relating and reacting not only to her but to the others at the same time. Each was reacting differently to her. And their reactions were not the simple, understandable ones she had anticipated. It was like juggling six balls in the air at once. Unforeseen emotions came out, outbursts occurred. She was obliged to telephone for help from several junior colleagues who had more experience with groups. Finally, after about six months she discontinued the group. She ended on a somewhat skeptical note as to whether psychoanalysis—at least as she knew it—could be effectively used for groups. Nevertheless, she still remained so impressed by its possibilities, if its techniques could be modified, that she encouraged setting up a research study project in group psychoanalysis at the Institute in 1945.

By the fall of 1944, Marianne had completed her analytic studies. Her personal abilities had soon been recognized in the group. Robbins had described her in his evaluation as "intelligent, sensitive and intuitive . . . one of the most gifted students . . . possessing genuine warmth and an unusual grasp of the total analytic situation." She was assigned a teaching position in a seminar with Karen and Muriel Ivimey, the young assistant dean, at the New School. Indeed, she had already been participating in the affairs of the Institute as student representative on the faculty council for a year. She was thus intimately familiar with the situation and the personalities involved. Even more than the others, as she had been during the Fromm split, she was again torn by conflicting impulses. Several of her close friends left with the medical school group. She needed to distance herself for a while. With her recent marriage, she also required time for her home and social life. To add to the urgency, her husband was being imminently called into military service, to be assigned to Europe.

Feeling unable to commit herself to the amount of time and work that would be demanded, she decided not to join the Institute. She would continue with her course at the New School, since that was only for a limited time. When she told her mother, there was a stormy scene. It is understandable that Karen, so wrapped up in her professional life, so limited by time, would have had difficulty in understanding this desire. Her daughters all sadly recalled from their childhood her exclusive preoccupation with her work at the expense of time and attention for her children. Now Karen reacted to Marianne's decision with hurt and resentment. As she wrote her daughter on this occasion, she felt this would give comfort to her adversaries and would lower the morale of the candidates. Curiously, the end of this letter indicated the deep feelings of affection underlying her surface resentment. It closed with "cordially," which she then evidently considered too formal, and then added another plea, to reconsider, followed by "love."

Marianne had also communicated her decision officially to the Secretary and to Robbins, who answered her with a long and friendly letter. After acknowledging her previous contributions, he expressed certainty that every member would be willing to lighten any excessive burden she might feel. The present time, he admitted, was a critical one for the group, but was not that "grim or arduous" because it was being taken "in the spirit of a good fight for our existence now and future growth." This storm would have to be weathered. He called attention to the uncertainty and anxiety the students had felt during the previous year. He thought, as Karen had, that this might be aggravated by Marianne's withdrawal. New students might also be deterred from applying. In closing, he noted that if, as he suspected, there were deeper, more personal and more problematic areas of conflict, these could surely be worked out with him. The optimistic tone of this letter, written in November 1944, was incongruous; Robbins had himself resigned from the group in February. It would have indicated that he still retained warm and close feelings toward the group and toward Karen.

A few months later, Marianne joined her husband in Europe. Later they were to return to settle in Washington, where she was to become an outstanding psychoanalyst in her own right. She never has aligned herself officially and exclusively with any of the analytic institutes.

But Marianne was not the only one Karen was concerned about. After recovering from her illness, Biggi had returned to Berlin, in spite of her mother's entreaties to remain in Switzerland. The year 1943 was to be the twenty-fifth anniversary of the UFA studios and Goebbels wanted to stage a super-spectacle in celebration. Goebbels planned to release *The Adventures of Baron Munchausen* to mark the twenty-fifth anniversary of UFA (and to prove that a German film could compete successfully with the popular Hollywood imports). Biggi was offered one of the starring roles in this super-spectacle, Empress Catherine of Russia. Its premiere on March 5 was a triumph, the last to be enjoyed by the Nazi film industry. It was shown perhaps twice in this country, then recalled because of problems over the film rights.

By this time, in the fall of 1943, with the downfall of Mussolini, the inevitable outcome of the war could be foreseen by even the staunchest German diehards. The bombing of Berlin had begun. Biggi and her husband remained in their house on the Kaiserstrasse in Babelsberg, just outside Berlin, where the UFA studios were located. Her car was confiscated, so she could not get around as before. She passionately took up cooking and knitting as a solace and pastime, just waiting until something happened, with her long-haired Hungarian shepherd dog as companion. The movie colony left one by one. Her personality had changed. Her actress friend Heidemarie Hatheyer urged her to come south to escape, but she could not—not yet. Finally, a short time before the Russians arrived, she succeeded in escaping via Salzburg to Switzerland.

Before leaving, she gave away her possessions, a typically generous gesture. During this time, Karen did not know if Biggi was dead or alive; with each report of the bombings, she wondered and worried.

Although Biggi was safe in Zurich, in March 1945 a mistaken report appeared in the newspapers, including the *New York Herald Tribune*'s obituary page, that she had died of tuberculosis. Biggi herself sent a telegram to Karen announcing her safe arrival and new job at the Zurich Spielhaus. But Karen never received it. Her worry and anxiety can well be imagined. Eventually Biggi sent an ordinary letter, which did get through, explaining the situation. Biggi was later able to laugh at the false notice, as Mark Twain did when confronted with a similar report, with his remark that "Reports of my death are greatly exaggerated."

In May 1945, Karen's fourth book, *Our Inner Conflicts*, was published. It brought together and systematized her previous ideas into a unified theory of psychic function and structure, both neurotic and healthy. "Inner conflicts" referred to the simultaneous, opposing pull between any compulsive yet contradictory, unconscious neurotic trends. The defensive attitudes which the person develops as solutions for such conflicts constitute the neurotic personality structure. The subtitle, "A Constructive Theory," expressed her basic philosophy of human nature as well as her personal outlook on life. Man is innately constructive; he only becomes destructive when obstacles are put in the way of his growth. This was a reformulation of her oft-stated belief in the power of self-healing, that life and time could be the best therapists.

The reviews of this book were generally favorable. Harold Lasswell commented that previously her theory had been "a list of items rather than an inclusive framework, and so, with characteristic honesty and persistence Dr. Horney has continued her quest. . . . This new perspective gives a more coherent account of the self than before. . . . There is an unmistakable note of optimism in her analysis, since she sees the personality as a going concern, capable of progressive adjustment. The book is distinguished by clarity, poise and mature judgement." But he then warned that "the problems involved are of the utmost complexity and the author's contentions can only be competently assessed by persons . . . highly specialized in Psychiatry and social psychology. The writing is so lucid that it will evoke the illusion of comprehension in uncritical and unqualified minds."[2]

After Karen completed this book, a reaction set in. The writing itself had been demanding for her, an emotional struggle. According to Kelman, during such periods of "creative passion," she was often moody, restless and intensely irritable, oversensitive to any criticism. He compared her state to a woman giving birth. And like many a new mother, she experienced a phase of emotional exhaustion and withdrawal from others during the slow recovery. Finally she would go through a reactive period of socializing and gaiety.

Only infrequently would writing flow easily for her. She often had to overcome temporary inhibitions in her productivity, when either nothing would come or her ideas were confused and needed clarification. More often than not, she would have to struggle with a page, then redo a paragraph or sentence here or there. She would sometimes have Gertrude retype it as many as seven or eight times. At times, when stuck with an idea, she would play a game of solitaire, while allowing her thoughts to flow freely. Then she would return refreshed to her work, and would be able to continue. In a newspaper interview in 1945, she admitted to having such "inhibitions in productive work—in my writing and formulating my ideas. But I get over them. Being confronted day by day with problems in your patients makes you think about yourself too much. Either that or you have to put an armor about yourself—which I haven't done."

Occasionally, when confused by some concept, she would bring it up in discussion with colleagues. Using their suggestions or examples, she would usually be able to clarify or modify her thinking and then expand it. Some of her colleagues and supervisees complained that she stole their ideas or case examples to present as her own. Possibly so. Sometimes during lectures she would mention Doctor so-and-so having given her this case history; sometimes she apparently did fail to give proper credit. More often her own ideas were the original ones, modified to take her colleagues' suggestions into account.

This ability to cut through the brambles of side issues was one of her outstanding traits. Many analysands commented how, during both her analyses and more public discussions, she would suddenly come in with an enlightening "This is what you really seem to be concerned with" when they were feeling absolutely lost in their free associations or thoughts.

XIX
OUR INNER CONFLICTS

In 1945, Karen's book *Our Inner Conflicts* presented a third, more articulated and refined version of her theory. In the interim, some modifications of the first version (*The Neurotic Personality of Our Time*) had been made in the book *Self-Analysis*. In that second version, the original four major neurotic drives adopted as a defense against basic anxiety had become ten neurotic trends. Although each was described separately, some were more closely related than others. Each of the ten trends was at the center of a small constellation of associated attitudes: needs, behaviors, values, feelings toward self, inhibitions, demands on others, secondary conflicts, etc. Such compulsive trends could thus reinforce, enter into conflict with or otherwise modify one another. The presumed "cure" of neurosis was then expanded. It consisted not only of character change through elimination of neurotic trends, but also of developing an incentive to realize one's potential, to grow.

Now in the third formulation, her focus shifted. The emphasis was still on the total personality and on neurosis as a disturbance of relations with others. But here the most important factor was the conflict between trends, the solutions used to resolve such conflicts and the consequences of unresolved conflicts.

Neurotic conflicts differ from normal, daily human conflicts. The latter are resolved by recognizing the issues involved, then making a largely conscious choice between alternatives, then following that choice—renouncing one alternative. With neurotic conflicts, this simple resolution is impossible. The forces acting are not only diametrically opposed but are unconscious and compulsively driven. Therefore decision, choice and responsibility are lost.

The ten trends she had previously listed in *Self-Analysis* are now grouped into three "movements" in relation to others. These are a "moving-toward" or compliant personality; a "moving against" or aggressive personality; and a "moving-away" or detached personality. These ways of relating begin to develop in childhood out of the child's "basic anxiety" in reaction to rejective or otherwise harmful neurotic attitudes of his parents. Infantile feelings of helplessness, hostility and isolation toward parents contribute respectively to each type of movement. Since each is driven by anxiety (or the need for safety), it becomes inflexible and pervades the entire personality. Although one of the three may predominate in behavior, the others become repressed into the unconscious. Nevertheless, because they remain powerfully and actively compulsive, they will cause conflict. This "basic conflict" forms the core from which the neurosis will emanate.

Each becomes a nuclear trace around which a broad constellation of attitudes will later develop in the adult, with complex ramifications in the personality. Even though they do not designate demarcated character "types," each orientation will come to include fairly consistent needs, sensitivities, avoidances, inhibitions and feelings about the self.

The person with a moving-toward-others personality needs to feel loved, accepted, needed, taken care of by others. He becomes hypersensitive to the expectations of others, which he must live up to. He is self-sacrificing, generous, undemanding. He avoids quarrels, competition, standing out. Blaming himself, and apologizing, comes easily. But there are inhibitions on any assertiveness or anger. He often feels helpless and inferior; or at least, his self-evaluation depends exclusively on what others think of him. Values like goodness, sympathy and humility are idealized, whereas their opposites—egotism, selfishness, ambition, domination—are despised. Yet despite the repression of these latter values, they can come through into conduct in the service of the permitted and expressed values. For instance, domination can be exerted through love, or detachment through impersonal affection.

The moving-against-others neurotic has diametrically opposite qualities. He needs to control, to succeed, to exploit and triumph over others. Prestige and recognition are part of this. He must be tough, hard and unsentimental—and always right. He enjoys competition, arguing, winning. However, inhibitions do exist on feeling or expressing any softer emotions: affection, tenderness, understanding, enjoyment.

Moving-away-from-others involves a form of emotional detachment in which the person becomes an objective onlooker to himself. He needs to keep emotional distance, noninvolvement, from others. Self-sufficiency, privacy and independence are additional needs. He is hypersensitive to external influence, interference, obligation, or any coercion, whether it comes from another person or from rules. Feelings in general are suppressed. He excludes both the softer emotions of the compliant person and the power-drive of the assertive one. To experience either would provoke conflict. But he needs to feel superior and needs external recognition nonetheless, in order to gain a sense of uniqueness. Marriage, as a long-term commitment, is apt to be difficult and anxiety-inducing. Sexual relationships tend to be short-lived. To be forced into closeness with another can bring about a panic state or other severe disturbance; it can be experienced as a disintegration of the personality or as a total inability to cope with the world. Detachment thus differs from the other two trends in being more stringently defensive against the direct emergence of conflicts.

There are four ways by which the neurotic attempts to defend himself against conflict. The first is repression of that trend which contradicts the predominant, needed one, which then becomes a total orientation toward life. This has just been described. The second is removal of the self from inner conflict through detachment. This also creates distance from other persons or situations likely to heighten or bring awareness of the conflicts. The third is the creation of an unconscious, irrationally idealized image of the self. The person may try to live up to this, eventually coming to believe he is that image. Or he may focus on his realistic self, poor by comparison; this was termed the "actual self." He then comes to despise what he perceives himself to be; this psychological entity was newly termed "the despised self." Or he may concentrate on the discrepancy between the two. Then he will constantly prod himself toward the degree of perfection he feels he should attain. The new concept "tyranny of the shoulds" was first referred to here in connection with this notion of driving oneself toward impossible inner demands for perfection.

The psychic functions of such a self-image are many. Its omnipotence substitutes for real self-confidence and genuine pride, damaged by neurotic development. It permits the person to feel superior instead of humiliated or unworthy. Its ideals, no matter how spurious, replace the impaired neurotic ideals. With it, faults are transformed into virtues. In it, conflicts are made to appear reconciled.

Yet despite its defensive advantages, this creation also has negative effects. It renders the neurotic over-vulnerable to any criticism; the image is threatened by it. He must depend on constant confirmation of this illusory self by others. If anyone fails to do so, he also becomes a threat. The neurotic will admire falsely those in whom he sees the idealized traits of his image; and will find intolerable those with his despised traits. Most important, it alienates the person from what he really is and can be: from his feelings, wishes, capacities and genuine qualities. It leads to a sense of pretense, even of unreality. Finally, the "shoulds" that the person imposes upon himself become an intolerable burden. These are eventually felt to be restrictions, an inner authority, to be rebelled against.

The fourth major defense is externalization, or the experiencing of one's own attitudes in others. This occurs when the discrepancy between the idealized image and actual self becomes unbearable. If this tendency is severe, it must result in an excessive preoccupation with others, an other-directedness and an over-dependency on external circumstances. It will inevitably produce a feeling of emptiness or shallowness.

Among the feelings most often externalized are self-contempt, rage at oneself and self-coercion. This is so because of the particularly intense, painful and destructive quality of these emotions. But this process leads to secondary problems. The person will come either to despise others or to feel despised by them. Or his anger can be directed at his own faults seen in others. Or it may be felt that others are angry at him for the same presumed faults. The same anger can be externalized onto one's own body, giving rise to psychosomatic symptoms. One's "shoulds," with their coercive force, can also be blamed on others. As a result, the neurotic may become hypersensitive—resentful or rebellious—to any external authority, however benign it may be.

However, even these defensive solutions to inner conflict can only provide an unstable equilibrium in the personality. Therefore a number of lesser protective techniques or "auxiliary approaches to artificial harmony" are required. Horney enumerates seven of these. (1) The development of "blind-spots" about contradictions between one's actual self and the idealized image. (2) Keeping contradictory attitudes or functions in separate compartments of one's awareness. These are logic-tight and impervious to reason. (3) The use of rationalization to justify obvious discrepancies. This is self-deception through falsely logical reasoning. (4) Excessive self-control can be exerted to prevent oneself from being overwhelmed by contradictory emotions. This can vary from the use of conscious will power to the unconscious checking of spontaneity. (5) Arbitrary rightness is a position taken to eliminate indecision and self-doubt. (6) Elusiveness is a constant shifting of one's position. This serves defensively to becloud, confuse and evade. Here the repression has been inadequate, and the idealized image is indefinite. (7) Cynicism consists of the denial of any moral values or fundamental beliefs. It is often unconscious. But it may be consciously expressed in the belief that appearances are all-important or that anything is permitted provided one is not caught.

Although all these major solutions and auxiliary measures may provide relief from conflict to some extent, each of them is in itself vulnerable to threat. Therefore they can, and usually do, generate additional conflict or other adverse effects on the personality. The imminent failure of either the overall protective personality structure or of specific measures in particular, can result in various fears. The fear of falling apart or of insanity really represents a fear that the precarious equilibrium of the personality will be disturbed. The fear of being found out, of being exposed, is a fear of discovering one's pretenses or imperfections. Fear of change indicates a fear of losing one's idealized image.

Besides fears, unresolved conflicts can produce an impoverishment of the personality in other ways. Usually there occurs a loss of interest in the self resulting from the misdirecting of one's energies toward impossible goals. This can show itself as a chronic strain, or inertia, or general ineffectiveness. Moral integrity is impaired, to be replaced by excessive egocentricity and a pseudo-morality. The latter involves having to keep up many unconscious pretenses, such as the pretense of loving, of goodness, of having knowledge, of honesty, of suffering, or of taking real responsibility.

Hopelessness is another especially important consequence. It can result from several possible sources. One is the realization that changing external conditions alone will bring no relief. The inability to extricate oneself from the web of conflict piling up upon conflict is another. A third is the realization that it is impossible ever to attain one's idealized self image. Finally, despair at ever becoming whole and whole-hearted, is still another. This basic hopelessness can be experienced as a chronic pessimism, depression or a sensitivity to disappointment. Without ever coming into awareness, it can cause the neurotic to try to lose himself in zestless, nonproductive activities, in drinking, sexual promiscuity or in vicarious living.

XX
SELF-QUESTIONING

"Recognition of self is as important as the recognition of other factors in the environment; to search for truth about self is as valuable as to search for truth in other areas of life. The only question is whether introspection is constructive or futile. I would say it is constructive if it is used in the service of a wish to become a better, richer, and stronger human being. If it is an end in itself, that is, if it is pursued merely out of indiscriminate interest in psychological connections—art for art's sake—then it can easily degenerate into . . . a 'mania psychologica.' And it is equally futile if it consists merely of immersion in self-admiration or self-pity, dead-end ruminations about oneself, empty self-recrimination."

—*Self-Analysis*

In September 1945, Karen turned sixty. Time and her sedentary life were exacting their toll on her. Her figure was thickening, her movements slowing, her hair thinning and graying. Otherwise her health was good, even though she was having difficulty in maintaining the pace she was accustomed to.

Her life settled into a scheduled, strictly regulated routine. She usually woke at five or five-thirty and spent the first hour or so sitting up in bed, with a cup of tea, her papers and books around her, reading or writing. (This habit persisted even on vacations. When she occasionally visited her friend Muriel Ivimey's summer home, she would generally be seated at the garden table on the lawn before her hostess came down at seven.) She would see her first patient at seven, or if need be, at six. An anecdote is related about one student whose analytic hour was scheduled for 8 A.M. He began to complain about having to come so early to the previous candidate, who had just finished at 7 A.M. session. The latter rejoined, "What are you complaining about, and to me? You ought to talk to the fellow who comes before me!"

She would habitually sit in her easy chair in front of the picture window overlooking the park. She often kept it open, even in colder weather, and wore a shawl or blanket around her shoulders, while the student shivered. It took courage to ask her to close it; not many did. If she had an evening lecture or social engagement, she might leave her hair up in curlers, for which she would apologize. She was not always so gracious, however. One former student recalls arriving at her door at 8 A.M. He tried the knob several times; it was locked. He rang several times, and while waiting, heard the bolt being quietly drawn back. Moments later, she finally opened it. She angrily scolded him for having rung when the door was open. They worked several hours on his timidity and inhibition. His vain protests that the door was really locked were brushed aside. It was one example of her difficulty in imagining—let alone admitting—that she might be wrong, at least in front of an analytic patient.

She worked until just before one. Her lunch had to be on the table exactly at that time and woe unto her housekeeper if it wasn't ready. Twenty minutes for lunch, twenty or thirty minutes for a brief nap, then time for a short walk with Butschy, her dog, in the park. She would then work until about six, leaving herself just enough time to prepare for any evening activity.

But if such discipline and organization was so evident in her time and professional work, it certainly was not in her handling of her paperwork, her money and her car. Her desk was usually piled high with a long-standing accumulation of papers, all jumbled together: bills to be paid, checks received from patients, letters to be answered, reports to be filled out. Then Gertrude or Karen herself, at Gertrude's urging, would try to clean it up all at once. Until the next time.

She seldom knew how much money she had, either in her purse or in her bank account. At times she might ask a patient to pay in cash instead of the usual monthly check just to have some for her immediate expenses. Her income was fairly good, never large; financially she was comfortable, never wealthy. She did not save much. Her fees were not high by current standards, even though she could have asked any fee she chose because of the demand for her services. Once her junior colleagues started their own private practices they soon asked higher fees and earned more than she did. She turned away many patients, referring them to colleagues. Some analysts today still feel rejected and therefore resentful at having been refused therapy by her. On the other hand, she would sometimes feel slighted when a candidate, in the initial interview with her, indicated a preference for another senior analyst. She had to make the decision! She preferred to work with patients whose problems she found interesting, or those she thought could influence others, i.e., other analysts, professionals, teachers, writers. Some say she preferred to work with men rather than women. This report is impossible to evaluate, because she did have a large number of women patients at all times.

Even though she might accept a slightly reduced fee in special cases, she felt strongly that the fee helped establish a healthy attitude toward the analysis. If you did not pay, you would feel the analysis worthless. This may have been a carryover of Freud's original position—later changed after the success of the Berlin Clinic—that sacrifice was a necessary precondition for analytic progress. It was for this reason that she would not practice analysis on credit. Some candidates would later complain that she was unfeeling and unsympathetic if she threatened to discontinue analysis when they were temporarily hard-up and unable to pay.

Her handling of money was a constant worry to her accountant and to Gertrude. Whether buying food, clothes, a little knicknack or a house, she showed an equal disregard for the expense. Shopping with Gertrude, she would often ask, "Can I afford that? How much money do I have?" She gave generously, directly or in gifts—to her daughters, her ex-husband, relatives and friends in Germany—with a uniform disregard for her actual resources. Only once is she known to have protested—after the war she received so many requests for money, food and clothes from Germany that she found it hard to comply with them all. Yet she liked to bargain. On one occasion, when the Association was negotiating for their new apartment on Ninety-eighth Street, she was told by the Committee that she could "*handeln*" (bargain). She was delighted and literally clapped her hands with joy.

Butschy, a black spaniel with long hair, floppy ears and pleading eyes, was a significant personality unto himself. She bought him for companionship and indeed treated him like a valued friend. As she confided to Gertrude only half-jokingly, it was at a time when she had been thinking of remarriage but decided against it. She would prefer a dog to a man for company. Everything was permitted Butschy; he was pampered and spoiled. If he wet on the floor, it was wiped up without a word. Once in the park with Sophie, her Norwegian housekeeper, he escaped his leash and wandered off. A policeman picked him up and levied a fine of five dollars. Karen laughed at the incident. "Just think," she said. "How cheap it is, only five dollars for a year's use of the park." If a prospective student arrived for an interview and Butschy jumped into his lap, then his acceptance was certain. Butschy would sometimes be admitted during an analytic session and lie at Karen's feet. Or he might jump on the couch. His biggest fault was his habitual loud snoring, which penetrated into the next room and kept Gertrude awake nights at Wildwood. Karen claimed she never noticed it or was never bothered by it. She had even psychoanalyzed him. As she laughingly told Kelman, his Idealized Image of himself was a picture of a dignified Great Dane and a fierce, courageous police dog combined. But when he fought with bigger dogs and got into trouble despite this image of himself, he would be realistic enough to run away. As he became older, he "settled down to being a dignified old gentleman who had never had a wife." Like Freud's dog Jophi he appeared in many dreams of both her patients and colleagues.

Although the week was so busy, the weekend from Friday noon was strictly reserved for "rest." At one o'clock sharp, Gertrude would bring the car, Karen would appear promptly, with Sophie, the housekeeper, carrying a large picnic basket, pulling or being pulled by Butschy. In the city Gertrude would drive, but once across the bridge, Karen would take the wheel. Her driving had not improved since Chicago. She still drove with the same blithe abandon. Renate recalls—as do others who sat beside her in the little red sports coupe—how she crouched down, quaking in fear, unable to move, while Karen brushed past other cars. Once, while visiting her analytic friends the Lowenfelds in their Long Island home near hers, Karen could not turn her car around to leave by the narrow, rutty access road. Whereupon she *backed* down at full speed, something no one had ever done before, leaving her hosts aghast.

But it was not absolute rest she needed on these weekends, but a change of pace. Not that she didn't love just lying in the deck chair. She could not take more than an hour or so of doing nothing. Not yet. Her mind was too busy, her energy level too high. She usually would bring some writing to do. Or she would garden, or walk, or go shopping with Gertrude in nearby Riverhead. Activity was a compulsive need for her.

The difference between being—in the sense of remaining inactive with herself—and doing, was not yet clear to her. This is one reason why the existentialist concept of "being" remained so difficult for her to grasp. Before being fully able to grasp the idea, one must have felt and experienced the thing itself.

Although Kelman claimed that her reference to this distinction in her 1932 paper on "The Dread of Women" proved her to be already an existentialist, this is not accurate. She used this distinction then in a limited and specific context, namely one of activity versus inactivity. The male must be active during sexual intercourse to be productive, to contribute to the birth of a child. The woman can be inactive, passive, frigid and still conceive. This was quite different from "Being" as an ontological state, involving consciousness or awareness. While Karen had been dilettantishly interested in the philosophy of such existentialist writers as Kierkegaard and Husserl, it was largely as an intellectual exercise. She could grasp its theoretical meanings but not yet its deeper implications. She was soon to turn toward the Eastern philosophies, though in the spirit of a religious quest rather than philosophical inquiry.

Between 1946 and 1950, as the country returned to normal after the war, many discharged young physicians returned home. The large number of draftees who were rejected as emotionally unfit for service made a strong impression on the medical community. The success of psychotherapy in treating the psychological "casualties" of combat attracted many of these returning doctors to psychiatry and psychoanalysis. These circumstances produced an influx of candidates into the Institute; by mid 1947, the number had risen to over forty. The Association also grew rapidly with the addition of the graduates from the previous five years and the recently arrived senior German-speaking refugee analysts. Several among them became lecturers or training analysts. Alexander Martin succeeded Kelman as president.

Karen remained busy with her teaching and writing. In 1946 she spoke at three Academy meetings. In one paper she discussed "The Role of the Imagination in Neurosis."[1] She believed that normally the imagination could serve constructively for planning, for consolation or—in the case of the artist—for conscious remodeling of reality in artistic creation. But the neurotic comes to live in his imagination when the internal pressure of conflict becomes intolerable. It is thus part of an unconscious self-idealiza-

tion, wherein the person sees himself as omnipotent and exempt from ordinary problems of life. Or failing this, he feels worthless. The reality of
self and of living thus becomes unreal; unreality appears as reality. This
idea was to be incorporated as a central concept into the final version of
her theory.

Karen's second paper was on technique. In "Criteria for Dream Interpretation,"[2] she claimed that in order for an interpretation to be plau-
sible, it must fulfil three conditions. It must stimulate further relevant
discussion, its symbols must relate to the patient's emotions, and its expressed solutions must connect with the patient's conflicts.

Her third presentation was on "Self-Hate and Human Relations."[3] It
was basically a summary of her course lecture on the same topic. She
made a distinction between healthy discontent with self, leading to constructive action, and neurotic self-hatred, which occurs when irrational
goals of superiority are not achieved or irrational claims on others not
met. These must be given up through analysis before one's real self-esteem and genuine potential can be arrived at.

In addition she taught two Institute courses: "Psychoanalytic Technique," and with Kelman, "The Meaning of Dreams." And finally, her
course at the New School was entitled: "At War with Ourselves: Self-Acceptance and Self-Condemnation." This series of lectures was to become
the basis for her new book, for which she began to gather notes in 1947.
Various topics from this course were discussed in greater detail during
several informal "interval" meetings with the candidates. These included
pride and self-hate, neurotic claims on others, and methods of handling
such attitudes in analysis.

During these years, the interval meetings were held on Sunday at her
home. Many analysts today still remember with much pleasure the free
give-and-take atmosphere there. Karen had to forego her weekend in
Long Island on those days, but it was the only time available for her. In
1947 the group rented an apartment on West Ninety-eighth Street which
was to serve as home for the Institute, the Association and ACAAP until
1955.

In May 1946, the fifth anniversary of the Association was celebrated at
the Henry Hudson Hotel. A series of short presentations preceded a
reception. The occasion was a joyous one but serious too. Many had tears
in their eyes as they thought of the hopes, the conflicts and schisms, the

travail of the previous five years. The celebration drew an immense audience, surpassing any previous meeting of this kind. Karen was accustomed to a full house at all her lectures now, at the Academy meetings as well as at the New School, where a large auditorium was usually reserved for her.

At the meeting, her old friend Harold Lasswell spoke on "Psychoanalysis and Power," the subject of his recent book. He reminded his listeners of the contributions psychoanalysis could make toward understanding the motives and personalities of those aspiring to power. Alice Brophy, then president of ACAAP, spoke of the impact that the newer concepts of analysis were having on public affairs: on business and personnel training, on education and childrearing practices, on nursing and public health, on social services. Kelman briefly reviewed the past history of the Association. In expressing his outlook for the future, he again expressed his hope for a new clinic.

Karen herself spoke on "The Future of Psychoanalysis."[4] As might be expected, she was concerned only with theory. She contrasted the "pessimistic basic philosophy" of Freud—that "man is at bottom driven by elemental instincts of sex, greed and cruelty"—with her own. "We believe that man has potentialities for good and evil and we see that he does develop into a good human being if he grows up under favorable conditions of warmth and respect for his individuality . . . Psychoanalysis has become for us a means for liberation and growth as a human being." After listing some of the recent changes she had been making in her own theory, she set forth several aims for the immediate future. These included finding methods of group analysis, verifying results of analytic therapy, clarifying the dynamics of psychosomatic states, developing techniques for treatment of the psychoses and shortening therapy of the neuroses.

One year later, in May 1947, ACAAP celebrated its own fifth anniversary. The tone and the guest list were much the same as the previous symposium, though the speakers were different. The overall topic was "Mature Attitudes in a Changing World." Margaret Mead spoke on "Maturity and Society," drawing upon her studies of primitive cultures, and Eduard Lindemann of the Columbia School of Social Work on "Maturity and Culture," defining the concept of maturity in relation to present social values.

In her own presentation on "Maturity and the Individual,"[5] Karen outlined the essential criteria for individual maturity. For her, there were two ingredients. One was to be able to appreciate the reality of oneself, of others and of situations. The neurotic is too confined by the narrow horizon of subjectivity and egocentricity. The second was the capacity to take responsibility for oneself and one's actions. The neurotic blames another for his difficulties—his parents, society, fate or his unconscious.

To knowing observers who saw them on the platform at these two meetings, the respective roles of Karen and Kelman had changed from what they had been five years before. No longer the student reacting to the older teacher, he had become his own man. If she was the star of the show, he was evidently the producer and director.

The normal effects of age, and the unslackening demands of teaching and her latest book, left Karen with less energy to devote to the everyday affairs of the Institute and the Association. As she began to depend more on her younger colleagues, Kelman naturally assumed more administrative control and Karen encouraged it. For example, when Ivimey, the rather quiet and unassuming assistant dean, complained in a letter to Karen that Kelman was exceeding his authority, she replied protectively that if he was, then it must be accepted because it was no doubt for the good of the Institute.

Those younger colleagues who succeeded Kelman as president of the Association—Martin, Ivimey, Elizabeth Kilpatrick, Paul Lussheimer— were all less assertive than Kelman and unable to challenge his behind-the-scenes influence, remaining uninvolved with internal power struggles.

Karen seemed always to be fondest of those who were most heavily involved with the Institute. Toward some she remained rather cool, albeit publicly friendly. Others became "favorite sons." Toward those who did not become as active and dedicated as she would have liked, her disappointment and occasionally her impatience could show.

Alexander Martin, today a distinguished member emeritus of the Institute, recalls how he preferred to stay out of internal politics. After having attended the famous Mental Health Conference in 1930, he had met Karen during her first talk at the Washington Psychoanalytic. While working at the Sheppard-Pratt Hospital there, he came under the influence of Silverberg and Robbins. His beginning psychoanalysis had been interrupted by the death of his analyst, Paul Schilder, Karen's old friend from Berlin. He was in analysis with Karen during the split from the New York Society, and he continued to work with her through her Hotel Essex days.

Apart from the qualities he found in her as an analyst—her intuitive acumen, clarity of thought, simplicity, emotional warmth and constructive encouragement—one incident at the beginning of his analysis endeared her to him. He was once given an 8 A.M. makeup appointment for a missed hour. By mistake he appeared at her office at 8 P.M. She interrupted her dinner to see him. This special consideration made an indelible impression upon him.

Attracted by her holistic approach to analyzing the total personality, Martin dedicated himself exclusively to clinical work. Although Karen was disappointed by his failure to become more active in the affairs of the Association and his advocacy of medical school affiliation, they remained staunch friends. They often visited each other's homes for pleasant social evenings. Martin was a jovial, congenial man, who enjoyed a risqué joke, but whose conviviality never detracted from his good manners. He detested psychologizing and all theory except Karen's.

At this time Karen found another friend of an entirely different type that she could turn to: Frederick Weiss. His wife Gertrude had been the young, enthusiastic college student who was so fascinated by Karen's talks on women at the Humboldt Hochschule in 1927. Her father had known Oskar, and had tried to help Biggi start her career. Weiss himself born in Berlin, had studied philosophy and psychology in Heidelberg and Berlin before taking his medical degree. During his psychiatric residency with Bonhoeffer, he had been analyzed by Alexander and had attended the Berlin Institute, where he had met Karen.

As the scion of the wealthy von Weiss family, he was a nephew of von Rathenau, the German Foreign Minister during and after World War I, and cousin of Bernard Weiss, the Berlin police commissioner during the Weimar period. But from adolescence on he began to rebel against this affluence and status. He became an ardent supporter of ultraliberal causes, an activist speaker, a volunteer physician at a workers' free clinic (where he knew Käthe Kollwitz) and a habitué of the student cafés. In the Romanische Café, where he sometimes met Karen, he was a regular at the poetry-literary and philosophy-psychoanalytic tables. His wife recalls that he and Karen "seemed to fit together, both not only allied against the status quo but also possessing a similar 'creative madness.' " Probably it was the rebelliousness, the vitality and the common bond of language and Berlin experience that drew them together from then on.

He looked up his former teacher when he arrived in New York in 1939. There was much to reminisce about. She encouraged him to enter the new group. Only another analytic supervision with her would be needed to complete his training. In 1943 he became a member of the Association and immediately began to write and speak at meetings. He was different from the others: emotionally volatile and impetuous, his incandescent vitality had to be constantly tamped down. Where most of the others were either self-effacing, inhibited or detached from the internal politics of the group, he could never be. He was used to being involved; debates and argument were his medium. Indeed, he needed to be the center of attention and resented those who he felt deprived him of it. Where most shrank from any challenge to Kelman's influence, he plunged in. An intense rivalry developed between them that was to affect the development of the group for the next twenty years.

But in 1948 Karen still exercised a powerful restraining influence on Weiss, and was frequently called upon to soothe his ruffled feelings after some imagined slight. (On one such occasion, she wrote him an admonishing note: "For God's sake, get at your psychic troubles!") He became her "reader," her eyes and ears on the psychoanalytic world. He was an omnivorous reader of the analytic literature. Because of a physical handicap, a spastic stiffness of his legs, he could not move around freely; his reading and extensive library were probably a compensation for this. Karen herself was too busy to keep up with the latest developments and publications in the field. So he would read everything—either on his own or at her request if she was interested in some specific subject—and summarize his reading for her on the telephone at least twice weekly. Or they would visit each other's homes for weekend social evenings.

During the summer vacations of 1946 and 1947 with Renate, Karen found her truly primitive paradise. It was in the small Mexican village of Ajijic, on the shore of Lake Chapala, with the steep slopes of the Sierras behind. They stayed in a colony of small adobe bungalows, without electricity, indoor plumbing or running water. The colony was owned by one

Don Pablo—a guitar-strumming German who loved to adopt stray dogs and donkeys. There she was able to swim to her heart's content or to paint the flamboyant sunsets, the picturesque streets, the banana palms and the fishermen along the beach among their nets. Every night a fierce tropical storm would break, the thunder and lightning echoing back and forth among the mountains, while Karen and Renate and her family, cozily esconced in their bungalow, would sing or tell stories. Karen began to work on her last book in Ajijic. During the second summer there, Kelman joined them for a few weeks and either worked on a paper of his own or helped with the book. Bernard Zuger, today a respected analyst, stayed in the town for a week and came upon them by chance. It was hard to tell whether he or Kelman was more surprised or embarrassed, but Karen was neither. They all spent the next few days either playing cards or climbing the hills together.

On occasion, Karen, Renate and the children would take the old, dilapidated bus to Guadalajara. The ride was usually a hair-raising adventure; Karen enjoyed every minute, drinking in the all-too-human reactions of everyone else. The bus took on groups of Indians at every stop, with their bundles, baskets, children and pigs, until it was so top-heavily swaying that they expected it to topple over at every turn. The driver would climb on top or crawl underneath at each stop to test whether the ropes holding the bus together were still secure. Yet they always managed to arrive reasonably intact. Karen's seeming sang-froid in face of the danger and her involvement with the tribulations of the other passengers was indeed striking, reminiscent of her similar reaction during the storm-tossed outings on the North Sea coast.

On her return to New York in the fall of 1947, Karen was confronted with the need for a reorganization of the group. The ostensible reason given was the increasing number of candidates, and with it, an increase in administrative work which could not be handled adequately by the dean and the Faculty Council alone. Under the new arrangement, the Institute would become an autonomous organization, independent of the Association. One of the realistic benefits of the change would be that the Institute would be chartered by the state as an accredited psychoanalytic teaching facility; its administrative power would then be vested in a board of trustees, chaired by an elected president. The dean—namely Karen—

would still be concerned with curricular and training issues. But as it happened, only one person seemed then qualified for the post of president, and that was Kelman. In effect, this made official what had long been unofficially true: the concentration of authority in his hands. Nevertheless Karen accepted this, either because she was then unable to appreciate clearly all the ulterior motives for the change or because she was too busy with her own work to pay attention.

Even though she was slackening her pace somewhat, she was still busy. In addition to her regular courses, she participated in a new course at the New School, "Literary Figures in Light of Psychoanalysis." The three works she chose to present herself were Ibsen's *Hedda Gabler*, Stendhal's *The Red and the Black* and Flaubert's *Madame Bovary*. The heroines of all three of these works, as Karen pointed out, represented a single psychological type: the apparently self-effacing woman with a great need to be loved, gradually revealed to be manipulative, vindictive and ultimately destructive.

During the academic year 1947–1948, Karen presented papers at two Academy of Medicine meetings of the Association on "Self-Effacing Attitudes"[6] and "The Value of Vindictiveness."[7] Both papers were drawn from her course and were to be included in her next book. She also spoke more informally at three interval meetings. At the first of these, she discussed her paper on self-effacement in greater detail. She distinguished between a pure self-effacing type and a mixed aggressive–self-effacing person. In this paper, the concept of alienation from self was introduced as clinically resembling, but different from self-effacement. At the other two meetings, she expanded on "The Meaning of Neurotic Suffering."[8]

In September 1948, she again spoke at a regular Academy meeting, this time on "Shallow Living as a Result of Neurosis."[9] Here she introduced the concept of resignation as an active means of avoiding inner conflicts. And in March 1949 she described "Man as a Thinking Machine."[10] She pointed out how the neurotic can use intellectualizing or a belief in the power of the mind, to escape emotional conflicts, and to maintain a feeling of power over others.

More important, however, in April and May she began to present her as yet imprecise formulations of the "Real Self—Its Significance in Therapy." Unlike the subjects she had previously written on, this concept of the "real self" was somewhat difficult to incorporate into the framework of her theory of psychic function. But as she pondered it, she became more and more aware of its implications and nuances. She knew already that the students had had difficulty in grasping it. At their meetings they questioned whether she was referring to an innate, pre-determined psychological entity, a kind of homunculus present in the person at birth, or whether it was some metaphysical force. Much still remained to be clarified, and her theory would have to take this into account.

As she worked further on this idea of the real self through 1949 while preparing her New School course, additional dimensions and ramifications became apparent to her. She realized that it involved such issues as the definitions of guilt and sin, morality, the nature of good and evil, the quality of material, spiritual and human values, the distinction between self-interest and selfishness, between altruism and neurotic interference in the lives of others. These were no longer only psychoanalytic questions; they touched on philosophy and religion as well, and she began to feel a deeper interest in these two subjects than ever before.

But this was not simply an intellectual interest. Some profound change in the way she was experiencing herself was taking place in her. Perhaps the change in the title of her New School course provides a clue to what it was. In contrast to the previous "At War with Ourselves," she now chose "The Search for Inner Unity." The emphasis had shifted from the conflict to its resolution. A healing process was working within her, some resolution of her own inner conflict between pride and self-condemnation. Its manifestations were still external. In fact she urged several colleagues to write on related aspects of these topics. For instance, Muriel Ivimey wrote a paper on "Neurotic Guilt and Healthy Moral Judgement," Weiss on "Psychoanalysis and Moral Values" and Lussheimer on "Psychoanalysis and Religion." In all likelihood, she suggested these topics in the hope that her colleagues' examinations of these questions would help her clarify her own attitudes.

In mid 1949, she began to discuss philosophical questions with Gertrude's daughter, Ursula, then an instructor at Hunter College. Ursula agreed to invite a few of her professors for an evening of informal, free-ranging discussion, something of a reprise of Karen's social evening debates in college and at the Berlin Institute. Gordon Clapp, Professor of Philosophy at Hunter, Max Knoll, Professor of Atomic Physics at Princeton, Erich von Karlau, a sociologist, and Joseph Campbell, a Jungian psychoanalytic ethnologist were on hand. Karen was so fascinated by the first discussion that she asked Clapp to give a series of lectures to the students at the Institute on the relation between philosophy and psychoanalysis. (She attended a number of these but said little.) The meetings at Gertrude's home and later at her own summer cottage, some twelve in all, continued through the spring of 1950.

In these meetings she participated actively, asking questions related to the lectures, trying to connect the philosophical ideas with her own and with herself. For example, she compared Plato's division of his ideal state into castes of soldiers, workers, farmers and rulers to the substructures within the self—the ego, superego, the urge to grow and the repressive inner authority. She preferred the Augustinian concept of the "city within the soul" to a simple parellel between society and the individual psyche. Internal and external factors did not coincide exactly one-to-one; it was more complicated than that. She disagreed with the Cartesian duality between mind and body, believing that this division hid the essence of both reality and the personality. The "*Cogito, ergo sum*" could too easily become a neurotic defense; she had recently written about such compulsive intellectualization. She was impressed by William James's concepts of the private and social selves; later she read his work more thoroughly and adopted some of his ideas.

Ursula was teaching and studying phenomenology and existentialism and Karen was eager to discuss these philosophies both at that time and later when she returned from a trip to Japan in 1952. She showed a surprising knowledge of these subjects, recalling her previous readings of Kierkegaard and Husserl. Kierkegaard's "either/or" seemed to her roughly analogous to her own emphasis on conflict. What appealed to her most was his position at the intersection of psychology, philosophy and religion. It was where she stood then. She disliked the phenomenologists since she felt their writings showed a "too great reliance on words, playing with them . . . there was much more to psychological roots . . . in the nature of experience, in a more direct sense."

Karen was also becoming more interested in religion. Since adolescence she had never been interested in organized religion; she had no special feeling for or against any particular sect. Starting with Ida Behrmann and Louis Grote in childhood, many of her personal friends had been Jewish. So had most of her analytic colleagues. Yet she was not philosemitic in the same way that Ernest Jones was, for instance. According to Harold Kelman, she was pleased and proud to be "elected an honorary Jew" by her colleagues at the Institute. Her daughters all married Jews. For her, religion had become more a philosophical and ethical issue: The Nazi persecution of the Jews had been distasteful not out of religious considerations but because it was an insult to human dignity in general. Fromm's avowed Jewishness had never interfered with their long-standing close relationship; she had accepted it as part of his heritage and personality. She believed that an individual's faith was only of importance insofar as it entered into his neurosis or enabled him to deal with the ever-present anxiety that is simply part of being human. She had often discussed this with Tillich, who felt as she did, that a person's faith was not necessarily religious—even an atheist had faith—nor was it a belief in God. It was an "ultimate concern," and doubt was an inevitable part of faith. He explained then, as he was to write shortly afterward in his book *The Courage to Be,* his belief that every human being—neurotic or not— must experience existential anxiety arising from three sources: awareness of one's inescapable death, awareness of one's failure to participate creatively in life, of one's meaninglessness and failure to fulfil one's potential destiny and the consequent guilt. These three forms of consciousness bring with them the threat of "non-being." Faith is the courage to affirm oneself in the face of this threat. These ideas of his excited and stirred Karen deeply, stimulating the vague thoughts then swirling around in her mind, which were to emerge later in her theory in a more psychological context.

Her new concern manifested itself in other ways. During one evening at the Weiss home, he lent her a copy of Aldous Huxley's *The Perennial Philosophy.* The book remained open on her night table for two years; she read it every night. When she returned it to Gertrude Weiss, many passages had been marked; it had been well used. Basically Huxley's book was an anthology of selections and aphorisms from the great mystics and prophets of East and West, all dealing with, in Huxley's words, "the metaphysic that recognizes a divine Reality substantial to the world of things and lives and minds; the psychology that finds in the soul something similar to divine Reality; the ethic that places man's final end in the knowledge of the immanent and transcendental Ground of all being."[11]

She also turned to her frail Japanese friend Suzuki, who had made such an indelible impression upon her. He seemed to have already found meaning and harmony, not only within himself but with the world around him. She was curious to seek out his answer in the ways of Zen and entered into a correspondence with him that was to bear fruit only a few years later.

She also began to attend Tillich's sermons at the Cathedral of St. John the Divine, not out of formal religious conviction, but because of her friendship for him and interest in his ideas. During their frequent visits at each other's homes, the best part of the evening was usually the lively discussion between them of some philosophical or theological question. With him Karen felt entirely at ease, unconstrained, whether in a relaxed give-and-take of exchanged ideas or simply in silence. It was not uncommon for them to walk hand in hand, not out of any physical intimacy but rather with a feeling of natural, unselfconscious harmony. This upsurge in her curiosity and self-questioning, focused mostly on religion—which she herself later described as a "positive discontent"—bespoke a kind of identity crisis. It was reminiscent of the similar self-doubting period during her adolescence, when she was also seeking meaning in life.

In 1947 and 1948, Brigitte was living quietly in Chardonne-sur-Vevey, above Lake Geneva in Switzerland. After years of separation and uncertainty, Karen was most anxious to see her daughter. So she spent two weeks in each of these summers visiting her. The joyous reunions were all too short. The rest of each summer was spent with Renate—although in 1947 and again in 1948, she made a short side-trip to Guatemala. Just before her second trip, she had received news that Kelman, who was vacationing there, had fallen ill with a pulmonary infection. She urged him to return immediately to New York, where he painfully recovered from what proved to be a lung abscess.

Through 1948 and 1949 she continued to work on her book. She was still not certain what to call it; in February she wrote Norton suggesting a preliminary title *Pride and Pity*. Then during the summer of 1949, she spent the er.tire two months with Biggi in a rented house in Moscia, above Ascona and their beautiful Lake Maggiore. She wrote Norton, "This is undiluted paradise. Sunshine, swimming, peace and mountains. With all that I am working hard. Do not yet have the title. Tentatively 'The

Human Tragedy in Neurosis'. Never again shall I write a book, but I have felt this way before." One wonders. Was this last cryptic sentence on her card the expression of creative outpouring into the writing she was doing? Or was it a premonition of finality? She was to spend all of the next two summers in Moscia as well.

During the Christmas vacation of 1949, she visited Renate again. She was so taken with their last vacation site, near Cuernavaca, that she decided to buy a permanent house there. This time she particularly enjoyed strolling around the nearby Aztec pyramid, communing with the ancient deities. As she expressed it to Renate, only half-humorously, "near the pyramid the Gods will protect and inspire me."

They did find a house for sale not far away, without a number on a street without a name. It was simple adobe in Mexican ranch style, with a high, thick-beamed, pitched ceiling, antique colonial furniture and big glass doors leading to the terrace. The garden was a typical lush and colorful Eden, with eucalyptus, oleander, bougainvillea and papyrus plants. Above all, it contained a delightful rock pool for swimming. Karen bought it for her daughter and family. She asked that a separate room be built later for her personal use over the garage. From it she could see Popocatepetl, first dim in the early mist, then silhoutted against the beautiful sunrise behind it each morning. She also requested that a number of tropical plants be planted in the garden: a lemon tree, coffee bush, bananas, bamboos and a palm tree. This desire for the exotic was another way of showing her difference, of her gentle rebellion against the ordinary. But she was not to use the room until the Christmas vacation of 1950.

Back home at the Institute before and after her vacation, Karen continued to be preoccupied with issues of morality and ethics. In December 1949, before leaving, she addressed the candidates on "Responsibility—Healthy and Neurotic."[12] She felt that three forms of responsibility could be distinguished: reliability in fulfilling obligations, caring for others, and most important, as a moral charge, the acceptance of blame for one's own actions. The neurotic either blames others or blames himself excessively. This tendency results from the demands of his neurotic pride in controlling his activities and difficulties, which leads inevitably to self-condemnation. Healthy responsibility means being truthful to, and aware of, oneself. It does not involve any blame. It requires freedom of choice.

In March 1950, she spoke on "Neurotic Disturbances in Work."[13] This was when she was most actively engaged in writing the book. In her talk she highlighted some of the problems she was having, which she had already reported on twice before. Now she described some of the difficulties connected with each of the various neurotic trends. The aggressive writer feels he can do anything; he overrates his abilities. Anyone who disagrees is jealous or attacking him. The narcissist spreads himself too thin and stops at slight obstacles. He hates details and loses interest quickly. The vindictive person works hard and with passion, but life outside his work is empty. He quotes others freely, contributing little of his own. He tends to be dictatorial and intimidating; he is unable to delegate work, since he feels he alone is capable of handling it. The self-effacing neurotic sets his aims too low and then plagues himself with criticism. He can work better for others and feels helpless working alone. If he realizes he is succeeding, he is seized by paralysis, inertia, forgetfulness or writer's block. Writing becomes a torment, since he is driven by unconscious perfectionism, and simply cannot stand errors. Then he craves constant approval, sympathy and appreciation for what he produces. Love affairs do not bring happiness, but he hopes they will. Thus he plunges into them, vacillating between love and work to assuage anxiety. The resigned individual suffers from inertia and hypersensitivity to coercion. He is defiant and rebellious, and must do things differently than others.

In April, before an overflow audience, Karen summarized her views on "Psychoanalysis and Moral Values"[14] at the annual ACAAP symposium. She defined her concept of self-realization, which was gradually becoming clearer. To help a patient attain self-realization, the primary moral obligation of the analyst is to remove obstructive forces. Now she elaborated on the three contrasting concepts of human moral conduct which had first been raised by Silverberg at the 1942 Boston convention. The "sinful, instinct-ridden and bad" concept of some religions requires conformity to superimposed moral dictates. The "something-essentially-good-as-well-as-bad" concept demands that the individual check his own sinful drives. This view permits help from without, from God or through grace, in order to be saved. She did not agree with either of these. In her own view, each person has inherent constructive forces within him which promote the growth and development of his own potentials.

Her last book was scheduled for publication in the fall of 1950. Yet in March she had still not decided on the final title. Those she had previously thought of just did not seem right. They somehow did not convey either the essential thrust or the comprehensiveness of her theory. In March she suggested to Norton *In Search of Self-Realization;* then *In Search of the Real Self.* Finally, after her return from her summer in Switzerland, she and Norton arrived at the final choice: *Neurosis and Human Growth—The Struggle Toward Self-Realization.* This included both the theoretical conceptualization of the neurotic personality and her newer emphasis on the process of constructive growth.

One anecdote is related about the book just before its publication. Bernard Zuger was preparing a lecture on neurosis and psychosis and was having difficulty in completing it. Karen offered to lend him the galley-proofs of her book. He called her shortly afterward to discuss some concepts he was not clear about. Her reply was that she herself was no clearer about them, but she had hope!

When the book was finally published reviews were generally enthusiastic—where they appeared. None came out in the classical Freudian journals. Benjamin Weininger, a former member of the Association, wrote in *Psychiatry:* "This is Horney's most important work since *The Neurotic Personality.* In her previous works she offered isolated insights into personality. Here the discussion hangs together as a unified theory. . ."[15]

Ashley Montagu, the sociologist, also called it her most important book. "Her admirers will be more than pleased; her critics, though they may come to damn, will, I think, mostly stay to praise, though they may demur at the author's irreverent treatment of Freud. Horney admires and respects Freud and his achievement, but does not worship him. She has made a creative use of whatever transference she had toward Freud, and in that sense remains among the best of Freudians . . . The book might be regarded as a work of moral philosophy."[16]

Objections to the book were generally focused on her concept of the real self. They were based on the same misinterpretations the candidates had had, which she had been hard put to correct. For one, "she talks as if a real self is standing by, waiting to come out when the neurotic self is worked through." For another, "[her] conception of the 'real self' is vague, and when not vague is downright metaphysical or flatly erroneous."

After finishing the book, Karen felt emotionally drained, depleted, empty. When she visited Renate that Christmas she was tired, tense, and more irritable than ever before. She complained of feeling excluded and was easily angered. But she recovered quickly after a brief explosion of her pent-up feelings—in time for the usual happy Christmas celebration. Possibly this mood was a reaction to her long-sustained creative struggle.

XXI
NEUROSIS AND
HUMAN GROWTH

Neurosis and Human Growth constituted the fourth and final version of Karen's psychoanalytic theory. It showed many changes from her earlier writings: in the style of writing, in emphasis and details of the theoretical structure and in the overall spirit of her thinking.

One modification was the different significance accorded to the idealized image of the self. Previously the creation of this irrational self-image had been seen as only one of four major defensive solutions to conflict. Now it became the nuclear process of neurotic development, a comprehensive solution that occurred in all neuroses regardless of their form. Spurred by the child's rich imagination, the process begins in early childhood as a reactive defense against basic anxiety. It has two stages. First is the creation of the fantastic idealized self image, starting in the child as a conscious process, later continuing in the adult as an unconscious one. It is derived from the person's special needs, abilities and experiences. In it, needed neurotic trends are idealized, contradictory attitudes isolated or transformed into positive traits so as to eliminate the conflicts. In the second stage, the person identifies with, actually becomes this image; it becomes an idealized self.

Several drives contribute to this self-idealization (otherwise known as actualization of the idealized image). These include the need for perfection, neurotic ambitiousness and the need for vindictive triumph. Such drives are compulsive, insatiable and absolute in their intensity.

Another new concept was self-realization. Growing in a healthy parental environment, the child would be able to develop his real native attributes, his given potentials. Such a milieu would require from parents a basic warmth, freedom of expression, encouragement and guidance, healthy friction and rational discipline. The child's positive qualities would include his spontaneous feelings, interests, wishes, personal abilities, will power and values. He can tap all his resources. Such a type and direction of growth is termed self-realization. The inner force which moves the person toward this end is the real self. It is not a specific form of personality or infantile homunculus; it refers to forces or energies, exerted in a certain direction, analogous perhaps to the Bergsonian "élan vital."

This healthy child can relate to others by pleasing, or drawing closer, by assertion or opposition, by withdrawal or being alone. As long as these attitudes are spontaneous, flexible and appropriate, they are complementary and easily integrated.

If, on the contrary, the child grows up in an atmosphere of neurotic attitudes in his parents, he can develop the feeling of insecurity, distrust and loneliness previously described as basic anxiety. His relations with his parents and others then become one-sided, rigid and compulsive, motivated by a need for safety and security. They become neurotic trends, in dynamic opposition with each other, therefore creating conflict. With each trend, particular needs, inhibitions, sensitivities and values also develop. The need to maintain such a defensive stance in the face of underlying conflicts and lack of self-confidence drives the neurotic toward actualization of an unreal façade, an artificial way of life and a false image of himself.

The neurotic expects to be treated by others as if he really were this grandiose self. His expectations and demands, unconsciously aggrandized, are endowed with feelings of entitlement, of being due him as if they were a right. They become claims on others or on the world and life. Their frustration brings an abused feeling, of being unfairly treated. Since demand is based on a neurotic need, its content varies with the predominant trend. It may be a claim for obedience or uncritical acceptance, for understanding, for happiness, for results without making any effort, for unconditional love, for immunity from aging or stressful events, for invulnerability to illness, suffering or change, for freedom from rules, problems, restrictions or limitations, for recognition of his superlative qualities, for special consideration or privilege.

All neurotic claims have several characteristics in common. They do not take into account the realistic possibilities of fulfillment. They are unreasonably egocentric and so do not allow for the needs of others. They should be satisfied without appropriate efforts. And as demands, they may include a feeling of vindictiveness. The degree of awareness of the entitled feeling can vary from conscious to completely unconscious.

But it is their effects that call attention to their presence. Frustration of a claim often leads to anger. If repressed, this feeling can be transformed into a psychosomatic symptom, a vindictive rage reaction, or a feeling of depression. The presence of chronic claims is often signaled by a chronic pessimism about life, an envy of others, or a general uncertainty about one's own rights.

The striving to maintain the idealized image is expressed differently toward oneself than toward others. Claims are directed toward others. The neurotic whips himself by a system of "shoulds" and "musts." These will also vary according to the major trend. As examples, he should be strong, stoic, enduring; loving, generous, self-sacrificing; omniscient, omnipotent; serene, tranquil, untouched by events; unemotional, in absolute control of feelings, or ultra-sensitive to emotions; wise, reasonable, understanding; infallible—the list is unending. And like claims, they ignore the reality of whether they can ever be achieved. Since they have an absolute quality, they do not represent attainable ideals or genuine moral standards.

Most important, shoulds have a coercive quality; operating from the unconscious, they exert a constant pressure. This attribute gives rise to their major symptomatic effects. Failure to measure up to them can produce a gamut of reactions: anxiety, self-criticism, self-hatred, depression, usually disproportionate to the apparent cause. Reactive feelings toward what is, in effect, an inner authority, can vary. One person may accept it, welcoming a system that checks disturbing feelings. Another may rebel against it passively, feeling only chronic strain, resentment or inertia. Or it may be an active rebellion, being "bad," acting out. If the inner authority is externalized on to others, he becomes hypersensitive to external authorities.

Finally, having to do, feel or be the way one *should* do, feel or be, results in a loss of spontaneous actions, emotions or attitudes. The neurotic's life becomes a spurious as-if façade or only a shallow unfulfilling existence.

What gives the idealized image its immense value and intense hold on the neurotic is that it becomes invested with pride. Such neurotic pride must be distinguished from a healthy form, real self-esteem. The latter is based on realistic factors: some true ability, a job well done, a real achievement, a sense of worth or self-confidence. Neurotic pride is based on the spurious, imagined irrational values of the idealized image. Therefore it is shaky, easily hurt, needed rather than appreciated for itself.

Depending on his neurotic structure, the person will invest his pride in specific attributes. For instance, he may pride himself on his prestige, his intellectual functions like knowledge or reason, his ability to control through power or will, his lofty standards like wisdom, honesty, good judgment or rightness, his goodness, his lovability, his invulnerability, his capacity to get away with things. It is here that the transformation of imperfections into virtues is best seen.

While such pride is needed to deny unwanted negative qualities, it inevitably leads to even greater distress. It renders the neurotic vulnerable to hurt pride reactions. Two of the most typical emotional reactions are to feel shame and humiliation. The former is felt when one becomes aware that the prideful standard is being disproved from within; the latter when it is violated in or by others, from without.

However, these simple reactive emotions frequently do not even come into awareness. Pride in self-control may cause their immediate and automatic repression. Or they may be unconsciously transformed into some other emotion, like grief. Or finally, only a secondary reaction to the shame may be experienced, such as rage or fear. In fact, a humiliating situation need not even occur. Sometimes even the anticipation of such a situation can produce the reaction—anticipatory anxiety or fear. Finally, when this rage does occur, it too may be immediately repressed and changed into depression, psychosis or somatic symptoms.

Several typical dynamic responses to hurt pride can occur as defensive means of restoring pride. Taking revenge is one way of assuring a vindictive triumph. Another is to lose interest in the event. A third is by frank denial or by forms therof, like forgetfulness or evasiveness. Still another can be the self-conscious use of humor.

When the neurotic identifies with his pride-invested grandiose image, he views his actual self from that vantage point. What he actually is becomes the ever-present obstacle to being the godlike creature he imagines himself to be. How he actually functions always highlights the discrepancy. He then must inevitably hate himself as he really is. Pride and self-hate are two unavoidable sides of the same coin, both encompassed by the term "the pride system." The neurotic is rarely aware of his self-hate, at least in its true intensity and ramifications. He only experiences its effects.

The expressions of self-hate can be grossly categorized into six forms.

First are the *coercive demands* on the self. Failure to fulfil or violation of shoulds calls down intense hatred upon the self. Second, *self-accusations* are directed at any faults, difficulties or pretenses that give evidence of weakness in attaining one's ultimate standards. They carry a tone of moral condemnation and give rise to guilt feelings. And they will be felt despite their obvious irrationality or even if the failure is beyond one's real control. They can also be externalized, and then experienced as accusations by others. Neurotic standards differ from healthy conscience, which is a reminder to the real self of realistic shortcomings.

Third, *self-contempt* (self-disparagement, self-belittling) is a way of negating any attempt at achievement or improvement. Its symptoms can be seen in the neurotic's constant comparison of himself with others and envy of those perceived as better. When externalized, it may be a hypersensitivity to criticism or rejection—real or misinterpreted. Or it may exist as a constant need for the regard, admiration or recognition of others as a means of compensating for feelings of inferiority. Fourth, *self-frustration* inhibits hope, striving, choice, potential, enjoyment, inner freedom. Fifth, *self-torturing* attitudes go beyond even the torments of the other forms. These can include severe hypochondriacal fears and obsessions, masochistic fantasies or impulses. Sadistic urges may be active externalizations of these attitudes.

Lastly, direct *self-destructive* impulses may be acute or chronic, conscious or unconscious. They can consist of minor activities like nailbiting or scratching; transitory thoughts of harming oneself; reckless conduct in sports or driving or neglect of physical infirmities; drug or alcohol use; accident-proneness; and possibly chronic illnesses like cancer or tuberculosis. Often such attitudes will only be expressed in a disguised form in dreams.

Alienation from self is now seen as the core process of neurosis. It is defined as a remoteness from one's genuine, spontaneous feelings, wishes, energies, self-directedness, values—from the real self. It can also involve the body, manifesting itself as a numbing of sensations, loss of identity, or feelings of depersonalization, "like being in a fog."

The many processes occurring in every neurosis combine to produce this result. All compulsive drives remove a person from his real spontaneity and autonomy. The movement toward actualization of the idealized image, with all its shoulds, determines a mode of existence other than what one really is. Externalization further removes one from all inner phenomena; they are experienced from without. Self-hate is an attitude of active rejection of the self. When pride governs feelings, then true feelings are ignored. The inertia resulting from inner conflicts saps one's energies. Lastly, the need to maintain spurious values denies one's genuine values and responsibility for oneself.

And yet, however comprehensive a solution like self-idealization may be, the personality still remains poorly integrated, unstable, caught in conflicts and tensions. Five additional factors must also be present in order to relieve such tension, corresponding to the seven listed in her previous book as auxiliary measures or approaches to inner harmony.

One of these is alienation from self, which is thus not only a result of the neurotic process but an active defensive measure. By blurring all inner experiences, it lessens the intensity of inner conflicts. The second is externalization. Any inner quality, whether admired or despised, healthy or neurotic, can be seen in others. Compartmentalization (or psychic fragmentation) is another. Inner processes are experienced as disconnected and isolated rather than as parts of a whole, or contradictory or causally related, as the case might be. The fourth is automatic control of impulses, actions and feelings. This can take place at their unconscious source or as they emerge into consciousness. The fifth is supremacy of the mind or intellectualization. This refers to the use of the mind or knowledge to avoid participation in one's feelings and conflicts. The person becomes a disinterested spectator of his own experiences. He may believe that knowing in itself means changing.

All these various dynamic solutions to conflict, comprehensive and auxiliary, operate in all neurotics, but they will be expressed differently in each type of personality. The three initial ways of relating were described as "moving-against," "moving-toward" and "moving-away from others" in the previous version. Now they are termed "major solutions," and grouped into expansive, self-effacing and resigned orientations. They are seen to involve not only attitudes toward others, but toward the self as well.

The expansive personality identifies with his glorified self. He is bent on mastery and superiority; he despises self-effacement—helplessness, failure, timidity, weakness. Three subforms of this orientation are distinguished.

Narcissism is the psychic state of loving the attributes of one's idealized image. The narcissist believes in his greatness, uniqueness, omnipotence, infallibility and freedom from limitations. He must impress others and needs their admiration. He overlooks flaws or transforms them into virtues. But his relations with others are poor; he imagines criticism and becomes easily enraged by it. He disregards the needs and feelings of others. His work suffers from being too grandiose in its aims. So he often incurs failure through real limitations. He may seem optimistic and happy, but just underneath the surface are pessimism and despondency.

The perfectionist neurotic identifies with his demanding standards and feels superior to others because he alone carries them out. So he denigrates and despises others. He needs to be perfect in behavior, attitudes and values. The discrepancy between what he believes he is (and tries to be) and what he really is is blurred by his self-deception. Since he feels himself to be fair, dutiful, just, he feels entitled to fair treatment, fortune or success. But he can collapse with self-hate when misfortune contradicts this claim, or when he makes mistakes.

With the arrogant-vindictive solution, the neurotic has identified with his pride. The need for vindictive triumph makes him highly competitive. He cannot tolerate losing and when it threatens, he can be subject either to violent rage or to distrust of others; they are out to beat him. Therefore he is constantly scheming to frustrate others. These attitudes enter into his sexual relations also. He needs to dominate and exert power. On this basis he builds extreme claims: to be right, to be respected despite his disregard for others, to be invulnerable and immune. His pride in strength, power and control is so absolute that any "softer" feelings like love, compassion or sympathy are crushed. When they might emerge, his self-contempt is tremendous. When he perceives these traits in others, he may feel disposed to punish them.

The self-effacing neurotic identifies with his despised self. He shuns, even fears any expansive qualities. Suffering and helplessness in fact have a certain unconscious appeal for him. He craves the help and care they could procure for him. He can accept failure, inferiority, self-denial. If any self-contempt comes up, it is passively externalized; others are looking down on him. He fears hostility in himself and in others. Arguments must be avoided. He must be loving, giving, understanding, self-sacrificing.

These attitudes are glorified into the "good," the lovable qualities in himself, even though it may mean completely eliminating his own interests. But intense self-hatred is generated when any awareness of his repressed hostility, pride or vindictiveness emerges. He needs others not only for love, but also to avoid being alone—proof of his being unwanted and unloved. When his claims for love or help are not met, he feels chronically abused. This can make for chronic resentment of others or for accusations against himself—often in the form of somatic symptoms and suffering.

Neurotic suffering serves several purposes. It acts as a justification for claims. It often is a means of being vindictive or exploitative without having to consciously admit it. One avoids accusing oneself by accusing others and suffering becomes an excuse for not making more of life. In extreme cases, helplessness, illness or even psychic suicide present themselves as the ultimate way out of difficulties. They can even be experienced as the final triumph over the world or fate.

Morbid dependency is an extreme form of this orientation, occurring mainly in erotic love relationships. The self-effacing person is often attracted to a dominating partner in whom he sees those traits that he misses in himself. These he admires in others, and concludes, consciously or unconsciously, that their absence in himself is responsible for his suffering. Besides, even though he wants to obtain love and sympathy, he can be repelled by another compliant person, who displays the same irritating weaknesses as himself. The need for surrender through self-degradation or self-elimination is compulsive. And once begun, the person is too fearful of asserting himself to take a stand—a situation that eventually makes for increased inner conflicts.

The third major solution, resignation, differs dynamically from the first two. Here the neurotic removes himself totally from all conflicts instead of simply repressing one contradictory side, as in the other solutions. It provides a freedom "from" the unpleasant rather than "for" something positive. Typically, he gives the impression of being an observer of himself and of life. This nonparticipation is much broader than the simple intellectualizing described previously. Here, the neurotic avoids being emotionally touched by anything that happens within himself. He eliminates awareness of painful conflicts by distancing himself from all feelings.

A second trait is the aversion to any serious striving toward a goal, to any effort or to any psychic movement. To achieve peace and serenity may be a conscious aim, but at a deeper level this means an absolute freedom from change, an unrealistic nirvana-happiness. Detachment from others is a typical quality, especially insofar as relations will demand emotional involvement. Sex is usually only physical contact.

Characteristic, too, is a hypersensitivity to coercion, influence, obligation, restriction, limitation, pressure or intrusion. This occurs because one's pride is invested in stabilizing or immobilizing the dynamic forces of two repressed orientations, both of which are still compulsive. The person still identifies with the attributes of his idealized image but he has renounced the active drive to make it real in life. He therefore may show self-effacing or expansive attitudes at various times, but these are not compelling drives. Nevertheless, he still feels the shoulds from both sets of attitudes. In addition, newer shoulds express needs for independence, stoicism, privacy, freedom from want or desire, passionless and unruffled serenity. This combination accounts for his sensitivity to any coercion. Then by externalization, his own inner dictates will be experienced as coerciveness and authoritarianism in others.

Different inner reactions to this basic process can be observed clinically. Persistent resignation may be low-keyed and still permit some activities. Feelings of inertia and chronic strain then often accompany sustained effort and work. Inner feelings are restricted, including interest, curiosity and enjoyment. If any of these are felt, they quickly fade. A deadness or emptiness is sometimes experienced. However, since freedom is always sought, this inertia always contains an element of passive rebellion.

Another reactive type is the actively rebellious person, who may rebel against the external environment or his own inner restrictions. To a limited degree this can be a healthy movement.

Behavior of the third group is characterized by shallow living. Increasing emptiness, loss of feeling, futility and lack of direction can result in an attempt to fill one's life with meaningless distractions. Emphasis is then placed on having fun: on parties, sex, socializing, amusements; or on opportunistic success, on money, seizing the advantage—but solely for the freedom these offer from life's difficulties; or on automatic adaptation to the prevailing codes and habits of others.

In the last chapters of *Neurosis and Human Growth,* some of the therapeutic problems posed by this character analysis are discussed. Actually, to speak of a "cure" of neurosis is not appropriate. Psychoanalysis only helps the patient overcome his growth-obstructing needs and attitudes, thus relieving his conflicts and obviating the necessity for solutions. This includes dissipating his illusions about himself. Then, and then only, can he grow in a healthier direction and develop his potentials.

But this goal of the analyst is not the goal of the patient in therapy. He feels that analysis should help him retain—even strengthen and perfect—his neurotic solutions and values. To renounce them would endanger his psychic existence. It would be too dangerous to obtain real insight into what he feels to be his shortcomings. He wishes to remove only the disturbing situation, the immediate problems, the painful symptom. Furthermore, since his unconscious expectations of therapy depend on his particular neurotic solution, he seeks change through his own will power and control, or without effort and involvement, or through the analyst's magic wand. Each growing awareness will bring some blockage: evasiveness, argument, hostility, spurious agreement, apathy or forgetfulness, periods of self-hate, anxiety, etc. All the specific defenses must be understood and laid bare: needs, claims, shoulds, prides, solutions, values. In this process, intellectual knowledge is insufficient. There must occur an emotional experience of each specific defensive attitude as well. This aspect of the therapy constitutes a disillusioning process, occurring during the first phase of analysis. At the beginning, conflicts are still blurred. The second phase must consist of delineating and mobilizing constructive assets of the patient. Then a gradual moving forward will occur, with more spontaneity and vitality. But this, in turn, will bring repercussions in the form of periods of self-contempt, with rapid up-and-down shifts in mood and symptoms. Rapid changes later in the analysis are indicative of the *central conflict,* the struggle between all the obstructive, neurotic forces and the constructive, healthy forces. Passing through each of these phases will eventually result in a strengthening of self-confidence.

In this book, the final version of Karen's theory differs from the previous ones in several ways. In the first place, she modified the theoretical structure of the neurotic (and healthy) personality. The role and importance of the idealized self-image have been changed. From simply one tactic (out of four) of resolving inner conflicts, it became the crucial defensive move of neurosis. The relation between self-glorification and self-hate were clarified. The entire concept of self-hate assumed a greater significance. The new concepts of self-realization and real self were introduced. This led to an expansion of the notion of conflict. It occurred not only between opposing compulsive solutions, but also between the pride-system and the real self (central inner conflict). Alienation from self was now seen to constitute a key process of neurotic development. Yet with all these modifications, the theory remained a personology, a study of character structure.

In the second place, this work is much more sophisticated and complex, both theoretically and stylistically. In her previous books, Karen's view of personality was relatively simple—perhaps even deceptively oversimplified. Here one senses a much greater realization of the profundity of the human psyche and the complexity of human relations, whether healthy or disturbed. Even a well-demarcated symptom like anxiety cannot be ascribed to some limited conflict between basic drives. It can result from active opposition between more complex trends or their secondary and tertiary products, like claims, values or shoulds. Conflicts breed further conflicts; reactions to conflicts may create new reactions, and so forth. The degree to which the neurotic is enmeshed in his web of defensive devices becomes more evident here. The intensity of feelings (or lack of them) is conveyed much more dramatically here, whether it be despair, self-hate, pride or emptiness.

In the third place, the theory has evolved in terms of psychodynamics. The concepts of peremptory forces, psychic movement and directions have become as important as descriptive traits and behavior types. Consider the concept of direction. In the first version of the theory, emphasis was primarily placed on the influence of the culture on the individual personality. The direction was mostly from the outside inward. In this final version, the main focus is on the influence of intrapsychic forces on interpersonal relations. The direction is from within outward. Even within the self, growth is seen to occur in a healthy direction (self-realization) or neurotic direction (self-idealization). The neurotic rises above conflicts and then looks down on others.

Direction also implies movement, both microcosmic and macrocosmic. The child moves toward, against, away from parents; alienation is movement away from self. Movement is implicit in the very notion of dynamic, active conflict and active escape from it.

Lastly, a holistic spirit is now quite evident here. Despite her emphasis on intrapsychic phenomena, she makes clear that these only occur in a context. The cultural, the interpersonal and the intrapsychic, the mental, the emotional and the somatic, the past and the present are all closely intertwined. Even though one aspect can be observed and studied, the other aspects of the individual are still very much present, and must be taken into account. In the first version of her theory, personal attitudes and inner conflicts were seen to be a reflection of similar factors in society. The two could nonetheless be easily differentiated. In this version, the distinction is not so clear. At numerous points we are told that what is described as past history may be a projection of one's present attitudes. What is seen as outside situations may really be an externalization of internal events. Subjective and objective are often difficult to separate. The individual produces his needs, claims, shoulds, conflicts at the same time that he directs their effects back upon himself; it is a reflexive influence, even though he may feel that he is being acted upon by "something" within himself. But hopefully, as therapy progresses, the person grows closer to his real self. Then he will come to feel active in his own being and life, responsible for himself and "the captain of his own ship."

This final version of her theory was to have many long-term effects that Horney neither intended nor would have completely wished, and in any event could not have foreseen. She was basically trying to systematize her concepts of personality but was attempting to do so by extending and building only upon her previous ideas. The major exception to this was her introduction of the real self and the process of self-realization. She often stated that any one of her ideas could not be really understood if isolated, taken out of context of the whole framework. When she did discuss her ideas in her classes or her Academy lectures, she always linked them with their dynamic emotional causes and effects. Unfortunately, others who have followed her and who have borrowed or "rediscovered" ideas she enunciated have either changed their meaning or have failed to convey their scope. And this is usually done without giving credit to her.

A number of her ideas have become incorporated into the then new ego psychology begun by Freud and developed by his followers. For example, her notion of pride, transformed from healthy into an exaggerated neurotic form, was elaborated upon by Heinz Hartmann, a distinguished Freudian analyst. He called attention to the neglect of this emotion in classical analytic writing and the need to give it its rightful importance. Horney's concept of irrational self-idealization was further amplified by Annie Reich, Jeanne Lampl-de Groot and Samuel Novey. It was redefined much as Horney conceived it to be, as a narcissistic defensive operation against anxiety, rather than simply as part of the normal ego-ideal. These authors still linked it directly to traumatic experiences of the infant; grandiose fantasies would be a compensation for feelings of helplessness. More recently, younger Freudian analysts like Heinz Kohut and Otto Kernberg have extended and refined her concept of neurotic, defensive narcissism, especially in relation to the "borderline" personality. Their work is replete with terms introduced by Horney, such as the splitting of the self into omnipotent and self-devaluative attitudes, pathological self-esteem and integration of the self.

Karen's idea that the relationship between the patient and analyst consisted of more than the simple repetition of the infant's attitudes toward parents has also been confirmed in recent years. Many classical analysts now speak of the broader "therapeutic alliance" or the "working" or "real" relationship during psychoanalysis. Following Karen—and Franz Alexander, who also stressed this point at about the same time—they believe that healthy, later-developed, here-and-now aspects of both patient and analyst enter into the analysis as much if not more than infantile ones. Her insistence on the need to experience emotionally all on-going feelings, that is, on emotional instead of only intellectual awareness, has appeared in the so-called experiential schools of psychology. These include the client-centered therapy of Carl Rogers, the Gestalt-therapy of Fritz Perls and Whitaker and Malone's experiential therapy.

One of her most far-reaching contributions was the introduction of the concept of self-realization—the innate tendency of the individual to grow in a healthy direction—into her systematized theory of personality and neurosis. Following this principle, there have appeared several schools of "self-actualizing" psychotherapy, the so-called third force in psychology to counterbalance the Freudian biological views as well as the culturalist approach. Notable among these are Kurt Goldstein's organismic approach (although he also influenced Horney and was himself previously affected by Gestalt psychology), and especially Abraham Maslow's theories.

Aside from these specific derivations, Horney's theory presaged other more general currents in psychological thought that have become popular today. One has been the increasing emphasis on socio-cultural factors as the causes of emotional illness. She would have found this overall trend congenial. But not completely! She would have disagreed with the degree to which society is blamed for neurosis and the resulting attempts to treat neurosis by simply changing social conditions. In point of fact, even though she continues to be considered a "Neo-Freudian culturalist" psychoanalyst, this classification is misleading. It was based on her earlier work; she remained individual-oriented and in her later work focused almost exclusively on the inner structure of the psyche.

The second current popular today is related to this, namely her holistic emphasis on the dynamic, continuous interaction between external cultural conditions, interpersonal relations and inner emotional experiences. This view is described today as "systems-theory." Her contribution to this trend was significant, though, like so many of her other advances, it has been largely overlooked.

XXII
THE FINAL YEARS

As 1951 began, friends noticed that Karen seemed subtly changed. Though she continued her usual socializing in her own home or at friends', it was less frequent than before. She complained of feeling lonely and appeared subdued. She took to reading light detective stories that she could go through quickly. George Simenon was one of her favorites. Several of his books were usually to be found on her night table. Often she would seek out old German or Indian movies in the small out-of-the-way art theaters, or lectures or dance programs in the YMCAs. She kept looking, for instance, for films with the Viennese comic actor Hans Moser. After Gertrude Weiss once ran into her at such a program, Karen would often call her for company on similar outings. "Please come with me, I've no one to go with." From time to time she would ask the Weisses if a social evening could be held at their house, when her own was disorganized after vacation or when she was having "housekeeper trouble." She took it for granted that her requests would be accepted and the Weisses were generally happy to oblige. She would always show her appreciation by giving them a plant or other small gift. Some of the guests at these evenings included Kurt Goldstein, Abraham Maslow, Alexander Mitscherlich, Clifton Fadiman, Max Frisch, Gustave Bally and Medardi Boss.

Her attitudes and relations were changing, not only toward the Weisses but toward Kelman as well. As she moved closer to them, she was distancing herself from him. It was rare for her to show anger, especially in public. This was why her outburst in Mexico during the Christmas 1950 visit had so surprised Renate. But from that time on, Karen began to express anger toward Kelman. At least three occasions are recalled by colleagues. Once when he was speaking on "Duplicity," she furiously asked "What are you really trying to say?" Another time, when he was lecturing on dreams, he introduced the theories of Andras Angyal, a holistic psychiatrist, as the basis for his own ideas. Karen jumped up and berated him, crying, "This is not my theory!" On another occasion, after he claimed that some degree of anxiety was normal and tolerable, she again angrily protested. It was the obligation of the analyst as a physician to relieve emotional pain, to heal.

She now no longer restrained Weiss in his rivalry with Kelman, even subtly encouraged him. From then on it was a rare evening when Weiss did not contradict Kelman. In his brief biography of Horney, presented as an introduction to his 1971 book on her theory, *Helping People*, Kelman questions why she might have changed in her attitude toward him. The proper question was not why, but why now. It was inevitable that his ambitions, his need to exercise authority, and desire to be his own man—which she had supported until that time—would have set him on a collision course. One example of the conflict was a scathing letter Karen wrote to Janet Frey, the long-devoted secretary of the Institute. Letters addressed to Karen were being opened in the office and were then being forwarded directly to Kelman for his action. Henceforth, she demanded, such letters should be sent only to her and she would decide who was to do what.

There might have been a number of reasons for the change in her attitude toward her protégé. After finishing her book, she began to turn more of her attention to the affairs of the Institute, as she had done several times before. When her inner creative springs dried up temporarily, she turned outward for new stimulation.

Another reason might be that she was becoming older and more mature—she had just passed sixty-five—and as well, that her needs and personality were changing through her constant self-analysis and emotional growth. Seeing herself more clearly, she was also seeing others more truthfully. She confided to Gertrude and several colleagues that she was only then coming to realize Kelman's "true" nature, that his interest in the Institute was ultimately dictated by personal ambition.

She also began to realize that the two things she cherished most, her theory and her Institute, were being threatened. She felt that Kelman's new holistic concept of neurosis challenged the validity of her own theory, and she resented his reliance on another authority, Angyal, rather than herself.

Furthermore, she felt that the antagonisms between members of the group were hindering its development. Certainly she had partly contributed to these rivalries, wittingly or not. Her compartmentalization of her social relationships into small, fairly consistent groups—with each group aware of the others, but uncertain of Karen's real preferences—created feelings of favoritism or exclusion and jealousy. But Kelman's attitudes contributed to these antagonisms to an even greater extent.

On one hand he had built a personal following among his analysands, and even among those who, while disliking his personality, still respected his intellectual brilliance. This constituted a power base in the Institute. At the same time, his autocratic, inflexibly demanding, unfeeling and abrasive attitudes toward colleagues had fanned resentment against him; the rebelliousness of Weiss, and others like him, could only be heightened in response to Kelman's overbearing behavior. As a result of all these factors, an extreme polarization of feelings was developing within the group.

Unfortunately, in his version of these events, Kelman dwells only on the conflicts Karen may have been experiencing. He depicts himself as merely an interested spectator, or even an innocent victim, of the deeds of others. He neglects his own role in these events, although, in fact, he seems to have been a principal actor. Karen and his colleagues were also reacting to his attitudes and actions, even if he himself was unable or unwilling to admit this.

Probably yet another factor was also contributing to her change in personality: her state of health. About this time she was beginning to have the attacks of right upper abdominal pain that were to continue for the next two years. Except for an occasional twinge of arthritis in her knees, she had been in relatively good health until then. One painful flareup of the arthritis had occurred in Chicago (where she had been rushed by ambulance to the hospital for a short stay). Another less painful episode had bothered her once while she was passing through Paris. She had since remained fearful of illness and physical pain, and of doctors. She refused to see one for a checkup, and she preferred to prescribe her own remedies for herself and usually felt she could overcome the minor infirmities—such as the Mexican diarrhea and the twinges of arthritis.

After a second attack of abdominal pain occurred in spite of her own self-medication, she finally visited a local doctor. At first it was simply considered an upset stomach and medication was prescribed. Then when she developed a persistent diarrhea, Gertrude took her to see Gary Zucker, an internist and excellent clinician who was the personal physician of several colleagues in the Institute. As he recalls, she seemed more

interested in drawing him out about his problems than in revealing her
own difficulties. She was cautious and reserved—even perhaps dis-
trustful—which all added to the problem of getting a thorough medical
history. He suspected a gall-bladder condition and had an X-ray taken,
which was inconclusive. When he suggested an exploratory operation,
Karen would not have it. She seemed to be fearful. In any event, she
agreed to continue the medical treatment. But throughout the rest of 1951
and 1952, the attacks of pain kept recurring intermittently.

In January 1951, the peripatetic Suzuki returned to the United States
to teach at Columbia University, helped by a subsistence grant from the
Crane family. Several analysts took his course in Zen Buddhism and called
it to the attention of Cornelius Crane and Karen.

To Western eyes, Suzuki would have seemed a strange, striking figure.
Throughout the Far East, he was revered as a sage by millions of followers of the esoteric Zen religion-philosophy—which was neither a religion nor a philosophy, at least not in the traditional sense. Teitaro was
his given name; Daisetz was a nickname given him by his Zen master,
meaning "one of great simplicity," or as he laughingly used to say, "of
great stupidity." He himself was neither a Zen master nor a monk. He
was not even a college graduate, the "Doctor" being an honorary degree
many times repeated.

Small, thin and wiry, gray and balding, his parchment skin gave him a
look of infinite age. Although his long eyebrows, pointed outward like
horns, gave him a ferocious look, this was contradicted by his eyes, at
once profoundly deep and naughtily childlike behind schoolmasterish
wire-rimmed glasses. He spoke in a low, slow voice, often rubbing his
forehead in a gesture of seeming uncertainty; and yet there was an air of
serene authority about him, as if he no longer had any ambitions or
illusions about life. He had come to terms with himself and with life. He
preferred to explain the elusive teachings of Zen in simple, direct language (since words were usually inadequate anyway) and enigmatic para-
bles (when even simple words failed). His childlike worldly-wise look, his
uncertain tranquillity, his knowing but enigmatic speech, all combined to
give him an impressive air of infinite wisdom.

Karen was drawn to him and a curious friendship developed which was
to last until her death. During 1951, she invited him to her home a

number of times, along with some of her colleagues. Suzuki, Richard DiMartino and Karen were also guests in Crane's apartment and Ipswich home several times. Suzuki recommended to her Eugen Herrigel's book *Zen in the Art of Archery (Zen und die Kunst des Bogenschiessens)*. She was deeply affected both by the book and by her discussions with Suzuki and she tried to relate Zen ideas to her theory, but found it most difficult.

DiMartino recalls their searching conversations during the rides home from Boston. She tried to compare the Zen notion of *Dukkha*, or the basic suffering and mental pain of existence, with her own concept of basic anxiety. However, as they explained to her, the Zen concept was more complex, with a transcendental aspect. It included three distinct states. Mental anguish was the subjective experience of ordinary imperfect existence. Then there was the separate painful experience of life's changes. This was frightening because change was usually interpreted as being for the worse. It contained an element of fear of the unknown, of mortality. And third was an awareness of the conditional state of life, of not being free. This last aspect made more sense. It could be related to the need for freedom she saw as a neurotic trend, to escape from the intolerable inner restrictions against feelings, needs, wishes, or impulses. But this, of course, was quite different from her "basic anxiety," which was rooted only in human relations: the feeling of the child toward subtly rejective parents. She knew of the existential philosophical idea of *"Angst der Kreatur,"* namely the helplessness felt by everyone as part of being only human in a world of powerful and inexorable forces. This was closer to the Zen concept. She also felt that a central problem of neurosis was the shift from one's feelings to other compulsive ways of functioning: from experiencing—or in Zen terms, from being—to an overemphasis on appearance or thinking. She quoted one of Suzuki's aphorisms: "Life is not a problem to be solved but an experience to be realized." She was so inspired by him that she began to think of going to Japan to see that culture for herself. She broached the idea to Crane, who began to make the necessary arrangements.

In the meantime, she organized a workshop for about a dozen members of the group, plus DiMartino, Dr. Otani, a master of the Shin sect, Suzuki, and Nokamura, his young secretary. They met at the home of Joan Harte, a candidate. There they discussed such questions as the Koan— the unanswerable question—the nature of consciousness and awareness, the possibilities of immediate experience and many others. What impressed them about Suzuki as much as his knowledge was his habit of dropping off for ten minute catnaps in the middle of a discussion. He would wake up and continue as if he had never stopped talking. Karen mostly listened, very intently; she said little. She attended only about three of these meetings, though fifteen were held. She never remained for the social amenities after the discussion, apparently wishing to avoid social contact with Harold Kelman.

At the beginning of 1951, Katherine Kelman, the wife of Harold Kelman's nephew, Norman, had the inspiration of setting up a lay group to raise funds for a psychoanalytic clinic. She suggested it, almost jestingly to Karen while they were riding home from a meeting together in a taxi. Karen welcomed it at the time. She wondered whether her lifelong dream was finally to come true. On second thought, however, as she admitted privately, she had some reservations. These were based on her old fear of loss of autonomy in teaching, painfully sharpened by her past experiences with the Chicago Institute and the New York Medical College. When she brought it up at the meeting of the board of trustees, these doubts were reinforced. Harold Kelman was still hoping that his original clinic plan would be adopted. He was therefore opposed to the new proposal and later remained so. Although a few others agreed with him, the board voted to drop the previous plan and support the new one. Karen questioned whether physicians would have the "business ability" to organize such an enterprise alone. She mentioned that she had already tried it with them and it couldn't be done. On the other hand, she would not want it to be run from a businessman's viewpoint alone. She felt they could be too sharp or cold in their dealings. Her image of a clinic administration was a blend of the idealized attributes of the doctor—kindness, compassion, self-effacement—and the businessman—aggressiveness, competitiveness, hardness. For her that would be the best of both worlds.

Throughout the year, Katherine Kelman, Esta Brody, Nathan Freeman and a few other members worked vigorously, through many meetings and debates, to form a sponsoring committee.

It is possible that the paper Karen wrote in February 1951 indirectly expressed the basic feelings responsible for her irritability toward Renate at Christmas time and her subdued behavior after her return. Its title was "On Feeling Abused." [1]

As if in apology, she pointed out that the neurotic may, by excessive compliance, invite inconsiderate behavior from others. Even so, he will respond with disproportionate feelings of vulnerability, hurt and victimization. These feelings may be kept from awareness by neurotic pride: in not showing anger, in keeping under control, in serenity. As a defense against awareness of this pride and especially the self-contempt that underlies it, the person will experience himself as passive, empty, without emotion. He will thus focus mainly on the outside world, on what others are doing to him. During analysis, the reversal of this process, namely coming closer to oneself and one's constructive feelings, can be quite painful. The person may then defensively try to change and manipulate others or lose interest in himself. His heightened self-hate can induce suicidal thoughts; or can be externalized as vindictiveness toward others. But when eventually worked through, the result will be a feeling of responsibility, a sense of value and the certainty of being "the captain of his ship."

In April, the annual ACAAP Symposium in the Henry Hudson Hotel, which drew the usual large, enthusiastic crowd, was devoted to "The Constructive Forces in Man." Karen spoke on "The Individual and Therapy."[2] She raised the important question whether it might not be Quixotic to believe in, and base therapy upon, the notion of inherent constructive forces in every individual. For her, the answer was no. Destructive trends in people cannot be denied, but they are not innate. They are generated by growing up in an unfavorable milieu. They can disappear when a person who has lost contact with himself no longer has to prove a need to be something he is not. The "bitter, pessimistic and destructive can and do again turn toward life."

In closing she quoted the "Eastern philosophers who have always believed in the spiritual powers in man. They have seen these powers develop as man stops violating his nature." Here was the source of the magnetism she felt emanating from these Oriental religions: their spiritual or uplifting power, so closely related to her own concept of self-realization. This was the first fruits of her reading and discussing with Suzuki.

In May, many of the group traveled to Cincinnati to participate in the annual convention of the American Psychiatric Association. Karen took part in a round-table discussion, along with Kelman, Weiss and Martin, on the now perennial subject, "Moral Values in Therapy." These out-of-town meetings were generally joyous breaks, mini-excursions away from her routine. They had begun three years before, to St. Louis, Montreal,

Detroit, now Cincinnati and the following year to Atlantic City. They were her only opportunity to meet some of her former Freudian friends, at least those who still welcomed her. She liked to gather her "group" around her during the meeting, usually in some ethnic restaurant. She seemed to feel freer than usual over a few drinks and a good meal. At the meeting in Montreal, for instance, in an Austrian rathskeller, she joined in singing old German songs. Even Kelman, who seldom unbent socially with candidates, sang along. She acted in a caring, motherly way toward her younger colleagues. And yet when someone made a remark to this effect, she objected sharply. Apparently she could not quite bring herself to admit to harboring the softer emotions—calling to mind Renate's observation, "sentimental she was not."

On another such occasion, in St. Louis, Nathan Freeman suggested a trip to a nearby gambling casino that was still open. Karen became excited; she exclaimed that she had always wished to gamble but had rarely had the courage. She even thought she had a system for winning. But when he started to round up a group, she insisted that the younger candidates remain behind. Gambling was wrong for them! The old puritanical strain was still present in spite of all her experience and self-analysis. Unfortunately, when they arrived, the casino was already closed. Karen's disappointment was all too apparent.

She loved gambling in its milder forms, like card-playing—rummy, double-solitaire, poker and canasta. During her vacations in Mexico with Renate it was a favorite pastime, using dried black beans (frijoles) for money; or with Gertrude at her summer homes near New York. On one train trip to the psychiatric convention in Cincinnati, she and Norman Kelman played cards constantly during the entire journey. She became so engrossed in the game that she was oblivious to hunger, until he reminded her that it was almost too late for dinner. During such friendly games she would openly and unabashedly cheat. When someone would protest, she would laughingly admit it and remark that he should have stopped her sooner.

Norman Kelman was among Karen's favorite younger colleagues at this time. Some suspected that he was being groomed to challenge the position of his uncle at the Institute. She did enjoy being with him and Katherine at their home or visiting their friends. These included Marie Rasey and Earl Kelley, both professors of educational psychology, Carl Sandburg, the poet, and Hiram Haydn, the critic and publisher. Young

Kelman loved baseball and would often talk about it; Karen knew nothing of it and was baffled by these discussions. Kelman was appalled. How could one be a real American without knowing anything of the great American game? Finally he got her two tickets to a game to prove it could be both instructional and entertaining. She came with Remarque. To have to explain the intricacies of the game to someone who has not been brought up with it is an experience few people forget, and Kelman was no exception.

June 1951 was the tenth anniversary of the founding of the Association. Both the Association and the Institute were continuing to grow rapidly. Following Martin, Muriel Ivimey became president of the Association. There were now over sixty candidates. The teaching staff numbered twenty-five, of whom eleven were training analysts. A birthday celebration was certainly in order and a gala reception was held at the St. Moritz Hotel. Karen appeared to be relaxed, but those close to her sensed she was under a strain, her gaiety forced; she did not dance as she had ten years before in Boston.

She had prepared a statement for the occasion, in which she briefly reviewed the history of the Association, mentioning some of the recent trials and tribulations, including the splits. But in the final paragraph, she revealed some of the thoughts that were troubling her. She admitted that "with different personalities working together closely, frictions were unavoidable. . . . We are still learning that in human relations focused on work to be done, personal factors such as righteousness, ambition, vulnerabilities and resentments have to recede . . . We need creative minds, good teachers and organizers. But the productivity of these very activities and their benefit for the whole group, depend on the aliveness and integrity of the individuals composing it. For knowledge may freeze into dogmatism; teaching may fall on barren soil and organizing may deteriorate into bureaucracy unless the group is pervaded by . . . an interest in the growth of all its participants."[3] This was both a wish and a warning. No one close to the situation could have failed to understand who the "organizer" was.

During the summer vacation, Karen returned to Switzerland to be with Brigitte. Her daughter, now divorced, was alone. Karen, too, feeling as she did, also needed someone. She persuaded Biggi to come to the United States and they applied for the necessary immigration papers. Their stay together that summer in Moscia was one of the most delightful she ever spent.

When she returned in the fall, the house in Wildwood Hills seemed small and inadequate. She asked Gertrude to look for another one. When Biggi arrived in New York, Karen introduced her to her friends at a series of parties at several of their homes. Biggi recalls how she felt somewhat uncertain before the first of these parties, her first experience of an American soiree. Karen gently chided and reassured her at the same time, with the comment, "In America, you're not supposed to be shy, it's an illness and a failure."

She continued to immerse herself in Zen during this time. In October, a young Japanese physician, Akahiso Kondo, was invited to an evening at the Norman Kelmans', along with the Wenkarts, the DeRosis, Suzuki and Karen. Kondo, now a leading psychiatrist in Tokyo, had been attending both Suzuki's classes at Columbia and Institute courses at the New School. His first encounter with Karen occurred in the street before going up to the party. He had a curious intuitive feeling of recognition and a sense of wordless communion while he was with her. "As she looked at me, her blue, bright and serene eyes were quite impressive to me. I felt a natural, congenial flow of communed feeling suddenly run between us. Then when he [Kelman] opened the door, I found the elderly lady already standing beside him. Just as he began to introduce me, she said in a cordial tone, 'We have introduced ourselves already.' Having been brought up in the tradition of Zen, such an experience of encounter was nothing alien to me. This most unforgettable moment was not only fulfilling in itself, but also decisively determined my life course."

That evening, like many others, was both social and full of free-flowing conversation about religious and philosophical ideas. Once, to illustrate a Zen method of teaching, Kondo struck Kelman on the forehead with his palm. As expected, he fell to the floor—to everyone's amusement. But he learned that asking the logical "why?" really explained little. The surprise and shock taught him much more.

Kondo was soon accepted as a special analytic candidate. He found Karen's theoretical views entirely congenial with Zen concepts. In one class, she gave him an ordinary weekly assignment to write on, "Intuition in Zen and Psychoanalysis." Imagine his surprise the following week when he found himself reading his paper in front of a large audience of students and faculty. It was a specially convened "interval" meeting. Speaking for the first time before an American audience, he soon discovered himself, and an inner store of self-confidence. The paper was later published in the Journal and Kondo was to be Karen's guide on her visit to Japan.

By December 1951, after a long and intense search, Gertrude finally found a charming little house in Rye, New York. Karen said, after she took it, that this one was to be "for good." Situated on the shore of Long Island Sound, it had a little pier and a view out over the water. Karen liked to sit and watch the tides coming in and going out, rocks and little islands disappearing and appearing, gulls wheeling overhead and crying raucously. The constant change fascinated her, visible symbolic evidence of her belief that life is change and a person changes with it as long as he lives. She was even able to see a few analytic patients there occasionally.

During the academic year 1951 to 1952, she had reason for legitimate pride in the regular growth of the group. Elizabeth Kilpatrick succeeded Ivimey as President of the Association. The number of Institute candidates had increased to eighty-five, with a special program for foreign graduates. A special series of courses was offered for nonanalytic medical practitioners. While this was being discussed in the Faculty Council, Karen thought back, perhaps with a trace of wistfulness, to her role in a similar program some thirty years before in the new Berlin Institute. This year she had been forced to give up her regular New School courses. It was just too much for her. She tired easily, and almost always suffered from chronic fatigue. Nevertheless, she still continued her regular full-year course on psychoanalytic technique at the Institute. She hoped that a book on this subject would be her next project.

Karen was not too tired, though, to visit the neighboring sculpture studio of one Madame Barzhanski with Biggi and Norman Kelman, who was already taking lessons there. While she herself did not do any sculpting, she posed for Biggi, who produced a fine bust of her mother. She succeeded in capturing a certain taut, melancholy quality that was her prevailing mood at the time.

By January 1952, by dint of much patient diplomacy, persuasion and negotiation, Katherine Kelman had succeeded in forming the new clinic foundation, helped by several Association members. Its list of sponsors read like a roll-call of Karen's friends, including Harold Lasswell, Kurt Goldstein, Harry Tiebout, Austin Davies, Alfred Lunt, Alvin Johnson, Jerome Nathanson, Ashley Montagu, Earl Kelley, Marie Rasey, William Lancaster, Carl Sandburg, Iago Galdston, Carl Zuckmayer, Daisetz Suzuki, Marianne Eckardt, Arthur Jersild, and Hiram Haydn.

When advised of the proposed new name, The Karen Horney Foundation (the clinic also was to bear her name), she wrote back: "You have not only my whole-hearted consent but I consider this to be the most meaningful honor I ever received or might receive in my life." Then in March, an Association meeting was held to discuss the use of psychoanalysis in a clinic setting. For the first time, her reservations about the clinic and the anticipated problems were aired to the faculty and candidates.

That same month she also participated in the usual annual ACAAP Symposium in New York's Town Hall. With her were Weiss, Kelman and her "Dear Paulus" Tillich. The subject was "Human Nature Can Change."[4] She again voiced her optimistic view of the ability of every individual to grow constructively. She gave evidence for this capacity in the child's development, in her observations of people driven to become unconsciously destructive toward themselves, and in her experience with such patients who changed during analysis.

What is clear, however, is that in all her presentations during that year, she had brought forth nothing really new. Basically she was repeating, re-emphasizing, re-examining what she had already written. She was like an artist who has painted his canvas and is examining it from every possible angle before applying any further strokes. It was as if she had emptied herself with the completion of her last book.

Therefore it was not surprising that the subject of her last important article, in February 1952, was "The Paucity of Inner Experiences."[5] And like so many of her other papers, even though it could have been derived from her own emotional state of the moment, it was what she actually saw in her patients, and it transcended both herself and them in being applicable to human nature in general.

Here she referred to a restriction not only of emotional life but also of thinking, willing and doing. While such faculties might not be available to consciousness in this state, they remain alive deep within the person, emerging, for example, in dreams. One result of this intrapsychic paucity is an overemphasis on interpersonal processes. "Externalized living" is one extreme and pervasive form. Another form is an overattention to the expectations of others: to the proper behavior, appearance, the impressions one makes. One is directed by rules and how to get around them. Another result is a compulsive substitution of thought and fantasy for feelings. The awareness of inner emptiness or nothingness constantly threatens to emerge, causing feelings of anxiety, boredom and loneliness. In reaction, compulsive defenses may be adopted, like compulsive eating, hectic activity, socializing or destructiveness. To deny such fears, the person may feel a pride in his stoicism, unemotionality, detachment or objectivity. Or he may simply feel a vague sense of something lacking in his life. During analysis, the patient must be enabled to confront not only his emptiness or deadness, but also his dread of coming to life. He must become aware of all the illusions and pretenses which avoid contact with his underlying painful emotional conflicts.

Although Karen seemed to be influenced by existentialist ideas in this paper insofar as she cited Kierkegaard's "fear of nothingness" and Tillich's "fear of non-being" as a source of anxiety, this influence was more apparent than real. She was not speaking on the same level as they were. She did not see her concepts of being, or of anxiety and fear, as ontological states but rather as emotions and forms of consciousness, therefore as psychological functions.

The distinction between these two forms of experience continued to puzzle her. What was the difference, for instance, between normal, essential, "existential" anxiety on one hand, and neurotic or pathological anxiety on the other? This problem was debated in a panel discussion at the April Academy meeting.[6] Kurt Goldstein, her old friend from Berlin, was trying to adapt Karen's notion of self-realization to organically damaged patients. Paul Hoch, another old psychiatrist friend, Rollo May, a young existentialist psychologist, Weiss and Harry Gershman, a candidate, all participated with her. Karen was still searching . . . still searching . . . still searching.

In the summer of 1952, the long-awaited trip to Japan finally took place. There were some anxious moments after Karen applied for renewal of her passport. The government at first delayed in issuing her one. She felt terrible; would she have to give up the trip? She wrote to Washington herself and asked others to intervene for her. Why was it being withheld; had she unwittingly sent money or packages to someone in Europe who was unacceptable to the government? Finally she received the passport with a letter of apology. She had been confused with another person of the same name who had been blacklisted.

Brigitte, Karen, Crane and his wife, and Suzuki went together. It was the highlight of her life, perhaps even to be the end of her search. Kondo had planned a series of meetings with important Japanese analysts and DiMartino had arranged visits to several Zen monasteries, where Suzuki's prestigious name gained them an immediate welcome. Karen said that her purpose there was "to study Japanese culture by getting into direct contact with people and places, by intensive discussion with a few well-selected persons, and by leisurely devoting time to the appreciation of nature"—rather than by a heavy schedule.

In the resort town of Hakone, she spent one day discussing Morita therapy with Professors Kora and Koga, with Kondo interpreting when necessary. She listened mostly, eager to learn. She summed up the similarity of her own theories with Morita's by saying that they both were trying to understand and treat the patient's total personality and immediate experiences.

While standing in the reception room at the Jikai-Kai Medical School, Karen instinctively picked out Morita's portrait from the many others hanging there. Some were astonished; some responded with a knowing smile. It added to her reputation as one endowed with some intuitive power. The lecture she gave, "New Developments in Psychoanalysis," presented her theory by contrasting it with Freud's. She particularly stressed the notions of constructive growth and self-realization, therapeutic attention to the whole person, the interweaving of intrapsychic and interpersonal factors, and the emphasis on immediate experience in therapy. These she related roughly to Zen principles. It was reported soon afterward that her lecture, especially her openminded attitude, was a breakthrough in the acceptance of psychoanalysis by the Japanese, and the introduction of Morita therapy to the West.

Much of her stay was spent in Kyoto, where she wanted to be among the common people. She took to wearing the pointed straw hat and plain loose dress of the Japanese farm women. A folk festival intrigued her immensely, as did the Kabuki Theatre. Visiting a bride's school, she appreciated how the young women were educated for their marital duties. If only Western women could be trained for marriage, there would be fewer divorces. But she also commented that such education in how to behave was basically artificial and did not change the women's real attitudes. A tour of Kyoto's red-light district may have recalled to her mind a similar excursion she had made at eighteen, when she went to Hamburg to see things for herself.

In spite of the hot weather, they visited many temples, shrines and monasteries, of both the Zen and Pure-Land sects. Karen, intensely curious, asked many questions, which were answered by Suzuki and Kondo in running discussions. She seemed to be in an intense ferment, digesting and trying to integrate what she saw and heard with her own ideas. The more abstract concepts like the Koans and the spiritual nature of consciousness seemed to make her uncomfortable; she found them too metaphysical. "How does one learn the Zen discipline?" she asked, trying to make a comparison with psychoanalytic training. In answer, Suzuki described the learning principle as "the individual being like a sponge . . . which fills itself with air by its very nature, so the person takes in the atmosphere of the monastery and of Zen naturally. One doesn't have to learn it."

The discipline involved in the training and daily lives of the monks intrigued her. How could this help in assimilating the Zen teachings? She saw this only through her Western eyes; it was admirable how they learned to cook, to serve, to garden, to eat and drink tea in a certain way. It was all useful. She could understand the explanation only with difficulty that *what* they were doing was irrelevant and immaterial. The importance of their actions lay only in the doing itself. Kondo tried to make clear that as the inner awareness takes over, one becomes the act, whether drinking tea, fencing with a staff or shooting the bow. Action, consciousness and life itself were held to consist only of the successive and fleeting moments of existence. Existence was evanescent, insubstantial; solidity or substance was delusion (*maya*). Each instant had to be caught in passing, since no one moment would ever be repeated. A deed, once committed, could never be undone. Suzuki used the *sumiye* ink paintings to illustrate: once the line is drawn, it cannot be erased or gone over. This was a total responsibility for one's actions much like her own concept of self-responsibility. To be conscious of an experience in thought, to state it or write it down, destroyed it. Indeed, the goal of all their labors and actions was to make the Zen disciple transcend and leave behind his logical and abstract thinking, by focusing on his down-to-earth physical body. This fitted in with Karen's emphasis on the patient's having to experience his emotions fully during analysis.

Karen also asked what happened during meditation, and what it accomplished. The answer was that it could also permit the student to free himself from his misleading trust in his thought processes. The student usually meditated on a question that had no logical answer. It was not a state of passive self-emptying. On the contrary, it was a mental struggle, involving a high degree of tension, conflict and doubt. With perseverance, it could provoke a mental crisis, ideally accompanied by flashes of that intuitive spiritual insight known as *satori*. The word "Zen" itself, derived from the old Chinese *Ch'an* sect of Buddhism, yielded the word *zazen*, meaning "to sit and meditate." Suzuki wrote that "Zen devoid of *satori* is like a sun without its light and heat."

She tried to define this concept of *satori* in terms of her own psychological thinking. Even for Suzuki, it was difficult to define in simple words. He could only describe it as an "intuitive way of looking into the nature of things, in contradistinction to the logical or analytical understanding. It means the unfolding of a new world hitherto unperceived in the confusion of a dualistically trained mind." Opposites were harmonized, integrated into a unified whole. But it remains a mystery and miracle nonetheless, even though it happens every day. Karen finally arrived at an equivalent for herself: "to break through the shell of egocentricity." Beyond this, the Zen concept of enlightenment, referring to a total point of view arrived at through repeated episodes of *satori,* could only be analogous to, though not exactly the same, as her own concept of self-realization.

The relation of the disciple to the *roshi* or "master" also impressed her. She agreed with its purpose—"to absorb wisdom"—but seemed to value the relationship even more. It was maintained by the student after he left the monastery. It was also unique in that the disciple could choose to remain as long as he wished, provided he was found meritorious, or could leave intermittently to return to his family, or could return to live there after the age of sixty-five. She felt this arrangement permitted both freedom from discipline and the possibility of periodic re-immersion in the training, which she likened to re-analysis, as urged by Freud.

Most of all, she was fascinated by one enchanting spot, the temple garden of Daigo-Sanbo-in (Temple of Three Treasures) in Daigo, just outside Kyoto. She returned there several times with Brigitte, DiMartino and Kondo. It consisted of an irregular pond, small pine trees and irregularly shaped rocks, all arranged in a design expressing esthetic harmony and simplicity. The sound of a small waterfall was calculated to counterbalance the silence by imparting a dynamic liveliness. It was all meant to enhance the visitor's contemplative spirit. On her second visit, Karen sat off by herself and became absorbed in the view; she remained for half an hour unmoving, in total concentration and meditation, oblivious to everything around her. Her Japanese friends felt admiringly that she had attained the ultimate spiritual attitude, a total oneness with nature. Kondo expressed it as, "Nature becomes me and I become Nature." He believed this confirmed his previous feeling of communion with her. When she rose and rejoined them, he recalls how her "face was beaming and lit with delightful contentment."

Each morning, Karen would discuss with him the events of and especially the people she had met the day before, asking him for a thumbnail personality description. She seemed to be trying to confirm whether her own assessments of particular people were valid.

At the end of the all-too-short month, she was sad to have to leave with Biggi. Kondo and the Cranes took off for a short stay in Tahiti; Kondo continued on to Hawaii. He met Karen and Biggi on their stop-over in Honolulu and squired them around again until they re-boarded the plane. When Gertrude met Karen in New York she found her looking wan and tired.

Kondo and his wife had been invited back on a scholarship sponsored by Crane. His paper on Morita therapy was presented in October at the Academy meeting. Karen gave an extended commentary.[7] Although she explained the Morita therapy as a product of the Eastern cultural background, it was more than that. She reported on what she had learned and experienced in her contacts with people and ideas in Japan. She tried to convey the subtle meaning of nature there, referring to her own inward turning and feeling. Most of the audience had difficulty in grasping her explanations. After all, she was describing subjective and personal experiences only she had felt.

A second such meeting was held in November, at which she developed the idea that the Japanese emphasis on nature was equivalent to her own reinforcement of inner constructive forces. In the East, the growth observed in plants acts as a stimulating external example for the individual. Their closeness to nature could prevent or alleviate the alienation from self found in the West to a much greater extent. Our stress on intellect and disregard of the body made it harder for us to know our true feelings and face inner emptiness. This step would be required as a preliminary to self-realization. In Japan, where the intellect is less emphasized, the habitual meditation and self-discipline would make it easier to accept one's emptiness.

DiMartino was present at these meetings. One burning question was still not clear to her and she asked him whether Zen could provide an answer. After you break down the patient's idealized self-image and other defenses, are specific efforts needed to stimulate his constructive capacities or do they emerge automatically? In his reply, he compared this notion with the Zen concept of death and rebirth. Both are aspects of the same spiritual experience. It occurs as part of human existence; nothing needs to be built. That answer satisfied Karen, too, and the issue was left there.

This was the last time Karen was to speak in public. Her physical condition was growing worse. The abdominal pains kept recurring and she was visibly thinner. But she had no time for doctors or sickness; she still had work to do. The book on technique was waiting. Besides, she had not yet found what she was seeking, though she felt closer to it. She invited Kondo to her home several times, both in the city and in Rye, to discuss his ideas on the real self she was trying to write about. Few people who heard her during that last meeting had recognized that in her references to intellect, disregard for the body, inner emptiness and self-realization, she had been speaking of her own inner search. Kondo had realized it. He still recalls the "free association" quality of their mutual musings, with Karen taking occasional notes, much in the style of Suzuki. He recognized her struggle, but no answer would come. She just could not yet express what it was that was haunting her.

If the answer was not forthcoming from the disciple, perhaps it could be obtained from the master. She continued to talk with Suzuki and her admiration for him was unabated. He was invited to address the analytic candidates at a special meeting. Just as Karen had tried to understand the

Zen principles in terms of her own theories, now he reciprocated; he tried to explain neurosis and mental illness in terms of Zen.

According to him, the personality consisted of five groups of attributes: one's physical form, the five senses (perceptions), feelings, intellect which organizes perception, and self-consciousness (*mana*). The latter is conscious, but is so constantly reflecting on inner experience that it is practically unconscious. One part of it is "discriminating consciousness" (*vignana*) that determines awareness. The "inner reservoir" of experience, corresponding partly to the unconscious, consists of individual, collective and cosmic experience. Mental disturbance, including neurosis, comes from not being able to adjust to changes in external situations. However, these are not objectively real situations but exist only as we conceptualize them, as the taking of symbols for reality is a natural human tendency. "We are all delusions." The true and original state of every being is a state of innocence or enlightenment. The acquiring of knowledge plus its accompanying emotions, constitutes a state of "original sin" or what is commonly called psychological consciousness. When this original sin becomes aware of the innocence underneath, the state is experienced as illusion, and all experiences as illusory. Thus, mental illness can be reduced to the metaphysical unconscious. When the unconscious can be understood through *satori*, the disturbances will disappear.

Few of the candidates understood him, not only because of the abstruse nature of the material but also because of his difficult style of presentation: slow, in a sometimes inaudible voice, darting from one thought to another. Only those with some previous knowledge of Eastern philosophy could grasp his meaning.

Crane invited the whole group who had been in Japan to his family home in Ipswich for a weekend. They all went on a picnic one day to a nearby island. Karen was bright and witty, her old social self. They all laughed hilariously as they each recounted their experiences and mishaps in Japan. Karen arranged another evening with them in her home, along with Kurt Goldstein and Tillich. Still another was held at the Weisses' with Erich Remarque and several others. She also met several times with the philosophy discussion group of Ursula Eckardt.

Why all this hectic activity now? Was some answer to her long and arduous spiritual quest now on the threshold of emerging? Perhaps she was waiting for a few words that would give it that final needed thrust, would give her some insight. Or did she have some instinctive feeling that her time was running out, forcing her to cram so much into the time that remained? Both Biggi and Renate, on a visit, noticed how thin she was. She was not feeling well in general, besides having her pains. Once she had to cancel a party for Suzuki at the Weisses' the evening before it was to be held. One Friday before leaving for Rye, she suddenly felt faint and had to go to bed. She was unable to lecture that evening to her class on analytic technique. Norman Kelman had to fill in for her, as he did for the balance of the semester.

For the next few days at home, she had difficulty in breathing, and pain in her chest. She called Nathan Freeman, another favored younger colleague at the time, who—as she told Biggi—she considered a "Rock of Gibraltar." He convinced her to call the doctor in the building. He found fluid in her chest and advised hospitalization. She was frightened and did not want to go. She feared that if she went in, she would never leave. But she finally permitted herself to be taken to the Harkness Pavilion of the Presbyterian Hospital. When the chest fluid was examined, they finally knew. It was a primary cancer of the bile ducts in the liver that had spread to the lungs, a condition seldom diagnosed during life. This was why she had been having the pain in her right side. Now the pressure of the fluid in her chest was weakening her heart and it, too, was giving out.

On oxygen, and with the fluid drained, she improved temporarily. She asked Freeman to tell her the truth. "Would she make it?" In a quandary, he responded, "You have had many fights. This will be your hardest." He felt that she would fight, and remained hopeful. Her young intern at the hospital was Robert Coles, today one of the foremost social psychiatrists in the country. He was in awe of her, knowing she was famous. Even though he visited her daily to check her and draw blood for tests, he hesitated to speak to her about personal things. It was only after he obtained a note from his professor of medicine, whom Karen knew slightly, that he dared. He noticed she was reading Meredith's *The Egoist*, and they discussed literature one day. Another morning they discussed women in medicine: the burdens of the years in training, the conflict it entails with marriage and motherhood, the objections or jealousy still felt by many men in the field. She recalled her conversations with the Russian diplomats; it was much easier for women in that country. But she still remained optimistic about the future. He was still young; by the time he reached her age, things would be better.

About herself, she seemed cheerful and serene. By the third day she

knew she was dying, and said so to him. But she seemed resigned to
the point of not feeling sadness, bitterness or despair. By the fifth day,
all realized her condition was hopeless. She went downhill rapidly.
Brigitte, Marianne and Gertrude took turns staying with her around the
clock. Two days before her death, she whispered to Gertrude and Norman Kelman that she was at last content to be leaving; there was just no
point in going on. She died in her sleep on December 4, 1952.

At the funeral, Harold Kelman cried as he had perhaps never done
before. Many of her colleagues felt crushed for weeks; some felt as if they
had lost a mother. Suzuki, now laconic, whispered softly to Kondo, "We
have lost one of the most wonderful persons. She was still too young to
die." There were tears in his eyes. Her passing had faraway reverbera-
tions. In Japan a period of silence was ordered at the medical school, and
prayers were said in many temples. In Germany, Karl Muller-Braunschweig canceled his work and classes for a day of mourning.

Even her foes grieved for her. Clarence Oberndorf wrote, "With the
death of Karen Horney, there passed from the psychoanalytic scene a distinguished, vigorous and independent figure. Notwithstanding her defec-
tion from the American Psychoanalytic, there seems little doubt that Horney retained a strong devotion to Freud's procedure of a thoroughgoing
investigation of psychic conflict and did not sacrifice conscientious work
with patients to rapid or superficial methods. Time will eventually decide
the value of Horney's ideology in psychoanalytic therapeusis. But her
responsive and warm personality will remain affectionately in the memories of many of her earlier colleagues as well as her later students and followers."

Her devoted Paulus said it best of all. "Few people were so strong in
the affirmation of their being, so full of the joy of living, so able to rest in
themselves and to create without cessation beyond themselves. . . . It
was the voice of people, of inner experience, of nature, of poetry. . . .
and in the last year, the voice of eastern religion, which grasped her
heart. If I were asked to say what above all was her work, I would answer:
she herself, her being, her power to be the well-founded balance of an
abundance of striving and creative possibility. . . . A light radiating from
her being was experienced whenever we encountered her . . . to her
children, to others in her house, to her friends, to those who worked with
her personally or publicly. She knew the darkness of the human soul, and

the darkness of the world, but believed that what giveth light to any one suffering human being will finally give light to the world. The light she gave was not a cold light of passionless intellect, it was the light of passion and love. She wrote books but loved human beings. She helped them by insights into themselves which had healing power."

As she had always shunned ostentation, it was fitting that only a small stone mark her resting place in Westchester's Ferncliff Cemetery.

After the funeral, her three daughters had to clear the oppressive atmosphere of the funeral parlor from their spirits. In spite of the crowd of friends and colleagues come to pay homage, the pomp and ceremonies had seemed so artificial, so alien to the freedom and vitality of their mother. They decided to go to the top of Rockefeller Center. Shaken, stunned by the loss, they stood there pensively, looking at the distant lights below, vaguely conscious of the muted noise. The cold air gradually refreshed and stilled their minds. Sadly they reflected on how their destinies had turned out. One was the artist and actress, another the humanist and psychoanalyst, a third the earthy mother and spiritual searcher. She had been all of these, for better or worse, in her own unique way. Each of them was different and yet in some ways similar. Each was an outgrowth of her being, still a part of her personality. If each daughter was asked to describe her mother, each picture would be, in effect, a different person, derived from different memories. Yet it would be the same; this was the paradox. Perhaps it was true, as Suzuki professed, that every person's essence transcends itself and becomes part of those around it, not only in the past but into the future as well. Mother had gone in the flesh; was it also the end of what she stood for? If Suzuki was right, then they were by their very nature fated to carry forward her ideals, her vitality, her strengths and weaknesses. The threads of their lives had separated and now had come together again, if only for one brief, sad moment. If he was right, then in spite of the separation they were indeed one, part of a pattern in the larger fabric. Perhaps this was the answer Karen had been searching for: it was the sense of completeness in herself, of oneness with others.

SOURCE NOTES

INTRODUCTION

[1] RUBINS, J. L., "Karen Horney: A Biographical Study," in *Developments in Horney Psychoanalysis*. Huntington: Robert Krieger Publishing Co., 1972, p. 12.

[2] NATTERSON, J., "Karen Horney: The Cultural Emphasis," in *Psychoanalytic Pioneers*, Alexander, F. (ed.). New York: Basic Books, 1966.

[3] KELMAN, H., *Helping People: Karen Horney's Psychoanalytic Approach*. New York: Science House, 1971.

CHAPTER V

[1] ABRAHAM, H. and FREUD, E., *Letters of Sigmund Freud and Karl Abraham*. New York: Basic Books, 1965.

[2] Ibid.

CHAPTER VI

[1] ABRAHAM, H. and FREUD, E., *Letters* . . .

[2] "The Technique of Psychoanalytic Therapy," reprinted in the *American Journal of Psychoanalysis*, 28, 3, 1968.

CHAPTER VII

[1] JONES, E., *The Life and Work of Sigmund Freud*. Vol. II, p. 70. New York: Basic Books, 1955.

[2] OPPENHEIM, H., *Die Neurosen Infolge von Kriegsverletzungen*. Berlin: Karger, S., 1916.

[3] SIMMEL, E., *Neurosen und Psychisches Trauma*. Berlin, 1918.

[4] Letter to Ernest Jones, in loc. cit. #1.

[5] FERENCZI, S., ABRAHAM, E., SIMMEL, E., JONES, E., *Zur Psychoanalyse der Kriegsneurosen*. Leipzig: Internationaler Psychoanalytischer Verlag, 1919.

[6] HORNEY, K., "Phantastischer Infantilismus bei einem Grenzfall zwischen Neurose und Psychose."

[7] RIVIERE, J., "Recollections of Freud," in *Freud As We Knew Him*, Ruitenbeck, H. (ed.). New York: Wayne State University Press, 1975.

[8] "Contributions to the Female Castration Complex," Unpublished paper presented in November 1920.

[9] GRODDECK, G., "The Psychic Origin and Psychoanalytic Treatment of Organic Disease." Leipzig: Hirzel, 1917.

[10] GRODDECK, G., *The Book of the It*. London: Vision Press, 1950.

[11] DURRELL, L., "Studies in Genius: Groddeck." *Horizon*, *17*, 384, 1948.

[12] Letter to G. Groddeck, cited in Grossman, C. and Grossman, S., *The Wild Analyst*. New York: Dell, 1965.

[13] GROSSMAN, C. and GROSSMAN, S., *The Wild Analyst*. New York: Dell, 1965.

CHAPTER VIII   •

[1] VERKAUF, W., "Dada—Cause and Effect," in *Dada—Monograph of a Movement*. New York: St. Martin's Press, 1975.

[2] SHAPIRO, H., "Acid: The Morality of a German Artist." *Intellectual Digest*, March 1973.

[3] JANCO, M., "Creative Dada," in *Dada—Monograph of a Movement*, Verkauf, W. (ed.). New York: St. Martin's Press, 1975.

CHAPTER X

[1] FLUGEL, Z., "Feminine Psychosexual Development in Freudian Theory," *Psychoanalytic Quarterly*, *43*, 385, 1973.

[2] DEUTSCH, H., *Psychoanalyse der Weiblichen Sexualfunktionen*. Vienna: Internationaler Psychoanalytischer Verlag, 1925.

[3] DEUTSCH, H., *Confrontations with Myself*. New York: W.W. Norton, 1973.

[4] HORNEY, K., "Discussion on Lay Analysis," *International Journal of Psychoanalysis, 8,* 255, 1927.

[5] HORNEY, K., "Gehemmte Weiblichkeit: Psychoanalytischer Beitrag zum Problem der Frigidität," *Zeitschrift für Sexualwissenschaft, 13,* 67, 1927. Presented as "Frigidität und andere weibliche Funktionsstorungen in Lichte der Psychoanalyse."

[6] FENICHEL, O., "The Pregenital Antecedents of the Oedipus Complex," in *Collected Papers of Otto Fenichel.* New York: W.W. Norton, 1953.

[7] PERLS, F., *In and Out of the Garbage Pail.* New York: Bantam Books, 1972.

[8] Deutsche Psychoanalytische Gesellschaft, *Zehn Jahre Berliner Psychoanalytisches Institut (1920–1930).* Wien: Internationaler Psychoanalytischer Verlag, 1930.

[9] ALEXANDER, F., *The Western Mind in Transition.* New York: Random House, 1960.

[10] BENEDEK, T., "Death Instinct and Anxiety," *International Zeitschrift für Psychoanalyse, 17,* 333, 1931.

[11] HORNEY, K., "Der Kampf in der Kultur: Einige Gedanken und Bedenken Zu Freuds Todestreib und Destruktionstreib", in *Das Problem der Kultur und die ärztliche Psychologie.* Vortrage Institut fur Geschichte der Medizin, Univ. Leipzig 4, 105, 1931.

[12] JONES, E., "The Phallic Phase," *International Journal of Psychoanalysis, 14,* 1, 1933.

[13] HORNEY, K., "The Dread of Women."

[14] FREUD, S., "Über die Weibliche Sexualitat."

[15] JUNG, C., "Geleitworb," *Zentralblatt für Psychotherapie 6,* 139, 1933.

[16] HORNEY, K., "Die Verleugnung der Vagina. . . ."

[17] FREUD, S., "Analysis Terminable and Interminable," *International Journal of Psychoanalysis, 18,* 373, 1937.

[18] FREUD, S., *An Outline of Psychoanalysis.* New York: W.W. Norton, 1938.

[19] WEIGERT, E., *The Courage to Love.* New Haven: Yale University Press, 1970.

CHAPTER XI

[1] HORNEY, K., "Zur Genese des Weiblichen Kastrationskomplexes," *International Zeitschrift für Psychoanalyse*, 9, 12, 1923. ("On the Genesis of the Castration Complex in Women," *International Journal of Psychoanalysis*, 5, 50, 1924.)

[2] HORNEY, K., "Flucht aus der Weiblichkeit," *Internationale Zeitschrift für Psychoanalyse*, 12, 360, 1926. ("The Flight from Womanhood: The Masculinity Complex in Women as Viewed by Men and by Women," *International Journal of Psychoanalysis*, 7, 324, 1926.)

[3] HORNEY, K., "Gehemmte Weiblichkeit: Psychoanalytischer Beitrag zum Problem der Frigidität," *Zeitschrift für Sexualwissenschaft*, 13, 67, 1926. ("Inhibited Womanhood: A Psychoanalytic Contribution to the Problem of Frigidity," *Feminine Psychology*, Kelman, H. (ed.). New York: W.W. Norton, 1967.)

[4] HORNEY, K., "Die Angst vor der Frau: über einen spezifischen Unterscheid in der Mannlichen und Weiblichen Angst vor dem anderen Geschlecht," *Internationale Zeitschrift für Psychoanalyse*, 18, 5, 1932.

[5] HORNEY, K., "Die Verleugnung der Vagina: Ein Beitrag Zur Frage der specifisch weiblichen Genitalangst," *Internationale Zeitschrift für Psychoanalyse*, 19, 372, 1933. ("Denial of the Vagina," *International Journal of Psychoanalysis*, 14, 57, 1933.)

[6] HORNEY, K., "The Problem of Feminine Masochism," *Psychoanalytic Review*, 22, 241, 1935.

[7] HORNEY, K., "Personality Changes in Female Adolescents," *American Journal of Orthopsychiatry*, 5, 19, 1935.

[8] HORNEY, K., "The Overvaluation of Love: Study of a Common Present-Day Feminine Type," *Psychoanalytic Quarterly*, 3, 605, 1934.

[9] HORNEY, K., "Das Neurotische Liebesdurfnis," *Zentralblatt für Psychotherapie*, 10, 69, 1937. ("The Neurotic Need For Love," *Feminine Psychology*, Kelman, H. [ed.].)

CHAPTER XII

[1] HORNEY, K., "Psychische Eignung und Nichteignung Zur Ehe," *Ein Biologisches Ehebuche*, Marcuse, M. (ed.). Berlin: Marcus and Weber, 1927.

[SOURCE NOTES]

[2] HORNEY, K., "Über die psychischen Bestimmungen der Gattenwahl," *Ein Biologisches Ehebuche*, Marcuse, M. (ed.). Berlin: Marcus and Weber, 1927.

[3] HORNEY, K., "Über der psychischen Wurzeln Einiger Typische Ehe Konflichte," *Ein Biologisches Ehebuche*, Marcuse, M. (ed.). Berlin: Marcus and Weber, 1927.

[4] HORNEY, K., "Die Monogame Forderung," *Internationale Zeitschrift für Psychoanalyse, 13*, 397, 1927. ("The Problem of the Monogamous Ideal," *International Journal of Psychoanalysis, 9*, 318, 1928.

[5] HORNEY, K., "Das Misstrauen zwischen den Geschlectern," *Die Psychoanalytische Bewegung, 2*, 521, 1930; slightly modified in *Die Arztin, 1*, 5, 1931.

[6] HORNEY, K., "Zur Problematik der Ehe," *Psychoanalytische Bewegung, 4*, 212, 1932.

CHAPTER XIII

[1] HORNEY, K., "Psychogenic Factors in Functional Female Disorders," *American Journal of Obstetrics and Gynecology, 25*, 694, 1933.

[2] HORNEY, K., "The Problem of Feminine Masochism," *Psychoanalytic Review, 22*, 241, 1935.

[3] HORNEY, K., published as "Maternal Conflicts," *American Journal of Orthopsychiatry, 3*, 455, 1933.

[4] ALEXANDER, F., *The Western Mind in Transition*. New York: Random House, 1960, p. 109.

[5] Published as "Conceptions and Misconceptions of the Analytical Method," *Journal of Nervous and Mental Diseases, 81*, 399, 1935.

[6] ALEXANDER, F., "Neurosis and Creativity," *American Journal of Psychoanalysis, 29*, 116, 1969.

[7] ALEXANDER, F., *The Age of Unreason*. Philadelphia: J. B. Lippincott, 1942.

[8] ALEXANDER, F., *The Western Mind in Transition*. New York: Random House, 1960, p. 109.

CHAPTER XIV

[1] HORNEY, K., "Restricted Applications of Psychoanalysis of Social Work," *The Family, 15*, 169, 1934.

[2] HORNEY, K., "Certain Reservations to the Concept of Psychic Bisexuality," *International Journal of Psychoanalysis*, 16, 510, 1935.

[3] HIGGINS, M. and RAPHAEL, C., *Reich Speaks of Freud*. New York: Farrar, Straus and Giroux, Inc., 1967.

[4] TAFT, J., *Otto Rank: A Biographical Study*. New York: Julian Press, 1958.

[5] ARMBRUSTER, C. J., *The Vision of Paul Tillich*. New York: Sheed and Ward, 1967, p. 29.

[6] HORNEY, K., "Culture and Neurosis," *American Sociological Review*, 1, 221, 1936.

[7] HORNEY, K., "The Problem of the Negative Therapeutic Reaction," *Psychoanalytic Quarterly*, 5, 29, 1936.

[8] SPIEGEL, R., CHRZANOWSKI, G., FEINER, A., "On Psychoanalysis in the Third Reich." Unpublished manuscript.

[9] HULL, D., *Film in the Third Reich*. New York: Simon and Schuster, 1973, p. 92.

[10] REISS, C., "Das Kommt Nicht Wieder," *Das Neue Blatt*. Berlin, August 1, 1967.

[11] Ibid.

[12] JONES, EC., *The Life and Work of Sigmund Freud*, Vol. 3. New York: Basic Books, 1957, p. 221.

[13] ALEXANDER, F., Letter to Mrs. Laura Fermi, March 3, 1964.

CHAPTER XVI

[1] HORNEY, K., "Can You Take a Stand?" *Journal of Adult Education*, 11, 129, 1939.

[2] Published in the *International Journal of Psychoanalysis*, 20, 480, 1939.

[3] DANIELS, G., "History of the Association for Psychoanalytic Medicine," *Bulletin of the Association for Psychoanalytic Medicine*, 11, 12, 1971.

CHAPTER XVII

[1] THOMPSON, C., "Penis Envy in Women," *Psychiatry*, 5, 123, 1942.

[2] HORNEY, K., "Understanding of Individual Panic," *American Journal of Psychoanalysis*, 1, 40, 1941.

[3] HORNEY, K., "Children in Wartime," War Bulletin VII, Association for Advancement of Psychoanalysis.

CHAPTER XVIII

[1] FROMM, E., "Sex and Character," *Psychiatry*, 6, 21, 1943.
[2] *New York Herald Tribune*, 1945.

CHAPTER XX

[1] HORNEY, K., "The Role of the Imagination in Neurosis," *American Journal of Psychoanalysis*, 6, 56, 1946.
[2] WILLIG, W. (ed.), "Dreams in Psychoanalysis," *American Journal of Psychoanalysis*, 18, 127, 1958.
[3] HORNEY, K., "Self-Hate and Human Relations," *American Journal of Psychoanalysis*, 7, 65, 1947.
[4] HORNEY, K., "The Future of Psychoanalysis," *American Journal of Psychoanalysis*, 6, 66, 1946.
[5] HORNEY, K., "Maturity and the Individual," *American Journal of Psychoanalysis*, 7, 85, 1947.
[6] HORNEY, K., "On Self-Effacing Attitudes," *American Journal of Psychoanalysis*, 8, 75, 1948.
[7] HORNEY, K., "The Value of Vindictiveness," *American Journal of Psychoanalysis*, 8, 3, 1948.
[8] HORNEY, K., "The Meaning of Neurotic Suffering," *American Journal of Psychoanalysis*, 8, 78, 1948.
[9] HORNEY, K., "Shallow Living as a Result of Neurosis," *American Journal of Psychoanalysis*, 9, 84, 1949.
[10] HORNEY, K., "Man as a Thinking Machine," *American Journal of Psychoanalysis*, 9, 94, 1949.
[11] HUXLEY, A., *The Perennial Philosophy*. New York: Harper and Row, 1945.
[12] HORNEY, K., "Responsibility in Neurosis," *American Journal of Psychoanalysis*, 10, 84, 1950.
[13] HORNEY, K., "Neurotic Disturbances in Work," *American Journal of Psychoanalysis*, 10, 80, 1950.
[14] HORNEY, K., "Psychoanalysis and Moral Values," *American Journal of Psychoanalysis*, 10, 64, 1950.

[SOURCE NOTES]

[15] WEININGER, B., review in *Psychiatry, 14,* 471, 1951.
[16] MONTAGU, A., review in *New York Herald Tribune,* Nov. 5, 1950.

CHAPTER XXII

[1] HORNEY, K., "On Feeling Abused," *American Journal of Psychoanalysis, 11,* 5, 1951.
[2] HORNEY, K., "The Individual and Therapy," *American Journal of Psychoanalysis, 11,* 54, 1951.
[3] HORNEY, K., Speech on Tenth Anniversary of the Association for the Advancement of Psychoanalysis, *American Journal of Psychoanalysis, 11,* 3, 1951.
[4] HORNEY, K., "Human Nature Can Change," *American Journal of Psychoanalysis, 12,* 67, 1952.
[5] HORNEY, K., "The Paucity of Inner Experiences," *American Journal of Psychoanalysis, 12,* 3, 1952.
[6] Panel Discussion on "Neurotic Anxiety," *American Journal of Psychoanalysis, 12,* 89, 1952.
[7] KONDO, A., "On Morita Therapy," *American Journal of Psychoanalysis,* 87, 1953 (with discussion by Horney).

BIBLIOGRAPHY

ARMBRUSTER, C.: *The Vision of Paul Tillich*. N.Y.: Sheed and Ward, 1967.

BANNACH, H. J.: "Die Wissenschaftliche Bedeuting des alten Berlinen Psychoanalytischen Instituts." *Psyché*, 4, 242, 1971.

BAUMEYER, F.: "Zur Geschichte der Psychoanalyse in Deutschland." *Zeitschrift für Psychosomatische Medizin*, 3/4, 203, 1971.

BRÈS, Y.: *Freud et La Psychanalyse Américaine Karen Horney*. Paris: J. Vrin, 1970.

BUSSE-WILSON, E.: "Liebe und Kameradschaft," in *Grundschiften der deutschen Jugendbewegung*, W. Kindt (ed.). Dusseldorf: E. Diederichs, 1963.

CHERRY, R. and CHERRY, L.: "The Horney Heresy." *New York Times Magazine*, Aug. 26, 1973.

DIÄGER, K.: "Bemerkungen zuden Leitumständen und zum Schicksal der Psychoanalyse in Deutschland zwischen 1933 und 1949." *Psyché*, 4, 255, 1971.

FERMI, L.: *Illustrious Immigrants*. Chicago: University of Chicago Press, 1968.

FRIEDRICH, O.: *Before the Deluge—A Portrait of Berlin in the 1920's*. N.Y.: Harper and Row, 1972.

FROMM, E., SUZUKI, D. T., and DIMARTINO, R.: *Zen Buddhism and Psychoanalysis*. N.Y.: Harper and Row, 1970.

GAY, P.: *Weimar Culture: The Outsider as Insider*. N.Y.: Harper and Row, 1968.

HONNEGGER, M.: *Georg Groddeck: Der Mensch und Sein Es*. Wiesbaden: Limes Verlag, 1970.

HULL, D. S.: *Film in the Third Reich*. N.Y.: Simon and Schuster, 1973.

JOHANN, E. and JUNKER, J.: *German Cultural History of the Last Hundred Years*. Munich: Nymphenburger Verlags, 1970.

KNIGHT, R.: "The Present Status of Organized Psychoanalysis in the United States." *Journal of the American Psychoanalytic Association*, 1, 197, 1953.

[BIBLIOGRAPHY]

KRACAUER, S.: *From Caligari to Hitler—A Psychological History of the German Film*. Princeton, N.J.: Princeton University Press, 1947.

LAQUEUR, W.: *Weimar—A Cultural History 1918–1933*. N.Y.: G. P. Putnam, 1974.

————: *Young Germany: History of the German Youth Movement*. N.Y.: Basic Books, 1962.

NELSON, W. N.: *The Berliners: Their Saga and Their City*. N.Y.: David McKay, 1969.

OBERNDORF, C. P.: *A History of Psychoanalysis in America*. N.Y.: Grune and Stratton, 1953.

REISS, C.: *The Berlin Story*. N.Y.: The Dial Press, 1952.

ROAZEN, P.: *Freud and his Followers*. N.Y.: Alfred Knopf, 1971.

SAPINSLEY, B.: *From Kaiser to Hitler*. N.Y.: Grosset and Dunlap, 1968.

STROUSE, J.: *Women and Analysis*. N.Y.: Grossman, 1974.

THOMÄ, H.: "Some Remarks on Psychoanalysis in Germany, Past and Present." *International Journal of Psychoanalysis, 50*, 683, 1969.

TILLICH, H.: *From Time to Time*. N.Y.: Stein and Day, 1973.

VON ECKARDT, W. and GILMAN, S.: *Bertolt Brecht's Berlin*. Garden City, N.Y.: Anchor Press, 1974.

WEIGERT, E.: *The Courage to Love*. New Haven: Yale University Press, 1970.

ZUCKMAYER, C.: *A Part of Myself*. N.Y.: Harcourt Brace Jovanovich, 1970.

ZWEIG, S.: *The World of Yesterday*. N.Y.: Viking Press, 1943.

INDEX